Passion for Place:

EMBRACING GLOBAL WANDERLUST

Joel I. Deichmann, PhD

D1525647

1st WORLD
PUBLISHING

Passion for Place: Embracing Global Wanderlust

Joel I. Deichmann

Published by 1st World Publishing
P.O. Box 2211, Fairfi eld, Iowa 52556
tel: 641-209-5000 • fax: 866-440-5234
web: www.1stworldpublishing.com

First Edition
LCCN: 2014922121
Softcover ISBN: 978-1-4218-8696-1
Hardcover ISBN: 978-1-4218-8697-8
eBook ISBN: 978-1-4218-8698-5

Dedicated to my sister Rachel,

And to my soul mate Karen, thank you for your love, encouragement, and support.

This book is a gift to our children Charles, Isabela, and James.

PREFACE

Allow me to introduce this book by conceding that I have been immeasurably fortunate. Through the travels that led to this book, I fully appreciate the value of a First World passport. Those who are born into or adopted by any wealthy country enjoy a tremendous luxury of opportunity, no matter how materially rich or poor they are personally, no matter what life has dealt them. There is no greater privilege than the opportunity to learn about life in other neighborhoods, and then return safely to one's protected home. On any budget, travel is the best education money can buy.

I am just one of the world's innumerable travel junkies. Travel junkies sometimes feel contented at their present location, but their minds are always drifting toward other places, and especially "the next adventure." For a variety of reasons, many people are unable to travel. I empathize with them, having been isolated on a small family farm in Western New York throughout my formative years, lacking any of the resources required for travel. Recognizing that travel is a privilege, I invite the reader to join me on this journey around the globe. I am now fortunate in so many ways- a loving family, a stable financial situation, a tenured professorship, and a comfortable home. I could easily sit back on my laurels for the rest of my days, yet it seems that I am always willing to put my most treasured resources at some risk in order to explore another hidden corner of the world. In pursuit of this global adventure, one stranger along the way accused me of being a skunk for leaving my young family; others have praised me for ambition and courage, unwilling to allow financial and time constraints to hold me back. Most likely I am guilty of something, according to your perspective. My obsession with travel is not deliberate; quite the contrary. I was born with a passion that was suppressed during my seemingly endless years on the farm, which only made it stronger.

Over the past twenty-five years I have sought out and embraced every opportunity to travel, with or without the resources most people would consider essential. My determination to get away might be a reaction to spatial confinement throughout my formative years. On the farm, I was at the bottom of a power structure that, at the time, seemed harshly repressive; one that imposed punishment for dissent and even sometimes for questioning its logic. I knew deep down that I would eventually be free from my childhood autocracy when I turned eighteen; nevertheless, I reasonably expected that marriage, family life, and a career would prohibit me from exploration. Fortunately I was completely wrong about that. I found a way to travel even after getting married and "settling down." Among my wife's greatest qualities are her trust in me and her support when I see a chance to get away. She has been the most understanding lifetime partner anyone could ever imagine.

As I look back now, a great many of my trips have been "seize the moment" responses to fears that any freedom I had would soon evaporate. There are several examples. At twenty-three, "I'm getting married very soon, and I need to grow up and settle down. I'd better take one last trip because things are going to change." At twenty-five, "my PhD program will be very demanding, so I'd better take just one last trip before I become tied down by work." Thereafter, "a baby is on the way, so I'd better take just one more trip with this manageable traveling family before it grows; when a baby reaches the age of two, it requires its own paid plane ticket." For more than a decade now, I am privileged to have a family, a mortgage, and a career, and I'm traveling more than ever. I take my position of professor very seriously, but there always seems to be room for "one more trip," and I view travel to be essential for my own professional development. My first "real" job after completing graduate school quickly offered me freedom (in the form of time) to travel overseas, but only at my own expense. Increasingly, the nature of my job supports international travel through research projects and teaching opportunities. After a quarter-century journey to see the world, I confess that I don't see any change in sight; I'm hooked for life even though traveling in a car can be tedious and dangerous (Chapter 3, *America by Car: County Idiots*), long flights in an airplane can be uncomfortable (Chapter 10, *Africa for Beginners: Ghana*), and spending more than one year away from home during this scheme can become lonely and frustrating. I share some of the latter sentiments in Chapter 12: *To Russia without Love*. But alas, this passion for travel appears to be incurable; only treatable… with travel.

This book is about perspectives and how they change over time. It begins from the perspective of a farm kid who dreamed of traveling to faraway places but never thought he would have the opportunity or the means to do so. Inexplicably, opportunities began to appear and gradually multiply, and nearly every chance to travel has been embraced. The result is a series of unlikely adventures to some of the world's most interesting places, each with its own purpose and cast of characters. The purpose of travel was never to write a story. The story was lived, and then it was written. The idea to write a book was born when friends suggested that I document my quest to visit every county in the USA. My response was and still is: "Thanks, but who would want to read an entire book about county collecting? Reading about trips to more than 3,000 counties would be a bit tedious, don't you think?" The idea has to be bigger: an isolated farm kid growing up and fantasizing incessantly about traveling to exotic places, then in adulthood meeting the world as those dreams come to life. As for that county obsession, I offer Chapter 3, which explains the quest, and highlights a few of the more salient expeditions that might be of interest to the reader. These chapters are not silos. Each one offers sufficient context to be understood individually, although I do hope to keep the reader's interest long enough to stay with me for more than one journey. Everything in this book really happened; locations, events, and people are real. I use pseudonyms in cases where I was unable to obtain consent to use real names.

A note about chronology: The chapters are placed in chronological order; however, because some of their themes, such as county collecting and leading students overseas, extend over several years, temporal overlap with other chapters is unavoidable.

CONTENTS

Introduction 11

1. *Zum Allerersten Mal* (For the Very First Time) 17

2. The Great Gypsy Train Robbery in Slovakia 31

3. County Idiots: America By Car 55

4. Joel & Karen's Rocky Adventure 93

5. Finding Traction: Traveling Overseas with Students 109

6. Chile: *Mi Amor* 127

7. Pictures of the Pope 143

8. China: Seeing is Believing 179

9. The Waiting Place: Never Cross a Border
   without your Passport 201

10. Africa for Beginners: Ghana 223

11. Nashua Lampoon's Zooropa: Europe with Kids 245

12. To Russia without Love 265

13. Winter Into Arab Spring: Bahrain and Neighbors 307

14. The Yellow Brick Road to Oz (and New Zealand) 325

15. Gelato Every Day: Italy, Croatia,
    and Bosnia-Herzegovina 345

16. A Sort of Homecoming: Mainz, Germany 385

INTRODUCTION

"I am a child of the Soviet Union, which is a small family dairy farm in Western New York. Or so it seemed at the time. The Soviet Union is where my story begins, and ironically, my passion for discovery ultimately leads me to live in Russia, where I first hear the call to write this book"

St. Petersburg, Russia (November 2007)

It is early on a winter evening in 1987, and my father and I sustain our routine daily quarrel while milking his cows. The details of the argument are unimportant; I am a seventeen-year-old high school senior, and my father works seventeen hours every day on a dairy farm to provide for his family. The stress has to do with whether I would be excused from the evening milking this upcoming spring so that I can try out for baseball after school. The tension in the barn is worsened by physical exhaustion at the end of a day that started with the morning milking at 4am. Then there's the omnipresent financial stress cloud that hangs above our family, all of the things that I should be doing better in life, and of course the apparent endlessness of this bitterly frigid and dark winter. An old-school autocrat, my father is always right; compromise and dissent are forbidden. Given the present atmosphere, it seems as though there is no possibility that he might be willing to drive me to the small city of Hornell when our chores are finished for the first round of interviews for the Rotary International student exchange.

Although a licensed driver, I'm not allowed to drive, and this is understandable. A seventeen-year-old on the family car insurance policy is beyond our means. I know that getting to that interview is my long-shot ticket to the world, but I refuse to resort to pleading. The man I work with every day is my father, not my boss. This farm is his life, not mine. And he is always right, even as I grow old enough to discover otherwise. In his house and his barn, he seems all-too fond of saying "what I say goes, and that's final." To this day, I have never had any success disagreeing with my father about anything.

My father and I finish the evening chores and turn off all but one light as we leave the dairy barn. In tense silence, we climb the frozen hill toward the farmhouse, snow crunching underneath the tread of our boots. We pass through the porch doorway and kick the snow off our boots, and then hang up our barn clothes. There are four of us at dinner: my parents, myself, and my nineteen-year-old sister Rachel, who is profoundly handicapped. Unable to walk, she spends most of her time in a wheelchair, and she needs to be spoon-fed three times a day. Rachel is unable to speak; everyone else at the table *chooses* not to speak in the wake of the argument that took place in the barn. My mother—accustomed to the tension between her husband and youngest child—eventually attempts some small talk, but the air remains heavy and she refrains from picking a side.

After finishing my dinner, I have lost all hope for a ride to Hornell. I excuse myself from the table and retire to the adjacent living room, where I sit alone and stare at the flames in the stone fireplace. My father built this masterpiece in the mid-1970s with rocks carried up our big hill from our creek. Five of my older siblings—all of whom have already fled this nest—helped with this major 35-foot construction project. The fireplace and chimney serve two purposes: our main source of heat, and structural support for our early 19th century farm house. I gradually succumb to the all-too-familiar feeling of desolation as the farm keeps me from doing what I think I need to do.

From kindergarten to my current senior year, this farm has been an insurmountable barrier to so many normal youthful desires and goals, from sports to social outings. Resisting the trap of self-pity, I remind myself that my profoundly handicapped sister is in the next room. She has never walked, nor has she spoken a word. She will never go to college, let alone Europe. Nonetheless, I regretfully begin to concede my chance at an underdog's once-in-a-lifetime opportunity. I have often thought to myself that living on this farm must be a lot like life for most non-Communists in the Soviet Union: lots of miserable work for a cause they don't believe in; no freedom of movement or expression and no pay, just room and board. It is 1987, and I am growing impatient just like the resistance in the Soviet Union. I take comfort in knowing that even if I don't have a shot at becoming an exchange student, at least I will be able to escape to college within the year.

Unpredictably, my father asks my mother to feed my sister Rachel her dessert, and says "Are you ready, Joel?" I am taken completely off guard by this sudden benevolence, and I think the man who said it might be surprised too. In a flash, I rush upstairs to change my clothes and splash some soapy water on my face, but there's no quick way to cover up the stiff odor of a cow barn in one's hair.

My father sits with me at a Hornell restaurant table while Rotarians Jerry, Bob, and Phil courteously ask me questions about my interest in being an exchange student. Why do I want to do this? Where would I want to spend a year and why? Bashfulness, nervousness, and lack-of-confidence have me in a stranglehold, and I feel defeated. As the questions keep coming, I anguish about the inadequacy of my answers. I can still smell the cow barn in my hair and on my clothes. At the end of the interview, the Rotarians explain that I should keep my expectations modest. Germany is very popular and therefore assignments are extremely competitive. Even if I am approved as an exchange student, I should be prepared to be sent to another country.

So why do I want to go to Germany? For starters, my ancestral roots are there somewhere, or so I think at the time based upon my name. Germany has been a major player in the world, a cultural and political epicenter generating both good and evil. On an unusual outing at nearby Alfred University months earlier, my father and I had attended a slideshow and discussion about Germany, led by a professor who was a returning Fulbright scholar. Afterwards, my father shared what it was like growing up during the Great Depression and World War II, with Germany as the main villain. Germany was so despised in America that the very pronunciation of our name was even changed to sound more Dutch than German. To me, it doesn't seem possible that my father would ever understand why I should spend time in Germany, the country that enabled some of the greatest criminals in the history of mankind.

Fights between this teenage son and his father are unpredictable and happen regularly. To their defense, my parents have always worked hard to provide their kids with life's necessities, and my father's forceful spiritual and political indoctrination is always well-intentioned, if increasingly resented. As for me, I'm not perfect, but at least I don't care about drugs, and I'm not pursuing sex too soon. I have a nice girlfriend and some decent friends, whom my parents would seem to prefer as their own kids. In our nearby woods, my friends and I drink beer around campfires and plot our respective independence movements. A student of the Cold War, I cannot help but think of the escalating struggles of my teenage years as expressions of resistance by a Soviet republic or satellite toward a reluctant strong-armed Moscow. They are usually met by repression, always psychological and often physical—but thankfully less and less so as my strength approaches that of the General Secretary. I know I am ever so fortunate to be a healthy American with food on the table and a roof over my head, but I crave freedom and opportunity! Because of my father's priorities in life, I have the dubious privilege of "earning my keep" by waking up to an alarm clock at 4am to feed, milk, and clean up after his cows before attending school, then doing chores again when I return home from school in the afternoon. I am an unpaid laborer obliged to accept party doctrine, which in my view works neither for the family business nor for the family itself. Throughout my youth, I cherish one song in particular by REO Speedwagon, and its refrain "…it's time for me to fly…I've got to set myself free…"[i]

Please allow me to reiterate the context for those who grew up in a *normal* environment, if such a thing even exists. We all have our struggles, and maybe there is no such thing as a "normal" family. But for what it's worth, the backdrop for *this* story is seclusion on a small family dairy farm, seven miles from the nearest town. We call it the boondocks. Reaching school friends over our family telephone requires both parental permission and twenty-five cents per minute. Driving is not allowed, and we are out of range of cable television. Internet, cell phones, and satellite television are but twinkles in the eyes of inventors. Music is so important in my life and for my sanity, so I play it from "LP" (long playing) vinyl records or the more modern audio cassette tapes. Stuck in one place, I am increasingly frustrated, sometimes enraged, and always yearning to discover the world. But in my present state of mind, I would settle for Pennsylvania. I am counting down the days until I can leave this farm, one way or another.

Both my father and I fully appreciate how pivotal for my future course in life it was for me to go to that Rotary interview. All of our ugly arguments aside, I'll always be grateful for his decision to drive me to that first interview.

1

ZUM ALLERERSTEN MAL
(FOR THE VERY FIRST TIME)

It is September 1ˢᵗ, 1987, and at age eighteen, I step off the first flight of my life from Rochester, New York, and into my life. I sit by myself at Pan American Gate 3 in JFK airport and reflect on my new reality. I just cannot believe that I was able to break away. I am overwhelmed by emotion after months of anticipation and preparation for something that I wasn't sure would really happen. It *is* happening! The cage fell away, and this is suddenly *my* life. I recall the walk I took this morning, along the rocky creek bed in the cow pasture. On that walk, I took time to contemplate with appreciation all the people in my life that I will miss: the nice girlfriend of one year that I just broke up with, my camping buddies, my family, and the new friends from Rotary who drove me to the airport. I forced myself to hold back tears of emotion, and maybe a few got out anyway. When I return from Germany next year, everything will be different. As I watch the planes taxi down the runway, I realize how fortunate I am to have this dream come true.

Eight hours later, the Pan Am jet delivers me faithfully to the jet way at Frankfurt International *Flughafen*. I walk with the other sleepy-eyed passengers for nearly twenty minutes, and as time passes the airport's magnitude blows me away. Baggage claim signs are posted on the ceiling in German and in English.

This is my first international trip, and it doesn't look like it will be so hard.

I have communicated with my first host family, the Kellers, only by postal letters, and I wonder what they're like in person. I'm eager to meet them. They have my flight information, so I'm confident they can find me in their airport. I manage to find my luggage at the carousel, and I wait there for my host family to pick me up. An hour passes, and the baggage claim area clears out. As a rookie traveler, I have no idea that only passengers are permitted to enter this enormous hall. I am afraid to go beyond the sliding doors, because the sign overhead says "EXIT. NO RE-ENTRY." What if they are just late to pick me up, or just unable to recognize me as a stranger? If I go through those doors, I won't be allowed to return to baggage claim, where my hosts must be expecting to find me.

As I try to figure this situation out, I see another confused looking young guy wearing blue jeans and a matching jean jacket. With a brush-cut and solid "military" build, he is clearly American. He approaches me and introduces himself as Kevin. He says I look confused and American also, but because of my slight mullet, I could be German. Kevin's luggage has been lost. I go with him to file a report, and together we figure out that we need to exit though the final customs check under the "NO RE-ENTRY" sign to be picked up. My host sister Nina recognizes me immediately from the photo I sent. She and her mother are visibly relieved to see me emerge, as it's now been two hours since my flight arrived. Kevin's German host family is nowhere to be seen, so he climbs into the Kellers' already packed Volkswagen Cabriolet with me and my luggage for the short Autobahn drive to Mainz. We arrive at the place I will call home for the next three months: Am Eselsweg #58 in Mainz-Bretzenheim. After a nice lunch, my host father, Dr. Keller, calls some fellow Rotarians and reaches Kevin's host club. Kevin then manages to reach his host parents, who had not been expecting Kevin to arrive today. Shortly afterward they arrive in Mainz to pick him up and take him to Langen, half an hour's drive away.

Am Eselsweg means "on the donkey path." My new home is beautiful and modern with a spiral staircase to my host siblings' bedrooms on the second floor. My own quarters are a first-floor sewing room converted to a bedroom for my use, curiously featuring a sink in the corner. There is a small garden, and a shed for the bicycles that I will use as my main mode of transportation, much to my eventual frustration. The members of my friendly host family look just like the photos Nina had mailed to me. Dr. Keller is tall, dark, weathered, scruffy, and smokes a pipe; Frau Keller is pretty with a constant smile, dark complexion, and big cheeks. Nina is my age, short with even larger cheeks than her mother, and Jan is young, tall, and wiry, and can best be pictured playing soccer or table tennis. All of them call me "Cho-el," as the "J" sound doesn't exist in German, and the first letter of my name is normally pronounced "y"). "Cho-el, you have had a long trip; you must need to *dusch*" says Nina. Being male, and thanks to three years of high school French, I infer that she is offering me a shower. I respond affirmatively, and I am shown the way to the "*WC*," (pronounced "*vay-tsay*) "What's a WC?" I ask. Nina explains that it means "water closet" in English. "Must be British," I respond.

The shower feels like a new birth, but I wonder how much can be seen through the barely opaque glass tiles that represent the outside wall, maybe a bit too much for my idealistic American sensibilities. After the shower, the five of us sit down to what will be our routine nightly gathering: *Abendbrot* (evening bread) is a light German dinner of bread, cheese, pickles, olives, meats, and wine. My hosts explain that Germans prefer to have their large meals at noon time, followed by a *Mittagspause* (afternoon break, a naptime or German *siesta*). Accustomed to large dinners and quick lunches, *Abendbrot* and *Mittagspause*[ii] immediately make a lot of sense to me. I retire to my room after a long, demanding journey. Before going to sleep, I take a few minutes to write in my *Tagebuch* (journal). I imagine (correctly, I'm sure) my host family members sitting at the table sharing their concerns about my nonexistent German faculty. Give me a month to get on track with that, I tell myself, as I listen to Boston's "Don't Look Back," a song whose title must become my new mantra.

Scholars such as Pedersen (1995) have enumerated the various stages of culture shock. I wake up on my first full day at the beginning of the Euphoria Stage, filled with elation and my fascination with the new situation. I need to miss school today, in order to get registered with the appropriate authorities and shop with Nina for school supplies. Nina shows me around Mainz: city life and bike paths, then I meet Nina's pretty friend Karina. I am in heaven, stimulated by adventure and my newfound freedom. No cows to milk today. No schlepping around at the grocery store for $3.35 an hour. No arguments with my parents!

During the first few weeks in Mainz, elation gives way to some measure of culture shock, and some minor things begin to annoy me, like how Germans spell *Amerika* and *Kanada*. I start to receive supportive but often very sad letters from a few girls at home, especially the lovely girl I just tried to break up with before I left. I received several letters from her in one week. I guess this flurry of writing was her coming to terms with the end because afterwards her letters stop abruptly. She had rejected the gentle rejection I tried to deliver in person weeks earlier. We cared a lot for each other, but we just didn't have the steam it would have required to survive a year apart, and I was able to see that before she did.

I begin private German classes in nearby Nieder Olm, as well as lessons at the Maria Ward Girls School. The latter are taught by *Schwester* (Sister) Maria Coronada, a sweet elderly nun who speaks no English (to us) and calls her walker a Mercedes. In her classes, I quickly make friends with three *Kanadian* girls from Winnipeg and two *Amerikan* guys: Craig from Missouri, and

Ronald from Montana. On weekends I join my host family on Rotary outings, and at the end of the month, I travel with my junior class (sixteen and seventeen year olds) to Italy for nine days. This is, along with my one-year German visa and insurance, paid out of the extraordinary generosity of the local Rotary Club, Mainz 50° North. I had truthfully told my host family that I lacked the money to go to Italy, and honestly I am more interested in settling into Germany than leaving again for another country, especially so soon. I haven't yet hit it off with many of the kids in my younger all-boys Catholic school, Markus being the exception. In-between classes, the sixteen year olds wrestle, squawk, and giggle in the hallways, and at eighteen I have absolutely no interest in taking part.

Our Italy itinerary includes Naples, Sorrento, Capri, and Vesuvius, but Italy does not impress. I write in my journal that "the water is full of garbage; it's disgusting, just like the streets here. The shop owners can rip you off easily too. This place is a real, dried up, crusty, you know… but it's great to see it anyway." The itinerary is packed, but with more walking in the oven heat and more museum time than I would like, and traveling blindly can be difficult in the absence of prior information and mental preparation. Unable to understand much German, I feel dragged around and I long for Germany. Shanleigh and Jill, the eighteen-year-old *Kanadian* girls, are with us on the trip and garner a lot of attention from the sixteen- and seventeen-year-old German boys. The girls always seem to be surrounded by a cadre, and I aside from my shyness I am loath to play along. I do manage to make two friends on the trip: Winnie from Hechtsheim and Zsolt from Klein Winterheim, both suburbs of Mainz. Winnie is a pale, skinny kid who loves heavy metal and alcohol. Zsolt is a tall, strong Hungarian-German obsessed with Frank Zappa and the USA. My naïve mentality and Zsolt's flattery of America inhibit my ability to recognize that he also has an intolerant streak. In their efforts to practice their English, both Winnie and Zsolt resist speaking German with me. Sadly, I find that most Europeans are far too willing to speak English. In Italy, I withdraw from gregarious Craig, who—on account of his advanced German—seems to be doing much better socially with the "cool kids" in our class.

Germany, my beloved destination of intent, makes even more sense to me when I return from Italy, and now I have two German friends and several more acquaintances to help me through the year. Weekends are filled with activities and outings with these folks, as well as Kevin, the Ohioan I met at airport on arrival day. My daily routine includes writing in my journal, and a good portion of the text discusses girls I know back home, as well as others as I meet them in Germany. As far as such matters go, I am really on the lookout and ready to find the right one, but not if it jeopardizes this special year in Germany. To keep things interesting for the reader, my favorite prospect is a blonde exchange student from Ontario, New York, whom I met only twice at exchange orientations. Coincidentally she is also studying in Germany, but in the northern city of Münster. There will be two opportunities to see her this year in Germany at Rotary-sponsored exchange student events.

It is a bittersweet ending to the first three months in Germany. I owe *Familie* Keller an enormous debt of gratitude and yet another apology. I reflect upon all of the stress I must have caused them when I innocently failed to emerge from baggage claim on the first day in Germany, when I had countless bicycle problems and ungratefully complained about that two-wheeled piece of *Scheiße*, when I rode that same damn bike across the city of Mainz to play hockey but didn't return until after midnight, and when I asked my host sister Nina to give me some space. Given my living environment *Am Eselsweg*, I was at best a B-guest-*Sohn*.

The Beer Family pulls me out of all this. Yes, you read the name correctly; the word *Beer* in German means "berry." This shiny, happy, lovely family of five breaks every last stereotype you and I might have heard about those stuffy and formal

Germans. The parents are Volker and Ingrid, and they have three girls: Steffi (my age), Susi, and Sabine. It's all smiles and giggles in their home, and lucky for me, my host father always wanted a son. He gives me the affectionate nickname *Luschbär* (something like "Lazy Bear") and instructs me to call my host parents *Papa and Mutti Beer*. I spend the next three months walking their Irish Setter Gypsy after school, playing Beatles hits on their grand piano, and thoroughly enjoying every day. The two points of contention are as follows: 1) each day my host sister Susi sleeps until the absolute latest possible moment, then slams down her breakfast and RUNS at full speed to our bus stop, dragging me along; and 2) I discover too late that I use too much time and water in the shower, and I let the faucet run in the sink while I brush my teeth and shave. Of course, by the time the exploded water bill is noticed, I'm more than a month into my home stay. On the farm where I grew up, water (albeit not hot) is supplied for free by a well. The idea that water costs money is new to me. Highlights at Beers include skiing and spending *Sylvester* (New Year's Eve) 1988 in Sorcuolm, Switzerland, and the many excellent day trips on which they take me, as well as the Mainzer Fassennacht Mardi Gras celebration in February.

Papa Beer inspires me like few other people in ways that will last a lifetime. His household is happy, loving, and carefree, but he still has his own space and fun. This is exactly how I want my future household to be. During the winter of 1988, Papa Beer leaves Mainz for two weeks to fly to Algiers for a Sahara Desert adventure with his buddies. Upon his return, his travel photos and stories—like how water freezes at night in the desert—blow my mind. From his collection of thousands of photo slides, I learn that he does these two-week adventures to destinations around the world regularly, often taking one of his three daughters with him. The idea that a father could explore the world, be a good parent, and still have fun by goofing around with his kids is something to which I aspire.

Papa Beer and I go running a few times in a Gonsenheim

park adjacent to the Autobahn. The sight of *Waldsterben* (forest death) near the highway will always be etched in my mind, and I'll never forget the choking stench of auto emissions combined with the odor of chocolate from the nearby Nestlé factory. I am accustomed to periodic short, three-mile runs, but his weekly one-hour regimen nearly kills me. Later, Papa Beer will die of cancer in 2005, and I can't help but wonder if running often in that pollution might have played a role in his demise.

I hate to leave the Beers, but my program dictates that I will be assigned to a third host family for the final three and a half months of the exchange. Peter and Ruth Eckes live in Nieder-Olm, an exurb of Mainz, and they have four children: Maximilian (my age) as well as his younger siblings Konstantin, Isabel, and Clemens. I quickly discover that the name Peter Eckes is extremely famous, associated with the liquor and fruit juice industries, not just in Germany, but also in Brazil, Switzerland, and elsewhere. Nearly everyone in Germany knows the name. Given my humble origins, I am extremely intimidated to meet Herr Eckes at first, let alone live as a guest in his home. This becomes especially true when I learn that Herr Peter Eckes, *Der Vater*, has a reputation for being a very strict disciplinarian, not unlike my own father. There is no way I will be able to address this man with the informal "du" rather than the very respectful "Sie," as he later insists. I am told that I should plan on dressing up for church and remaining groomed each Sunday for a fine dinner that would be prepared by the family cook, unless nice weather permit Herr Eckes to grill for us. The family—even the patriarch—is warm and generous to me. Although Max is absent while studying at Douai School in Reading, England this spring, his family and I ski with him in Switzerland during Easter holiday. I am told that at the end of my school year, they will send me to Great Britain to ride trains with Max and his friends. In the meantime, my only responsibilities are daily "walkies" throughout the beautiful vineyards with Jana, the rather ferocious family boxer, going to school, and politely allowing Mutti Eckes to correct my quickly-improving street German and guide me away from associates, who might get me into trouble.

At the end of a year abroad, most exchange students buy a Eurail pass (then called Interrail) and travel around Europe at their parents' expense. Absent the requisite money, I hatch a more modest scheme to purchase an inexpensive month-long Germany-wide youth rail pass called *Tramperpaß* (tramper pass). Germany is simply the single country in the world that interests me most, and I am here for the express purpose of learning about it. At the end of nine months, it's almost time to go home to America, but I haven't seen enough of what I came for. So far, I was privileged to travel to Grevenbreuch, Münster, Heidelberg, Wiesbaden, Worms, Aachen, and divided Berlin, but I intensely want to experience other places I've heard about, including Bremen, Hamburg, Stuttgart, München, and Köln. Without seeing these places, I would consider my year in Germany less than a complete success. I make my case to the Hornell Rotary club, which is required to give consent for me to travel. I discover later that because of my limited budget and perceived risks, the trip was nearly a no-go; however, my request is approved thanks to Rotarian Jerry Brown, and some unexpected support from my mother. This trip will be made on a shoestring budget, and it pushes me to return home and start working in mid-July rather than mid-August. My friend "Ohio Kevin" and I will camp or stay with other exchange students we've met, or on rare occasions spend nights in youth hostels. Our travel itinerary is based upon a list of cities that at least one of us wants to see, often where we've already made the acquaintance of other exchange students. The ticket costs 234 Deutschmarks (about $150), and is valid for unlimited travel on German trains for one month. What an incredible opportunity; a new level of true freedom!

Kevin travels from his host family's place in Langen to meet me at the Mainz *Hauptbahnhof* (main train station) and we begin our joint trip northward along the Rhine. The May weather is inordinately cool and rainy, and our supplies are limited to the packs on our backs: one tent, two sleeping bags, two knock-off Walkman cassette players, and of course an absolutely necessary small Casio keyboard about one foot in length. In each town, we buy supplies such as bread, cheese, chocolate, and water. With insufficient money for luxuries such as hostels and campgrounds, we pitch our tent wherever we can find a place.

During our idle time on the trains, Kevin and I look out the window and fancy ourselves some sort of goofball songwriters, and one song really sums up the way we travel Camping in Someone's Backyard.

Riding around on all the trains
Schleppin' around in the pourin' rain
Sufferin' from that backpack pain
What did we do when the nighttime came?

Where do we run to, where do we sleep?
Gotta stay quiet, don't want to breathe
Pricker bushes everywhere
Set up the tent but there's a house over there

CHORUS
Joel: Campin', campin', campin', campin' in someone's backyard
(Kevin: doo doo, doo doo, doo doo, doo doo, doo doo, doo doo)
Joel: Campin', campin', campin', campin' in someone's backyard
(Kevin: doo doo, doo doo, doo doo, doo doo, doo doo, doo doo)

Mornin' comes, the ten o'clock rain
Gotta 'search out' another train
Back to that good old pack pain
Tomorrow, for sure, we'll have to do it again
Gotta stay quiet, afraid to breath
….Got no water for brushin' teeth
Flashlights off when the sun goes down!
Or the tent's like a glow bug on the ground

For us, the trip across Germany is probably the best education that anyone has ever received in one month. On the long train rides, Kevin and I exchange our observations of people and landscapes, share stories and jokes, and sometimes even discuss our shared Christian beliefs. In all, Kevin is what one would describe as a very good kid, and to me it's remarkable what great times and laughs we share without drinking—even the occasional beer—in Germany. Can you believe it? While traveling, we take turns as trail boss, and continuously check each other's navigational work so that we don't end up on the wrong train or in the wrong side of town. Throughout the country, we meet up with exchange students and German friends that we know from Rotary events. In the cases where we know someone in a city on our bucket list, we are sometimes invited to stay inside a German home. The hospitality of our German hosts overwhelms us, and we learn lessons to carry us forward in life through the generosity of Germans, not to mention the captivating discussions with them about current events.

In our efforts to maximize our rail passes, Kevin and I travel to Germany's southern border and walk across the Swiss border to Mittenwald, then visit the border towns of Lindau, Germany, and Salzburg, Austria. There, in Mozart's hometown, we run into an American exchange student named Nancy, whom we had met at an earlier Rotary event. She is also doing *Tramperpaß*, but all alone. Next, Kevin and I take night train to Germany's northern border, backpacking from the German line's terminus and into Denmark. After that, yet another train takes us to the island of Sylt on the North Sea, where we camp in the cold wind-blown dunes with the resident sand mites. Unbelievably, we run into Nancy yet again in the city of Lübeck! Nancy doesn't have a place to stay that night, so Kevin chivalrously invites her to sleep between us in our two-person pup tent. It turns out to be a cozy night. Innocence, respect, and honor prevail effortlessly. The next morning, Kevin and I agree that it seemed pretty cool to sleep beside a girl for the first time.

Speaking of innocent fun, this short account of one year in Germany that virtually began with Italy now ends with a trip through Great Britain with another group of great kids. The ring leader—my host brother Max Eckes—is one of the funniest and nicest gentleman travel companions you can imagine. With his friends Alexis (French), and Nicola and Ivan (Hungarian-Colombian brothers), ours is a group of enthusiastic youths on a mission to maximize five one week BritRail passes. These one week tickets cost more than the one-month German tickets, but my host family generously covers all of my expenses. The trip begins in London, continues to Cornwall, then Wales, Bath, York, and Edinburgh, and finally back to London. Sleeping in beds at hostels, eating in restaurants at least once a day, and experiencing much better weather in Britain than we did on the continent, this trip seems posh compared to the *Tramperpaß*.

By the end of my time in Germany, I write my daily journal in the local language to signify (and maybe showcase) that I have embraced the entire experience. A suddenly fulfilled eighteen year old inks his final overseas journal entry at the Frankfurt *Flughafen*, translated to English here.

Aus und vorbei, oder nicht? ("Over and done with, or not?")… On the day that I chose to return home, I'm here sitting confidently in the same Frankfurt airport that had me intimidated and confused less than a year ago. My flight to Newark has a 90 minute delay. I'm not very excited about going home, but I know that the time is right. I just need to come to terms with the fact that I am leaving Germany, and the dream is ending. I have spent ten and a half months here, about one twentieth of my life so far. As the gate area fills with people, the girls keep looking better and better to me. Most of them are Americans, so I guess that's what I'm after. I'm going home!

The entry is less than profound, but life has begun. Next stop: university! I will not have a chance to return to Europe until 1992, nearly five years later. Life gets busy for me at the State University of New York at Geneseo. While enrolled as a full-time undergraduate at Geneseo, I work nearly full-time hours while co-founding and participating actively in a fraternity. Most importantly, however, I will engage in a magnificently entangling and enduring relationship with that *American Girl.*

2

THE GREAT GYPSY
TRAIN ROBBERY IN SLOVAKIA

It's late spring 1993 when my *American Girl* Karen and I graduate from Geneseo State University. With the consent of her father Jerry and following three years of dating and ten months of engagement, we get married on the last day of July. She is 22, I am 24. Karen is just lovely, with blue "intoxicating" eyes, as my friend Rich was fond of saying in an endearing, non-threatening kind of way. Our wedding and reception couldn't have been better. Like waiting for the flight to Germany, as I wait for this beautiful woman to walk down the aisle, I feel like I am taking off on the great adventure of life. Except this one is the big game, because marriage—unlike Germany—is "until death does (us) part." All at once our lives change dramatically. The generosity of our well-wishers overwhelms us, and we squirrel away a portion of our wedding gift money to add to our (mainly Karen's) modest stash for a planned but still unscheduled trip to Europe. Karen had passed up the chance to study in Europe while in college, so I promised to take her there and introduce her to the places and people that I know, as well as discovering some new ones together.

After ten days' honeymoon on Edisto Island, South Carolina, we move from New York State with our cat Ferne and a small U-Haul trailer full of worldly belongings to southwestern

Ohio, where we have both been admitted to graduate school at the University of Cincinnati. I leave my beloved employer, Wegmans, in favor of a geography teaching assistantship that pays my tuition plus $800 per month on which to live. This is plenty given our frugal lifestyle, a loaned car from Karen's parents, and the affordability of living in Cincinnati. As newlyweds, Karen and I manage on $13,000 of income, earning two Master's degrees, and miraculously taking on no new debt. We spend that first year of marriage enjoying each other's company, working through graduate school, and planning our one-year anniversary trip to Europe.

At the end of my first year in the Master's program, I am asked to teach a summer course at the University of Cincinnati entitled "The Geography of Europe." I have never taught before at the college level, so I'm terrified. However, given my passion for Europe, how could any subject matter possibly be more appropriate for me, and how could a summer course be more timely given that I'll be traveling there soon?

In mid-August, we drive from Cincinnati to Poughkeepsie, New York, where Karen's parents live. Karen's oldest sibling, Jon, still seems pretty skeptical of this young guy who married his even younger sister before they have Master's degrees, let alone jobs. "What does a geographer do, anyway?" is the question I fear most at every holiday family get-together. I'm working my way through graduate school, and I'll figure out something when the time comes. Karen arranges for her father to drive us to Newark International Airport, and somehow convinces Jon to pick us up in one month.

Karen and I sit at Gate 106 of Terminal C awaiting our departure to Germany. With no deadlines to meet, we respond to Continental's request for seat volunteers. When boarding is complete, it turns out they don't need to bump us after all, but in appreciation for our cooperation they upgrade us to business class. That's good business, Continental! Ample leg space, good food, and useful amenities kits; items from which enter into this chapter a bit later. Things can't be better, and this young couple feels blessed to no end. We're headed for one month in Europe with our only challenge being a plan to survive on $50 a day. Given this constraint, I don't feel like we should spend $20 on a tour book, but some might say there is a fine line between financial prudence and folly. I am confident that by accepting invitations and advice from European friends including my three former host families, we can manage. We will save money by sleeping in the homes of friends, on night trains, and occasionally in hostels. A band called The Kinks uses the term "never never"[iii] to describe the forbidden fruit known as the credit card, and even though we have a couple of them, we are determined not to tap them on this trip unless we face a dire emergency.

After we land in Frankfurt, we visit a travel agency and purchase two one-month, unlimited rail travel tickets valid throughout most of Europe. Then I enjoy day-long dates with my young wife in Heidelberg, Mainz, and elsewhere. In Mainz, we are treated with the greatest hospitality by my three host families and my friends from my former school Willigis Gymnasium. I am so excited to introduce my wife to my host families, and I observe mutual approval. When we leave my third host family, Herr Eckes puts an envelope in my shirt and says to me "bus fare" with a friendly smile. *"Danke schön,"* I respond awkwardly. Whatever is inside, he surely thinks we can use. On the bus, I open the envelope and find 1000 Deutschmarks, about $600. To us, it might as well be a million dollars, as our budget is so incredibly tight! Back onto the Deutsche Bahn to Bingen, Köln, Ruhrgebiet, Bremen, Rostock, Neustrelitz, each place handpicked for one reason or another, and nearly all of them enjoyed.

Just north of Berlin, Neustrelitz is our strategic staging point for the next day. We need a place to camp before exploring Berlin, an exciting city that was still divided by a wall in 1988, the only other time I had visited. Upon disembarking in Neustrelitz, I immediately observe tension in the atmosphere. "Sure feels different from the west," I remark to Karen, trying not to show any undue concern. Schlepping our backpacks, we walk the streets away from the city center searching in vain for any wooded area where we might be able to camp. To no avail, I ask several people if there is a campground or forest nearby. We receive only glares that seem unfriendly, or maybe I'm being over-sensitive. I haven't noticed any other foreigners here, either. Karen observes that "they're closing their shutters" as they see us walking down the sidewalk. Could they really be this xenophobic in Neustrelitz? The sky grows dark and we can't seem to find a secluded place to set up our tent. There are houses and people everywhere! We become tired and rather uneasy, especially Karen. Exhausted and desperate, we decide to set up our tent between glistening new vehicles in a brilliantly lighted Volkswagen dealership. I reason that if we cannot get away with going stealth, an alternative solution is to hide in plain view, under the protection of the lights.

It turns out that the new Volkswagen dealership in Neustrelitz is also the town's teenage party spot. Just as we nod off to sleep, several German youths gather in the parking lot with their assorted libations and tobacco products, then proceed to carry on all night long. In comparison, my youthful overnight parties with friends in the woods of Western New York seem tame. My ears twitch with the shrill North German dialect that I cannot even fully understand. Could this be one of the nationalistic youth groups that I've read about, bent on keeping foreigners away from Germany? Heavy metal music and drunken laughter oppress us for the duration of the evening. In random intervals, we hear the forceful shattering of glass bottles on the parking lot tarmac. I think Karen might be crying. She doesn't sleep a wink. We pray in whispers that the youthful revelers will leave. Karen recites a string of Our Father's and Hail Mary's. I lie on my back with my Swiss army knife drawn and ready on my chest, unsure how to react if we are approached. Could our luck have run out? Not yet.

At some point during the night, the cacophony subsides. With the sunrise, Karen and I pack up camp to leave on the first train out of Neustrelitz. We hurry back to the station and board the Deutsche Bahn to Berlin, reaching the city by seven o'clock. Exhausted with the uncomfortable—indeed terrifying—night behind us, we splurge for coffee and apple cake at a street side café. I show Karen the Gedänknisskirche, Charlottenburg Schloß, Siegesäule, and Brandenburg Gate, as well as other highlights that I know from my 1988 visit to West Berlin. I'm hoping that Karen is impressed when random Germans ask me for directions, and I respond confidently in German. We walk all day, easily ten miles. In East Berlin, I take a lot of photos and video to contrast the old and the new, observations from the centrally-planned and market-driven periods. I'm sure we took some amazing photos that we will never see.

At nightfall, Karen and I sit on a bench near Zoologische Garten (Zoo) Station, sharing a half-liter beer to reflect upon and celebrate our incredibly fun day. The beer seems to enhance the city's vibrant colors and energy as darkness falls. Entranced by Berlin at night, Karen and I spend a bit too much time people watching and taking it all in. "Crap—we've got to go, or we'll miss our train to Prague" I exclaim, looking at my watch.

We dash back into the station and up the broken escalator with our enormous packs, reaching the platform just as our train pulls out of the station. I realize there is still a chance to get on that same train at a station on the eastern side of Berlin. "Come on—we're gonna have to hurry!" I shout to Karen. Already breaking a sweat, she and I race back downstairs and into the Underground station to wait on the platform for the next eastbound U2 (Underground line 2) to Ostkreuz. Energized by seeing "U2" on the sign, I can't help but allow the driving industrial riffs of U2's song "Zoo Station"—written about the place we just left—to pound in my head as our train snakes through the tunnel… "Time is a train… makes the future the past… you're standing in the station…your face pressed up against the glass" (Zoo Station, from *Achtung Baby*, 1991).

"We still have a decent chance" I reassure Karen. Berlin's subway is extremely efficient, and Ostkreuz is a major station where intercity trains might wait just long enough for us to catch up. Sweat is flowing freely now, if not from the summertime heat, from our self-induced predicament. At Ostkreuz, we surge out of the U2's doors, and then race up to the platform and climb aboard just as our train to Prague starts to move again. The scene couldn't have been scripted to be more dramatic. Even though missing our train at Zoo was a stupid mistake, I know that Karen is impressed that I got us on board here. Now, I am thrilled that we are on our way deep behind what had been the infamous Iron Curtain, a daunting image cast and perpetuated throughout our lives by the Western press. What could be more exciting?

One of my professors told me that Prague is not to be missed, but the reason why was not obvious to us at first. When our train pulls into Prague- Holešovice station, it takes us a long time to get on track and find the "sweet spot" of the city. When we do, we are flabbergasted by Prague's beauty. Words cannot adequately describe the Old Town's medieval charm, brilliant colors, and glorious architecture in assorted Romanesque, Gothic, Renaissance, and Baroque styles. Just a few highlights include Our Lady of Týn Church, the Astronomical Clock, Charles Bridge, and Prague Castle. We are simply in awe. Our European rail adventure has been spectacular, but today in Prague brings it to a new level!

It is 22.30 on August 25th when I make my daily travel journal entry.

Greetings from Praha. What a day! Slept five hours minus two interruptions to get tickets "Czeched" by both German and Czeck (sic) conductors. Upon our early morning arrival in Prague, we slept on benches in the Holešovice station. Uncertain about safety, we were reassured to see a policeman *telling bums to wake up and get off the floor, and then pick up the garbage they had left there. We left the station and walked about one mile without finding the "sweet spot" of the city with all of the cool sights. How were we to know that the train station was nowhere near the city? I could have used that $20 guidebook today! Disappointed, I asked some Canadian tourists where to find the cool part of Prague. Following their advice, we got all day city transit passes for 50 Kč, or less than $2 each. We took the subway to Florenc station, wandered in the wrong direction, and got lost again. Karen was ready to abandon the city, but we didn't know where we were on the map and we couldn't find our way out because we couldn't find any street names. Asking directions helped a bit, but not much. We spent most of the day wandering through Prague. We stumbled upon the Old Town while trying to find our way out of Prague. I think we saw most of the major landmarks. Some locals were very rude to us. I guess it's because we're traveling Americans and they're not. But it really just pisses me off when people abuse visitors, probably out of jealousy, assuming we are wealthy. Yes, we're fortunate to be on a trip, but we are also on a very tight budget, and we even slept in a parking lot two nights ago. I'm just tired and cranky right now, but I hate it when people create unnecessary tension. Why be a butthole when you don't even know a person? Specifically, I'm referring to servers who brought us kava this morning and fettuccini this afternoon. Hosers, the lot of them! Then this evening, the waitress who brought us beer cried when I tipped her. Finally, at the luggage check in Holešovice station we lost 40 Kč because we couldn't understand the lock instructions written only in Czech and Russian. I challenged this luggage woman when she told me I need to pay again, but lost the argument, which took place in a haphazard mix of German and English. Other than these incidents, we were really impressed with*

Prague and the Czecks (sic) we met. They seem to be a fit, attractive, and happy population (22:50).

After our exhausting day, Karen and I are jubilant to be safely aboard the train that is just about to depart Prague for Budapest. Our compartment has a door, and gives us a feeling of safety from the strangers aboard the train. There is only one other passenger in our compartment of eight seats. I don't like myself for thinking this, but the man looks filthy and somehow nefarious. Neither Karen nor I make eye contact with him, but like everyone does on a train, we try to identify his nationality. We can't decipher the language on the cover of the book he is reading; the characters don't seem to be from Latin or Cyrillic alphabets, the only two I would recognize. Suspicious of the shady guy in our compartment, Karen and I realize that we need to take care. However, as we get tired, we also begin to get sloppy and let our guards down. Eventually, our vigilance gives way to a flirtatious argument about me eating a can of spicy pickled fish, which Karen finds repulsive. I take selfies of us, and then narrate the day's video summary, one that I'll never see. I write in my journal, then at Karen's urging I dig my toothbrush out of my backpack, inadvertently showcasing our other possessions in the process. She pushes me out of the compartment. When I return, we each tuck away our belongings and get cozy.

The nefarious-looking man gets out of our compartment at the next stop. "Sketchy," Karen says. "Yup, I concur… glad he's gone," I respond. At last, we relax and put on our elastic sleep masks from the Continental Airlines business class "amenities kits," then begin another unrestful sleep. We are interrupted far too often by the train conductors and border patrols in the Czech Republic and Slovakia, who repeatedly want to see our passports and tickets. These intrusions seem to occur at least every hour, worsening our extreme fatigue. After digging for our secured tickets countless times, we tire of the process and leave them out on the window side table right next to our heads and far from the sliding door. Hours later, we awaken to the thundering voice of the Slovakian ticket controller's voice saying *"Dobre rano, Lístky prosím."* As the uniformed man looms over us with a ticket punching-gun, we infer correctly that he wants to see our rail passes. We suddenly realize they, along with Karen's handbag and my camcorder, have been taken from the table that is situated right between our sleeping heads!

The controller speaks neither English nor German, and is clearly losing his patience with us. A Slovak gentleman in the corridor hears my attempt to convey to this man that we were just robbed, and he comes to our compartment door offering to help. As the train begins to move again, Karen and I are made to understand that without tickets, we must get off the train at the very next stop, somewhere in Slovakia. The controller moves down the corridor, and the Slovak gentleman sits down next to us.

Slovak lawyer Pavel Korvín introduces himself in German and explains to me that he will escort us off the train in Nové Zámky. He guides me and Karen to the run-down police station and explains to the officers what has happened. Immediately, the Slovaks conclude that this crime was committed by Gypsy thieves. Pavel gives us the phone number of his flat in Bratislava then heads off to work. He promises to pick us up here in the evening. For now, he instructs us to go first with the large, bearded, armed policemen to their small, green, rusty Škoda decorated with "POLICIA" on each side. With no verbal common ground, the police gesture to us to put our backpacks in the trunk and get into the back seat. The officers stow their guns in the trunk beside our backpacks. The crammed trunk remains open during the drive to wherever we're going, its lid bouncing incessantly with the bumps. On unpaved roads, they drive us through a city of Soviet-planned *Herrenhäuse* (prefabricated block high rise apartments) to another police station, more accurately described as a police fortification. I'm not sure why at the time, but we need a different type of police to deal with this crime. The front door of the station is protected by a heavy steel gate. Our police escorts unlock the gate and the door, then we are led upstairs to another barred gate. Inside are two young, clean-cut, cool-looking officers relaxing in their chairs, Ivan and Branislav. The office walls are plastered with hundreds of photos of nude women, cut from porno magazines. A feeling of uneasiness descends upon me and Karen as we sit silently waiting for an "English specialist." She will help the police translate our story into the Slovak language for a formal written report, which will be notarized and mailed to us so that we can use it for insurance purposes. As we wait, I pull out my travel journal and jot down a few notes.

It is 9:30 in the morning in Nové Zámky, Slovakia on August 26th, 1994. Here we are in a police station, and we should be in Budapest by now. Man, we slept well last night! We slept so well, in fact, that our bags were stolen from right next to our heads. This happened when our train was stopped in Bratislava. At 6 o'clock in the morning, the conductor, flanked by armed police, came into our train compartment to check our tickets. Unable to produce them, we were told to get off the train... We didn't know what to do, and I tried in vain to explain that we had been robbed. None of the men spoke English or German. Our Eurail train passes are gone. Our plane tickets are gone. Our camera and camcorder are gone. Karen's wallet is gone, as well as her travel journal and the brand new scarves she bought in Prague. She is devastated. They didn't get our passports, thank God. And at least I still have my money and my journal.

This event knocks us sideways after the high points of Berlin and Prague. We were easy targets, young, smiling, and naïve.

By local standards we are wealthy, simply by virtue of the fact that we are traveling in Europe, but we are probably among the poorest young American backpackers ever to set foot in the Old Country. Karen hits the nail on the head when, between teary outbursts, she proclaims that Pavel is an angel for helping us through this.

"English, soon" is promised by Ivan. Sure enough, after some time a young, plain looking woman enters the room wearing a shirt with the imprint "US Unlimited," and introducing herself as the local school's English teacher. She takes us to another upstairs room where a (non-electric) typewriter awaits. In broken English, she asks us what had happened. During the extensive questioning (first separately, and then together), I request a bathroom break. The men's room smells like stale urine. The urinal is a trough that drains out the end of the second story and directs its contents down to the ground. The police officers downstairs will surely know whenever the bathroom is in use. Hands go unwashed, as there is no running water in the sink. By late morning and with the help of the officers who had talked to Pavel, the English teacher translates the four-page report into Slovak, which the police promise to send to Beers, my second host family in Germany, whom we plan to visit again before flying home to the USA.

Officers Ivan and Branislav show us their collection of purses with slit bottoms and ask if any of them belong to Karen. They demonstrate how such bags get cut along the bottom while women hold them tightly under their arms. The contents are taken out, often without the owner noticing. Purses are snatched, emptied, and abandoned in the street or in railway station garbage containers. Playing charades with a few interspersed Slovak, English, and German words, the officers explain to us that when we fell asleep, somebody came into our compartment, grabbed our belongings, dashed out, then jumped off the train as it started to leave the station. They tell us that Gypsies are well-known for this technique, as they seldom have their own tickets to ride the trains. The stolen rail passes are then sold, or used to commit more thefts aboard trains.

With the report finished and the English specialist on her way back to school, Officers Ivan and Branislav invite us to lunch and we oblige, happy to leave the stale, dingy, pornographic police station. Lunch turns out to be Golden Pheasant *pivo* (beer) at a small, outdoor sit-down kiosk[iv]. Ivan can speak a tiny bit of German, and he says he knows about our home city of Cincinnati which he pronounces "Chin-chin-natt-ee." Branislav produces from his pocket a dog-eared postcard from Montana, USA. He indicates that his brother lives there, or went there, or wants to go there, I'm not sure. We have a great time drinking with the police officers, and do our very best to piece together enough French, German, and sketches to keep the conversation going. Whenever caveman language fails there is beer to fill the gaps in the conversation. When the party is over, we've each had several .5 liter beers. Ivan gestures for the bill. As it arrives, he proceeds to remove a large stamper from his belt, applying its black and red ink mark to the bill. Could it be that the officer just certified that "this beer is for cops," and therefore no charge will be incurred by the defenders of justice? Maybe Ivan was simply instructing the waitress to add it to the daily tabs and bill the police at the end of the week. Either way, beer with the cops made our terrible day infinitely better, and we express our gratitude to the officers when Pavel returns to take us back to his flat in Bratislava.

The present moment in time is a profound one. We had been moving forward with child-like glee in our happy new marriage and in this amazing trip, and now we are headed backward, to Bratislava—a city we had no intention of visiting in the first place. And, we are relying upon the good will of a stranger we just met on a train.

Pavel the Slovak lawyer leads us to his central Bratislava flat. His domicile is quaint, compact, and dated, but clean and functional. Pavel apologizes that there is no hot water. Given my rural farming background, I didn't know any lawyers in the USA, but I am pretty sure they didn't live in modest apartments like this one. Pavel explains that tonight, his wife and new child are away at the *dacha*, a weekend house. We are instructed to put our backpacks down in the host's bedroom, which we are told will be our guestroom. Pavel then takes us to the nearby K-mart[v] and buys Coca-Cola and popcorn for us, *oblátky bryndzové slané* (a local cookie), and a freshly-cut rose for Karen. She is visibly overwhelmed by these gestures, and can't stop a few more tears from escaping. We return to Pavel's flat, and as we drift off to sleep in comfort, we marvel at everything this kind Slovak has done to try to correct our misfortune and make us feel better. Karen reiterates to me that she "is convinced that Pavel is our guardian angel."

The next morning, Pavel takes us around Bratislava's city center to find out if it's possible to buy two one-week train passes that would enable us to keep traveling rather than returning directly to Germany. So, the "bus money" that Herr Eckes had tucked into my shirt pocket saved our adventure, as the price for our two new passes is $700—almost exactly what he gave me. Admittedly, Herr Eckes, among others, had warned us to stay away from what many Germans pejoratively call "Eastern" Europe (locals insist that they live in "Central" Europe). From Pavel's concern throughout this ordeal, it is clear to us that he doesn't want these two impressionable visitors to remember his beloved Slovakia by yesterday's misfortune. Most people would have ignored the robbery and passively watched us get kicked off the train to find our own way home; instead, Pavel stepped forward to show compassion, and he saw the situation through[vi].

Early the next morning, we thank Pavel profusely and board another train to Budapest. Although a Band-Aid covers our troubles, everything seems different now than it was before Prague. We're emotionally distressed, and we've lost our zeal to move on. I pull out my travel journal and a pen. "They say that making light of a bad situation is a good way of coping with it," I say to Karen. With apologies to Pavel and the other friendly Slovaks I've met in my travels, in the aftermath of our plight I jot down this parody of "Hotel California."

Riding east on the rail line
On the Balkan Express
Post Socialist picture show
Litter, concrete, and mess

Overtired from the cities
Spent the past day in Prague
Sunset on the horizon
Gloomy fields of fog

So we made ourselves cozy
And got set for the night
We passed out into a deep, deep sleep
Shady man, pale light

When we woke in the morning
Suddenly all bereft
Destinations on the loudspeakers
Bastard robbed us and left

Living it up at the Hotel Bratislava
A God-forsaken place
Not a smiling face
Getting ripped off at the Hotel Bratislava
Makes us want to leave
Why can't we already leave?

Arriving at Budapest's Keleti station, we do our best to get out of our funk. We are in a new city –Hungary's capital— and the show must go on. From a posted map, we discover that Budapest is actually two cities: Buda and Pest, and we gaze across the

Danube toward the citadel on Gellért Hill. Given such amazing attractions on tap, our day in Budapest feels like it should "feel" better. Something seems to be missing from this incredible city, but maybe it's just that something is missing from us. Our confidence and optimism have been shattered, and we view almost everybody on the street with suspicion and in some cases contempt. Cautiously, I take out some Deutschmarks to exchange for enough Hungarian forint to get us through the day, then we negotiate the Metro to Lajos Kossuth Square and surface just outside the spectacular Hungarian Parliament.

As we emerge from the Metro, a large group of children encircles us in the square, and some of them reach deep into our pockets. This occurs so quickly that neither of us has the opportunity to launch a physical response. Personally, I already feel so violated by the robbery on the train that I'm angry enough to punch anyone, even a punk child thief. Fortunately, our pockets were already empty. From the start of the trip, while in cities Karen and I had both taken the precaution of putting our money and tickets in German *Geldbeutel* (money bags), which we secured to our belts and tucked behind our shorts pockets.

Still, really? We just get back on our feet and a pack of child thieves tries to rob us? Karen and I fluctuate between being deflated and just simply pissed off. Budapest is beautiful, and we'll spend our day here, exploring Pest and hiking to Buda's Gellért Hill. However, our excursion behind the former Iron Curtain is not going well, and we cannot even blame the Communists; crime is not part of their legacy! We decide to "splurge" on a hostel to get another good night's sleep. However, we aren't very pleased when the hostel's director explains that girls and guys need to sleep in separate rooms. The rules seem reasonable for most backpackers, but it's already been a few days since together-time for this freshly-married couple. We challenge the system and get away with some bunk time together, any sounds getting drowned out by the loud party taking place in the hostel's adjacent common room. The joke turns out to be on us though, as the party becomes as loud as a dance club and continues all night long.

The next morning, defiantly holding a strategic meeting at a Budapest McDonald's, Karen and I decide that we need a completely different game plan. The idea of exploring "East of the Iron Curtain," exotic at first, has been spoiled by the train theft, the attempted theft in the square, and the sleepless night in the hostel. Our new plan involves getting the hell out of here and going to more predicable lands. In our frustration, we jot down a list of reasons under an entry entitled "BUDAPEST (szajci)"[vii]

Top Ten Reasons We're Going Back to Western Europe

1. *Eastern Europe (sic) sucks*
2. *We're desperate enough eat at to McDonald's*
3. *One of us (Karen) was promised some beach time*
4. *It would be nice to shit, shave, and shower without having to pay for it*
5. *We're sick of being clueless*
6. *We're tired, sick, and sick & tired… dirty and swampy*
7. *Gypsies*
8. *Need working phone to call our bank and cancel our stolen credit card*
9. *Do laundry, drop off useless charging cords for the our stolen cameras*
10. *Look into—just maybe—two plane tickets back to the USA???*[viii]

On the morning of August 28th, 1994, we present our shiny new tickets to board our train of deliverance from what seems to have become hell. The itinerary will take us to Vienna, Linz, Salzburg, München, Frankfurt, and finally Mainz. Among the things I write in my journal are observations about the region in 1994, including the extreme "pollution," and my recurring quote that "people here need to lighten up and have a laugh."

Not all is negative, though, and there are a few good things to remember: 1) Pavel the Slovak lawyer, our guardian angel; 2) prices so low that we can afford to eat in restaurants; 3) the magical ambience of Prague; 4) the friendly, spirited beer-pounding policemen in Nové Zámky; 5) knowing that when we're done exploring here, we can go home to the USA. We leave this place with our lives, some good stories, and the possessions that fortunately still remain in our backpacks.

Despite Vienna's splendor and the dramatic Alpine mountain setting of Salzburg, the train ride back to Germany seems to take forever. There are no Gypsies in our train compartment this time, only two friendly drunken Austrians. As the colorful landscape graces our afternoon, they bring out some mood enhancers procured on their most recent trip to Amsterdam; we politely turn down their generous offer to partake.

Arriving in Mainz feels like putting on a warm, well-worn glove. It sure feels good to be back in Germany: a clean, orderly place that simply makes sense to me. From the train station pay phone, we manage to reach neither the Beers nor the Eckes. Perhaps they're out of town. With few options, I decide that it's worth going to the Beers' house, where at least we can drop off some gear. Karen and I ride the tram to Gonsenheim and to our disappointment confirm that nobody is home. Now what? We unload our backpacks on their back lawn and wash our laundry by hand with shampoo and cold water from a hose. As Karen and I hang our clothes on patio furniture and wait for them to dry, we decide that we might as well go to Italy tonight.

On the tram back to Mainz, I map out our route, taking us from Mainz via Basel, through the Alps to Milano, then Bologna, Florence, Pisa, and Antigiato Playa, where we hope to find a satisfactory beach for Karen. Yes, it's true that the trail boss admittedly overlooked a few amazing cities along our route, or maybe his companion was just over-eager to get to the beach. The night on the train continues our string of bad luck. Approaching sunset, we cross the border into Italy and head toward the Golfo di Genova. Missing our intended stop, we need to backtrack with our packs and begin our search for an affordable hotel. At the reception desk, we are horrified to discover that the cheapest price for a room is 160,000 lira, or $120. For us, it might as well be a million dollars. We cross the busy motorway and walk in the darkness along a trail that seems to head toward the beach based upon the absence of artificial light. Again physically and mentally exhausted, we decide to sleep under a small tree. I feel like an idiot. Thinking we were finished with camping, just yesterday we left our tent and some other gear in Mainz. Karen and I will need to share a single sleeping bag and a blanket, and use a raincoat for cover. We do our best to get comfortable, but struggle to sleep at all, thanks to patrolling insects and the nearly incessant roar of the highway we crossed an hour earlier. At night, noises always seem louder, and the dangers seem closer, especially in a strange place. "I wonder what it will look like here when the sun rises," I muse out loud, trying to cheer up my wife.

We spend the following glorious day at Antigiato Playa. The beach rejuvenates Karen, although I doubt she'll ever forgive me for making her sleep on the ground under that tree last night. After we get our fill of sunshine, we head back to the train station, which is equipped with a small grocery store. She and I pick up some supplies while waiting for our train to Rome. Our shopping list includes two large bottles of water—one of which we gulp down immediately—two pears, two apples, some grapes, pretzels, cookies, and a bottle of white Tuscan wine. We'll have a veritable feast on the train! After a couple of hours of watching eight trains roar through the tiny station at full speed, we start to wonder if any trains bound for Rome actually stop in Antigiato. Eventually, a nice older couple walks past us and sits down on the bench across the platform. I greet them with a timid "*bongiorno.*" What comes next—I think—is their polite attempt to explain that it is already evening, and that there may be no more trains headed in our direction today. So, I look for the station attendant's office. Communicating in gestures and German, I am able to find out with a reasonable level of confidence that the final train yet to stop at Antigiato tonight is "bound for Grosseto, direction Roma." *"Grazie signore!"* We'll be on it.

Our train reaches Grosseto far too late to connect to Rome, and the station looks particularly sketchy. "Karen, I promise if we can find a room for $60 or less, we're going to stay in a hotel tonight." The train doors open and Karen announces that she sees a sign from God… several hotels just outside the station. One hotel's flashing neon signs advertises $60 rooms. Yes, the bright blue price is shown in US dollars. Far be it from me to ignore divine providence, especially after what we've been through these past few days. After three weeks, our first hotel of the trip! Hallelujah! The simple things in life have been missing: a nice clean bathroom with fresh towels, soft pillows, and a huge fluffy bed. The first hot shower in sixteen days! We eat the food, drink the wine, everybody having a good time. At last, Karen and I have a chance to get reacquainted and get our feet back on the ground. The next morning, we both maximize the extensive breakfast smorgasbord by packing a small sandwich and some Nutella packets for the train, and Karen borrows towels for future beach use. We are ready for Roma!

Who says you can't do Rome in eight hours? We have no money for entrance fees, so we won't get bogged down with the level of detail one encounters at museums and other attractions. We simply enjoy walking the streets and squares, marveling at the monuments and churches, and watching the locals and tourists.

With a successful day in Rome behind us, now we're moving on to France on a night train. We love the freedom of a rail pass. The event on the Balkan Express was a humiliating kick sideways, but we have faith that the best bits of our trip remain ahead of us. As the sun rises and we approach Marseille, I look over Karen's shoulder and notice that she just wrote "From Hell to Heaven" on the top of the page of the new journal she just bought.

In Provence, we visit with Craig and Jane, a lovely and über-generous American couple from Los Angeles whom we met two weeks earlier in Mainz. About the age of our parents, Craig and Jane had hosted my German host sister Susi in their home near Aix-en-Provence while she studied French. In Mainz, Craig and Jane invited us to visit them in France. They live in a beautiful Provençal home with dogs named Pauillac and Jammer. Jane is a gracious hostess, and Craig is an excellent cook.

After dinner, I pass my own journal to Karen, encouraging her to add her observations. I remind her that she is much better with the details. For example, in Aix-en-Provence, she observes "narrow and quaint" alleyways, and "gutters down the middle of the avenues," and she uses words that are unfamiliar to me like "breathtaking" when describing squares and fountains. Karen even reports in French what we just ate: *aperitif* at dinner, *chèvre chaud, canard avec pomme de terre.*

In the morning, Craig takes us wine tasting by bicycle. Along the way, we stop at a vineyard, where Jane drives her car to meet us. After a couple of samples, Craig begins to express frustration with his juvenile, thirty-something adult son back in America, who doesn't seem to be finding much direction in life. He flatters us by praising the confidence and purpose we seem to have in getting married so young. Neither Karen nor I know exactly what to do when we finish graduate school, but Craig assures us that we will find success.

Unfortunately, we might have overestimated the sincerity of Craig and Jane's polite offer to stay a third night in their house. Yes, I believe we are guilty of overstaying our welcome in Provence. In doing so, we learn a valuable lesson[ix]. To this day, we remain overwhelmed by the kindness and generosity extended to us by Craig and Jane, and we wish we could find them again to tell them how much those three days in Provence meant to us.

The next morning, Karen and I are alone again, and we take the train to Cassis. I become completely attentive in the midst of the many topless women sunning themselves all around us on the beach, and I encourage my wife to do like the locals. Alas, all good things must come to an end, so over the next days we visit the beautiful cities of Arles and Avignon. On Karen's insistence, we visit the Van Gogh museum in Arles, to discover that Vincent was a very naughty—if talented—dirty old man. We sing *"Sur le pont d'Avignon"* on the bridge of Avignon, nostalgically appreciating our respective French classes at Alfred-Almond Central School and Our Lady of Lourdes High School. We reluctantly bid France *"adieu"* for now by changing trains in Beziers, Cerbêre, and Port Bou.

Madrid was on our original itinerary, but our budget prevents us from getting there. Who could imagine that $30 kept two of us from experiencing Madrid? Here's how it happened: on the train bound for Barcelona, we discover that Spanish trains impose a "seating" fee for holders of Eurail tickets, amounting to about $5 per person per journey leg. For us, going all the way to Madrid would represent about half of our new daily budget of $25^x, and then we still need to make it back to France! So we have to settle for one day in Cataluña. Given all of the linguistic miscues I've made, I shouldn't judge anyone, but I can't resist teasing Karen after I hear her greet a lady at the Barcelona rail station information kiosk with "Buenos Aires."

Barcelona does not show us its best. Our poorly-planned, self-guided tour includes Gaudi's fanciful church La Sagrada Familia and the Olympic Facilities, as well as a cursory look at some other squares and buildings. We remain discouraged by the greed of the Spanish rail company, and concerns about cash cloud our day in Barcelona; moreover, the virtually abandoned and graffiti-riddled 1992 Olympic facilities fail to impress us.

Rather than exploring Spain, we opt to spend our final few days in Bordeaux and Switzerland, riding the trains and picnicking—an absolutely splendid low-budget bonding experience!

We subsist on fresh baguettes, cheese, chocolate, and assorted fruit, washing the food down with bottles of water and inexpensive wine of formidable quality. On the train, we confirm the French stereotype that many people smell like sweat and/or cheese, and we reckon that we do as well. We stop briefly at Lyon and Geneva to peek at these cities during our short layovers. En route to Paris, we see a picturesque Swiss village named Brig. Spontaneously, I tell Karen "hurry- grab your backpack." We clamor off the train to explore. We decide to buy some supplies and have a picnic in a town center park, completely surrounded by a magnificent view of the snow-capped Alps.

Karen and I culminate our amazing backpacking adventure in Paris. Paris is simply spectacular, just like the other French cities we've seen, but so much larger and busier. Again due to time and money constraints, we focus on monuments and churches rather than the contents of museums. Our checklist includes the Eiffel Tower, Hôtel des Invalides, the Conciergerie, Notre Dame, the Louvre, Place Pompidou, the Opera House, and Sacre Coeur. We discover that the tourist circuit of Europe is surprisingly small. Three times on this trip—in Munich, Barcelona, and now Paris, Karen and I randomly run into Sharon, a lovely Korean-American girl from Houston who is traveling across Europe by herself. Following l'Arc de Triomphe, I insist upon an unconventional tourist stop at La Defense, the ultra-modern suburban downtown planned by the French government in order to protect the architectural integrity of central Paris. I learned about La Defense in the textbook of the first college-level class I ever taught, earlier this summer at the University of Cincinnati. Based upon our short experience in Paris, Karen and I are inclined to dispute the widespread stereotypes of French rudeness. Our rejection of such generalizations gains even more credence after staying with Karen's gracious family friend Luïc and his wife in Orléans, close to Paris.

There is one final story to tell about this incredible month-long learning and bonding odyssey that the two of us managed to complete on about $3000, plus the "bus fare" that Herr Eckes gave us. We arrive at the Frankfurt airport three hours before our flight in order to pay the replacement fee for our tickets. The Continental desk agents don't want to issue new tickets to us, and their English is clearly worse than my German. "Vutt you are talking about… *replacement* teekits," asks one haggard agent. Calmly and politely, I explain the Great Gypsy Train Robbery in Slovakia to her. After forty-five minutes, Continental rightly re-issues our tickets for a fee of $50 apiece, and just in the nick of time we are permitted to pass through security and board our flight.

Karen and I spend the flight time back to Newark writing in our journals. For each of us individually, the trip has been an emotional roller-coaster ride. But let's think about this… what a great experience for a newly married couple! They mean it when they say "for better or for worse, for richer or for poorer." Wow, how fortunate we are to have had this opportunity! A microcosm of marriage itself, this trip's delights and the struggles alike will certainly strengthen our relationship!

3

COUNTY IDIOTS: AMERICA BY CAR

It's almost daybreak as I steer Rich's red 1980 Toyota pickup truck off Interstate 75, into his driveway and then onto his front lawn, laughing sadistically to myself. I had stayed awake at the wheel over the past three hours only by drinking burned gas station coffee, hanging my left arm out the window to feel the refreshing nighttime breeze, and taking puffs on a cheap cigar—the latter a last resort for this non-smoker. When I began my driving shift hours earlier, Rich had decided to stretch out in the bed of his pickup truck, under the cap, as unsafe as that might seem for interstate highway travel. The last time I saw him was more than three hours ago at a gas station in Crawfordsville, Indiana. There, as I filled up the tank, I pounded on the cap's darkened window to wake Rich and ask if he needed anything, then waited for a response. Nothing. So I pounded again. Still no response. Wow, Rich must really be out of it! I just drove 200 more miles across Indiana and back to Cincinnati, then parked Rich's vehicle diagonally on the grass in front of his house. Satisfied with my mischief, I walk down Riddle Road and up to my fifth floor apartment. My wife Karen is just waking up for work. As I enter the bedroom, anticipating a comfortable collapse into bed, she tells me that I just missed an urgent phone call from our friend Jeff, as well as the big note he taped to our apartment's door:

"JOEL: CALL ME ASAP!!!." Immediately, I call Jeff back and listen in disbelief as he explains to me that Rich had crawled out of the truck's bed in western Indiana to use the bathroom, and I drove off without him.

Cincinnati, Ohio, Spring 1995.

This chapter is dedicated to the memory of my dear friend Richard A. Spohn, 1945-2008. Without Rich, the thought of "collecting counties" would never have entered my mind. This challenge entails visits to every American county, and there are 3143 of them. Collecting counties requires careful planning, enduring patience (for collector and fellow passengers alike), safe driving, and lots of good luck. I keep track of my progress with various-colored highlighter markers on blank county maps of the USA, and I maintain my "tally" in an Excel file. Collecting counties is a game of conquest for the passionate modern geographer who missed the true American era of exploration.

I didn't come up with this idea myself, and I won't be the first to complete the challenge. About thirty people (mostly retired, many deceased) have already traveled to every US county. Including me, 500 or so report their ongoing progress with the Extra Milers Club[xi], which I discovered some time after beginning my own quest.

As important as counties become to me, more important by far is that if it hadn't been for Rich, I probably never would have pursued a career in academia. This means, among other things, that most of the adventures in this book simply don't happen. In short, without Rich, I would probably be that typically discontented guy doing a job he hates. With Rich I shared an interest in going to faraway and exotic places like Prague and Chile, places that have become quite familiar to me, but tragically also places that Rich never had the opportunity to visit. It was on a road trip with Rich that I first discovered the magnitude and dramatic beauty of the American West, where his mortal remains lie. Rich shall forever rest in peace at his favorite place on earth: Jenny Lake in Grand Teton National Park. One could not imagine a more devoted and loyal friend than Rich, and I can only hope that I was a good enough friend to him.

The story begins in 1994, and Rich is my boss in the Geology-Physics Library at the University of Cincinnati. Rich began working here when he started graduate school three decades ago, and got so busy with his job that he never found time to finish his thesis.

My responsibilities at the library are to work the circulation desk, and sometimes re-shelve books. I do less of the latter after Rich discovers that I don't have a good grasp on the Library of Congress coding system. While at the circulation desk, between helping patrons I am allowed to do homework and experiment with a budding technology: text-only email.

Rich tends to be rather eccentric. His appearance might be described as a smaller version of Albert Einstein. In his mid-40s, he is all of 130 pounds, and has curly white hair. It is characteristic of him to begin and often end each sentence with a "hmm" sound. Rich spends an inordinate amount of time chatting with patrons, with me, or other student workers. When he's not chatting, he quietly plans trip routes or highlights maps for his unconventional hobby: attempting to visit every county in the United States. I am at first dumbfounded at how such an apparently intelligent person could engage in such a monumental waste of time, money, and gasoline and put himself at physical risk. Such a senseless distraction in life! Doesn't he know how dangerous the road is? But I am simultaneously both envious of his freedom and curious about this strange passion. Rich is single, has friends everywhere, and a job that supports the things he cares about most: travel and discovery. I am a financially-constrained graduate student from the Northeast who has not yet seen the Rocky Mountains. In fact, just before I got married last year, I made a final bachelor's jaunt to visit my brother in Austin, Texas, thinking the whole time that the party is over. I'm okay with my own expectation that marriage and graduate school will stifle any hopes of travel. I'm looking forward to a career and kids with Karen, and I anticipate the constraints these responsibilities will inevitably impose on me.

After a few weeks of working in the library, Rich starts calling me "Jid the Kid," which he derives from the initials of Joel Ian Deichmann. "Hmm… hey Jid, I have a new project for our geographer in training. How would you feel about sorting maps… like tens of thousands of them?" he asks, laughing. "Sure," I respond, having no idea what he is talking about. He leads me to the enormous map cases in the far corner of the library. Fifty or so steel filing cabinets, chin-high and four-feet wide, are lined up against the walls. On top of those cabinets are stacks of large topographic maps—approximately three feet square, each representing a seven mile wide swath of the United States. Rich explains that more than 100,000 maps were donated to the University of Cincinnati by the US Army Corps of Engineers. From now on, rather than working at the front desk or re-shelving books, I would be charged with sorting maps. What a break! I am not exactly the best book re-shelver on the team, and this map project virtually guarantees several months of employment! Even at modest work study wages, this assignment would augment my meager $800 monthly teaching assistant stipend.

A few days into the project, with maps piled on tables in the study area, Rich suggests that two other graduate students and I deliver some of the maps of respective local relevance to universities in the Midwest and South. All young geographers, Jeff, Mike, and I leap at the opportunity! Destinations include places where Rich has close ties with other map librarians: the University of Illinois, University of Kentucky, and the University of Tennessee, among others. Rich offers to subsidize our expenses in order to find a new home for the valuable maps. I gleefully go along on a handful of such trips, surprised and enthralled by this new sort of junket that requires very little investment from me. Having moved here from New York State, I am very interested to explore the US Heartland and South. The only requirement from me is time, and I have plenty of that. In fact, I find my graduate program to be anything but intensive compared to my undergraduate years at Geneseo, where as a full-time student I worked 30 hours a week and led a fairly active social life.

One day as I sit at the Geology/Physics library's circulation desk, probably looking bored to insanity, Rich appears with a poster tube, greets me with "Hey Jid," and out pulls a 24-by-36 inch map, then unrolls it in front of me on the circulation desk, holding the curled ends down with books. The map features thousands of county divisions, and about half of them are colored with a yellow highlighter. "Hmm, this is my county map, Jid... I'm a county idiot." I don't know Rich well, so I'm not sure what to say. "Haven't you ever heard of the CIA... the County Idiots Association?" He asks. Rich shuffles merrily through the back room, turns on the light in his office, and returns with a blank map for me. He cheerfully explains that it might be interesting for me to trace the highways I've been on in my lifetime and mark the counties they intersect. "Okay," I think to myself, "I have nothing better to do while making $4.00 per hour."

With a Rand McNally road atlas and a yellow highlighter, the exercise of re-tracing my footsteps turns out to be incredibly fun! I was born in Connecticut, raised in New York, and I was on a handful of trips in the northeast as a child: camping in Vermont and New Hampshire; overnights at my friend Matt's house in Jackson, New Jersey and the State Fair in Syracuse, New York. I recall clearly which routes I had taken, so I mark them with a yellow highlighter on my new, blank county map. I then re-trace the three precious road trips I took in college during Geneseo's unconventional two-week spring breaks: to Austin, Texas and Daytona Beach, Florida with co-worker Jaime in

1990, Daytona with Karen in 1991, and Austin and Daytona Beach with college buddy Chris Meetze in 1992 via Big Bend National Park and Mardi Gras in New Orleans. Sadly, most of that rubber was laid on the same ribbon of interstate asphalt. Such a waste! I love to travel, and Rich was correct when he said that by re-tracing my tracks, I would re-live some of the joy of my road trips! Rich has a look at my map, which is colored yellow across a fair bit of New England and New York State, plus a yellow swath from to the center of Texas, along the Gulf Coast to Florida, and I-95 north to Washington, D.C. "Hmm, Jid, you've got a long way to go. Hmm. We'll have to start planning our first county adventure together!"

The honeymoon ends only a few months later when I buy a plane ticket to join Rich and Jeff——another UC work study co-worker—at a librarians' conference in Norfolk, Virginia. After a full day at the conference and several hours of driving to what I can only call "Tidewater nowhere" during the middle of the night, I sit in the backseat gritting my teeth and cursing to myself. Our intention was to visit my college buddy Rick at the University of Virginia in Charlottesville at 9pm. It's now 1am, and we are driving back roads with no idea when we will get there. Rick is expecting us, and I am beside myself with anger, trying to keep my language clean. In the front seat, Rich and Jeff navigate obscure routes looking for signs welcoming them into new counties, periodically stopping and examining maps under the dashboard light. They make U-turns or K-turns after entering each county or noticing they are on an incorrect route. I quickly tire of Rich's otherwise endearing "hmm"-ing tick, and Jeff's triumphant "harhickey," the exclamation that he utters each time we cross a new county line. Little do I know that a few months later I will succumb to the desire for counties, and even borrow Jeff's celebratory trademark.

The seed planted by the map delivery trips in the Midwest withstands the storm of frustration unleashed by the insanity of the "Tidewater midnight run." The academic year of 1994-95

yields a bumper crop of counties (714 out of 3143) and gal-
vanizes my determination to continue. For now, my base in
Cincinnati is most favorable; it allows me to travel in nearly
any direction on good roads with relatively few physiographic
barriers, except for the nearby Appalachian Mountains. Enabled
by my part-time job and part-time freedom, cheap gasoline, a
family to visit spread all around the country, and support from
brothers-in-arms, I am hooked. Soon, I decide that I will be
enthusiastically introducing the hobby to others and taking
my own wife captive as reluctant participant on these senseless
detours!

Classes come to a close after the first quarter of my second
year of graduate school. Meanwhile, the travel bug gestates and
grows. With little action at the library circulation desk over
break, I dream of faraway places and ruminate upon ways to
reach them. I don't have much money, but for the first time in
my young adult life I do have the luxury of time. Karen and
I refuse to take on debt during our two years of studying in
Cincinnati. She and I will both be working extra hours over
break to pay for her tuition, but my winter break from classes
will be an entire month long, and the library is closed for half
of that time.

I hatch a plan. It has been eighteen months since I've seen
my big brother Jonathan in Austin. My college friend Dave
Schoenl, who lives in Syracuse, just might be crazy enough to
go on a road trip to Texas. I decide to call Dave on the weekend.
"Let's do it," he says without hesitation.

On the morning of December 10th, Dave arrives in Cincin-
nati after his ten hour all-night drive from his home in Syracuse,
New York. Shortly after leaving the Queen City of the (old)
West at 11am, we agree to make a stop "on the way." We will
visit our mutual friend and fraternity brother Tom Doupe at
Alamogordo Air Force Base in New Mexico, 400 miles west of
Austin. By my calculations, if we stop to spend fifteen hours
with Tom, Dave will have spent 48 out of 63 hours in the car,

and I will have spent 38 out of 53. You need to "be" the car; this is what county collecting is all about!

This is my first major road trip together with Dave, so he and are figuring each other out. As Mark Twain wrote: "There ain't no surer way to find out whether you like people or hate them than to travel with them."[xii] As Dave sleeps, I drive toward my first planned exit from Interstate 74. I wonder how he is going to react when I make a quick detour to get a new county. Until I see how Dave responds, I have very modest goals for countries on this trip.

Fully caffeinated and sufficiently rested for now, Dave is already prepared to take over in Indianapolis. Damn, this means I will have to ask *him* to make the detour. We pay $.83 per gallon in Cuba, Indiana, and then I do some calculations. We need to drive 1409 miles to Tom's place, and to get there in 24 hours we'll have to average 60.4 mph. We gain two time zones heading west and lose one on our way to Austin. We'll be there in time for NFL kickoff for east coast games. If we average 65 mph, it will only take 21.6 hours to get to New Mexico. As it begins to snow I notice that Dave is maintaining the speed of 70. Cool, I think to myself, Dave is a confident driver. I'm sure he's a safe one, too. After all, he works for an insurance company!

As Dave continues to drive, I take copious notes of irrelevant details. I just love to travel. We exit the highway in Terre Haute, Indiana, "Queen City of the Wabash Valley," and follow signs for the airport, where we plan to add Dave as a legal driver with Hertz. The posted speed limit is 3mph in front of the adapted air hangar that is the terminal. At the tiny airport, we find no Hertz office and are told that the company only has an office downtown. "Screw that," says Dave, "we don't have time."

After driving all day and through the night, the sun begins to rise in our rear view. We watch the colors outside change from gray to reddish earth, and Santa Fe trains seem to appear everywhere, along with abundant road kill that seems to have assumed the flatness of the pavement, marked only by stains.

We make our own road kill, luckily out of tumbleweed. In the morning in Portals, New Mexico, we call Tom and give him our ETA. We ask him if we can have lunch at a place where we can watch football. Unlike Tom, who is a New York Jets fan, Dave and I are both Buffalo Bills fans, and our team has won four consecutive AFC Championships, or lost four consecutive Superbowls, depending on how you look at it. Under Jim Kelly, they remain competitive at 7-6, facing the 7-6 Minnesota Vikings this afternoon. The day turns out unhappy. Unable to find an open sports bar at 11am, we listen to the game on AM radio. The Bills lose 21-17, and Jim Kelly suffers what might be a career-ending injury.

José is Tom's Mexican-American friend and Air Force colleague. We invite him to join us for the post-game excursion to Mexico. Unwilling to drive our rental car across the border, we park at a fenced-in outdoor lot on a sketchy street in El Paso. We confirm that the gated lot is open until 11pm—plenty of time for us to return. The attendant takes our car keys as we leave, in case he needs to move the car. Uneasy about leaving the keys, we walk across to Ciudad Juarez for some refreshing Dos Equis with lime, authentic tacos, and souvenir shopping. After some "shock treatment" (as José calls tequila) at Fred's, José and his gringo companions return to the USA on foot by 10pm.

We walk swiftly down the shadowy and perilous street to find that the gate to the parking lot is locked. "The little fucker is gone," Dave observes verbally, as we ponder what to do next. It's a cold December night in El Paso, and our jackets are locked in the car, which is locked inside the fence. We use our new souvenir Mexican blankets for warmth. Large run-down sedans circle us like sharks, rocking to bass beats. Their passengers, local tattoo-laden homeys, slow down to take a look at us. Thank God José is with us; he might save our asses from the gangs. As our body temperatures drop and our level of discomfort surges, we agree that we cannot remain on this street indefinitely. Suddenly, Dave's had enough. He asks me to help him climb the fence, so I form a step by interlocking my fingers, as if helping a rider mount a horse. With a boost, Dave scales the fence, smashes the window of the attendant's small shack, crawls inside, and recovers the keys for the Hertz rental and the front gate. Don't mess with Schoenl.

In the small hours of the morning, on the way back to Alamogordo Air Force base, José insists upon giving us a short night-time tour of White Sands National Monument. The dunes are highly visible and quite eerie in the bright moonlight. As we've known José for less than one day, I nudge Dave and say "I hope Tom picks trustworthy friends—it would take forever for the police to find our bodies out here."

Dave and I say goodbye to Tom and José, then spend the next ten hours in the car on back roads to Austin, collecting counties as we go. This makes three nights in a row for Dave. Even I am sick of driving after two nights in a car, and I need bed. We have hardly eaten in the past two days. Hopefully we can find hot food in Lampasas, which seems to be the only town of decent size along our route.

We arrive on Harper's Ferry Lane in Austin, and are greeted by music "on 10" (loud) and a huge cooler stacked to the top with cold Budweiser cans and ice. "Let me introduce you to Big Bertha" says Jonathan. He takes us out back and proudly shows us a black, smoking monstrosity that looks like a tractor without the normal large rear wheels. He opens the top to reveal a feast of chicken, various sausages, and beef brisket. Oh, it's always a pleasure to see my brother, his wife, and the kids! We spend the next several days enjoying "Texas Cookin'" (Jonathan's authentic food, as well as Guy Clark's song). While my brother is at work, Dave and I take short excursions from Austin to collect a few more of the 254 counties in Texas. As I've completed more of Texas than Dave has, he then goes solo with the rental car to collect a few more.

Dave and I leave Austin for the drive back to Cincinnati on December 17th, 1994. Dave continues onward to Syracuse,

and Karen and I drive to Poughkeepsie, New York with our cats
Ferne and Bearcat for the holidays with her family. At the Kadela
neighborhood Christmas party, a steady stream of my new in-laws
and their friends approach me with great puzzlement about my
absurd obsession. Their questions about counties are slightly less
onerous than "What are you ever going to do with a geography
degree?" At that time, I never could have predicted that the New
Year would become my most productive county year ever. In
1995, I would visit 740 counties—about one quarter of the US
total, while finishing up my Master's degree.

The ensuing road trips are shared with various co-pilots:
Rich, Dave, Jeff, and others. The trips take many forms. As a
Master's student in geography, my visits and interviews for PhD
programs at the University of Kentucky and University at Buffalo
became integrated with county excursions. Some other great
early Cincinnati-based memories include the nine-hour trip to
Lexington, Kentucky (eighty miles as the crow flies), a two-day
drive around Lake Michigan with Rich, and my first trip to the
mountains of the West (Willcox, Arizona) with Rich, Dave,
and our mutual friend Chris, with whom I had earlier driven
to Texas and Florida. Rich enables me by giving me his 1987
light blue Ford Escort station wagon that has only 30,000
miles of use. "I will accept only one dollar and your friendship
for the car, Jid; save your money for buying gas" he insists. Rich
also helps me achieve the goal of completing all three hundred
counties in the tri-state area (Ohio-Indiana-Kentucky) before I
move from Cincinnati to Buffalo. I end my time in Cincinnati
with a two week a road trip to the Pacific Ocean and back with
Karen, featured in Chapter 4.

Before my four magical years in Buffalo, New York begin,
I've completed most of the northeast, and it becomes very
difficult to reach any uncharted counties exclusively by car.
So, my *modus operandi* changes and a new exercise becomes
familiar: pick an far-flung corner of the country with national
parks or other places of interest, plan a trip with Karen or another

county-collecting friend, find and purchase an inexpensive flight to a nearby city, rent a car, and clean up a swath of counties. From Buffalo, my flight destinations include Phoenix, Denver, Seattle, Santa Ana (CA), Minneapolis, and Austin. My brother Jon's house in Austin provides a base for road-trips throughout the largest and as "most countiferous" (as Rich would say) state in the continental US with 254 administrative units. Strategically located academic conference selection enables trips to Fort Worth and Hawaii, as I explain below. At other times, I simply take exceptionally lengthy road trips with interested friends, like my Buffalo neighbors (he from Oklahoma, she from Austria) to the Badlands of South Dakota, or with Dave to places with the express purpose of collecting new counties. I drive from Buffalo to Austin, Texas; Denver, Colorado; and Lake Michigan. On the latter trip, as Karen and I "Loop the Lake" we drive some sixty hours during a three-day weekend. When my older sister relocates from Rochester, New York to Denver, Colorado, Dave and I volunteer to deliver her belongings to her in a Ryder van. As compensation for our assistance, we collect a few dozen counties along the way, which is covered by her moving expense allowance. Because most counties are not accessible via interstate highways, it's usually necessary to navigate along back roads, the ones William Least Heat Moon calls *Blue Highways*^{xiii}.

As children enter the household I'm building with Karen, life gets infinitely more complicated, and I need to prepare myself to postpone my county quest, maybe until retirement. But at that point I'll probably too old and wise for such folly. For now, why would anyone want to spend even one minute more than necessary in a car pregnant or with small children, and what about diverting scarce family resources? Well it turns out not to be so bad: Karen's pregnancy with Charlie, our first child, includes county collection during a January break trip to visit her sister in Phoenix, and after my cousin's July wedding in Denver. Most opportunities to travel with Karen and eventually our kids to see family in New York, North Carolina, or Maine would yield a tally in Pennsylvania, Virginia, or New England.

Lest the reader assume that county trips invariably lead to the abuse of reluctant family members, it is worth reiterating that most of the missions take place with equally committed county-collecting friends. One of the more dicey examples is the aptly titled "November Peril 1996." The trip begins on a dark, foggy late autumn night in Buffalo, New York. As graduate students, we own older vehicles that aren't entirely reliable for such long trips. So, I set out with Karen to pick up a rental car at the Buffalo International Airport. I exit route 33 at Union Road and take a right to find an ATM only to learn from a policeman that no right turn is allowed on red. So, two miles from home, I have already received a moving violation. Moments after I drive away with my ticket, the ATM eats my bank card with the explanation "Card expired; will not be returned." "Any chance you want to reconsider this trip, Joel?" Karen asks, as she gets back into our Honda Civic to drive to Syracuse to meet her high school friends. "Naw, it's too perfect…Rich has Monday off, Schoenl is free, I'll only miss one day of class, and you're not going to be here anyway… it's a perfect opportunity for all of us." More like a perfect *storm*! I will drive the rented Ford Contour from Buffalo the next day and meet Rich in Charleston, West Virginia.

True to form, I excuse myself from Friday's Research Methods class early to buy some bananas and pretzels at Tops and return home to quickly plan a route through Cameron and Mifflin counties. If successful, this journey will finish Pennsylvania on the way to Charleston. As darkness falls, I'm cruising down tiny roads through narrow Appalachian valleys. Water seems to pour from everywhere and splash from other vehicles onto the road. Street flooding results from backed up drains and streams ponding on roadsides. Unable to safely take my eyes off the road, I take travel notes on a cassette tape recorder.

I search for a slice of good small town pizza in Kylertown, PA to get a break from the insanely dangerous driving conditions and celebrate the completion of my tenth state: Pennsylvania. Hours later, I find myself still on similarly darkened "blue highways" between Grant and Barbour counties in West Virginia. I pull into the motel in Charleston, West Virginia at 2am, completely exhausted, and a weary Rich opens the door to greet me with an ice cold Labatt Blue. "Top of the mornin' to ya, Jid" he exclaims as he laughs, then offers a friendly handshake.

I revel in the safety and comfort of this cheap but tidy hotel, and the beers bring glorious decompression after the long, stressful drive. Rich is upset about Weather Channel reports of a big storm heading for the Northeast. "C'mon Rich, I live in Buffalo," I try to reassure him. "This is nothing compared to what I drive in." My comments don't seem to help, as he's worried about his own drive home after I'm gone. "Jid, this storm is going to be worse in Ohio than along your route," he says. Having not seen each other in some time, we enjoy catching up by exchanging news and memories until the beers are gone: about 5:30am. Two hours of sleep will have to suffice; we'll leave here at 8am.

I awaken at 10:45am. "Hey Rich…" "Hmm, crap, we overslept" is the response from a pile of blankets and pillows on Rich's bed." We set our new departure time for 11:30. Rich remains troubled about the weather, and is still considering shortening the trip. Stubbornly, I tell him that after already driving so far, I can't lose this opportunity to collect. I want to take US 119 south to Kentucky and pick up five new counties, but Rich prefers I-64 west to I-75 south with no new counties, mainly to be in position to get back to Cincinnati quickly if required by the storm. Fair enough, "we'll meet somewhere in Kentucky," we say nearly simultaneously. Rich astutely suggests the London, Kentucky Walmart store's electronics department, where the first one to arrive will have time to browse music and movies, another interest that we share. Heading off individually again, we shake hands and wish each other a safe trip. I head west on I-64 one exit to get Putnam county, then south toward Williamson.

Arriving at Walmart at 3:40, I grab a "Good Morning, Vietnam" VHS for $6.96, and ask the cashier if she's seen Rich, as I describe him with long, curly white hair. "He looks like Albert Einstein," I add. As I turn around, there he is. "Rich, you need to pay for this video tape because I wouldn't have found it if you hadn't told me to meet you here." "Not funny, Jid," Rich is visibly not in the mood. It seems that since we split up, he had some inclement weather on I-64 and almost decided to head back to Cincinnati.

Walmart allows overnight parking for free, so Rich's idea to meet here was a good one. And in a small town like London, Kentucky, a huge Walmart won't be hard to find. We will leave Rich's vehicle here and continue toward Tennessee in the rented Ford Contour.

As I begin driving, Rich passes out cold within seconds. Hours later, the lights of Chattanooga appear above the median of US 27, and I wake up Rich. Rich and I discuss how we both really like this town; not only because of its setting, but also because it seems to have so many trains. Rich directs me onto I-59, which we follow into Georgia before exiting already at interchange 2. Heading back into Alabama, I drive up a long hill in search of the county sign for Jackson County. I miss the turnoff while reading the map with the dome light on. No problem, we'll just take the next turn-off. Easier said than done. Driving eight more curvy miles up a hill under the pitch black night sky, we finally get Jackson County. "Harhickey" I shout. "Hmmm, we'll remember this one, Jid," says Rich, as he laughs.

Rich and I make it to Gadsden, Alabama by 11pm. I pull into McDonald's out of desperation. I need a cup of what I call "dependable coffee." In a pre-gourmet age of mass-produced coffee overcooked on gas-station burners, one can count on McDonald's. While we're stopped, I need to leave off my previous cup of coffee. It takes the clerk ten minutes to get the irritable manager's key and unlock the restroom. I should have gone outside. We're wasting time, I'm running out of steam, and I have the jitters and sour stomach from too much caffeine. Rich groans in acknowledgement of my return. "I won't last long," I tell him. "I'll quit when I have to." I return to I-59 south, which I follow to exit 166 and on to US 231 south and then US 280 south(east) for St. Clair, Talladega, Shelby, Cossa, Tallapoosa, and Chambers counties. That was a good run, but now a letdown ensues.

By Alexander City, the caffeine's effect has gone smooth, and I feel like I need to be done driving, so I nudge Rich to wake him. "I can't drive now, Joel" he says. He's clearly angry with me for pushing on and trying to ride the storm out. To his defense, I was against making a stop at the Knoxville airport to sign him on to the rental contract. He adds that he doesn't want to risk it after having taken his medication just a few hours earlier. "No worries, Rich, but I'm spent too." I pull off the highway and snooze for a few minutes behind the wheel.

Shortly, I wake up from the cold and from the need to "find a friendly tree," as Rich is fond of saying. I am borderline fit to drive, and having to do so solo, the odds just seem to keep stacking up against us. Still on US 280, the sky is black, but in the headlights we see more and more deer, most along the roadside and some in the road itself. I continue onward, very cautiously. My travel budget does not include damage to a rental car. Three deer appear on the right side of the road. I brake gently at first, then out of necessity almost hard enough to squeal the tires as I move slowly into the oncoming lane. Rich makes eye contact with one of the deer and evidently pisses it off. "D'oh," Rich exclaims as an adult deer jumps directly into his door, face-planting itself against his window. Leave it to Rich to get his sense of humor back at a moment like this. I pull off the road to check for damage. It's too dark out to see any dents, so I sweep the extent of the passenger door with my bare hand. Slime on the door could be blood, snot, feces, or brains. But the car appears to have suffered no dents or broken glass. Phew!

We manage to reach our friend Dave Schoenl's Auburn, Alabama apartment by 1am, then have a couple cold Molson Canadians and talk about counties and tomorrow's plan. We manage to get to sleep by 5am. The plan is to wake up at 8am or so, complete a short double-swath in Alabama, and get to a sports bar just in time for the Bills' noon kickoff in the Central Time Zone. Suddenly remembering that Alabama is a dry state on Sundays, Dave informs us that we'll need to go to a Columbus, Georgia sports bar if we want to watch the game. Football without beer is like Thanksgiving without turkey. I drive as we re-enter the Peach State, and even at eight miles over the speed limit, cars are passing me on both sides. I notice that Rich doesn't look like he feels well, and I regret that I pushed him to be here now. I try to cut the tension and lift his spirits with small talk. "Hey Rich, know why they call it I-85?" "Why, 'Droll?' (as he calls me sometimes)" "Because everyone drives 85." "Hmm, ugh....that's really bad you know...you're incorrigible, Jid" says Rich. That's a good sign, at least he's calling me Jid again.

As luck would have it, the Bills/Eagles game is the only game this sports bar *wasn't* going to feature, so the three of us lobby the bartenders to put our game on. "Ma'am, the teams' combined record is 13-5," I argue, as Dave points out most of the games being shown aren't even being watched. Wings, beers, and the Bills: what could be better? Rich seems to be doing fine now. We take it very easy on the beers because we need to drive again afterwards. The Bills win 24-17, and Dave heads for home.

On the way back northbound, Rich and I take US 80 east to grab Talbot and Marion counties, and then continue on I-185 north to snag Harris, Troup, and Heard counties and head back into Alabama. Rich drives for fifty miles and then announces "Jid, I'm kicked." I drive as far as I can manage. When I can go no farther, Rich and I nap for a few uncomfortable minutes in the parking lot of Food World. With tornado-like clamor, a street sweeping machine wakes us just after midnight. "Lookout Joel, it's a Tennessee Zamboni!" says Rich. We're back on the road through Fayetteville, Tennessee and to the McMinnville Walmart Super Center, which will be another safe place to nap. I am useless for driving at this point. With the engine off, the car becomes teeth-chatteringly frigid. Luckily we brought our sleeping bags to keep us from freezing. We sleep until 6:30am, when we are awakened by another Tennessee Zamboni. For sure, I am paying the price for my overzealousness.

I drive along Tennessee Route 111 north in order to make a one hour detour that will get Bledsoe County, one that we barely missed on our southbound trek. After that, we take a lonely Monday morning road into the Village of Hilham to get Jackson County. Going a few miles over the 30mph limit, I pass a sheriff; at least no children are present, which would make the limit 15. "Our damn New York plates," I say to Rich. "We're screwed." The sheriff shakes his finger at me and I nod at him respectfully to acknowledge his warning. "Too bad we need to come back through here," I say to Rich. We need to return in a few minutes after our county U-turn. I drive into Clay County on TN 292, and then back into the Village of Hilham. Sure enough, the same sheriff car is in position, waiting for speeders. I pass cautiously at 25mph. Timidly, my eyes peek into my rear view mirror. Yep, he is following us. "Damn New York plates!" I exclaim again, shaking my head. The sheriff follows for about two miles, probably to the town line, and then turns onto a side street, leaving us alone.

Now we need to make time… Rich's storm is moving into the Midwest. I drive into Kentucky on route 111 for a quick farewell lunch with Rich at a very modern looking KFC in London. Rich heads his way back to Cincinnati on back roads, and I head mine on the interstate. No more virgin counties to take this trip. Averaging 75mph, in two hours I pass through Cincinnati. In Columbus, I have to make a detour on 315 to avert a traffic backup on I-71. By now, Rich should be back in Cincinnati safely. AM radio is dominated by talk of snow peril. Two feet have been reported in some Midwestern cities and more is expected. I elect to take I-76 east into Pennsylvania to stay away from Lake Erie, which turns out to be wise. There are whiteouts on my route after Akron, but it's nothing like the weather I'm avoiding. My eyes follow fresh tire marks in the snow to a Chevy Blazer in the median. I crawl at speeds as low as 20mph. In the sky above Lake Erie, I can see mighty storm clouds, well-illuminated by the lights of the nearby cities. I take I-79 north to Erie, as a Buffalo weather report announces that the New York State Thruway remains clear all the way home.

A journey of great peril indeed, but I am home by midnight with great accomplishments to share with Karen: forty six new counties! Two in Pennsylvania, ten in West Virginia, fifteen in Tennessee, thirteen in Alabama, and six in Georgia.

This is just one example of what might be called a "dedicated" county trip, but over the next decade, my appetite for counties would impact my selection of family vacation spots and pro-fessional conferences alike. Everywhere, I would travel armed with a my county map, a Road Atlas, and a selection of colored highlighters to mark my territory.

In March 1999, I combine professional conference with family vacation, and counties! It is already five years into my county quest. Our son Charlie is less than one year old, our fetus Isabela is due in October, and I have an opportunity to take them and their mother to Hawaii. Kids under two—as well as fetuses—fly for free. But the main justification for this trip is to attend the main annual conference for my academic discipline. My brother Jonathan offers me enough miles for two round-trip tickets from our home in Buffalo to Honolulu. Unable to pay the actual ticket price to the airlines, I send him $500 in appreciation. Even so, this trip will be a huge expense. A worthwhile investment for me, however, as this conference will get me my first job interview and an invitation to Bentley for a second interview. I am particularly excited because Karen and I will be the first in our immediate families to visit the islands. After my conference, the trip will allow us to see Haleakala and

Hawaii Volcanoes National Parks, and will possibly give me the chance to visit all of the counties in the state.

We fly via Chicago and Los Angeles. Charlie embarks on a half-hour screaming episode over the otherwise pacific Pacific Ocean. I'm sure the flight attendants and other passengers will never forget it. To decompress after the long flights, we drive our rental car to a pebble covered beach, loaded with "pearly shells." We are staying at the Outrigger Hotel in Honolulu—the cheapest room on the island—for $80/night. We have a small balcony, and we are only a couple blocks from the beach. Charlie enjoys making sand angels in the sun, and the parents enjoy the weather, which is generally mild and breezy but not at all hot. Charlie is acting sluggish, so I leave Karen on the beach and take him to a nearby clinic just to be safe. Charlie endures x-rays, a urine sample, and a blood test, and four hours later we race back to the beach to join his very worried young mother. The trip had simply been stressful for seventeen-month-old Charlie—he has an ear infection, and he is tired, dehydrated, and jet-lagged.

The next day is the first day of the AAG meetings. I do my best to attend faithfully, and present my paper on the "Subnational Distribution of Foreign Direct Investment in Poland," part of my PhD dissertation that I intend to defend this upcoming summer. While I play the role of diligent graduate student at the conference, Karen and Charlie go swimming in Maunalua Bay near Diamond Head.

After the conference meetings taper off, we have a chance to do some sightseeing and county collecting. From Maui, I will be able to carefully manage inter-island flights with a packet of six one-way ticket vouchers on Hawaiian Airlines. So, Karen, Charlie, and I fly to Maui for two days and visit Haleakala National Park, and of course to tally Maui county. On Maui, we are struck by the most dramatic topographic and climatic changes imaginable between the leeward and windward sides of the mountain. Even more amazing is the drive along the poorly-maintained (and sometimes mud-covered) Hana road on the eastern side of the island. Just south of Hana, we camp for free, as seems to be the Hawaiian custom.

A gentle, cool, and moist midnight wind gradually ramps up into near-hurricane force as we sleep. Our tent trembles violently as if it will be blown up the mountainside with us inside! Standing up inside tent to hold the windward corners in place, I try to calm Charlie and reassure Karen. I ask Karen to stand on the lifted corners of the tent floor as I run outside to move the car to that side, protecting us from the angry ocean's assault of spray. Eventually, the wind subsides, and my companions fall asleep.

Next, to claim the island county of Kauai, I will need to make a solo round trip there and back, with my ultimate destination of the Big Island. So, at 5am I leave Karen and Charlie at the hotel on Maui. Karen has enough to handle with the baby, the baby bag, and the car seat, so I am caring for our huge Bauer hockey bag full of camping gear, which seems awkwardly out of place in Hawaii as I check it in for our flight. My short flight to Lihue arrives at the outdoor airport terminal, where I retrieve our Bauer bag. At the counter, I re-check it onto the same plane to return to Maui, then briefly exit the small airport's gates for a quick look at the mountains before re-boarding the plane. I wish I had more than a few minutes here, as the "Garden Island" looks absolutely stunning. Moments later, I'm back on a flight to Kahului, Maui, where I meet Karen, Charlie, and of course October Fetus, on the quick layover to Hilo on the big island.

On Hilo, to prevent a repeat of our stormy Maui camping nightmare, I rent a cabin at Hawaii Volcanoes National Park. Because volcanic fumes are dangerous for children and pregnant women, I hike the lava trail toward the red glow all by myself. Not much fun, really, and maybe even a bit scary as night falls.

So, the trip to Hawaii turns out to be extremely worthwhile. I had my initial job interview at a place called Bentley

College, somewhere near Boston. Confident that I'll be invited to campus for a follow-up, I return to Buffalo with a bit more incentive to finish my dissertation on schedule this upcoming summer. In addition to the Honolulu conference experience and a few job prospects, I end up with four new counties, ostensibly completing Hawaii; and my wife and baby boy inherit three: Oahu, Maui, and Hawaii. As a special family souvenir of this unlikely but worthwhile trip, a song I'm reminded of from my own childhood joins the bedtime routine of Charlie and subsequent kids: Burl Ives' "Pearly Shells."

We are living in Nashua, New Hampshire in 2008 when I get the news via email that my friend Rich died in his sleep. I call our mutual friend Jeff Hall in Cincinnati for our occasional telephone visit, and we discuss all the good times we had with Rich, at the library and on road trips. Unfortunately, because of family and work obligations, neither Jeff nor I are able to attend Rich's funeral ceremony at his favorite location of Jenny Lake in Wyoming. Rich probably started collecting counties before I was even old enough to drive, but he died without finishing. I don't know what Rich's county total is, nor do I know if his family kept his records. Jeff and I decide to honor Rich's memory with a major county trip to Oklahoma. This will be my final major trip, and hopefully it will allow me to complete five of my remaining eight states. Specifically, I hope to finish what remains of Oklahoma, Kansas, Nebraska, Iowa, and Missouri. Jeff and I will culminate our trip with a U2 concert in Norman, Oklahoma.

Up at 4am on October 15, 2008, I putter in my Nashua kitchen casually drinking coffee and making lunches for Karen and the kids. I booked a travel award with United Airlines on flights with codeshare partner USAir. This should be easy, as my flights are from the closest airport to home: Manchester, New Hampshire (MHT). I arrive at 6:10am, intending to take a 7:00am flight to Chicago, with my connecting flight scheduled to arrive in Oklahoma City (OKC) at 11:30. The check-in

agent calmly tells me "Mr. Deichmann, your flight is closed."
"That can't be," I respond, pointing to the 7:00am departure
on my flight confirmation. "Yes," she says, "your plane will
take off in eight minutes." Somehow I wasn't informed that the
flight schedule had changed. The United agent guesses that the
notification must have been lost in the codeshare with USAir.
The moral of this story is to always double check your flight the
day before you travel, and as is possible nowadays, also check
in on line and print your boarding pass. Everybody knows
that! So, over the next hour I explore several re-routing options
and I'm on my way to Oklahoma City on a three-leg trip…
via Denver! My unfortunate friend Jeff Hall has a short, direct
flight from Cincinnati to OKC to arrive at 10:30am. Despite
my best efforts to convince him to take a bus into the city and
spend the time exploring, he assures me he would prefer to wait
for five hours in the arrivals hall.

I pass through security for my flight to Philadelphia, and the
USAir agent asks if she can check my carry-on bag to my final
destination at no charge. "Absolutely…thank you!" On flight
1553 from Philadelphia to Denver, I find time to update my
county list for the first time in three years, and I'm at 3010.
Wow- this actually seems to be within reach! Still, I'm not sure
if my goal of finishing five states this trip is too ambitious.
When we decided to take a trip together, Jeff told me he wants
to drive only 8-10 hours per day. Autumn daylight is getting
shorter, I'll be arriving at OKC hours later than planned, and
Jeff and I have U2 tickets for the Norman show on Sunday
night. So, there is a lot of pressure. I'll do my best to finish the
task, but I refuse to risk missing the concert, let alone jeopardize my friendship with Jeff. I just really don't want to return
to this region for a handful of stray counties, especially after my
jinxed plane ticket—intended for Austin, Texas in June—had
already incurred a re-deposit fee of $150 when I cancelled that
trip to keep the peace at home.

I arrive at OKC at 4pm as (re)scheduled, but my gate-checked suitcase does not. I meet Jeff at baggage claim, and exchange excited "har-hickey" greetings, handshakes, and man-hugs. He and I file a lost luggage report, then line up at Avis to pick up our rental car, only to find that the company's new geographic restrictions to states contiguous to Oklahoma will keep me from reaching my goal of Nebraska. "I'm sorry Jeff, I need to ask around." Jeff is ever-patient in such situations. None of the nearby desks have cars available, so I make a phone call to Alamo, which is located off-site. They hook us up with a black Mazda for the same price, and although the car doesn't have the luxury of cruise control for the long trip ahead, we are not restricted from entering Nebraska.

At the airport, nobody seems to know directions to Interstate 44 west, the major interstate that connects the airport to…well, everywhere. When I find someone who thinks they can help, they tell us that it's at least two miles away. I watch the odometer carefully, causing me to miss the ramp for I-44 after a half mile. We need to turn around. The trip is not starting off well. To break the stress, Jeff asks me "Any idea why the license plates say 'Oklahoma-OK'?" "No idea, Jeff." "It's because Oklahomans don't know how to spell 'mediocre.'"

Happy to be out of airports and away from the city, Jeff and I clean up six counties in the southwest corner of the state. We guestimate Elk City as our target for the evening and Jeff calls to make a reservation at the local Motel 6 so that I can give United an address for delivering my luggage. We buy Subway and supplies as the sun goes down in our bug-splattered windscreen. Glancing at the road atlas while eating at Subway, I discover that US 62 represents the county line between Kiowa and Tillman counties. We already drove that road, but it's unclear if it enters both counties. Damn! We might have missed a county. With a vengeance, I make a half hour detour to pierce the county in its mid-section by crossing the fork of the Red River on OK 5. The time spent backtracking helps me appreciate Oklahoma's magnitude, and as the hours of this frustrating day pass, Jeff and I increasingly long for the refuge of our Elk City motel.

Just before we lose cell phone coverage, United calls me to explain that although my luggage arrived at Oklahoma City tonight, they will not be able to get it to Elk City until Saturday. For county collectors, this presents a problem! I have no idea which state I will be on Saturday night, let alone which town or hotel. "Never mind, keep it for now," I tell them, I will try to swing by OKC (two hours out of the way) to pick it up tomorrow, or call back early with another hotel address for tomorrow night. Worst scenario (so I think) is that they can deliver it to our Comfort Inn in nearby Norman for Sunday, just in time for me to fly back home in clean clothes. Jeff and I pull off the road, turn on the dome light, and try to find a shortcut between the towns of Reed and Carter (US 40 interchange 20). Instead of a time saver, we find ourselves on some crazy unmarked winding back roads (some of them unpaved), guided only by an illuminated cell phone tower in the distance. We use the tower as a beacon, correctly guessing it is back in the direction of US 40. It is a safe ending to an otherwise disappointing day.

Thanks to an in-room coffee maker, I'm up by 7:30. Elk City's Motel 6 is a fair motel at a decent price. When we check out, my luggage is still absent; no surprise. We are headed northbound, and I decide there is no way to make time for a detour back to the OKC airport to check on my suitcase. Instead, I make a quick stop at Pamida department store to buy socks, underwear, and a toothbrush. The drive on US 183 northward through Central and Western Kansas yields Comanche, Barber, Edwards, Pawnee, and Woodman counties for me, and a few additional ones for Jeff, including Sheridan and Logan with quick deviations near Colby before heading north again on KS 161. We keep getting farther away from Oklahoma City and my luggage! As we cross a quadruple swathe that I had already obtained on east-west trips, my next new county won't be until late tonight or tomorrow morning in Nebraska. Seems like a lot of driving this afternoon and evening, and we are both out of steam. Jeff had been hoping for eight-ten hours/day in the car, and we are already at twelve when we cross the state line into Nebraska. No luck finding any motels, so wearily I drive onward. When we finally reach Ogallala, Nebraska, we find another Motel 6 that turns out to have a vacant room with two large, comfortable beds. Despite moments of discouragement, it has been a good day. Examining our progress on the map, I know it will be possible for me to finish the five states, but it is far too early to reaffirm my insane ambitions with my co-pilot, who had spent part of today under the weather.

Today will be a marathon day in Nebraska. After a good rest, we begin late (8ish) northbound again in thick fog on NE 61 and then eastbound on NE92. From the start, I know that Day 3 of this trip will be decisive. Eastbound now as the fog lifts and we drive into the morning sun—a day that would end westbound toward the evening sun two or three states farther south. This after driving the length of Nebraska! We continue on 92 across the state to the "City of Wahoo", then I-680 around the north of Omaha and into Washington County on US75. Omaha can impress; to me it seems like a smaller version of Austin, TX. We drive into Iowa and south to US34 east, already racing against nightfall. Somewhere in Nebraska, Jeff realizes that I intend to return to four counties in Iowa that I missed last year due to lack of time, so I reassure him we can get a *double-swath* so that he would collect twice the number that I get. This turns out to be a great decision, and well-worth lobbying my weary friend. Unfortunately, US 34 east is congested and requires us to pass through countless towns to finish Iowa. The westbound return route we picked to add a swath of counties for Jeff goes through Lenox, Guss, and Essex. Luckily, it turns out to have great roads and very little traffic.

In the gloomy flats around the Missouri river, I drive as fast as I dare as Jeff does a masterful job of navigating us into the NW corner of Missouri to finish that state. The surroundings seem incredibly dark and eerie. I am desperately fighting slumber as Jeff dozes, but I know that we need to get a closer to Wichita if I am to have a chance of finishing before the concert. Sensing my weakness, Jeff wearily mutters "Uh, Joel, I'd like to get to the hotel as soon as possible," then nods off again. "Geeze" I think to myself, "if we're going to a hotel anyway, why not collect a fresh swath on the way there? Getting back on the interstate seems wasteful to me." I'll keep driving, Jeff can sleep. I take KS63 south across the Kansas River to Interstate 70. We are approaching stupid o'clock. At a rest area near Junction City I relent. Jeff is right, we can't claim the counties if we're dead. I pick up a booklet of bargain hotels and find an inexpensive vacant room just fifteen miles down the road in Abilene, Kansas.

We pay $38 to stay at the worst hotel imaginable. The air in the room smells like broken dreams and shame. Jeff and I are both terrified about bedbugs and untold other nasty things in the sheets. The previous visitors had left an unlabeled vial on the nightstand. Jeff unenthusiastically declares he doesn't want to get up until 8am. Realizing that 8am is not going to allow us to finish before the concert, I offer to bring Jeff hot tea if he agrees to be ready to jump into the passenger seat at 7:30am. Sold! Jeff goes to sleep quickly but uneasily, trying to minimize contact with the sheets and the stale air. I can tell he has the filth of the place on his mind. He's probably not very happy with my assertiveness either. It would probably be in bad form to remind Jeff how I felt years ago driving all night through "Tidewater nowhere.

When I get off the road from a long drive, I enjoy a couple of Buds to wind down, and tonight is no exception. On the vintage television, the Yankees win ALCS Game Two over Anaheim and seem to have the magic this year. As I sip my beer, I think to myself "we can do it." My whole body is celebrating the accomplishment of finishing Nebraska, Iowa, and Missouri today. Kansas and Oklahoma must fall tomorrow!

Up at 6am and out solo by 6:30am to claim Ottawa county—

an easy round trip of thirty miles each way in the dark. I *know* this is possible—we need to finish southeastern Kansas and northeastern Oklahoma, then clean up a few mid-state OK counties and get to the U2 concert. I am reticent to again discuss my intention to finish until I am confident that Jeff can see for himself that it is possible. I need to be sensitive to the fact that whether or not I finish, he still has more work to do in Oklahoma. By virtue of Jeff's reluctance to collect counties last night and trade a half hour of sleep for Ottawa County this morning, he doesn't share my blind ambition. I also know Jeff is skeptical but doesn't want to shatter my hopes. I return to the hotel to pick up Jeff, who is ever so happy to leave.

I embrace the awkward silence to concentrate on my driving as the adrenaline nearly bursts my veins. I drive 77mph on Highway 77 south under perfect collecting conditions: extremely rural roads that are straight, flat, dry, and have no traffic. By 11am in Independence, it becomes absolutely clear to me that this can be done. While driving, I triumphantly show Jeff the map on the road atlas and explain my route to him as I take a much-needed driving break so that he can scoop some pretty easy counties just across the state line.

At mid-afternoon we are reminded of the scale of these states. I can taste victory, but the pressure is palpable. I call an audible when we unexpectedly encounter road construction and detour signs. The result is a minor strategic error in our route. I'll spare you the details.

After the delay, I can tell that my drive (figuratively) to drive (literally) and finish this quest really pushes the envelope with Jeff. I want this very badly, and I try to explain to Jeff why I push so hard on such ventures. I just don't want to have to fly out here again—I need closure. I'm not going to live forever, aand I'm determined to get this job done. I'm sure that the U2 concert serves as comfort to Jeff. Deep down, he knows that there is no way in hell I would ever jeopardize experiencing a performance by my favorite band.

As we approach Oklahoma City and Norman to its south, we see traffic on the interstate grind to a halt in front of us. I ask Jeff to drive and I navigate us around fifteen-to-twenty miles of interstate parking lot. We simply take I44 around the western part of the city to US62 east and Santa Fe Avenue through Moore and into Norman. I don't know Oklahoma City, but its road layout is a grid, and this ain't my first rodeo. I'm seasoned by other U2 stadium shows. I had witnessed the same level of congestion recently in Boston, the New Jersey Meadowlands, and Raleigh. Jeff and I check into our hotel just in time to watch the Bills beat the Jets in overtime. For me, the stage is set and the day is ending perfectly. In the lobby, we meet two smoky older women from Tulsa and share a cab with them. We arrive at the OU stadium mid-way through Muse, the opening act.

Although our seats are not together, Jeff and I both have excellent views of one of the best concerts either of us has ever seen. I take a deep breath, look around, and revel in the successes of the weekend. It is a beautiful day, and our work is done. Life is great!

After the show, we walk two and a half miles back to the hotel faster than cars can drive through the gridlock. It is midnight and we still haven't had dinner. Jeff says "Hey man, let's go through the Wendy's drive-through." We stand in line for twenty minutes before reaching the counter. "I can't serve you, you're not in a car," the woman says. "Why not?" Jeff counters, "We waited our turn in line like everyone else, but we aren't polluting the environment…. And we have a car too…. it's parked just down the street." We stubbornly stand our ground, and the manager agrees to take our order. We are served some greasy, breaded, and most-likely spit-upon chicken tenders.

Only two hours of sleep for the weary travelers. With bleary-eyes and no shower, I drive to the Alamo rental return at OKC. The sky is pitch black at 5:00am and Alamo's rental car return's gate remains locked. My flight is at 6:00am. A security guard arrives to ask us what we are doing there. We explain that our flight is in one hour. Hoping for the best, we reluctantly leave the car with him at the curb in front of the gate. Several other drivers emerge from their waiting cars and follow our lead, ditching their cars with the security guard.

I ask for a window seat on the right side of the plane to Chicago. It gives me a fine sunrise view of America and a fresh appreciation for the enormity of the landscape that I have traveled. I look out the window and ponder the fact that I have been all over this vast, incredible country, crisscrossing it at intervals of forty miles or less. I feel like I have experienced my country's geography. I reflect upon life on my family's farm, and consider this county quest an enormous privilege. I am almost done with this project. In just two weeks, I intend to complete Georgia. After that, some serious work remains in Alaska, followed by minor clean up in Virginia, and maybe the former leper colony Kalawao in Hawaii, if I decide that it really counts as a county.

That evening, I arrive home in Nashua after work to find my unopened Oklahoma-bound suitcase at my doorstep, nearly five days after I packed it.

The year 2011 is the first one without any new counties since I began this pursuit in 1994, and in fact probably since 1989. The next year yields eight boroughs in Alaska. Late on a January evening in 2013, I sit at the kitchen table drinking my favorite Chilean *Concha y Toro* red wine while goofing around on Facebook as Karen finishes up work. Here is my libation-inspired post:

> *10:17 on a Friday night. Karen is still working at the other end of the table, and I am bored enough to tell my FB friends a story in case they are bored enough to read it. In November 1994, my University of Cincinnati GeoPhysics Library boss Rich —later to become my good friend—inspired me to join him in his quest to visit EVERY COUNTY IN THE USA. Rich died too early in 2008 without finishing, but not before he and I completed many road trips together.*

Thanks to Rich, I discovered the spectacular American West, and by 2011, I needed to visit only 29 more counties of 3143. I got eight more of those in 2012 with my big brothers and good friend Dave Schoenl, and I am hatching a scheme to finish this ridiculous mission by November 2014 (20 years after I began). As I only need a few counties in Alaska and Virginia, there will be much rejoicing in some TBA independent Virginia city to conclude this quest in November 2014. You are all welcome to join me for a drink! ☺

That is my first universal public pronouncement of the goal, and I know that going public will motivate me to finish sooner. Many of the 40+ Facebook comments suggest that insanity is at work; others advocate for a book about the quest. I thank them for this idea, responding that such a book would be tedious to read: itineraries, travel notes, and a few interesting anecdotes. Instead, I decide that a brief discussion of county collecting might be sufficient material for a single chapter in a broader travel book project like this one!

Later that month, on a bitterly cold day in January 2013, Dave and I spend three evening hours on the phone with one another. We are plotting out our strategy to finish Alaska. The first step is for each of us to get an Alaska Airlines credit card that awards us each with a 25,000 mile enrollment bonus and two $99 companion tickets. We set forth a tight flight schedule with minimal downtime. Our sightseeing will be from 30,000 feet. Just hours after we arrive in Anchorage, our itinerary includes three, round-trip tickets to the far western reaches of the state and one flight to Kodiak to spend three days in the Aleutians on the Alaska State Ferry. Through this exercise, we have learned Alaska Airlines, Era Aviation, and PenAir networks like the back of our hands. The initial plan will leave only North Slope and Yukon boroughs in Alaska, which I will visit in 2014 with my sons and my brothers.

Walking back from the mailbox in May 2013, I open my Alaska Airlines credit card statement. There is a credit for $814 from the Alaska State Ferry. I call the ferry service, and I'm told the June sailing to the Aleutians has been cancelled, so my reservation has been refunded. Dave and I have one month to retrofit our strategy and find a way to get those three boroughs, as well as the others that are already set in stone. When I call, Dave tells me he will be in Alaska a few days early with his friend Lee, and that Lee is not into collecting counties. Plans may be in jeopardy.

On June 11th, Dave meets me at the arrivals hall in Anchorage. Lee is waiting outside to pick up my checked backpack with his rental car and take it to the hotel while Dave and I fly onward to collect boroughs. Man, that was nice of Lee," I say to Dave. Dave and I re-enter the terminal and fly to Dillingham and back that night, then meet Lee for Buffalo Wild Wings and an enthusiastic discussion of our plan for the week. We decide to use Spring Suites as our home base, with the shuttle and rental car as transportation back and forth to the terminal, where we will catch our flights.

The next day, Lee travels to Juneau for fun while Dave and I fly to King Salmon. From King Salmon, we secure passage on a packed single-prop plane to the remote fishing village of Egegik in Lake and Peninsula Borough with a pilot and five other passengers. With the salmon run beginning soon, passengers are stacked up waiting to get to the cannery. Egegik is a village of sixty or so Aleuts that swells to 3000+ during the salmon run. There is nothing to see, the liquor store is open for one hour per day, and the state police need to fly in from another borough in the event of an emergency, as happened following a recent murder. Dave and I stand out like sore thumbs, and in retrospect it's a wonder that we didn't get our asses kicked just for being there. "Are you Joel and Dave?" A local woman named Solvi asks us as we walk through the village looking for a ride back to the gravel landing strip. "That's us." Dave and I look at each other as if to ask how she might have guessed—we're the only two men over twenty who aren't native Alaskans. "Your ride will be here soon," Solvi says. This is our only day in Egegik. Our most memorable experience is on the flight back to King Salmon when the single propeller plane makes an unscheduled landing on the beach "runway" to pick up two tons of frozen fish. Not wanting to stand around looking arrogant, Dave and I roll up our sleeves and help load the boxes. As we take off again for King Salmon, it's only the pilot, Dave, and I, along with two pallets of frozen fish on a bumpy but mesmerizing 900-foot altitude flight.

Dave had already gone to Barrow before I arrived in Alaska, originally hoping to complete the state with me this week on the Alaska State Ferry. With the ferry's grounding, I fly to Barrow and back via Prudhoe Bay while Dave and Lee sightsee in Anchorage. My jet's path is directly over Mt. McKinley; the weather is perfect and the view is absolutely spectacular! I see fortresses of mountains, millions of lakes, and ribbons of rivers; there are no towns, cars, or roads to be seen. I cannot take my eyes off the jet's window. I am in awe, and at this moment I don't care if the plane crashes in this amazing place. I can think of worse places to die than Alaska. I later learn that this week in June 2013 is the warmest stretch of weather ever recorded in Alaska: 80s and completely clear every day.

Dave and I dutifully follow our amended plan. We fly to Nome, Kotzebue, St. Mary's, and Bethel, and for some time, we are convinced we will finish the state this week. In Dutch Harbor, however, our hopes get shattered. Dave reserved seats on Grant Aviation's flight from Dutch Harbor to the nearby island of Akun, in East Aleutians Borough, which would complete Alaska for both of us. Dutch Harbor has a small terminal, typical of Alaska and something special for most travelers to see. In a small hangar about the size of an average house, one can find check in, departures, security, arrivals, and baggage claim. We wait in vain at the terminal for ten hours. Neither the desk staff nor the pilot shows up for our scheduled flight to Akun. With two hours until our flight back to Anchorage, we abandon hope and explore outside the airport for some fresh air. Back in Anchorage, Grant Aviation staff offer us no explanation, only an apology. The completion of Alaska will require one more trip, and I will return with pleasure.

Two months later, I still need just four county equivalents: two in Virginia, one in Hawaii, and one in Alaska. I find time to put together a plan to finish this project once and for all. I had planned to save two Virginia counties until the very end so that I could have a party to celebrate with friends and family. Now, I think it would be a silly idea to have a party for myself. So I book an award flight for April on US Airways to travel to Honolulu. On the way to spending Thanksgiving with Karen's family in North Carolina in November, I make two quick detours from I-81 and I-77 in Virginia. The cities are called Salem and Galax. The detours run roughly parallel to the interstate, so they barely add to our travel time to North Carolina, and neither Karen nor the kids bat an eye at the deviations. Three days later, my father-in-law Jerry Kadela raises a glass for the accomplishment in front of extended family at Thanksgiving dinner. Some might think that finishing university, writing a dissertation, keeping a job and earning tenure, staying married and raising kids are true tests of resolve. They are indeed, but honestly, even if collecting counties is an exercise in folly, following through with anything this big is an enormous challenge. I truly feel honored to see that my family appreciates this.

Over the Christmas holidays, I return to Nashua and take account of my Alaska Airline miles. I need to spend $300 at Home Depot or Lowes to earn enough triple miles that will get me my $950 round trip ticket from Anchorage to Sand Point (East Aleutians Borough) for free, or I should say for a $10 ticketing fee. Accomplished in January! Flight booked in February! I'm going to Sand Point on August 9th, after spending a week in Alaska with my two sons, one nephew, and two brothers Chuck and Jonathan.

In April 2014, I travel to Hawaii and back to Boston in four days as if it's a work assignment, but on a tighter budget. I stay at a cheap hotel with a free airport shuttle, and subsist on granola bars, apples, water bottles, and my small flask of "travel scotch." One day out, the next day to fly to Kalaupapa County and take the National Historical Park leper colony tour, then one day of buffer just in case something were to go wrong, and a final day to get back to Boston. Nobody could possibly understand. Other than my immediate family and confidant David Schoenl, I don't think anyone even notices that I was gone.

Just north of Homer, Alaska, on August 9th, 2014, I help my two brothers, two sons, and a nephew pack up our soaking wet camp. Nervous about making my flight to Sand Point, I drive the six of us several hours to Anchorage, where we hastily unpack our rental car at the Courtyard Anchorage Airport. My flight is in two hours. I shower and leave everyone else at the hotel to decompress and prepare for tomorrow's flights home. It seems a shame—this hotel is too nice to serve as a staging ground for our wet and smelly gear.

I take the hotel shuttle to ANC, and then check in with PenAir for my 4:30pm flight to Sand Point. I ask if I can also check in for my 7:15pm return flight to Anchorage, but the counter agent apologetically says I'll need to do that when I get to Sand Point. Oh man! There is a high likelihood that I'll get to Sand Point within thirty minutes of my (re-) departure—too late to check in—and then I'll be at the mercy of PenAir to get back here. Tomorrow is a Sunday, so there are no flights back to Anchorage. If I can't make this immediate return flight, my boys and I will miss our flights home tomorrow.

Two hours of stress about getting back tonight, and PenAir doesn't sell beer on this flight. I see only clouds outside my window throughout the bumpy 800 mile flight to Sand Point. My neighbor, a nice Aleutian lady named Jenny Wood, is intrigued by my quest, and I'm fascinated by her story of getting rejected for a US passport because she was born in 1957, and is "older than Alaska." The State Department failed to recognize that she is a US citizen because Alaska was not yet a state. Our PenAir twin-prop descends onto the airstrip, and as I step off the plane I thank the flight attendant and pilot for the safe journey, dropping the news that I hope to be flying right back to Anchorage with them in a few minutes—The captain tells me to "see Bridget" at the bottom of the stairs and ask her if I can still get my boarding pass.

Wearing a bright yellow safety vest, Bridget greets me on the tarmac with a smile. I try to explain my tight situation to her with as few words as possible—time is of the essence. She laughs and says "congratulations and welcome to Sand Point!" Puzzled, I thank her, and then look at her with a face full of confusion. "Your friend checked you in, and your boarding pass is waiting for you on the counter inside." I follow the other passengers into the one-room airport. Just inside the door stands Dave Schoenl, who greets me with a congratulatory handshake and commemorative Sand Point hoodie in Alaska's state colors. "Hurry, we don't have much time," he says. Having arrived last night to complete Alaska for himself, Dave rushes me outdoors to the front of the airport for a photo opportunity with a sign that says "Popov Island: Welcome to Sand Point."

The quest for counties has been a magnificent obsession, and easily my life's most resource-intensive project, with time being the most essential ingredient. Many entire (twenty-four hour) days were spent in a car, with only short stops for gas, drive-through food, and bathroom breaks. To survive so many miles under all manner of conditions, one needs to be not only a careful driver, but also a lucky traveler. Too many good drivers die in wrecks, and I am ever so grateful for travel mercies and competent co-pilots. I am so fortunate to have shared my adventures with dear friends like Rich Spohn, Dave Schoenl, Jeff Hall, Chris Meetze, Dann Karlson, and Valerie Hartung, who happen to also be county collectors. Other excursions were with family members like Karen Kadela Deichmann and our kids, reluctant to spend even one extra minute in the car to get a county, but still willing to ride along and accommodate my passion. Now, my quest is at an end, so thank you Karen, from the bottom of my heart, for understanding the child inside your man.

4

JOEL AND KAREN'S ROCKY ADVENTURE

"Stood alone on a mountaintop, staring out at the Great Divide
I could go east, I could go west, it was all up to me to decide
Just then I saw a young hawk flying and my soul began to rise.
And pretty soon my heart was singing… Oh roll me away!
Gotta keep rolling, gotta keep riding, searching 'til I find what's right."

"Roll Me Away"
Bob Seger, *The Distance* (1983)

Every adventure needs a name. "Rocky Adventure" is a title that was chosen long before we left our home in Cincinnati for the West—in part to be geographically descriptive, in part to be witty, and in part as a precaution against unrealistic expectations. This adventure turns out to be anything but rocky, at least until we return home just in time to pack up and move 400 miles to a new city the very next day. This trip represents the culmination of many goals and dreams. The immediate objective is to string together some of the national parks we've long wanted to see, and to do it on a shoestring. The road trip also allows considerable progress in the county quest of Chapter

3. But what makes the trip even more exciting is that Karen and I don't yet know where in the USA we will ultimately find jobs and raise our family, and as Bob Seger says, we *"gotta keep ridin', searchin' 'til (we) find what's right."* It could be somewhere along this path that lay before us! With our very first opportunity to see a large portion of America, I am about to fall in love with my country like never before, and at the same time I will fall much more deeply in love with my wife Karen. Beautiful, open-minded, funny, and last but not least forgiving, I am learning that she is a pretty cool travel companion. To adapt my favorite *Twainism*, "there's no better way to learn whether you like someone than to travel with them for two weeks in a small car, taking breaks only to hike together in oven heat or to sleep together in a tiny pup tent in the wind and freezing rain."

Karen is still at work in downtown Cincinnati as I spend August Friday afternoon packing what I can fit into our 1991 two door Green Honda Civic. At 5:30pm, I pick her up from Great American Insurance on Walnut Street before heading west. The car is new to us with 160,000 miles, and the best vehicle either of us has ever owned. We have been married for only two years, living in a one-bedroom apartment near the University of Cincinnati, where this month we are both finishing our Master's degrees. I have been on many county trips with my friends, but this trip is going to be very different. Yes, it is a trip to *terra incognita* that will yield counties, but this time I am bringing my soul mate, someone I can talk to about lifetime goals, someone I can touch and kiss, and we are exploring uncharted territory together. My heart is singing. Colorado or bust!

The sun sets as we cross the Mississippi, pass the Gateway Arch to our right, and cruise through St. Louis. We have been driving six hours on Interstates 74 and 70. We are so pumped with adrenaline that we drive all night without realizing how tired we are, stopping only for gasoline. At eighty cents per gallon, gasoline is cheaper in Missouri than back in Cincinnati.

Our enthusiasm is fueled by music all the way: Over the Rhine, Sting, U2, Hootie and the Blowfish, and the upbeat cassette mix that I prepared for our trip, which includes all of the above. When the brilliant sun rises behind us in the morning, nearly blinding the driver in the rearview, we are already cruising through the emerald green rolling plains of central Kansas.

As the sun climbs into the sky and shines on our shoulders, the outside temperature rises quickly. For air conditioning, our Civic has only what my father-in-law ("FIL") calls a model 380: open both windows and the sunroof and drive 80 mph. Crossing into Colorado, we take US 40 to Aroya, then CO 94 toward Punkin Center. On advice from Rich, this is the shortest distance from Cincinnati to Garden of the Gods in Colorado Springs, our first destination. Although our trusty new vehicle is extremely fuel efficient, I am concerned about the scarcity of villages and even greater scarcity of working gas pumps. We might have an issue. Town after town lacks an operational gas station, and it's still a long way to Colorado Springs. The open sunroof seems to create quite a drag. To conserve fuel, at least in our minds, we slow down to 60 mph, close the sunroof, and roll up our windows. After nearly two hours of anxiousness, we roll into Punkin Center on fumes. The sign says "Cash only; no credit." I pump only as much gas as we need to get us to Colorado Springs. At 99 cents per gallon, gas at this podunk crossroads town seems astronomically expensive.

Garden of the Gods is absolutely magnificent: red rocks in every conceivable shape, and several short foot trails that allow us to stretch four legs that had been cramped in a small car for twenty hours. Heavy traffic getting back to I-25 makes driving the stick shift excruciating. Thankfully, August daylight is long, so by nightfall we make it west on US 160 to the junction with CO 150, then travel north to Great Sand Dunes National Monument. I inquire at some spartan wood cabins for today's best rate, hoping it's not too much. The cheapest room available is $25, discounted because its television doesn't work. "We didn't come here to watch TV did we?" I ask Karen. "We'll take it!" Out of the car at last, and amazed to meet the Rocky Mountains for the first time, Karen and I are absolutely in awe of the Southern Colorado landscape. Life is good! The sun casts shadows on the red sand dunes and descends beyond the purple Sangre de Cristo Mountains.

At sunrise, Karen smiles for a photo with the mountains as her backdrop as she eats yogurt and a granola bar. "I feel like I am in a Grape Nuts commercial with John Denver's 'Rocky Mountain High' playing in the background." We set out early, but the air gets hot as we hike the dunes, whose base is at 8500 feet above sea level. It can be challenging to describe the difficulty of hiking the Great Sand Dunes during the summer. The sand feels like it is burning through our sneakers, and the air is thin. We scale one dune—two steps forward, then sliding one step back—only to find that an even higher dune is hiding behind it. Some of the dunes tower to 700 feet, or as high as a 70 story building. The conditions are challenging, and I feel a bit of vertigo, something I've never experienced before. On the top of one of the dunes we discover something that—were it a rock—geologists might call an erratic. It's a black-eyed Susan, mysteriously positioned in the sand. After further inquiry, I discover that the flower marks the spot of someone's buried excrement. At first, I take some comfort in the observation that several dogs are playing in the dunes, but after further thought, I doubt that a dog would squat on a summit. Following our descent, Karen and I hike up the stream for half a mile to Saquache County. I had planned the hike using maps from the university's collection, and I identify its county line based upon the stream's curves and surrounding landforms.

Again thankful for long summer days, we race westward to Black Canyon of the Gunnison National Park, listening to John Denver's "Rocky Mountain High" and "Farewell Andromeda" albums. My sister Heidi in Rochester, NY, told us it is the most amazing place, with "canyons so deep you can't see the bottom, but you can hear the rapids." On her recommendation, Karen and I are excited to see it, or at least hear it! We make it to the western end of the park just before dark and spend our precious remaining time getting sunset photos. We are left with only frigid darkness for setting up our tent. I'm not sure if we are prepared for the extreme daily temperature swings, but we'll do our best to keep each other from freezing tonight.

The next day, we set off for Utah at the crack of dawn, again on secondary roads. We pull off CO 90 to photograph the colorful welcome sign "Utah: Still the Right Place." "Wow, Utah seems completely different than Colorado," says Karen. "Yeah, it's as if the state lines were drawn and then they put in the scenery," I add.

Beginning Phase II of our Rocky Adventure, we visit Arches and Canyonlands National Parks. The parks are both enormous, and well-maintained roads invite us to take some slight liberties with speed, blasting U2's *Joshua Tree* on our stereo as we cruise from trailhead to trailhead. "This *is* God's Country," I remark, adding that "It's easy to see how the American West influenced some of the songs on this album." The mid-August day is bright, hot, and lengthy. Unlike last night in the high elevations of Colorado, the Utah night in our tent seems even hotter than the day in the car. As this is peak tourist season, we are fortunate to have found a camp site at all; ours is at a noisy roadside campground near Dead Horse Point State Park. I observe that he lyric, "sleep comes like a drug in God's Country" seems like a lie this noisy and uncomfortably hot night.

With time being short, Karen and I set speed records for all of the major overlooks at Canyonlands. Sweaty and dusty at the end of the day, we are at a pivotal point. We have yet to explicitly set our ultimate objective on this trip. Should we try to make it all the way to the Pacific Ocean? Or, should we just take it easy and head north toward Yellowstone? At the outset, we decided that whether we see salt water on the trip depends upon our progress during the first three days. From an easterner's point of view, Colorado feels like "The West," and Utah is even farther west from there, but anyone who lives in Moab will tell you that it's nowhere near the Pacific. The voice of reason reminds us that we need to move our worldly possessions to New York State in less than two weeks. The following Monday, I start my PhD program at the University at Buffalo. Cautious about pushing our limits, we decide to do so anyway. When, if ever, will we have a chance to do this sort of thing again? Our sights are set on Crater Lake National Park, Oregon, and onward to the Pacific!

We blast through Utah and past the Great Salt Lake under blistering sunshine. After finishing my shift of driving, I enjoy a couple ice cold Coors Lights and marvel as the parched desert landscape passes. Mercifully, the air cools off as we enter Nevada, whose state line is marked by casinos in the desert, desert roses of a different sort, or cathedrals in the desert, or are they just mirages? Ah, beer. My thoughts wander.

In Elko, Nevada, I buy some nasty gas station coffee only out of desperation, relieving a fatigued Karen from the wheel. We drive our trusty Civic toward Oregon on US 95. Northwestern Nevada shows us some of the darkest, loneliest, and most desolate stretches of highway imaginable. Seeing abundant signs of wildlife—especially road kill—we remind each other that we're in a very small car, and the impact of hitting even a small animal might be devastating. We continue for hours, and it's difficult for me to stay awake, especially with Karen sleeping.

I turn left onto route 140 and enter the Sheldon National Wildlife Refuge. It's Karen's turn to drive. No sooner do I fall asleep than I am jolted awake by my wife's scream, followed by a loud "KLUNK." I'm thrust forward in my seat as Karen hits the brakes and pulls to the side of the highway, upset. "I think I just killed the spotted white owl," she exclaims, visibly shaken. Having seen something terribly large hit the windshield, I fumble in the glove box for my glasses. "I feel horrible," Karen exclaims, "we're in a wildlife refuge." We step out of the Civic for a breather, share a hug, and with apologies to whatever we just killed, we thank God for our own safety. We could use just a bit more of that safety stuff tonight!

I take over driving again. As Karen sleeps, the only thing for me to ponder in my solitude is a sign that says the next gas is 95 miles ahead. In the meantime, we drive on straight, flat roads, with nothing to see except the occasional tumbleweed or scampering varmint in the headlights. All at once, I wonder if I've lost it. I find myself rubbing my eyes and doing a double-take at a brightly reflective road sign warning about a sharp right turn in one mile, followed by a steep eight percent grade over the next four miles. How can this be? This road has been straight and flat forever, and I'm pretty sure we're not on a mountain. Fortunately, I obey the sign, slow down, and we begin our steep cliffside decent. In the dark I can tell there's a rock wall on our right, and nothing but seemingly endless blackness to the left. How far down could it possibly go? Having also had her brief slumber broken by my audible reaction to what must be the Great Abyss of Oregon, Karen manages to doze for a couple more hours before taking over again at the wheel.

As we emerge from the dark remoteness of the intermountain West, Klamath Falls, Oregon seems like a metropolis. We stop in town for gasoline and supplies. In sharp contrast to last night in Nevada, this morning is cold and foggy, everything is green, and the air smells of conifers and snow. We enter Phase III of our trip: the Northwest. Getting to the entrance gate of Crater Lake seems to take an eternity. The road winds upward, then upward and upward again, lined with tall evergreens and babbling brooks, dotted with roadside picnic areas and campgrounds. We have driven more than 2000 miles and visited four National Parks in the past four days. Critics might ask "But did you actually *see* anything?" The firm answer is "Yes, one would be surprised." Already, this is quickly becoming one of the best travel adventures imaginable.

When we arrive at Crater Lake, we revel in our freedom

and ability to walk the trails, and maybe even a little in being alive after driving through two of the trip's four nights so far. We discover that a volcanic pumice desert is more than just a funny name. One trail feels like walking on Bran Buds or feed pellets, and these begin to sound crunchy under our feet as the temperature drops and the snow starts to fall. We are sunburned and hiking in the snow. Yesterday we were suffering through heat of more than 100 degrees, and today it is windy and nearly freezing.

Karen and I hike Cleetwood Cove Trail, which leads down to the Crater Lake. The water is the deepest blue I have ever seen, almost. "It's almost as blue as your eyes," I tell Karen. "Thank you, Honey Baby." Crater Lake was formed with the collapse of a caldera, and with a depth of 1958 feet, it is the seventh deepest lake in the world. We are told that a helicopter crashed in the lake a few weeks ago and could not be retrieved. When we complete the steep descent to the lakeside dock, we find out the final boat tour of the day was cancelled due to choppy water. Karen is devastated. Quietly, I am relieved given the price of tour tickets, let alone the thought of the choppy water and the story about the helicopter.

Our campsite is beautiful and spacious, and to make the night interesting, the rangers just posted a bear warning—the first I had ever seen. We set up the tent together, and with mixed success, Karen uses her foot-pump in her best attempt to fill the air mattress while I build a campfire. As I start to cook dinner, she's still struggling with the foot pump. Being stubborn, I am reluctant to assist, but I do remind her I was against bringing that useless piece of junk on the trip. After all, it takes up so much space in our small car! We dine on kielbasa in fresh rolls with potato chips and very cold Coors Light. I am fond of Koozies, but tonight we really don't need them to keep the beer cold. Instead, we use them to keep our hands from freezing. I sip my beer and ponder how much I love to sleep outdoors in a tent. This is our first night on the trip getting into the tent before dark, and we do so in order to warm each other up.

We wake up with snow on the tent...in August. I build a fire. Shivering, I light the propane burner, pour water into the kettle, and make coffee. Excited for whatever we'll see next, we head west to I-5, then northward. As soon as we leave the coastal range, the weather becomes noticeably warmer. Driving through Portland, Oregon in the pouring rain, we notice a convertible with its top down. Karen glibly yells to the driver, "Excuse me, isn't it raining over in your lane?" So far, this trip has been extraordinary: the landscapes are dramatic and unique beyond our wildest expectations, and they seem to change with every turn we make. Everything seems to be working out; I feel so in love with America and my wife!

Partly because Astoria, Oregon was the setting for the film "Reality Bites," and partly because of its cool name, I am happy that it lies along our route. We drive along the Columbia River, and as we do, I push my luck with Karen by queuing up our trip mix and singing along to the Woody Guthrie song "Roll On, Columbia." She has little tolerance for folk music, so I receive a frown of disgust. Astoria is interesting but not as attractive as its name. We stop at Burger King, eat a quick meal, and leave wearing our BK crowns. After the long drive, it feels good to be youthful and goofy.

We cross the long Astoria Bridge as the sun sets to our left. We reach Washington State on the other side of the Columbia River. With relief I realize that the toll shown on the map no longer exists, at least in the northbound direction. We drive on US 101 in the dark to South Beach campground in Olympic National Park. We set up our pup tent in front of the Civic. In a test of courage, we walk together in the moonlight to dip our toes into the frigid, dark, and terrifyingly lively Pacific Ocean. It is a cool and breezy August night, and the hot and humid city of Cincinnati seems infinitely far from here.

Olympic National Park is massive and diverse, featuring both seacoast and rainforest. At the time, I'm unaware of one of its best and most unique parts—the drive up Hurricane Ridge. This is another example of being too cheap to purchase a $20 guidebook. You might recall that the same thing happened in Europe. I also have a tendency to compromise preparatory research depth for breadth of travel.

Karen and I are particularly intrigued by the rainforest drive and hike, and the "nurse logs" that give nutrients to baby trees, as well as the bright shades of green and brown, and the massive golden slugs.

At the Rainforest Visitor Center, I call my friend Rich in Cincinnati to check on my cats, and to ask about things at the university. "Hmm, hey Jid! How's the road trip? Nice to get your call!" He explains that my master's thesis committee is ready to set a date for me to defend my project. "I told your professors you would be back on Friday, so we scheduled your defense for that afternoon." I have to pause for a moment to figure out what day today was. I am pretty sure that today is Sunday or Monday. "Thanks Rich!" I respond, without fully appreciating that now is the immediate end of being carefree on vacation. So, we will drive across the country, visiting Uncle Peter and Aunt Greta and Yellowstone National Park on the way, and I'll be mentally prepared to defend my Master's thesis in four days. This is the thinking of a 23 year old. For now, it's back to our vacation! I don't want to give up a single day of discovering America with my young wife. After all, I am moving to Buffalo, New York to start my PhD in less than a week, and I don't want to have to backtrack to Cincinnati just to defend my master's thesis.

Karen and I spend the day exploring everything we can manage in Olympic National Park. That night, we take the Bremerton Ferry across the gloss-black water of Puget Sound to Seattle. I have never been to Seattle before, and the thought of visiting the fabled city seems unusually exotic to me. From photographs, I have a vision of its signature Space Needle and modern skyline rising above the waterfront and set against the snowcapped peaks of the Cascade Mountains. Growing up, I often chose to represent Seattle sports teams when competing against friends: tabletop football, HORSE basketball, and so on. I like blue and green, and I always thought the Mariners' and Seahawks' insignias were cool. As we approach the dock, the city is magnificently lit. Free from the steering wheel at last, I have the luxury of taking in the spectacular view. The loud arrival announcement sends us to our cars. After driving up the ramp and onto solid ground, the steepness of the streets challenges me. I struggle to negotiate the Civic's five gears, clutch, and brakes, while searching for signs to I-90 east. A Seattle Mariners game is letting out now, and pedestrians are tangled with surface traffic and highway ramps.

In the wake of Seattle's shimmering energy, the drive into Washington's darkened Coastal and Cascade ranges leaves us extraordinarily drowsy. I pull off I-90 at Snoqualmie Pass to take a short nap. Hours later, we awaken to the noise of morning interstate traffic. "God, it's freakin' cold," I say, shivering. "Freezin', wheezing," exclaims Karen. I start the engine and crank up the heat. I muster enough alertness to drive again, just long enough to find some coffee and breakfast in Easton. Fully charged, we blast eastward through Spokane and Idaho toward our next stop: Montana!

East of the Cascades, the air is noticeably hotter and dryer. After last night, our return to the intermountain region brings a welcomed change of climate. I coyly make detours from I-90 for a few easy counties along the way, fearing Karen's reaction. We pull off I-90 to get a picture of the Welcome to Montana sign as we enter the state. Not only is it a bucket list item for me to visit Montana, but being from the Northeast, it seems kind of cool to approach the state by car from the West. I am ecstatic at the prospect of visiting Uncle Peter and Aunt Greta in Bozeman, and in their home! Growing up on the farm in Western New York, we got to see them only when they made the long trip across the country, which was every two years at best. Being captain of our own Honda Civic, I feel like the world has grown smaller. I suddenly have the luxury to visit loved ones, even distant relatives.

Bozeman is a beautiful small college town. It takes us twelve hours to get there from Seattle, but when we arrive, my Uncle Peter and Aunt Greta are gracious hosts. I suddenly feel like an adult, visiting my father's youngest brother and seeing the home he and his wife have made; the place where they have spent most of their lives. I can readily see that I am in a Deichmann home. Everything is so well cared for. I think that all four of us have problems deciding when to end the conversation. We are all visibly exhausted but are unable able to figure out each other's cues—another Deichmann handicap! The next morning, Uncle Peter and Aunt Greta pack a cooler with sandwiches and drinks, and we head out for what Uncle Peter calls the "lazy" Madison River, or Lazy Madison River, which here flows northward into the Missouri, which in turn of course ultimately flows to the Mississippi and into the Gulf of Mexico. It seems a lot to fathom that this water flows into the Gulf of Mexico. Speaking of fathoms, the water was so shallow that we often need to dip in and push along the riverbed to dislodge the rubber rafts, which frequently got caught wherever the heaviest traveler sits. We stay in Bozeman for a second night.

Enter Phase IV: Yellowstone and the Grand Tetons. It seems tiresome to ponder the fact that Karen and I still have two national parks to visit. After a great breakfast and sad goodbye, we set out early in the morning for the 90 mile drive southward to the northern Entrance of Yellowstone. Yellowstone is larger than the states of Delaware and Rhode Island combined. I have to think carefully about how to approach the figure-eight route layout in order to maximize our experience with the limited time remaining. I thank Karen for allowing me to be trail boss and plan our route.

Our final day of sightseeing includes what seems to be all conceivable landscapes, soil types, beasts, fowl, and weather. At one point Karen and I look at one another, exchange a sigh of exhaustion, and exclaim that we are simply "parked out." Maybe it's possible to have too much of a good thing all at once. The torrential rain isn't elevating our moods. The first campsite reservation I probably ever made in my life was back in Cincinnati, having been warned that Yellowstone is crazy busy during high season. Sure enough, we arrive at the campground after dark to find that someone else is camping in our spot. Exhausted, I set up our tent only a few feet away in what appears to be an improvised fire ring. Karen and I sleep rather uncomfortably, uncertain how this happened on the only night that we actually had paid camping reservations. At the break of dawn, just to be safe we wake up and pack up before the multitudes of nearby campers emerge from their tents.

The next day we stop at the main overlooks along the figure-eight-shaped route that accesses Yellowstone National Park, taking snippets of video along the way. Running out of steam at Kepler Cascades, our rain jackets become our amour against the driving rain. We hike the short trial to have a look at the violently rushing river. Instantaneously soaked, we rush back into the car and share our last Coors Light. "Yup, I'm definitely parked out" says Karen, taking a sip. "Yes, me too," I agree. "Now, let's figure out how to get from Western Wyoming back to Cincinnati in twenty-four hours or less."

We drive southward out of the rain. It must have been blind youthful ambition that kept us from turning eastward and taking the shortest route home through Cody and Greybull. Instead, we continue south through magnificent Grand Teton National Park under a cobalt blue sky, stopping for snapshots along the way. This is a place to return to, maybe with kids someday. Now, it's just the two of us, young, together, lucky in love, but today not so lucky with time. I heed previous prudent advice from Rich about overzealous speed enforcement in Jackson Hole. At the very least the police are thorough, as patrol cars seem to appear at least once every mile marker, many of them busy with victims. "Wow! It's a surprise to see so many police in the proudly laissez-faire state of Wyoming." If anyone on the road has a reason to speed today, it is I on my 1650 mile journey back to Cincinnati, but I follow the rules, that is, exceeding the speed by no more than 10 mph.

After we descend from the Wind River Range into the town of Green River, there isn't much left to look at in Wyoming. We continue on I-80 as the sun sets in the rearview. Entering Nebraska, darkness falls and it starts to rain, then pour. Though tired and dealing with sub-par road conditions, our options are gone. I have played my cards to maximize our time out west, and now it is Wednesday night. We have no time to stop, and it would be too wet to camp anyway. With a budget of $500 for a six thousand mile trip, hotels are not an option. We continue a bit slower as it begins to rain harder. We see some of the largest lightning bolts that God ever unleashed in his angriest state. The rain pounds the windshield so hard that we can barely hear the stereo. We slow down to a pathetic speed and study the white lines in an effort to stay on the road. The storm lasts all night, but it seems an eternity.

To our relief, the sun comes up as we cross from Nebraska into Iowa. We have been spared the perils of the dark, the flooded highway, and now everything seems new. It is now safe for us to take turns driving and sleeping again. The plains are lush and green, just like the ones we had seen in Kansas twelve days before. Conquering the road before us seems like a formality now. The dangers are controllable. The storm is over. We are still alive.

I have been keeping a secret from Karen the entire trip, and it has to do with counties. This particular scheme invigorates me, and might have even helped me stay awake while driving through last night. It is secret plan, if you will. Until now, this plan is on a need-to-know basis, and I didn't think it would be prudent to let anyone know. As everyone knows, Cincinnati lies at the center of the Indiana-Ohio-Kentucky region, and I went on record with my goal of completing all of the counties in these three states before moving out of the city which will happen this weekend. Only three counties remain that I need to "get," and all lie a bit south of Interstate 70. Karen is asleep and I am driving at the time when we reach the fateful interstate exit. Adrenaline rushes through my veins. I gently make for the exit ramp. My face is red and burning with excitement… I can pull this off. I almost burst out in laughter when she wakes up and angrily demands… "Joel, what are you doing? Joel, are you getting a county? Joel, we can't do this now, we don't have TIME for it." This is one of the few times when the most easygoing travel companion in the world almost kills her husband. I knew all along that this could be incendiary, but I am on a mission. For Karen, the issue is not so much that I need to defend my thesis tomorrow. Rather, we have been gone for two weeks, we aren't home yet, and we need to move our stuff and our cats Ferne and Bearcat 400 miles to Buffalo, New York this upcoming weekend. "The detour is right off the highway" I declare, nonchalantly, "and there are actually three counties, not one, but they're all in a row and in a direct line toward Cincinnati." I drive eastward on Indiana State Route 236 to collect Vermillion, Parke, and Putnam Counties and complete the state. I confess that this episode certainly sets Karen off un-necessarily just before our move to Buffalo.

We arrive in Cincinnati safely, very late that afternoon. I change my clothes and defend my Master's thesis. Then, my friend Sam Patello joins me to help pick up an eight-foot U-Haul trailer for tomorrow's move to Buffalo, seven hours' drive from Cincinnati. The trailer is a whole lot smaller than I had expected, and it has an open top. As I pull up to our apartment building, Karen sees our rig and a storm blows up in her eyes. The good news, I tell Karen, is thanks to the open top, we can stack our things even higher!

The next day, Rich, Karen, and I travel as a 45mph convoy toward Buffalo on Interstate 71 north. Our overloaded U-Haul experiences a violent bridge joint bump near Medina, Ohio.

The jolt rips the tow hitch off Rich's Toyota pickup truck, and I drag the rig off the highway, sparks flying. Karen, takes the cats in the Honda Civic and says "Good luck guys, see you in Buffalo."

5

FINDING TRACTION: TRAVELING OVERSEAS WITH STUDENTS

"Choose a job you love, and you will never have to work a day in your life."

Confucius

This story is important to tell because it helps me embrace two of my discoveries that are counter to my upbringing: first, that one's contribution to an employer need not be measured as life's hours sold for cash; and second, travel is something that you can do for work, not just for vacation. I fully appreciate the enriching qualities of travel. Not only do I enjoy seeing the world, but I've come to learn that travel is the best education money can buy. So the question evolves from "How can I afford to travel in the first place?" to "How can I travel without paying for it out of pocket?" to ultimately "How can I make travel into part of my professional responsibilities so that I can get paid to do it?" I reflect upon a trip report I wrote following my first-ever travel grant award, which covered my expenses to Budapest to join a colleague's travel class. As I read the report, I see a young professor—not even on tenure track— keenly interested to learn that faculty could get paid to travel, but at the same time shocked about observations on that trip. We can do so much better.

Excerpt from "Budapest Travel Report"

The travel course to Budapest was an unqualified success for all participants- instructors and students alike. For me personally, two events stand out as being particularly rewarding: the lecture on Hungary's economic transition by former President of the Hungarian National Bank Professor Peter Akos Bod, and a bus trip to a refugee camp near Debrecen in eastern Hungary.

As an economic geographer studying foreign direct investment in transition economies, I was very interested to meet Professor Bod and learn from his expertise in my area of research. Professor Bod was generous in providing valuable data for my research and lectures on Central Europe. These meetings will likely lead to future work on investment in Hungary.

Our bus excursion across Hungary to a refugee camp located near Debrecen—Hungary's second largest city— exposed us to Hungary's physical and human landscapes beyond the capital city. The camp was situated within an abandoned Russian military base, and many of its residents were Gypsies, Iraqis, or refugees from the Balkan War. The class broke into small groups to meet with the refugees in their rooms. These discussions opened our eyes to the realities of refugee life and helped us understand one of Hungary's crucial dilemmas: balancing the flood of asylum applications against the restrictive immigration policies of the European Union, which Hungary aspires to join in a few years.

While these activities stand out in my own mind, the week was full of many other worthwhile events. We learned our way around Budapest and explored numerous sites of historical importance. We also completed a tour of parliament and several expert lectures at Budapest University of Economic Sciences and Central European

University, followed by social events with students and faculty.

Waltham, Massachusetts 22 March 2000

My Budapest travel report is a sanitized diplomatic account of a travel study that went horribly wrong. It would be ungallant for me to expose the full details of the trip that contributed to a former colleague's demise and raised eyebrows about the very nature of educational short-term programs. But the experience made me start to ask myself the question of whether I should attempt to take other people's kids abroad. Why would I want to risk such a debacle myself? Because I know that given the chance, I will do better, and why not share my passion for Central Europe with students while developing my own regional expertise and enjoying the time in the field? It seems like it would be a win-win. I just need to figure out how to get my chance. Toward the end of my first one-year contract, the Budapest course cultivates me as a rookie professor. Having been made a scapegoat for some of my ill-fated colleague's negligence, I begin to see how adept self-serving professors can be at promoting themselves at the expense of younger colleagues.

What went wrong on the Budapest trip? A generous commentary would suggest that the group was too large, and the students were unprepared in every way. Tension grew between a clique of rich international students and a handful of middle-class American students, and the tension went unchecked. Some rich students refused to stay with the class at its modest designated hotel, and found their own more luxurious accommodations nearby. Others skipped group meals at local restaurants and went to McDonalds. Indeed, it's a shame when students skip class, sleep in class, or leave a senior professor's lecture to vomit in the hallway from the previous night's over-indulgence. It's much worse when faculty leaders do the same thing. It may be excusable for faculty leaders who spent months living in

Budapest to get the class lost and cause the entire group to show up late for a lecture, but it's inexcusable for them to pass blame for their shortcomings on to a colleague who is visiting the city for the first time.

Hoping to rally support for another year of employment at Bentley from the few faculty I've managed to meet so far, I refrain from implicating my colleague for the fiasco-on-tour that he led, but his abuse continues after our return to Boston. Any optimism about getting a second-year contract fades when my trip-leading colleague takes advantage of my freshly-minted PhD energy and rookie neurosis by asking me to "help him" run data analyses, then write summaries, which he includes in papers submitted for publication under his name alone. I'm later asked "What do you think about this manuscript? Can you write a few comments?" Again, sole credit is given to the abuser. Eager to please and maximize my chances at another one-year contract, I comply passively. Teaching four courses per semester on a one-year contract, I could have used a crumb.

My survival at Bentley is nothing short of a miracle. Thrown under the bus and possibly guilty by association when the student course evaluations flood in, I search for jobs that begin the upcoming academic year.

Early one morning on the final week of school in April 2000, it is quiet and dark in the corridor of Morison Hall where my office is located, and my door is open as I prepare my classes for the day. The Vice President for Academic Affairs walks past my office, stops, turns around, and returns to my door where he and I exchange salutations. He asks me how I like working at Bentley, and whether I think I should stay for another year. I've barely ever met this man, but I'm aware that he's revered and/or feared by the entire faculty, so I'm nervous about his question. Is this an impromptu interview? The details of what I say in my trembling response don't matter. One week later, I receive my second one-year contract in the mail.

After a successful second year of teaching nine classes, I

am thrilled to receive a third one-year contract. The tragedy of September 11th creates enormous demand for classes in our International Culture and Economy ("ICE") program, and with a great team effort, our program is on track to grow into an International Studies Department[xiv]. The colleague who ran the circus to Budapest is no longer at Bentley after failing the test of the tenure process. Other skeptical colleagues have begun to either recognize my potential or value my contributions. Things have gotten immeasurably better for me as I've started to crack the code of university-level teaching, and I've established my own post-PhD research program. I recognize that I've really got to travel overseas in order to succeed as a faculty member in an <u>International</u> Studies Department, but money is not handed out freely to faculty to travel the world.

So, I return to the idea of travel studies. For someone who is not even on tenure track, it seems to defy prudence to take groups of someone else's kids overseas. At least I have been warned against this by senior colleagues. But I guess I am a bit of a gambler. If I could take students anywhere, it would be Prague. Why Prague? Self-interest, mainly. I want to get to know that incredible city better. Surely students would love it as much as I do, even though I know at this point I'm not really qualified to teach them much about it yet. Whetting my appetite for Prague were my one-day visit in 1994, followed by my second visit in 1998 as a one-day stopover on my 1998 dissertation research trip to Poland. My third visit was a data collection trip in December of 2000, for a new research project in the area of international tourism. I approach a potential collaborator Tomáš Cahlík by email at first. Tomáš is a professor of economics at Charles University who becomes a close personal friend. He would eventually come to the United States with his family and teach at Bentley for one year. Yes indeed, taking a chance can be worthwhile.

So I gamble on Prague, which I consider to be the most incredible city on earth with apologies to proud friends in other amazing cities of the world. Not only am I mesmerized by Prague's Vltava setting, architectural beauty, and brightly painted buildings, but I'm also captivated by the thought of the changes its residents experienced since the end of their repressed state of affairs under Soviet-imposed Communism. Maybe growing up in my father's autocratic house helps me relate to Czechs. Whatever the cause of my attraction to Prague, the first brief but inspirational visits have left an indelible mark on my compass.

My strategy for teaching internationally is taking shape: I will take students to Prague not only to introduce them to its many splendors, but also as a case study of post-Cold War transition. As a benefit to me, this experience will enable me to deepen and broaden my professional and personal knowledge base by doing something I genuinely love: spending time in Prague. If I succeed in this endeavor, I will do it again….and again.

For the class, I draw up a one-week itinerary of the "touristy" things I think I would want to do during my first full week in Prague, which this will actually be. After that, I add a visit at Czechinvest, a government agency that helpfully gave me data for my master's thesis a few years back. I email the Czech Parliament, Radio Free Europe, and a handful of US companies operating in Prague to request visits for my class. I email Pavel Vacek, Tomáš' graduate student who helped me collect data last year, and ask if he wants to be my local "expert" in exchange for modest compensation. He would love to! I draw up a syllabus for a 1.5 credit course on Prague and the Czech transition. Its deliverables include basic Czech expression quizzes, a travel journal, and a final thematic paper. I receive approval to offer the course based upon my "expertise" on Prague—so far only three day-long visits—and I begin promoting the class around campus.

As our class shuttle arrives at Logan Airport, I wonder if my boldness will pay off or ruin me. On the flight, I study my guide book for the best way to get from the airport to the city. Fortunately, Hotel City Centre is easy for me to find, and we settle in to decompress before meeting to take our *welcome* meal and discuss first impressions. I spend the week only a short step ahead of the students. I remain vigilant so that none of the negative aspects of *the Budapest debacle* will befall my group. I am scared to death for eight days, and I earn a modest stipend of $1000 for abandoning my wife with a five year old, three year old, and one year old to travel with a nice group of students whose ages I barely exceed. The experience is incredible, but I doubt that I'll get another break like this one again: paid to spend one week on professional assignment in Prague!

Over the next months, I realize that my students didn't only return to Bentley alive, but also "turned on to things international": ecstatic, enlightened, and generally much better for the experience. For me, this is a breakthrough, an "a-ha" moment as some would say. In one short week, not only have I more than doubled my time spent in Prague, but I have developed stronger friendships there. In addition, I now have a better rapport with my students, and a stronger reputation in student circles. In other words, I didn't anticipate the formation of a small student cadre of supporters that view me as something more than the mediocre young professor that I feel I am. I'm going to make the world my classroom. I think I've found my niche, and I've got to learn how to make this work… if Karen lets me!

In March 2002, one morning toward the end of my second student trip to Prague, I knock on Pavel's hotel room door so that we can go for breakfast. Without hesitation, he opens the door to reveal a nude couple in his bed, sharing the white comforter. Pavel invites me in and introduces me to his brother Petr and Petr's girlfriend Miša. Petr immediately stretches his hand out from beneath the covers to shake mine. I decline with a polite wave, and a badly pronounced "*Těší mé*," (it's nice to meet you). It seems that Petr came from the village of Vermerovice to meet his Ostrava girlfriend in Prague and make use of the "family" hotel room. "Gee, you and Petr have a pretty tight brotherhood," I estimate, as I wait for the elevator with Pavel. Any awkwardness fades quickly. I don't really expect to see Petr again anyway.

Meanwhile, toward the end of my third year at Bentley, I am informed that I will be allowed to apply for my own position, which Bentley has converted to tenure track and advertised internationally. After I win that tenure track position, I have two years to assemble my tenure package. Gradually throughout this process, friendships are forged in Prague, students are taught—clumsily at first—academic papers are published, and Prague emerges as my most familiar destination outside the USA.

After leading my second successful wife-approved university trip to Prague, I find myself on a flight to Santiago de Chile with Dave Schoenl, a best friend from my undergraduate years at Geneseo, and county collector extraordinaire. Dave shares my enthusiasm for travel; he goes wherever he can whenever he can. Passing the time on our flight, I share with Dave a recent conversation I had with a "gatekeeper" at Bentley who wields the prerogative to approve or reject faculty-led programs abroad. Casually, I had asked her when I would be permitted take students to Chile. After all, at that time I had spent more time in Chile than I had spent in Prague. She derisively snubbed me with her response that I "could do it when (I) learn to speak Spanish." "Okay, then, I don't exactly speak Czech either, but I know enough of it to find my way around, as I do Spanish." That conversation didn't go well. During years of working with that same "gatekeeper" before she moved to another employer, she never did validate my response about Chile, but I noticed that more and more of my faculty colleagues became sanctioned to take students to countries where they have little or no knowledge of the native language. In safe and friendly places, I think that's a great way to learn!

The memory of that frustrating interaction lingers in my head on a hot January day in a tiny grocery store in Temuco, Chile. I'm with Dave, searching the shelves for basic drinking glasses so that we can enjoy a bottle of wine on the night train back to Santiago. From the ceiling speakers, I barely make out the faint tune of "Stay, Faraway, So Close" by U2, that Irish rock band that wrote the playlist of my life and recorded the soundtrack of my relationship with Karen. The song and its video are inspired by a film that was set in Berlin, by the name of "Faraway, So Close." The fact that the song plays at this time of searching for my next big idea immediately resonates with me. I don't speak much Spanish or Czech, but I certainly *do* speak German. And it's got to count that I witnessed a divided Berlin in 1988, then visited with Karen in 1994. Thousands of miles from home, and even farther from Berlin, a new plot is hatched. In January of 2003, Berlin becomes my next big idea. As for Chile, as my small academic department continues to grow, I will personally make it a priority to identify and support a candidate who knows the place… and who speaks Spanish! South America is absent from our very short list of course offerings, and what better place to start than Chile: another landscape of tragic history and triumphant emergence! As for me, I will continue to develop and expand the similarly nascent regional competency I hold for Central Europe.

With Berlin in the back of my mind, I lead my third class to Prague in March 2003. My Czech local expert Pavel just began his PhD program in economics at Cornell University in the USA. He offers me his brother Petr as a substitute. "The guy I met in your bedroom?" "Yes, that's Petr." So my second meeting with Petr is at Ruzyně International Airport in Prague, where he awaits me and my students in the arrivals hall, and this time he and I exchange a firm handshake. Petr mainly charms the class with his unique Czech version of English, which is one hell of a lot better than any of our Czech. He earns the respect of the class by finding my two Korean students when they stray in the city, and he charms them with his sense of humor. As a native of a distant village in Eastern Bohemia, like me, he is learning Prague by doing Prague; however, I think Petr enjoys the spotlight of leading more than I do. I just want to be in Prague. Petr is a popular name in Pan-Slavia. One of my students from Slovakia is also named Petr, so in order to keep them straight, the class starts referring to them as Petr the Czech and Petr the Slovak. This works fine until we later meet a second Petr from Slovakia, whom the students dub Petr the Angry, a reference to an incident that they never fully divulge.

My next step is to propose a short-term program to Berlin, and I will do it in combination with Prague, which I have come to know fairly well. I send emails of introduction to geography professors at Freie Universität Berlin, as well as its affiliated *Gesellschaft für Erkunde zu Berlin* (Berlin Geographical Society), and over the next few months I arrange visits for my class.

I arrive in Berlin with twelve students, highly dependent upon my guide book and fold-out Streetwise map. I am taken aback at the extent of change that has occurred since my last visit, and immediately realize this visit will be as educational for me as for my students. Imagine a capital city of global significance divided by a wall for twenty-eight years, resulting in two completely separate sets of infrastructure. Ways of life diverged under governments of opposing ideologies. West Berlin developed as a satellite of the United States, and East Berlin as the capital city of the Soviet Union's German puppet. It emerged as a showcase of the Communist Bloc, an optimal assignment for Russian troops. Each Berlin became a visual manifestation of its system: capitalism and freedom with all their decadent vices versus socialism and repression and the associated material deprivation. And then to everyone's shock in 1989 the Wall is dismantled, reunification of the German state ensues, and the long process of political, economic, and social reintegration begins. And what makes Berlin so interesting is that it is so completely different from Prague, amazing in other ways. Because of its internal contrasts, Berlin is made for this course, and I am ecstatic to discover the treasure trove of opportunity that has been under my nose the entire time. Berlin is the perfect case study of the post-Cold War, and I subtitle my "Transition Economies" course "Case Studies in Berlin: Reunification, Reconstruction and Reintegration."

As a young professor, I appreciate the fact that I've finally had the opportunity to spend a generous amount of time in the European countries we call "transition economies," and develop some expertise there. I am passionate about Central Europe, and I pursue any and every opportunity to visit the region. I recognize the need to broaden my scholarship beyond the sort of foreign direct investment approach I've taken thus far, so I develop a plan to look at "Czech perceptions of the international tourism industry." I apply for a Bentley research grant to collect data in the Czech Republic, returning two months after my March class. In 2004, Pavel is still working on his PhD in Economics at Cornell, so I check to see if his older brother Petr is interested in helping me. My grant will cover all of our travel expenses; all I require is Petr's time. In May, Petr agrees to drive with me throughout the Czech Republic and collect data. The trip coincides with ten new countries joining the European Union, including the Czech Republic. Petr and I witness the spirited street celebrations in Prague.

As several "transition economies" stabilize and join the European Union, I start to ask myself when we'll stop calling them "transition economies." When you think about it, every economy in the world is in some sort of "transition," even "advanced" ones like the US and UK. Already well-established in Central Europe, my regional interest begins to expand eastward and southward to the former Yugoslavia, where it seems a lot of major change remains to happen. The bloody war ended ten years ago, and this region must be an incredibly interesting corner of Pan-Slavia. Out of curiosity, I convince Petr to travel with me through the Alps to Ljubljana, Slovenia and Zagreb, Croatia, cities that emerged early from the Balkan War of the 1990s. My time in Europe is very tight, so true to form we spend only one day in each city, garnering a sense for the lay of the land; both seem like complementary places to Prague for future travel case studies.

The following year, I propose and market a 3.0 credit travel course to Berlin, with side excursions to Munich and Mainz. Anyone remotely familiar with Germany knows about the enormous contrasts within the country, especially between north and south. Everything from physical geography to culture, economy, and political disposition varies greatly over this space.

An important opportunity appears. Our expanding International Studies Department has a new chair, Shiping. Under pressure to staff our increasingly popular courses, Shiping asks if any full-time faculty would like to take on an extra, full section of a course entitled International Studies 104: "Cross-Cultural Understanding," which meets Wednesday and Friday from 8:30-9:45. Overburdened already, and against the advice of at least one colleague who rightly points out that it would set a bad precedent for full-time faculty to work for adjunct compensation, I accept because I need the money. This turns out to be one of the best career moves I've made, not because of the money, but because I find a way to market my short-term programs to this group of students. I somehow hit it off with this group in particular, and they help populate future short-term programs to Central and Eastern Europe. For me, this travel facilitates professional *traction*: some very solid research output and personal friendships in the region. One important tangible result is that in my tenure package, I can point to four successful short-term programs (three to Prague, one to Berlin). At the end of the semester, I apply for a grant to travel to China, arguing that it better qualifies me to teach my World Regions course. I assist my chair Shiping with his travel course, giving me some new ideas to improve my own future short term programs ("STPs").

The tenure cut-off point for "up or out" is just about the same time of year as May STP offerings. At the point when I apply for tenure, about fifty students had survived my trips. That number will treble over the next five years, and I will continue my strategy of expanding and broadening my stomping grounds (or, regional expertise as we say). Siniša Ubiparipovic, a former student in my "adjunct-salary-graveyard-class" makes it possible for dozens of students to visit the former Yugoslavia with us. Thanks to the goodwill of local experts who are proud of their countries and tolerate—if not love—Americans, these trips are possible for me to lead. In most cases, I would be hard-pressed to run them alone.

In May of 2008, I lead my third student group to Berlin. At the end of a long day, I muse as follows…

> *Twenty years ago I visited a divided Berlin. Never could I have predicted its current state of being. I never could have predicted my current state of being. We are both doing okay, Berlin and I. For success, you need to work hard, but you also need to be lucky. I would like to hang on to this special place. Tonight in the fog, I went up in the Alex (TV tower) to observe the sunset. This was only the second time up there in my life; the first time being in 1988. Berlin, like the rest of Germany, was divided. As I look out at the reunited bustling city, the silent sleek and speedy trains, and the automobile traffic, I realize that Germany is an unusual place that really makes sense to me, a place where stuff gets done and things function properly. And because of my visit to divided Berlin in 1988, this is a city that will always have special meaning to me.*

As time progresses, I further refine my Berlin program and have the pleasure of watching the city continue to evolve: the Reichstag is completed and opened to the public, Potsdammer Platz (Potsdam Square) grows out of "no-man's land," the world's largest train station is built, and new U-Bahn lines are installed. Former East Germany's Palast der Republik (Palace of the Republic) is being demolished to begin reconstruction of the 15ᵗʰ Century Baroque Berlin Castle that was destroyed in 1945.

I cherish the opportunity to replicate, adapt, and expand my "overseas classrooms." Gradually, I become one of Bentley's most experienced, or senior, faculty leaders of short-term programs. On several occasions, I declare the privilege of traveling students to be "the best part of my job," and contribute the expression "taking Bentley to the world," which seems to find circulation in administrative circles.

As Prague and Berlin become "transitioned" cities, I speculate that Poland might be another interesting laboratory for learning, and my curiosity about the Balkans also grows. Warsaw is perhaps the city that was most devastated in World War II, but has risen again like a phoenix from the ashes. Other cities including Kraków and Wrocław offer excellent contrast that I find useful for my programs. My generous friend Adrian in Warsaw, whom you'll get to know in Chapter 7, is eager to assist me in showcasing his country. Adrian is one of the most intelligent and aspiring yet also friendliest people I've met. He works for the Polish Agency for Foreign Investment, and interacts frequently with corporate executives from abroad in an effort to facilitate investment in Poland. His kind offer to assist (indeed lead) as local expert will eventually open the eyes of twenty-two students to Poland. I succeed at luring in some skeptical students by adding St. Patrick's Day in Dublin as a convenient stopover on our way back to the USA. I estimate that this will also provide a welcome and pleasurable break for the students following the rigors of an intensive program led by my dear friend Adrian. Some triumphs and at least one pitfall that occurr while taking students to the Balkans with Siniša are unveiled in Chapter 9. Taking the good with the bad, there have been so many opportunities that turn out to be "trips of a lifetime," both for me and for many of my students.

So the years fly by like paper in the wind. Czech Republic, Germany, Ghana, Poland, Croatia, and Bosnia have become homes away from home, places of considerable familiarity. After leading fifteen trips, I am seasoned more than tired. There are a few valuable lessons to heed. First, a one-size-fits-all-happy-adventure abroad is simply not possible. Every student is different, so successful courses need to include a wide range of activities in hopes that each student will find enough good stuff for them. Students must be selected carefully and prepared for symbiotic learning. The most important thing is their attitude. Some students care mainly about learning, others care more about partying. Most students fall somewhere between the extremes. The professor needs to get to know all of the students as quickly as possible, and try to engage each one individually. Generally, in designing a course I think the trick is to combine structure with freedom, preparation with adaptation, and instruction with fun. If a host professor or parliament cancels our visit, we need to be ready to go to a hockey game or opera. A maximum of two scheduled events should be planned each day, with free time for the students to safely pursue their own interests, which is usually some combination of shopping, socializing, dancing, and sleeping. Professors also need free time to meet with local contacts and maintain their sanity by checking in at home. Students should also recognize the importance of certain behavior codes: that they are ambassadors for their country and their institutions. Beyond that, it's the buddy system: nobody leaves their buddy behind—ever! My wife Karen often advises me to remind the students about Natalee Holloway. Her friends should have never let her go off alone with a stranger. Always expect the unexpected, and anyone who needs to leave the group must let the leader know where they and their buddy are going.

Things don't always run smoothly, as captured in Chapter 9. There are a few memories of accidents, sickness, late arrivals, lost luggage, and bad attitudes. Twice, students needed medical treatment. Other students were reckless, hung-over, or disre-spectful, and there were even a couple of American princesses who should have traveled somewhere first class with their parents instead of taking my course. One day in Bosnia to tactfully encourage a complaining princess, Siniša and the students came up with the expression "Slav up" (meaning: *toughen* up). This rally cry reminds everyone if they're traveling in this group, they should be prepared to adapt, compromise, and exert effort; lean travel around the Balkans is no pleasure cruise.

After spending half a year of my life exploring other countries with college students, I've come to fully appreciate the value of short-term programs as student learning opportunities. I could not afford to travel like this as a college student myself, so it's a great privilege to have such spectacular opportunities later in life. Petr the Czech often says the simple words "the best way to learn is to travel." My trip format seems to work for young adults who cannot manage an entire semester abroad for financial, personal, or other reasons, and for those who prefer to sample multiple places rather than spend an entire semester at just one location. Equally important, these programs enable faculty to deepen and broaden their expertise on a given place and its culture, which is valuable in the classroom and in scholarship alike.

At some critical point, Bentley decision-makers showed confidence in me as a young faculty member. My passion for Central Europe resulted in a rather solid streak of fifteen embedded academic courses overseas. For about half of the students, this was their very first trip outside USA. It brings me great joy that the first trip outside of New England for a student from Vermont was with me to Croatia and Bosnia-Herzegovina. Two of my students who met in Berlin are now married with a child. Many of my students told me their travel course was pivotal in their lives; an experience they'll never forget. This is exceedingly gratifying to hear. Ten percent didn't do so well, or felt that I didn't do so well; nevertheless, my simple request to go to Budapest during my first year of full-time teaching opened up Prague, Berlin, Zagreb, Sarajevo, Accra, Warsaw, Kraków, Dublin, and indirectly even Chile to scores of Bentley students. It enabled me to build first-hand academic credibility in Central Europe, and to initiate and cultivate many great friendships.

One day when I have time, I want to travel solo on a journey to my favorite destinations in Central Europe. I will visit the cities to which I've taken students and spend a little time reflecting with my friends who live there, but without obligation. I won't be conducting research, I won't be leading students or other travel companions, and I won't need to deliver a paper or an expense report. Admittedly self-indulgent, this adventure will simply provide a refreshing opportunity to appreciate the people and places that mean so much to me, and to reflect upon the significant amount of time I've had the privilege of spending in Europe thanks to thanks the nature of my profession and support from my employer.

6

CHILE MI AMOR

Chile, mentioned in passing in Chapter 5, is worthy of its own chapter in this book. I can think of a couple of reasons why Chile became a priority to me, and why I had to find a way to get to there. Rich, the county-collector friend that I respect so much, knew a guy who went to Chile and returned to describe it simply as "beautiful like California, except everyone speaks Spanish." "What do you mean, Rich, doesn't everyone also speak Spanish in California?" I asked. "Droll Joel," was his reply. The other reason is U2's song "Mothers of the Disappeared" and the reference in "One Tree Hill" (both from *The Joshua Tree*) to Victor Lidio "Jara" Martínez, a Chilean poet and peace activist who was murdered and dumped in the street of a slum near Santiago. That's how Chile got on my mental map and bucket list. I also have a professional reason for going: I teach about all regions of the world, but until going to Chile, I had traveled only in North America and Europe. The reversed seasons provide yet another incentive; it is now winter at home and summer in Chile.

Shortly after I book my frequent flyer award ticket, I find out that we are pregnant. Five weeks prior to my departure, Karen is due to have our third baby. Because the trip is so close to her due date, we request a special checkup with our doctor. Everyone seems confident that the baby will gestate its full term. To a fault, I am very reluctant to change course in anything that seems right to me. After all, my free plane ticket is older than fetus-yet-to-be-named.

I've learned that Dave is usually up for a trip to interesting places, and he's a great travel companion for me. We share common interests about places, similar travel habits of ambition and frugality, and we have comparable tolerances for risk. It's almost three months after September 11th, and despite some concerns by friends and family members, Dave and I agree that this is probably the safest time ever to fly. We are certainly not willing cancel a long-awaited trip out of fear!

I will spare you most of the details of how I get to Chile, but a few comments are germane here. My ticket is free on Continental miles, the only airline at the time that offers miles that don't expire. So far, I have flown on airplanes only a handful of times, and this trip requires 75,000 miles, most of which I've accumulated using my Continental VISA card over the past five years. Because of route restrictions, the original plan is to fly from Boston to Newark to Los Angeles, then with partner Copa to Panama then finally Santiago over thirty-six hours. A cursory look at a map of the Western Hemisphere reveals that Los Angeles is not on the way from Boston to Santiago. In fact, Santiago is almost due south of Boston. Fortunately, I manage to convince Continental agent Mrs. Malowitz to amend my original itinerary over the phone. When she tells me "I can save you the flight to LA, overnight, and eight hours in Panama," I think it's too good to be true. Well, it *is* too good to be true. Unbeknownst to me, she changes my December 7th flight to December 6th. So she turns my flight itinerary into a forty-eight hour itinerary by moving up my departure date.

Guess what happens when I attempt to check in for my flight on December 7th? "Mr. Deichmann, your flight departed yesterday." Of course nowadays with on-line check-in, this could never happen. As the sweat puddles under my backpack, the Continental desk agent informs me she can get me out of Boston to make my original arrival time in Santiago, but only with an impossibly tight thirty-six minute layover in Miami for my international connection to Panama. It's worth a try. In tropical Miami, another sweaty airport dash ensues, and it's confirmed that even a relatively young and fit traveler needs more than thirty-six minutes to change terminals, pass through security again, and board an international flight at least the requisite thirty minutes before departure. With a petition that was apparently adequately articulate, I manage to get the Continental desk in Miami to book me a one-way direct Lan Chile flight to Santiago. As I'm handed my new boarding pass, the agent adds "Mr. Deichmann, please remember that even if we make an error, it is not our policy to buy tickets for passengers on competitor airlines. Enjoy your flight."

The Lan Chile experience is simply lovely, especially after the day I just had. Because I no longer need to connect in Panama, this flight gets me to Santiago three hours before Dave's scheduled 1am arrival. Now would be a good time to have a cell phone, I reason. I have no way of communicating my itinerary change to Dave while we're traveling separately. Upon my arrival in Santiago, I am extra relieved to intercept him as he emerges from the arrivals hall, right on schedule. Dave is surprised to see me, and we are excited to have a three-hour jump on our adventure.

We spend two days exploring Santiago: Cerro Santa Lucía, Providencia, government palaces and monuments, and an excursion to the coastal port of Valparaíso. I learn quickly that Chileans don't speak Spanish or *Español*; they speak *Castellano*. I also learn that most of the stereotypes I've heard all of my life about Latin Americans are simply wrong. People here are ambitious, intelligent, polite, and clean. Speaking of cleanliness, although it's summer, I notice a conspicuous absence of the kind of body odor that pervades public places in southern Europe. Or perhaps I just don't notice it because of my own traveler's stench. With the end of the fall weather at home, it's nice just to be where it's warm. Just the thought of being in such a fascinating place is intoxicating. South America!

After two days in Santiago, we board Intercity Bus #63 to Mendoza, Argentina. In the paper that I picked up at the station, I see that Argentina is today's top news story: the country is virtually bankrupt. The ticket man takes my $10,000 Chilean pesos for the eight hour ride over the Andes mountains—the second highest range in the world. This will cost us each $15. After a few hours, I find an empty seat with more space; Dave and I both doze off, with our respective rucksacks secured in our arms.

I awaken as the bus comes to a halt. The engine is turned off, and I nudge Dave with my elbow. The air is cold and thin. It is dark outside. I hear the sound of anxious Spanish-speaking voices amid loud snoring. Electronic Christmas tunes of "Jingle Bells" and "Oh Come All Ye Faithful" seem to be coming from the seat backs. Looking out the window, I see that we are at the border crossing to Argentina. For some reason, the seatbacks— even those directly in front of us—are stuffed with musical Christmas cards. A Chilean man rushes through the bus distributing jeans and sneakers to all of the passengers except for me and Dave.

"Everybody off the bus," we are commanded by the border police. In the frigid Andes evening air, we assemble on the side of the road and wait for the locals to answer customs questions and for our American passports to be stamped. There is no reason for us to say anything unless asked. A large blue and white billboard on the side of the road exclaims "*Las Islas Malvinas son Argentinas*!" (The Falkland Islands belong to Argentina). Wow—up here in the Andes, islands seem pretty far away! Relations between Chile and Argentina are tenuous at best, even though decades have passed since Chile allowed the UK to launch airstrikes against Argentina in the Falklands War. I see that one of the Chilean smugglers is being interrogated inside this Argentinean police office, and this holds up our departure.

After ninety minutes of stoppage, we are on the move again.

I surmise that somebody was paid off to overlook the smuggled goods, as all passengers seem to be back on board, and the Christmas songs continue to play. They, as well as the jeans and sneakers, get passed back up to the Chilean entrepreneurs, who respond with various tones of "gracias." I later learn that the limit on imports into Argentina is $300. So this is how Chinese products are transported over the Andes for Argentinean markets. Travel can be educational. The Argentine peso is pegged to the U.S. dollar at 1 to 1, so the country represents a strong (and large) market for illicit goods.

We arrive in Mendoza at 5:30am, just about sunrise. The land is flat, gently sloping eastward from the Andes. We get coffee at a restaurant near the bleak bus terminal. At the cost of $1.40 a cup we realize that Argentina is going to be expensive. The business of smuggling is making even more sense to us now.

Dave and I lock up our bags in the bus station, and then set out to explore Mendoza. The city is what one might expect for Latin America; beautiful plazas decorated with thousands of colorful ceramic tiles, nice shade trees, and modest houses but tidy. Everywhere, friendly people go about their daily business. They notice that we are strangers, but don't seem to mind, especially when we smile and try to speak *Castellano*. The locals—like Americans—seem to be less fit than Chileans (who are more like Europeans); although, maybe this is more of a big city-small city contrast. The storm drains also strike me. They are deep and wide—Mendoza must really get torrential rain at times. They seem so carefully designed, that maybe they are used to collect water for irrigating the seemingly ubiquitous vineyards. Mendoza's region is famous for the increasingly popular Malbec wines, and it is fascinating to have a glimpse of their origins.

A city cab takes us to the regional airport, which is surrounded by vineyards. The flight to Buenos Aires is short and uneventful. The flight attendant brings us each a crustless sandwich and a Quilmes beer in a decidedly un-masculine but patriotically Argentinean light-blue can. The sandwich is small, and I wonder what they did with the crust. Then it occurs to me that maybe they mass-produce these sandwiches from a large loaf of bread in a huge machine and cut it into neat little triangles. I guess I'll never know about the crust.

Our local city bus ride into Buenos Aires takes well over an hour. The driver has made his seat area a shrine to his football team the Boca Juniors, his kids, and Jesus Christ. Using just our hotel's address, Dave figures out that our hotel is only seventy more blocks of speed bumps and aggressive drivers that would make any American city look tame. What we think is gunfire turns out to be some sort of bombs that teenage boys throw at vehicles and passersby. Dave and I alertly jump off the moving bus and into the crowd at Plaza Congreso, the nearest stop to our hotel.

As we check in, the receptionist warns us that it will be difficult for us to obtain cash. Citizens are lined up at ATMs and banks to withdraw their daily limit over fears that the local currency will be devalued. Dave and I will need to depend mainly on credit cards to get by for the time being.

After quick showers and a change of funky "bus" clothes, Dave and I execute our routine approach to find the sweet spots of the city. We break out a map and string together the main attractions: Calle Florida, the obelisk, and the renovated docklands. We end the day with our first proper meal: pizza and *agua gaseosa* at a street-level table near the hotel. An impoverished woman with open hands and her sickly looking daughter approach as I take out money to pay our bill. As we walk back to the hotel, another dirty-faced, emaciated urchin mutters a plea in Spanish. Our guidebook calls Buenos Aires the "Paris of the South," but Dave and I are both struck by the extreme poverty that we witness in this beautiful city.

Up early to catch the Buquebus hydrofoil to Montevideo, Uruguay. Why not, when will we have this opportunity again? On the trip, we sit near two hefty retired women—Marge and Iris—from Washington State. We begin a friendly conversation with them, exchanging stories. I tell them this is my final trip before my family expands. I probably offer too much information when I add that I left my eight-month pregnant wife at home with two young kids. Without hesitating, Large Marge says "I think you're a skunk." Maybe I am, I think. I sit in guilty silence as we approach the dock, reminding myself that the South America plan pre-dates our pregnancy, and trying to reassure myself that being here is okay.

We arrive in Montevideo at 2:30pm with great expectations. A nice lady at Buquebus photocopies a map for us and points us in the right direction for the city's cool stuff, or historical center. The exercise is simply to check the place out quickly. Our target is Palacio de Ciudad and its surroundings on Plaza Independencia. The residential areas are modest but cared for. There seems to be far less poverty in Uruguay's capital than in that of its larger neighbor. Our lunch will be *schopp* (draft beer) and a *porteño*, a hotdog in a bun with ham and melted mozzarella.

Dave and I lazily kill our pre-return time in the shadow of a fortified wall on the waterfront, which we judge by taste to be the salty Atlantic Ocean rather than the muddy Rio de la Plata. As we relax for our final ninety minutes here, Dave reads our guidebook's section on the city to see if we missed anything. "Hey Deichmann…It says here that Montevideo is one time zone <u>east</u> of New York." "Crap, if that's true we're going to miss today's boat as well as tomorrow's flight from Buenos Aires." Suddenly, all happiness is lost. We proceed to ask three different pedestrians what time it is, and at last we become confident that it's only 5:20 now and not 6:20.

Dave and I make our way back to the dock, and purchase travel supplies from a small shop. While waiting, we discuss what we've seen. We agree that we've seen nothing special in Montevideo; it was just sort of cool to visit another country. We spot a fleet of twelve to fifteen ships and take a few photos. "That must be the entire Uruguayan Navy" I infer, suddenly realizing that photographing military equipment might not be wise, as it might not be entirely legal. Our return to Buenos Aires is graced with a one-hour discussion with a neo-fascist Italian-Argentine. It's possible to meet the most interesting people while traveling.

On the walk from the dock back to our hotel, the atmosphere on the street has turned for the worse, and it can be described simply as "angry." Dave and I stop to observe animated chanting in Plaza de Congreso, just outside our hotel. "This must be about floating the currency, don't you think?" Dave nods in agreement. Safely inside the hotel, we learn from hotel staff that the protests are led by *Peronistas* who are opposed to the austerity measures just announced by the government. Argentines are livid about a $1000 daily limit to withdrawals from their savings accounts. There is talk of a general strike tomorrow.

The next morning is December 11th 2001, and it's is exactly three months after hijackers crashed two airliners into New York's World Trade Center. Dave and I are up early for our planned flight to Iguazu Falls on the border with Brazil and Paraguay. We pack for the day then go to the lobby to call for a taxi. The taxi driver dutifully takes us to the airport, where we learn for the first time that the national airline Aerolineas Argentinas is also on strike. "It would have been nice of that bastard cab driver to tell us," says Dave. There would be no Iguazu Falls for us this trip, and we will have to seek a refund after we get home. We take another cab back to the hotel, then watch CNN, which is featuring a taped address by Osama bin Laden that was just released. Bin Laden's goal is to explain to the world why he did what he did. There's not much to do, as most everything on the street is closed. Lines have formed at the banks. Nothing is functioning in Buenos Aires today, so Dave and write in our journals and watch the news as we sip scotch. As daytime retreats, we observe an escalation of unrest in the plaza and streets below.

On our final morning in Buenos Aires, we wake up unsure if there will be anything to do in the city. The BBC and CNN confirm that the strike is over and indeed Argentina will return to work today. The feeling is bittersweet; although we missed Iguazu Falls, a planned highlight of our trip, the city is ours, and now we can make the most of our remaining time. Long lines remain at the ATMs and banks, so we still cannot obtain cash for subway tickets there. As a last resort, we exchange a few US dollars at our hotel, then leave for the day to visit La Boca and San Tome. After that, we'll visit the district of Recoletta to see its colorful houses and Eva Peron's grave.

The next morning, we are up at 4am and in a cab within an hour to get to the Buenos Aires Jorge Newberry Airport (AEP). I'm curious why we arrived at EZE, but must fly from a different airport to return to Mendoza from Buenos Aires. I wonder if we got that right. The driver does his best to negotiate traffic chaos, which is mainly gridlock already. This must be as bad as it can get. As we approach our departure time and AEP, I hope that there was no mistake and that we are going to the correct airport.

We land in Mendoza with too little cash for the $8 cab fare to the city, so we take trusty bus #63 instead. We lug our bags around the city to explore more plazas and discover the largest Christmas celebration we've ever seen, sponsored by none other than Coca-Cola. I empty my pockets of $6.83 to buy *cervezas* (beer), water, and cookies for the eight hour bus ride over the Andes.

By design, we take the bus across the Andes in both directions. The westbound views are very different, especially by day. The most dramatic mountain landscapes imaginable; I have never seen anything like this! Intertwining roads and abandoned rail switchbacks tower over distant green valleys. On the rail line, long sections of track are washed out and many of the snow sheds have been crushed by avalanches. The highpoint in the road is at Paso de los Caracoles, at 5669 meters (18,500 feet) above sea level. "Hey Dave, this pass gives new meaning to the word 'highway,'" I wink. We see several ski areas and a provincial park nearby. Enormous parking lots accommodate the vehicles of summer hikers, who are scattered along challenging steep cliff trails.

We are asked to disembark and stand by our bags for border inspection, and find this is much easier westbound than it was in the other direction. After the chaos of Argentina, returning to Chile somehow feels comforting; it feels kind of like coming home. Along this road somewhere are the *Concha y Toro* vineyards, home to a product I know and love. In my opinion they offer some of the best inexpensive wines, even in American markets, and I give them more than my share of business. The bus returns to Santiago's Central Station via Los Andes, and I help a girl from Philadelphia figure out which metro stop to use to get to her hostel.

At the market, Dave and I take turns watching our luggage and looking for some nice souvenirs for our respective families and friends. I could find nothing reasonably priced in Buenos Aires, but here in Santiago I can find few things that anyone back home would probably want. Unsuccessful, we return to the modest Riviera Hotel on Miraflores via the San Lucia stop.

For me, it's a quick and uneasy sleep, concerned about making my 4:50am flight. My flight to Panama City must be the earliest flight anywhere in the world. I wonder if the cab I requested will show up at 1:50am to give me a ride. It might be too late at night or too early in the morning, I'm not sure which.

Only half awake with my bags outside the room, I close the door without leaving Dave a "*ciao*" note. He will fly late in the day, and while sightseeing he will watch for souvenirs for me.

I walk quietly down the carpeted stairs to meet the taxi. I am out of Chilean pesos, so I ask the driver if he will accept $10 for the $6500 fare ($8.50). I bite off more than I can chew on the drive; I know enough *Castellano* words to make observations and ask questions, but not to understand the answers. An awkward silence begins as I exhaust my few "small talk" expressions.

At 2:27am, the SCL airport seems frighteningly deserted. Imagine my relief to see a line in front of the Copa Airlines counter! I struggle to stay awake at the gate, and then collapse after boarding. I sleep over the darkened Andes, and then sunrise shows me God's view of Ecuador and Colombia. Given that I have only fifty minutes to transfer, I am relieved that I'm not required to pass through customs in Panama. Luckily, my flight to Newark departs only two gates from my arrival gate.

I sit with two married Korean-Canadian Baptist missionaries who are on their way home to Toronto after work in the Panamanian jungle. They are a pleasant couple, and I am more impressed with them than they are with me. I am sipping a Gossamer red wine as we talk, and eventually I tell them that I just became a confirmed Catholic. Funny how labels can change conversations—they don't seem impressed with this revelation, or with the cup of wine in my hand. I explain to them that my wife is Catholic, and my parents spent much of their marriage fighting over their differing religious perspectives (Protestant versus Catholic)."I'm not going to put our kids through the same thing," I insist. I try to make light of the deteriorating conversation by adding "You know, my wife and most of my best friends were raised Catholic, and they seemed to turn out okay." Anyway, I have no choice but to reject the attitude that my belief system is perfect and anyone else's is wrong, or vice versa. Isn't the state of human imperfection our fundamental assumption as Christians? There is far more common ground than differences across Christian denominations. End of sermon.

All is well until air traffic control puts our plane in a thirty minute holding pattern over Central New Jersey. After landing in Newark, we wait on the tarmac for fifteen more minutes. I pass through customs and re-check my bags.

I miss my connection to Manchester, New Hampshire by five minutes. It was the final flight tonight, so I am re-routed to Boston. My flights on this trip seem jinxed, but luckily they do not suffer any real catastrophes. I cannot wait to see both kids. I couldn't find them anything in Chile, so I buy them overpriced toy airplanes that light up and make "whoosh" noises.

At Boston's Logan Airport, my third trimester wife and two sleepy kids pick me up. The hugs and smiling reception reassure me that Large Marge's "skunk" comment on the hydrofoil to Montevideo was misguided and that I'll be allowed back into my own home and bed. We stop at Applebee's in Nashua for a quick "cheeseburger in paradise" on the way home. Baby "Jack" James is born four weeks later.

Reflecting upon the trip, this is my first use of hard-earned award miles on international travel. My total expenses are barely over one thousand dollars, not a bad price for exchanging one week of New Hampshire winter for South American summer and a quick exploration of three countries.

Driven to explore more of Chile, my next trip there—again with Dave—takes place two years later. This time, the goal is to see some of Patagonia's natural wonders. I have my mind set on visiting Parque Nacional Torres del Paine, and Dave is keen to see Parque Nacional Magdalena Isla de Pengüinos, home to a colony of one hundred thousand penguins. To get there from Santiago, we fly "the milk run" with Lan Chile, stopping at Puerto Montt and the air strip of tiny Balmaceda on our way to Punta Arenas. The mountainous geography of Tierra del Fuego is nothing less than spectacular; its greens and blues mirror Alaska at the other extreme of the American landmass. In rough waters on a musical boat trip to glaciers in Parque Nacional Bernardo O'Higgins, a nice Chilean man grabs the hood of my coat to save me from sliding off the wet deck to a frigid death. In Punta Arenas, while Dave and I are deliberating whether to spend $1200 each and accompany an overnight scientific expedition to Antarctica, storms set in and decide for us that we will be lucky enough just to fly back north to Temuco, where we catch an overnight train for our final day in Santiago, then fly back to the USA.

In January 2006, I'm thirty-six years old, and I've been

enthusiastically promoting this incredible country of Chile to everyone I meet. I'm on my way back to Santiago for the third time, helping out as co-organizer and co-chaperone with my new colleague Kristin and her fourteen students. Our friend and Global Studies colleague Doreen is assisting with the trip as well, as she broadens her repertoire of travel experiences.

This particular trip is a two-week intensive academic course designed by Kristin. I had worked with her on the proposal and logistics, and to complement Santiago, I took care to add natural wonders of interest to me and arguably worthwhile for the students. These include Parque Nacional La Campana, Parque Nacional El Morado, and the coastal towns of Viña del Mar and Reñaca. To me, these are some "sweet spots" of Chile, not to overlook the tragic history of Pinochet's human rights abuses and their ongoing aftermath, the main topics of the course. The trip turns out to be an academic course not just for the students, but for me and Doreen as well. This is a fantastic opportunity to travel for free and learn so much more about Chilean history.

Still young enough to think I might become a rock star or at least competent enough on guitar to perform a song for my family, on a free afternoon I sit alone on Pio Nono in barrio Bellavista and write down some lyrics to a song. I am sipping a glass of *Castillero de Diablo*, thinking of Karen, and observing my colorful urban surroundings. The rhythm is slow, reflecting the stride of the passersby on this hot summer day in January.

PIO NONO
At a joint called La Palmera
Sidewalk table, Pio Nono
Shoulda brought me my sombrero
Waiter begs me not to go

It's hot and fine in January
Good to get back in the sun

Santiago Chile baby
Sip some wine and have some fun
In the LAND of the SUN
When it's COLD at HOME
God I LOVE your SUN
But I MISS my HOME

And the world it does spin
And it spins in spite of me
You know I'll sink if I can't swim
God help me swim in spite of me

In the country of El Perro
Gray street cat just talked to me
In the City of Love
I'm still blind, I want to see

Castillero del Diablo
Like to hear the people talk
Should put on my 30 sunscreen
Love to watch the people walk

Santiago mi amor
As the mountains shine in the sunlight
I have you now I want you more
Let us shine in the moonlight

On our travel study's final day in Chile, Michele Bachelet is elected president. She is the very first female head of state in Chilean history. Politics aside, this is an exciting day for everyone, except maybe male chauvinists, and there are plenty of those in Chile. Cars stream down the streets with drivers honking their horns incessantly while jubilant passengers hang out the windows waving Chilean flags. It is quite a spectacle, and I will never forget it.

As we fly back to Boston, I feel satisfied to close the chapter on Chile in my life. I have seen it, I love it, and I understand that it's time to move on. I first traveled to Chile for a reason, and today there is a lot to show for it. Even though I don't directly deserve credit, I played a small part in a successful program that lives on, and my own courses are better for my on-the-ground experience. Although I would like to visit Norte Chico someday, I have too many other things to do first. Blessed closure! My core competency is in Central and Eastern Europe, and others can competently represent Chile at Bentley. It will probably be a long time before I will again have the pleasure of seeing Chile, *mi amor*.

7

PICTURES OF THE POPE

Under a blood red sky
A crowd has gathered in black and white
Arms entwined, the chosen few
The newspaper says, says
Say it's true it's true...
And we can break through
Though torn in two
We can be one

"New Year's Day" by U2, *War* (1983)[xv]

Today is April 27, 2005, and Pope John Paul II passed away earlier this month. Coincidentally, I'm on my way to Poland on a research trip. Every once in a while I need a travel fix, but traveling abroad is the last thing I should do right now. It is the end of the semester. I have been busily preparing my application for tenure at Bentley, due in two months. My kids are all at immeasurably enjoyable but also very demanding ages for parents: seven, five, and three. My conscience weighs heavy for leaving their mother to care for them alone while she works full time. I also wonder if I'm a fool to miss another week of their lives when nobody is forcing me to go anywhere.

So why am I going to Poland? I want to extend what I believe to be upward momentum in my career, and make my long-overdue return to a country that intrigues me like few others. Academics are expected to develop a regional expertise or specialization, and having grown up during the Cold War, I have a deep and abiding interest in the European countries that were isolated behind the Iron Curtain; however, given my responsibilities as a relatively young parent, I have thus far failed to travel as much as I would like in Central Europe, which has quickly become my "wonderland." With limited time to travel, it will take perseverance to learn as much as I should about this massive and complex region.

My most recent, and my only, trip to Poland was in 1998, seven years ago. In all honesty I was fascinated more than impressed. I got a lot of mileage out of that visit; I wrote my dissertation in part based upon informational interviews I held with U.S. investors in and near Warsaw. At that time, Poland's success and return to Europe was far from a sure thing. I cannot wait to observe the state of affairs in Poland now, as it becomes one of the first Warsaw Pact countries to join the European Union.

This trip represents a leap of faith: I knew I had to do it, but didn't know how I would pay for it. I bought my Lufthansa plane ticket at my own expense, and then my project began to evolve. I put together a research plan, drafted an interview script, arranged meetings in Poland, and then applied for a modest research grant to cover the most basic travel expenses. Sometimes without faith nothing happens.

I have grown accustomed to the intensity and incessant motion of days like today. My heart races as I dutifully take the minutes at Bentley's Faculty Senate meeting, which has already run over its allotted time and into my final class meeting of the semester. After five more minutes, I pass my "secretary notepad" to the vice president and excuse myself to rush into the classroom in the next building, where twelve students wait to present their semester projects. Out of necessity, I enforce the five minute per student time limit strictly, ending class punctually at 3:25pm. I am on a mission.

I rush to my office computer, then locate and print three hotel vouchers I requested this morning. They were emailed to me over the past three hours while I was in meetings and class. Just as I leave the office, I receive an email informing me that my funding has been approved, and a happy rush of adrenaline soaks my spine. This morning's feeling of trepidation gives way to this afternoon's sense of elevation. All I care about now is to be checked in and at the gate for my 6:45pm flight.

It seems like a small world. My shuttle driver asks in a New England accent "Where ya off ta?" He explains that his wife is Polish, and he demonstrates a remarkable knowledge of Poland's modern history. He is taking Polish classes and will return to Warsaw for three months in the summer. I think to myself "Wow, it's remarkable that in America, even shuttle drivers can find a way to fund their passion for place. Three months in Poland would be nice!"

I board the 777 and stand in the first class cabin, waiting in the queue to get to my designated seat in economy. I notice the front page of a German-language newspaper. President George W. Bush and Crown Prince Abdullah are holding hands like childhood friends in a garden at Bush's Crawford, Texas ranch.

I find my seat and open my journal, exhausted. The metaphor that comes to mind is an emaciated animal that has mobilized all of its meager existence to support the gestation of a baby. This trip to Poland is my baby.

The last few days have been extraordinarily intense. On top of it all, preparation for this trip was a rat-race. In the office and at home, I have been grading end-of-semester papers and quizzes, preparing study guides and final exams, and attending end-of-semester committee meetings. And I needed to do everything well, especially now. I go up for tenure in two months. On top of that, I've been booking flights, surface transport, and hotel reservations in four Polish cities, and setting up non-conflicting interview appointments with seven people in five cities.

As husband and father of three young kids, I've been running around Nashua doing last minute shopping for eight days of groceries, finding dairy and produce that are fresh enough to last until my return, listing food inventory for Karen and the kids, assembling an eight-day babysitter "roadmap" of activities, arranging extended daycare, packing my suitcase, and cleaning floors as I backed out of the house. Last but not least, I thought I should toss that neatly-stacked cord of seasoned firewood into the garage for its own protection. Karen considers it to be unsightly, and I was afraid she would give it away while I am gone.

After five minutes of just sitting still on a plane contemplating all of the traffic in my head, forward momentum takes over and I nervously pull out my travel journal and start writing something. I'm not used to sitting still, and there's so much action in my mind that I have to do something, so I write some garbage that sounds decidedly unpoetic, but nevertheless captures my present state of mind.

I sit on Lufthansa flight 425 to Munich, and after that I will connect to Gdańsk, Poland. The plane is not full, and I'm hoping for an empty seat next to me—maybe some extra space for comfort. Driven by my passion for Central Europe, I'm excited for new knowledge and the adventures that I'll have.

Spring has arrived in the northern hemisphere's mid-latitudes—New England and Poland alike. Although it is cool and rainy now, summer visited briefly last week, prompting me to begin outdoor projects at home. It is a relief to be in flight; the separation forces me to take a break. I did double kid duty (Charlie is seven, Isabela five, and Jack three) for four days last week as Karen traveled to North Carolina for work. It is spring vacation week for public schools, which means that in my absence, Charlie needs special daytime daycare arrangements. I took him with me to work at Bentley both Monday and Tuesday; after that, I was fortunate to find room for him in a vacation program for the rest of the week. Uncertain how children in the workplace might be perceived by my new department chair, I kept my on-campus hours brief and worked at home as much as possible. This work was sandwiched between dropping off and picking up the other kids to allow Karen extended hours for her human resources work, which this month involves a series of multiple-shift layoff meetings and dealing with ensuing fallout. I was so busy these past weeks that most of my logistics for this trip were completed as late as 11 o'clock this morning.

Thinking it would be good for me to read something in German, I pull a copy of the newspaper *Süddeuthsche Zeitung* from the seatback in front of me. Struggling to make sense of the stories, I am reminded how rusty my German has become. A lot of the headlines deal with EU expansion to ten new countries, and I become interested in an article on German Chancellor Schroeder's visit to France to promote the EU Constitution before a May referendum. There is a cartoon of a sow labeled "EU" being sucked dry by ten little piglets (the 2004 accession states), with Romania and Bulgaria gleefully rushing to join in and struggle for a nipple. Another article expresses concern about Japan's sex life and repopulation issues: one third of married couples aged eighteen to forty-nine haven't had sex in the past month. Maybe my German is not so bad after all, if given an interesting story to read! I doze off for an indeterminate period of time. My catnap is interrupted by a brief announcement in a heavy German accent "Ladies and gentlemen… ve don't vant you to vait too long for your first drink, so ve vill begin cabin service right a-way!" Ahh- Lufthansa really knows how to make people comfortable while traveling in coach class! Having traveled only in the US lately, I've forgotten how nice it is to fly an airline that doesn't charge for a glass of wine. Or maybe the Germans are just pushers—I later notice in my Lufthansa in-flight magazine a full-page advertisement featuring young, attractive blond flight attendants and the statement "Now you can drink your miles," clarifying that frequent flyer miles can be spent on duty-free alcohol!

Upon arrival in Munich, it is already getting light outside, but it's only midnight back home. Walking drowsily through the terminal, I lament that there seems to be at least one flight to every other major Polish city prior to my departure time for Gdańsk. At my departure gate, I stretch out on a vacant bench and secure my carry-on backpack, then doze off with two alarm clocks resting on my chest. I re-awaken almost immediately, afraid that I might sleep through the boarding process. Bleary eyed, I force myself to sit up, walk to the rest room, and splash cold water on my face. I return to the gate to watch the extra features of *Schindler's List*, a task I meant to complete before leaving home. I will be visiting Kraków on this trip, and I want to fully appreciate one of the brighter stories of a city that many associate with nearby Auschwitz, the most notorious Nazi concentration camp.

As we descend through the clouds over Gdańsk, I notice that everything is gray. It's as if the springtime colors of Boston and Munich have been sucked out of the day that began in brilliant hues of green and blue. At first sight, northern Poland looks like anything but a cheerful place, but I'm on a mission for knowledge, not cheer.

Upon exiting the Airbus, I am immediately struck by the age and small size of the airport terminal. To my relief, I succeed in withdrawing 600 złotys—about $200—which should be about enough cash for the entire week. And now, I'm off to find my way to Novotel, the cheapest 3-star accommodation for my one and only night in Gdańsk.

I locate the correct 1970s vintage public bus to the city

center, and confirm its destination with the driver, who grunts affirmatively when I ask *"Centrum, prosze?"* The trip would cost only 5.2 złoty (about $1.30). I pay with the smallest bill provided by the ATM, 20 złotys. The driver grunts again as he counts out my change—I think it includes every last coin from his arsenal. My fare is represented by three connected tickets of 1.40 złotys (two for me, one for my bag). When I insert only one ticket into the noisy validation machine, the driver shouts something toward me in the back of the bus, and then repeats it. This draws the attention of every passenger on the bus. A friendly lady asks me if I speak German, then instructs me to validate the other two tickets as well.

On the ride into the city I can't help but notice countless pictures of recently-deceased Pope John Paul II on billboards, in windows, and at the centers of makeshift street shrines. Pictures of Poland's beloved Pope are everywhere!

As the crowded bus stops and starts at its assigned stations, I struggle to balance myself with my backpack. My eyes strain to make out any street names or landmarks recognizable from the bulky travel guide I'm holding. No thanks to the book, after forty-five minutes I manage to identify the stop that is probably pretty close to Novotel. I'm relieved to see that that the Old Town is within walking distance. Gdańsk has no modern skyline to speak of, only a cluster of attractive buildings reflecting the city's Catholic, Hanseatic, German, and Polish heritage. After exiting the bus, I walk right past Gdańsk's main train station. While I'm here I should check the schedule and buy tomorrow's train ticket to Poznań—I might be rushed after my tomorrow morning's meeting at GE Capital Money Bank.

I approach the ticket counter and wait for my chance to shine or fail, repeating to myself three or four Polish words that I am trying to string together. When my turn arrives, I point to my printed train schedule and ask for a ticket to Poznań. A bald, stumpy white man looks over from the line at the next window and asks in a Midwestern accent if I am American.

Good grief! I've come here to get away from America!. I guess my appearance and disabilities in Polish didn't fool this genius. When he insists upon helping, I reluctantly accept. I really want to work through this adventure myself, and I didn't come to Poland to depend upon overzealous Americans.

As my train ticket is being issued, I tell the man that I speak German, and that will get me by if necessary. His dander rises immediately, as he argues that "speaking German in Danzig is highly inappropriate and in fact offensive to locals." Danzig is the German name for Gdańsk. Yes I know this piece of history, but no I don't believe German will offend the Poles these days, at least not the young ones; nevertheless, I decide not to bicker with this *über*-helpful gentleman. I collect my train ticket, then we chat while walking the thousand meters or so toward ulica Długa, the main street of the central city's pedestrian zone.

Resigned to the likelihood that this apparently well-intentioned man will shadow me for a little while, I introduce myself. Vern from Green Bay, Wisconsin does the same. Vern says he has an afternoon meeting in the Old Town and would be happy to show me the way there. I thank him, and ask him what he's up to in Poland. He teaches American English for business at Gdańsk University of Technology. Vern explains that he will probably go to China to teach soon. I tell him about my research and I give him one of my ten remaining business cards. Before going his separate way to the meeting, Vern points out his favorite local restaurants to me, none of which look like they'll fit my budget. I say farewell to Vern as he heads off to his meeting and I to find my hotel. I would not see him again until the next day at the train station. He is watching people from above a stairway, and I avoid his gaze.

I cross Zielony Bridge to Spichrzów Island and find Novotel easily. The receptionists are visibly pleased—or amused—to hear me *try* to speak Polish. Like other Poles, they smile and listen patiently until I get stuck, which never takes long. Then, I ask in reckless Polish if they speak English, or maybe German.

My embarrassment becomes worthwhile when the receptionist asks for my passport and *seems* surprised to see that it is from the US. She could be playing a game, but I smile with satisfaction anyway. In these turbulent times, there are few places in the world where Americans are more welcome than in Poland, but even friendly Poles seldom expect us to experiment with their language, as difficult as it is.

I try to take a power nap in my room, but adrenaline keeps me awake—I'm so excited just to be on Polish soil! Anyway, I've learned that naps are a bad idea after crossing the Atlantic eastbound. Travelers should force themselves to stay awake until the local bedtime. Absent a nap, I shower, dress in fresh clothes, and head off with my camera and oversized guidebook. The first day in Europe is always what I call "The Longest Day": a day that seems to go on forever, or at least a week.

I explore Gdańsk's historic core during the next couple of hours, taking in the sights along the Motława River, notably the picturesque churches, alleyways, and the iconic Gdańsk crane. Pictures of the Pope are hanging ubiquitously in shop windows. As the sun moves to the west and the temperature drops sharply I am thankful for every shred of clothing that I packed. This evening, I am dressed in my warmest items: layers of shirts, a sweater, and a leather jacket. Partly to warm up, I find a simple restaurant and order a Żywiec beer with a plate of eight small *pierogi* —a very small and bland portion that needs salt and Worcestershire sauce for character. As I eat in the warm room, fatigue sets in with a vengeance. I leave the restaurant to face the chilly evening air, purchase a phone card at a tobacco kiosk, and find a phone booth. Thanks to the bus driver, I have some coins for calling home to give proof of life. It is noon back home, but I am ready for bed. I brace myself against the frigid, damp Baltic wind and head back toward Novotel. On the way, I find another restaurant, and order onion soup so that I can sit down and take in a partial view of the sunset over *Złota Brama* (Golden Gate). I delight in the warmth of this restaurant as I look out at the bright setting sun. From the immediate effects of first-day jetlag, my body threatens to shut down completely. I can't remember ever being this tired in my life, and I find it excruciating to keep my eyes open. Fearful of passing out, I do what many in my circles would consider a cardinal sin: I leave a half glass of excellent Polish beer on the table. As I arrive at my hotel I notice that it is still a bit light out, so I have been defeated. I enter my room and collapse immediately on my bed without even taking time to brush my teeth.

I awaken at 5am, and receive the opportunity to recharge some batteries…those of my human body and my laptop computer. No diapers to change, no classes to prepare! I lie half-awake, drifting in and out of slumber while watching the world news in German, coverage of a Donald Rumsfeld interview about the Iraq war. He calls Central and Eastern Europe, "New Europe." I am no fan of Donald Rumsfeld, but I do appreciate the distinction, and I am pleased to hear him praise "my" part of Europe.

Nerves set in while thinking about my 11am interview at GE Money Bank. I have no idea if I will interview a senior executive, an underling, or a team. Am I prepared enough with my questions? Crap, I suddenly realize that in my haste to finish up at my Bentley yesterday, I neglected to print copies of my interview "script." I open that file on my laptop and sketch a handwritten outline to use as a general framework and list of questions. This problem is nothing a pen and pad of paper cannot solve.

Shortly after 9am, I leave the hotel on foot to find GE Money Bank, location of my interview. Whoever decided to put wheels on suitcases was a genius—I've been told it was a woman. I take my suitcase to the train station lockers for storage, then search for ulica Elżbietańska, the location of my 11am interview. GE Money Bank's office is not far from the main train station, which makes it very convenient for me. I locate the facility and the "hidden" unlabeled door inside the parking corral that I had been instructed to use. Now that I've located the bank, I have a few minutes to spare before my interview. I use the time to visit the Old Town Hall, the Great Mill, and the Church of St. Catherine, all of which lie within a short distance along the Radunia Canal.

Bartosz, the tax director at GE Money Bank, insists that I call him by his first name. He makes my first informational interview pleasant and stress-free. Approximately my own age, he is collegial and easy to talk to. As the bank is in the midst of a routine audit by visitors from the USA, he thanks me for coming and excusing him from any "morning interrogations." My research questions revolve around the reasons behind GE Money Bank's location selection in Poland and in Gdańsk. Bartosz is helpful, but admits as tax director his responses may not be authoritative. Moreover, the bank was already here when he was hired. He candidly expresses his frustration with the Polish Information and Foreign Investment Agency (PAIZ)[xvi]. I find this interesting, as I used PAIZ data for my dissertation and subsequent projects. Our meeting runs over our scheduled hour. I become increasingly uneasy about the possibility that I might need to interrupt it to catch my train.

As our meeting comes to a close, Bartosz extends an offer to answer further questions over email or phone, and to extend a welcome to future student groups in Gdańsk. As I walk to the train station, I appreciate that Bartosz epitomizes New Europe. He is optimistic, motivated, and knowledgeable. This makes me optimistic about Poland's prospects.

Rushing to the station in my American-cut pinstripe suit, I buy a sandwich and retrieve my suitcase just in time for the 1:08 *pociag* (train) to Poznań. On this holiday weekend, the station is bustling. Luckily, my train halts with a door positioned precisely where I stand with my suitcase on the crowded platform. My reserved cabin is full, with seven other passengers already seated. I manage to find an overhead home for my small American suitcase, which is large by European standards.

Across from me sits a young man named Paweł, with whom I initiate a conversation. He and two fellow students from the Gdańsk University of Technology are on their way home to Toruń for the holiday. "Are you celebrating with your family?" I ask. "No, I have been working very hard at university and I am going home to drink beer with my friends." Paweł is wearing a red t-shirt with a white maple leaf and "Toronto" stencil. I ask him if he's been to Canada, and he replies, "Yes, I went to visit Canada when my US visa was denied." Not knowing what to say, I express some remorse. "My government seems to have a difficult time distinguishing between its friends and potential threats," I add. Although Poland and the Czech Republic were quick to snub what Rumsfeld called "Old Europe" (Germany and France) by joining US efforts in Iraq, their citizens still require visas to visit the United States. Paweł asks about international summer work programs in the USA. I confess that I don't know anything about the programs, so I hand him one of my few remaining cards and I invite him to email me, promising that if he does, I will try to get him some information.

When Paweł and his friends leave the compartment, I eat my lunch and read everything my DK guide has to offer about my destination Poznań, which takes all of thirty minutes.

As advertised by the textbooks I use, the North European Plain is as flat as flat can be. Poles chop the limbs off their tree branches, leaving short "stump" limbs, as opposed to the "thinning" style of pruning that is common in the USA. I'm not entirely sure why. After two and a half hours of the four hour train ride, I become bored with the silence so I begin speaking to the guy across from me. He speaks very little English, but I manage to figure out that he is a mathematician from Zielona Góra ("Green Mountain" like Vermont) who works in Gdańsk. Knowing that maps can be great facilitators of conversation when language itself fails, I pull out my map of Poland and some difficult but interesting discussion ensues.

We arrive in Poznań at 5:25pm. I have no interviews here—I

just came out of curiosity; it's a well-known city and my interviews tomorrow in nearby Konin and Koło justify this route rather than traveling directly from Gdańsk to Warsaw. A huge Polish queue (defined as a pushy crowd curving slightly to the right) waits at the ticket sales counter, so I'll wait until the next morning to buy my ticket for Konin. As I leave the main station on foot, my inability to orient myself leads to the conclusion that this travel guide is not worth the weight it adds to my backpack. For starters, the city map has an icon of a *pociąg* in its legend, but not on the map itself. In other words, my current location is not on the city map. I have no idea which direction or how far I need to walk to my hotel, just off Stary Rynek (Old Town Square). And that's where my hotel room waits for me. I don't mind embarrassing myself again in Polish, so I ask the same question of eight to ten people along the way, all of whom point me in approximately the same direction. As they respond I suspect they might be warning me that it is too far to walk, but this is part of the fun. An hour later, I check into the cheapest hotel of the trip, and what a great location!

My goals for Poznań are realistic: see the main sights, adjust to European time on the first full day in Poland, and prepare for an early departure for the following day's meetings. I sit at a bistro table and order a beer for people-watching, one of my favorite things to do in Europe. An efficient team of two clean-cut guys scans the street and trash cans for empty bottles and cans, collecting them and guzzling any leftovers as well as smoking what is left of abandoned cigarette butts. I've heard some cruel observers call these "bottom feeders," but doesn't society need such folks to reduce waste and keep things clean?

As the afternoon progresses, the din of holiday weekend traffic crossing Stary Rynek gives way to very loud live street music. For less than $10, dinner is a fresh Greek salad and pizza *capriciosa* with the fantastic backdrop of the illuminated Renaissance Town Hall.

I retire to the hotel by 10:30pm. I turn on CNBC to wind

down and find out what's going on in the world. After spending the day struggling to decipher a few understandable messages, it's remarkably easy to watch English-language news. Oil falls below $50/barrel after record highs. I wonder if this has anything to do with Bush and the Crown Prince holding hands in Texas earlier this week. I set twin alarm clocks to make sure that I won't be late for my morning meeting with Zbigniew in Konin.

Street noise from Stary Rynek until 4am results in an unsettled sleep. I'm omni-cognizant of my whereabouts, and I drift in and out uncomfortably all night. I manage to appear in the breakfast room for coffee and yogurt when it opens at 7am. I'm really not hungry yet, so with the kitchen's approval I make a ham and cheese sandwich on whole grain bread to take for the train ride. A taxi to the train station costs PLN 7.70 (about $2.50). A walk or tram to the station would have taken half an hour and given what I learned yesterday, it might have been disastrous without a proper map. It is nice to know that I saved $2.50 yesterday by walking to the hotel, though! I buy my ticket with ease, and then board the train. I take my reserved seat in an eight-person compartment that is already occupied by three women and a girl.

This part of the story needs a diagram…

West (morning origin)   East (evening destination)

Poznań → Konin → Koło → Kutno → Warsaw

My train leaves Poznań at 7:40am, and according to the itinerary I made with times pasted from web site of PKP, it's a two hour trip to Konin. As the train reaches full speed, I look out the window. Hmm, it really shouldn't take two hours to get to Konin, I think to myself. This train seems to be moving fast, and on the map Konin doesn't look like it's all *that* far from Poznań. Reassuring myself that I did my homework, I return to my crowded compartment and settle into James Michener's *Poland* without a care in the world. At about 8:30am we make our first stop. As the train began to roll again, I look out the window in horror to see the Konin station sign passing to the rear of the train.

Oh well, maybe the train will stop in Koło and I can call Zbigniew before the time we are scheduled to meet in Konin, the city that just passed the window. I prepare my bags to jump off the train at Koło station, but alas this newer high-speed train does not stop. Instead, it pauses curiously for several minutes in a field a short distance thereafter. Next to the track, I see what I think I recognize as the Wood-Mizer assembly plant I visited seven years ago. Confused, I am ever so tempted to get off the train, but there is no platform outside and a wire fence separates me from what I believe to be the very location of my 11:30am meeting; moreover, I am wearing business casual, and I would look silly walking through the tall grass and scaling the fence with my suitcase. As the train starts to move again, I see scores of brand new Wood-Mizer portable sawmills at the side of the building. Yup, that was Wood-Mizer, and now I'll be late for my meeting. Although my ticket is only valid for travel to Konin, the conductor doesn't hassle me. He probably pities my ignorance and is too much of a gentleman to throw me from a speeding train. I stand at the door for a half hour more until we reach Kutno, the next station.

I step off the train and study the schedule placard at Kutno's miniature station. Crap, the next westbound train back toward Koło and Konin doesn't leave until 10:50am, an hour and a half from now. That train *might* get me to Koło station in time for my 11:30am appointment at the factory. Damn, I've got to call Zbigniew and tell him that I screwed up. His response is, "No worries, Joel." It turns out he had been waiting at the Konin station to pick me up at 8:30am. "Stay where you are," he instructs me, "I'm coming to get you."

Mortified by my mistake, I kill time by exploring the train station's surroundings. It is a warm, gentle spring morning and the street is lined with grass and dandelions that haven't yet been cut this year. I sit on a bench in the sun and catch up with my journal, chronicling my first mishap of the trip. Let's make this the only one. A taxi driver waits by his cab wearing a Buffalo Bills cap. For only one brief moment the familiar symbol at an unfamiliar location causes me to smile at him involuntarily and prepare to talk to him. At once, I realize I don't have any way to help him understand my connections to Buffalo, one of America's "most-Polish" cities. Maybe he has family or friends in Buffalo who sent him the cap. My thoughts shift. Somewhere to the west, Zbigniew is speeding toward me at 100km/hour in a green Renault on a two-lane road. I puzzle over how I could have misread the train schedule. I hate making rookie mistakes, and wondering where I went wrong is driving me nuts. I can't wait to re-check the train times on the internet. Ultimately when I do, I discover that I had typed the time wrong on the two-page itinerary I prepared for my trip.

Wow, I'm humbled that Zbigniew is driving eighty kilometers to make up for my oversight. He arrives about one hour later. E30, the main highway from Berlin to Warsaw and on to Moscow, runs parallel to the train track I was just on, but has only two lanes and is fraught with congestion. It is also considered the most dangerous road in Poland. As a result of the heavy traffic, it takes him twice the time to get to Kutno.

Zbigniew parks his Renault and approaches me in a plaid red, white, and blue shirt, jeans, and dress shoes. Although we only met once briefly seven years ago, he and I recognize one another immediately. I greet him with an apologetic "*Dzień dobry*," and we exchange firm handshakes.

Having little common history to go on, Zbigniew and I manage to keep our conversation going as we drive westward. Last time we met—which was the first time we met—he was production manager for Wood-Mizer industries in Koło, the world's largest producer of portable sawmills, or sawmills on wheels. His new venture, called Prologistix, is a management consulting team that specializes in all phases of production in any industry. Zbigniew has invested hundreds of dollars and countless hours of study in management books, which he shipped from amazon.com to a friend in the USA, who then forwarded them to Poland. He is looking for new clients, which of course can be difficult for a start-up. He imparts that one of the barriers to business in Poland is corruption. As a small consultancy, he feels his firm is blocked out by the country's dominant oligopoly. He asks me to share my PAIZ database of US firms in Poland, and I happily do. Sadly, my list only includes contact information through 2001, which means even if firms are still active, email addresses have changed with personnel changes. In addition, some of the data wëre entered sloppily and need to be cleaned up.

Zbigniew twice refuses my apologetic offer of 100 PLN for gas ($30). Gas here costs the equivalent of $5/gallon, three times what it costs in the USA. Polish per capita income is $5000, about one sixth that of the USA. Not wanting him to lose face, I decide not to push the issue any further. He goes on to explain that he doesn't want gas money from me, instead he wants me to "take (him) to America… this country is fucked up, I say."

I mean no disrespect by describing Zbigniew's behavior as curious. Instead of going directly to Wood-Mizer or calling its CEO Dan to confirm our new appointment time, Zbigniew takes me to a "socks and underwear" store where he buys exactly twenty-three pairs of dress socks. While doing so, he speaks to nearly everyone in the store, employees and customers alike. Friendly guy about town, I think to myself. Zbigniew explains with pride that he negotiated his socks in bulk at the wholesale price. As we leave the store, he dials Dan's cell phone and hands the phone directly to me. Dan instructs us to meet him at a local restaurant, directions to which only Zbigniew knows. I return Zbigniew's phone to him.

Dan, from Indiana, seems very approachable for a CEO, and it's good to see him again. I am both grateful and surprised that he made time to meet me on a Saturday when he is expecting houseguests. So here is my chance to ask questions, I think to myself. What do I want to know? It is very difficult to fit in a single question with Dan. To my right, Zbigniew seems to have his own agenda for the meeting, and Dan does not seem interested in my questions; he has his own things to say. For example, he explains that when he hired many of his employees, they were living in houses with dirt floors. He loaned them money to build homes. I appreciate that he is a good Christian, but I am perplexed by this entire conversation. The meeting was supposed to be about foreign direct investment decision making, but I feel like my questions are being ignored, maybe because of some strangeness between my two acquaintances. Zbigniew no longer works for Dan, but clearly wants to do business with him again. He is here to win Dan over as a business client. Aha—that must be why Zbigniew offered to bring me here to Koło, all the way from Kutno! Wow, this is fascinating. The meeting with Dan was my idea, so I spring for everyone's lunch.

After lunch, we drop Dan off at his home, and then Zbigniew invites me to accompany him to Kalisz, a nearby historic town. "Fuck, I say, I'm going shopping there anyway, so you might as well see something." I'm starting to realize that Zbigniew is very fond of the "F-word," and likes to chase it with "I say." I want to tell him that it's not really appropriate to use that word in respectable English, if ever. Anyway, I've been invited to see another Polish town, and I'm excited about that. I accompany him as he window shops for some kind of motorcycle magazine. He explains that stores close at 2pm today thanks to the holiday. After buying his magazine, he proposes that we go for coffee and dessert. I don't do dessert, and could really use a beer, but I oblige to be polite. At an outdoor café in the main square, he instructs me to hold two seats while he makes four trips indoors to bring out two coffees and three desserts. He explains that the ice creams are for me. Again I notice that Zbigniew talks amenably to employees, customers, and passersby. "Hey girls, would you like to come and have ice cream with me and my American friend?" Thankfully, they decline. Yes I'm sure it would be fun to talk to Polish girls, but my naiveté is slowly giving way to a better understanding of Zbigniew's game.

Zbigniew evades questions, so I must repeat them. Even then, he is difficult to read. Generally he seems depressed, unhappy, and otherwise genuinely disgusted. Are things so bad for him in Poland? We remain at our table for another hour. He says he wants to take me to a famous castle nearby, but he is clearly in no hurry to leave. He explains that someone stole his business plan from a shared computer drive, and he fears the consequences. Conversation returns to the widespread corruption in Poland. He explains that firms won't buy his consulting services because "they prefer not to clean up their act." We are interrupted by a call from Zbigniew's younger brother. He is urgently looking for the Renault, which I now realize belongs to the brother. "Fuck I say, the castle trip is off," he announces. Kalisz is trumped by a return to Konin, the socialist block high-rise city that Zbigniew reluctantly calls home.

We arrive at the Zająçzkowski domicile in Konin at 6:45pm to pick up Zbigniew's brother. We walk directly past an older couple sitting in the kitchen, whom I presume to be their folks. I nod and utter a polite *"Dzień dobry,"* but Zbigniew doesn't introduce me. I later ask him if those people were his parents, which he affirms with a simply nod.

While we still have the car, we drive to the station to buy my train ticket for tonight's trip to Warsaw. We pick up some half liter beers and snacks, then return to his flat to hang out until it's time for me to catch my train. He directs me to sit on his futon while he puts on a live DVD of Sadé. Zbigniew plays the song "Smooth Operator" several times. He boasts, "Fuck I say, this sound system costs $1000," and to demonstrate its power he cranks it to maximum volume, which seems to shake the concrete construction. This is great fun for me, but I've got to go.

My train will leave from platform 2, which I estimate is located under the sign *Peron 2*. As I await its arrival, I contemplate whether I am more eager to leave Konin or get to Warsaw. Seeking relief from the strangeness of the day, I take refuge in the assigned train compartment with my compact disc player. My travel companions are two unglamorous lovers who cuddle and smooch with mutual zeal, while an old man in a threadbare suit drinks hard liquor from a faded Tang sport bottle. As for me, my thirst is quenched with a Warka beer that Zbigniew gave me for the trip. The train is full of revelers, drinking openly in spite of prohibition by PKP, the Polish rail company, and filling their lungs with cigarette smoke in the non-smoking corridor. Onward to Warsaw!

I arrive in Warsaw according to the train's schedule but hours after the arrival I had envisioned. I am exhausted, but grateful to Zbigniew for the curious adventures of the day. There will be plenty of time to (re-)explore the capital city on my own over the next three days. I walk briskly and purposefully for a half hour from the main station on well-illuminated Aleje Jerozolimskie (Jerusalem Avenue) and ulica Marszałkowska (Marshal Street) to MDM Hotel. Those who have been to a Central European train station know how important it is to walk deliberately— like you know where the hell you're going—especially alone at night with a big 'ol American suitcase on wheels. Such train stations might actually be portals to the underworld. I cannot decide whether the ubiquitous presence of policemen should scare me or comfort me.

On the last night of April, I check in at the MDM Hotel on plac Konstytucji (Constitution Square), enjoy my obligatory nightcap, take a shower, and go to sleep.

May 1ˢᵗ is *Święto Pracy* (Labor Day) in Poland. I sleep until my eyes pop open at 8:30am. I have in my sights a beautiful, free day for exploration; all that stands in the way is a complete breakfast. No alarm, no wake up call, no meetings, no classes, no kids; only great weather! I know that it's cliché, but "Life is

Good" sums up how I feel right now. There is truth to the incredibly popular slogan by the New Hampshire t-shirt company.

I ask the hotel receptionist if there would be any events to commemorate May Day. With her finger on a city tourist map she traces a parade route along Aleje Ujazdowskie, then folds the map and hands it to me. I run back to my room to pack my day pack with a liter of water, my guidebook, and my camera. As I walk outside, I notice a thermometer displaying 22 degrees C, which is about 72 Fahrenheit. My route is ulica Piękna, which I roughly translate to be Warsaw's "beautiful street."

At plac Trzech Krzyży (Three Crosses Square), I see a group of pensioners assembling under *Solidarność* banners. I proceed to what I expect to be the parade route, where a group of Communists ("New Left") is getting organized into marching formation. Brightly dressed and carrying banners in red and white, flanked by police in black and yellow, they seem more interesting than the pensioners, so I follow them for 500 meters taking photos from the sidewalk as they march on the street. Their parade is led by two young women pushing babies in strollers. I'm invigorated by what promises to be an interesting May Day in the sun. Not expecting to be heard or understood, I wonder out loud, "Are those babies really marching for the Communists?"

At the Nicolaus Copernicus monument, I notice another group of people surrounding a well-dressed speaker and forcefully waving blue EU flags as they cheer. City police try to keep the red (Communist) marchers away, but their leader and a handful of others infiltrate the "blue" (EU) crowd. They climb up to the podium, wrestle the microphone away, and give a short, fiery, speech to their political opponents. I'm not sure, but I believe the new speaker "won" the microphone for himself by citing "freedom and democracy" from the EU party's own speech and reasoning with them that he should have the right to talk in a free and democratic country. The media are everywhere, and the police are clearly positioned for possible escalation. I am in the right place at the right time! I only wish I could understand better what is happening. Just as things start to quiet down again, four people in caricature bobble-head costumes drive up on a small truck's bed: Frankenstein, Satan, and two likenesses of politicians from a rival party.

The commotion ends shortly, the crowd disperses, and another crowd forms around a speaker at the nearby plac Marszałka Józefa Piłsudskiego. As I walk in that direction, I am again taken aback by the multitude of Pictures of the Pope on shop windows, in addition to countless bouquets of flowers and burning candles that adorn makeshift shrines along the street.

To rest my legs, I settle in at an outdoor table at plac Zamkowy (Castle Square) in the Old Town, in full view of Sigismund's Column. Here, I watch the rising tide of pedestrians as they pass the Zamek Królewski (Royal Castle). I'm in my happy place. I see musicians, clowns forming balloon animals, horses with buggies, a "Native American" of dubious authenticity dancing to mystical sounds as they emanate from a battery-powered amplifier, parents with strollers, tourists, and older folks. A pack of English tourists approaches and one of them reads out loud the menu placard next to me: "'Something for the beer: bread with the lard'…Right, no thank you!" He shakes his head, has a laugh, and saunters away, English style.

Three Polish men arrive and sit down immediately behind me, as drunk and loud as people can possibly be this early in the afternoon. The oldest and loudest of the three is flanked by two young men, probably his sons, drinking with fortitude and singing Polish folk melodies on this holiday. They sound pretty good, but I fear that one of them will fall into my table. I use a short WC break as an opportunity to relocate to another table where I can appreciate their merriment at a safe distance.

The day ends near the Palace of Culture and Science, an imposing structure that is alternately referred to as essential historical artifact and heinous eyesore. This enormous wedding cake building was given to the Republic of Poland by the Soviet Union after World War II as a gesture of friendship. I eat a light meal at Sphinx, a Polish restaurant chain of Middle Eastern fare offered with an ambience that might remind one of Applebee's.

Although I overlooked a Polish holiday when I scheduled my time in Warsaw, I am fortunate that Adrian Grycuk makes time to meet with me[xvii]. Adrian is Manager in the Business Intelligence Department at the Polish Information and Foreign Investment Agency (PAIiIZ). I was aware of May Day, but I didn't plan on Tuesday being Constitution Day, nor did I anticipate that most Poles make this a four-day weekend, taking off the intervening workday on Monday as well. I am, therefore, overjoyed when Adrian shortens his holiday weekend to spend an hour discussing my recent research paper with me. This is the day that I would meet one of the nicest people on earth, with whom I would collaborate on teaching and research.

I meet Adrian at 2pm at MDM Hotel's front entrance. We introduce ourselves and shake hands, and then Adrian shows me to a nearby café and designates where I should sit. Without asking, he fetches two half-liter beers. My kind of guy! We discuss my paper entitled "Special Economic Zones and Foreign Direct Investment in Poland," one that I co-authored with my colleague Socrates the economist, not to be confused with Socrates the philosopher. The paper has just been accepted for publication in *Applied Economics Quarterly*. I am quite enthusiastic about the paper, but this meeting is a humbling experience. The paper uses econometrics, but Adrian is a case study guy and his first-hand experience with PAIZ unveils some weaknesses in our approach.

Within an hour, I realize that in terms of personality and general outlook on things, Adrian is the "Anti-Z," which of course is a double negative. It would be more appropriate to call Zbigniew the "Anti-A," and I would if I had met the two in reverse order. Like Zbigniew, Adrian is friendly; however, Adrian is eternally positive and his optimism is projected through his constant energy and smile. New Europe, indeed. Maybe Rumsfeld is onto something.

After deconstructing my research and making constructive suggestions for improving it, Adrian announces that he wants to show me "Hidden Warsaw." "Joel," he says, "I want you to know the real Poland." He takes me to several sites of World War II remembrance. On Złota Street and Sienna Street, we visit two of the few remaining fragments of the Nazi-erected wall of the Jewish Ghetto. Placards and boundary lines are provided for visitors, who read and photograph silently out of respect. Next, we visit a monument artistically designed to resemble the cattle cars that carted off victims of Hitler's regime from Warsaw to concentration and death camps, located at a place known as *Umschlagplatz* ("gathering place"). Adrian points out that many foreign heads of state visit this location while in Warsaw. Next, we visit the monument to the Jewish (Ghetto) Uprising of 1943 and the Warsaw Uprising of 1944. Although these uprisings were ultimately unsuccessful and devastating for what remained of the city of Warsaw, my own personal reflection at the memorial sites evokes something far beyond empathy for the resistance; I would describe it as a sense of pride for Poland. We conclude with a visit to Willy Brandt Square, on the north-western corner of the park where the future Museum of the History of Polish Jews will also be located. There are many Jewish tour groups, and several of the youth are carrying Israeli flags. Adrian tells me that the many Jewish tour groups bring with them their own security guard from Israel. Members of one group in particular gaze at us suspiciously as we visit the same monuments. We pass the enormous Catholic Powązki Cemetery, adjacent to the Okopowa Jewish Cemetery, which in turn borders an Evangelical cemetery. This visit raises a conversation with Adrian about ecumenicalism. We seem to be on the same page with regard to mutual respect among religions, a spirit of coexistence that had deep roots in Polish soil until the Nazis came to town.

It quickly becomes clear that Adrian is the trail boss, and that he's on a mission to show me his city. All I need to do is keep up and ask any questions that come to mind! For a refreshing contrast to the sites of death and destruction we've already visited, he leads me at a rapid gait to the new Arkadia shopping mall, one of the largest shopping centers in Central Europe. By this time I am well aware that Adrian walks swiftly, and that he enjoys walking. I like to walk too, especially in Europe, so I am puzzled that he persists in asking me if he is going too fast. "Am I slowing you down?" I ask. "Not at all," he insists, and then explains that one time a visiting investor fainted on a tour of the city while trying to keep up with him. "He must have been American," I say. To my surprise, Adrian responds, "No, he was Belgian." I tell Adrian that "compared to my young American students, I am still strong and fast, but compared to you, not so much." Knowing that Adrian values strength, as the day progresses and I eventually grow tired, I conceal any signs of fatigue from Adrian.

After our break, Adrian and I board a tram that crosses the *Wisła* (Vistula) River via the Śląsko-Dąbrowski Bridge. Adrian affectionately describes this district of Praga as "Old Warsaw." Praga is probably the most historically authentic part of the city, as it wasn't completely destroyed in World War II. It's also where the Soviets waited for the Germans to suppress the Warsaw Uprising. After visiting the Orthodox Church of Saint Mary Magdalene, we again cross the Wisła back into the core of the city. I am infinitely grateful to Adrian for showing me "Hidden Warsaw." Honestly, I have never had such a thorough tour of <u>any</u> city on earth; furthermore, many of the sights we visit aren't even listed in my guidebook.

We eat dinner at 7:30pm in the New Town. I insist upon treating, as a small gesture of thanks for the excellent tour that has just come to an end; or so I think. *Borscht* (beet root soup) is followed by *pierogi* dinner and on Adrian's recommendation, it ends with a shot glass of Żubrówka, an amazing vodka from Poland's northeast, not far from Białystok, Adrian's city of birth. Żubrówka is uniquely flavored with a single local blade of grass, giving it a subtle herbal flavor. Until now, I didn't know that vodka could actually taste pleasant.

I ask about Adrian's family and hometown. He explains that many people his family knew and cared about were carted off in trains during the war. Most of them went to Treblinka, which is located about halfway between Warsaw and Białystok. We learn that we share a great deal in common, not only in terms of professional interests, but also personally. I explain my ancestral roots, which I believe to be mainly Slavic and similar to his—perhaps this explains why we seem to be getting along so well. Adrian tells me about Laurence Rees' new book about the Holocaust, *Auschwitz: A New History*, which I promise to read upon my return to the states.

We then continue southward along Warsaw's Royal Route to a district where Adrian points out several additional squares, buildings, and monuments of present-day and/or Communist-era significance. Back near my MDM hotel again, we take a break at a restaurant. "What would you like to eat, Joel?" he asks. "Maybe some small traditional Polish food," I reply, asking him to recommend something. He orders two plates of an eastern Polish specialty: pickled herring on a large bed of spiced leeks, which he calls forest onions. Adrian explains that the dish is normally served with forest mushrooms, but that the restaurant had run out of them. Dinner is great, although I fail to eat all of my leeks. It is late, and I assume our tour is over. I thank Adrian for showing me around. "Actually Joel, there is more," he says. He leads me through the government quarter, and some zig-zagging ensues, allowing us to see some additional high points, including the Central Statistical Office. Then, we take public transportation to ulica Krakowskie Przedmieście. We take a few photos of the Polish Presidential complex. I am amazed that we don't get confronted by the guards. Adrian comments that this most important of Polish government complexes has less security than the American Embassy that we saw earlier today.

May 3rd is Poland's Constitution Day. My feet are sore from hiking sixteen hours in dress shoes yesterday. I sleep until 9:00am, which is the latest I remember sleeping in my adult life. After breakfast, I set out alone on foot. Confident that I can navigate public transportation, I purchase a ticket and jump onto a tram that follows ulica Marszałkowska to Ogród Saski, a beautiful park lush with green spring foliage and colorful blooms. On plac Marszałka Józefa Piłsudskiego, I walk to the fountain just behind the Tomb of the Unknown Soldier. A crowd is gathering, as are police, military, and the media. It looks like something interesting is about to happen here.

I take a seat on one of the benches and watch spectators congregate. Soldiers and cavalry march on the lawn as brass bands play patriotic sounding music. At the intersection of paths, venders display both Polish and EU flags. I recall a conversation I had with Adrian yesterday about the EU and its upcoming Constitutional Referendum in France. It seems to us that the French think they epitomize high civilization. Adrian had said that the French believe "everyone else is living in the trees," and I realize now that maybe the French are correct, at least about Poles. High above me, I see several Polish children climbing trees to catch a glimpse of the ceremonies.

Emerging from whimsical contemplation about the French, I feel a sudden chill of terror as I make a new observation of my surroundings. Except for me, every last one of the hundreds of people sitting on the now-crowded benches is elderly. I guess I missed my cue to give up my seat. I look for the next opportunity. As an old woman walks toward me along the path, I nonchalantly look at my watch and hurry off. Not knowing what to expect from the rest of the celebration, I decide to stick around and observe. I spend the next ninety minutes studying the Varsovians, periodically standing on tiptoes to see over their shoulders and listen to political speeches that I cannot understand.

Shortly after noon, I leave the patriotic celebration and make a run for Łazienki Park. While I'm in Warsaw, I don't want to miss its monument to Chopin, and the Palace on the Water. In the interest of time, I catch a bus along the Royal Route. I really enjoy strolling through these well-manicured grounds. Łazienki Park also offers a festive holiday atmosphere. In the garden, there are actors playing out scenes from Polish history.

Afterwards, I meet Adrian once again, who selflessly offers another afternoon to be sure that I learn as much as possible about Warsaw. He leads me past Parliament and some embassies, then points out the Warsaw Stock Exchange and National Bank of Poland. He then shows me his favorite bookstore, which could be compared to Barnes & Noble; a wide selection, multiple floors, plus lounge chairs and a café for "test-driving" books. Afterwards, we visit countless other far-flung sights around the city including the Warsaw Citadel area, and Wilanów, 17th century residence of Jan III Sobieski,

As we stand outside St. Anne's Church, I ponder both the death of the most beloved Pope, and the tragedy of riches that is Adrian's "Hidden Warsaw" tour. I've never before seen anyone take such time and care to share their city to a visitor. A crowd gathers for evening mass. Yesterday marked one month after the death of Pope John Paul II, and Poland's celebration of its favorite son's life doesn't seem to have waned a bit.

Adrian is eager to give me more feedback about my research paper, so we sit at an outdoor café table and order orange juice. As I receive more constructive feedback on my paper, we are interrupted by the passing of a rowdy drunken group as they sing songs in Hebrew. Without hesitation, Adrian tells me these are Israeli students, sent on a pilgrimage to Holocaust sites in Warsaw and Kraków. Astounded by this cacophony, I diplomatically say, "I can't blame them; I guess they have some steam to let off." Adrian has made many wise observations already, but I take special note when he says, "people are like water; they are made of water and can accordingly boil or freeze with surrounding conditions."

Full of traffic, my head hits the pillow at midnight like a rock. I remind myself that tomorrow I have meetings in both of Poland's two capitals: Warsaw and Kraków. Still, any anxiety about these meetings doesn't prevent me from fading immediately off to sleep.

It's my last full day in Poland, and I'm up at 6am to shower, pack, and prepare mentally for three meetings: 3M in Nadarzyn, just southwest of Warsaw; Oracle in Central Warsaw; and then CH2M Hill in Kraków, two and a half hours to the south by the new fast train. To manage the logistics and arrive punctually will be challenging, and I depend heavily on taxi cabs to get me to uncharted territory on time. I decide to pay the driver to wait for me during the forty-five minute 3M interview in Nadarzyn so that I can keep my luggage in his trunk rather than lock it at the train station. As we drive eastward I am okay with seeing the first cloudy, drizzly weather of my time in Poland—it somehow helps me focus on the task at hand. It's showtime. In twenty-four short hours I will be homeward bound. 3M and Oracle meetings are both interesting for me and very useful for my project on challenges facing US-based investors. Both gentlemen also express their willingness to meet with my students, should I ever decide to bring a class to Poland.

This visit to Kraków is my second; in 1998 I simply visited Auschwitz and Nowa Huta, two places I had learned about in high school and university classes. After that, on my sole evening in Kraków, I spend the late night hours in Rynek Główny before leaving early the next morning. It is a short, but magical visit to a beautiful city.

Thrilled to have a chance for a second visit to Kraków, I walk from the train station to Hotel Campanile. I change my clothes and take a city bus to CH2Mhill. I have an informative meeting with the office manager/head, and then return to my hotel in the drizzle. I change into jeans, and head around the corner and into Old Town Square. The rest of the day is mine, but I notice the Cloth Hall's booths are already closing.

Suddenly, it occurs to me that I haven't bought anything for my family yet. Quickly and with minimal negotiation, I buy some local souvenirs: a handmade metal necklace for Karen, a hand-painted locally-made box for each of my kids, small "Polska" glasses for two Polish-American friends, and a hand-carved, wooden, accordion-playing musician figurine for my shelf of collectibles. I make a quick stop at Hotel Wawel to drop off my booty, then leave again to check out Wawel Castle.

Perched on Wawel Hill, the ominously dark castle overlooks the city this damp and chilly springtime evening. I approach the gate only to find that the entire hill is closed until morning. I'll need to return to Kraków! I take a couple of poor quality nighttime photos then sit down at a nearby patio restaurant for a Żywiec beer and some reheated chicken as rain pours from the awning above me. My view of the darkened castle is obscured by sun umbrellas.

Unwilling to forfeit my last chance to explore, I walk to Kazimierz, the Jewish quarter of Kraków where much of *Schindler's List* was set and filmed. As I grow tired, I find a place to sit at *Rynek Główny* (main square) and admire the City Hall Tower, Church of St. Mary, the monument to Adam Mickiewicz (Poland's "national" poet), and the Church of St. Wojciech. Weather and fatigue drive me inside by midnight.

The next morning at 4:30, I take a cab to the airport for my 7:00am flight. The driver's meter exceeds the fare that he offered me. Beyond that quoted price, I am out of złotys, except for a few small coins that I earmarked as souvenirs for my kids. At the risk of being viewed as an ugly American, I realize this guy will have to do without a tip.

As I step away from the cab and gaze toward the terminal, I feel like I just stepped out of a time machine. The only evidence of the past half-century is a handful of modern cars and a tall Coca-Cola bottle dominating the traffic circle in front of the terminal. I enter the terminal hall, where all the functions of an airport seem to take place in one room, except for post-security waiting. Hundreds of Hasidic Jews dressed in black funnel through the doors and line up with British and Dutch tourists to check in for their flights. The counters are nothing more than a row of desks with luggage carts behind them. There appears to be no baggage conveyor. Just as I decide it might be rude to photograph the spectacle, the Asian man in line behind me starts eagerly snapping away with his big camera. It's my turn to check in with Lufthansa.

I wait to board at a multi-flight gate, thinking it might be the only gate in the terminal. It's difficult for me to figure out what is going, and there are enormous crowds for the new low fare airlines serving Kraków from London and Amsterdam. There are no signs for my flight, so I've got to stay alert. The scene of ubiquitous Hasidic Jews pulling suitcases is a troubling reminder of the film *Schindler's List*, which I recently watched.

As I write, I notice that a group of people is rushing through the un-labeled gate. It is now 6:35am and the waiting hall has become disturbingly empty. I ask the woman at the drink bar if Munich had been called. She responds, "no," but I'm not sure if she understands me. Just to be sure, I ask at the door that remains open to a bus. This time, I receive an affirmative nod and a gesture to climb aboard. The bus takes us to a small white LOT Airbus waiting on the tarmac. The jet, desperate for a paint job, boards from both ends and becomes filled only to half its capacity.

I take my seat in the last row of the plane, and pass out immediately. I wake up after missing the breakfast call. Sitting by the window opposite me is a large guy with less than his share of hair and more than his share of belly. He drinks beer at 7:30 in the morning and looks pretty contented with his lot in life. I feel contented too after eight days well spent. There are so many rich memories. Maybe someday I will write my own contemporary version of Mark Twain's *The Innocents Abroad*.

My expectations were that this short data collection trip would lead to the next stage in my career; instead, it wraps up a formative stage in my career, while presenting me with a new friendship and the beginning of a magnificent obsession with Poland.

I visit Adrian again in December 2007, as a refuge from a rather cold and inhospitable Fulbright assignment in St. Petersburg, Russia. Based upon my experience in both countries, the contrast between Polish and Russian cultures could not be starker. Maybe it's just that I was lucky enough to meet an exceptionally friendly individual in Poland, and not in Russia. Despite four months of my best efforts in Russia, I encounter precious few friendly locals there, let alone a single person willing to engage in cultural exchange with an American in the interest of improving relations between our countries.

Following my family Christmas in the USA, Adrian invites me for a brief winter visit to Poland on my way back to Russia, so I fly to Warsaw instead of St. Petersburg and plan a surface route through Poland, Lithuania, and Latvia during the Orthodox Christmas holiday. Adrian offers to complement the "Hidden Warsaw" tour he gave me with a tour of "Hidden Poland." First, we travel by train and explore Malbork Teutonic Castle. Next, we have a look at Poland's industrial history appropriately in the city of Łódź, where Adrian manages a production facility that makes razor trays for Gillette. Adrian arranges accommodations at the Sulejów Cisterisian Abbey, special because most tourists do not have the opportunity to stay in an abbey. After that, we visit the Black Madonna of Częstochowa, the Ogrodzieniec castle ruins, and Gabarka Holy Mountain. In northeastern Poland, we drive in the snow to Białowieża National Park, then stay at the tidy and comfortable Zaścianek Inn in Borsuki. Finally, I have the distinct pleasure of exploring Adrian's home town of Białystok. This beautiful city is shrouded in a freshly-fallen blanket of snow, and Christmas music plays for skaters on an ice rink in the square. I am surprised to observe a large American flag flying, and the sight sends a chill of happiness down my spine. Had I flown directly back to Russia, I would be waiting out my final few Fulbright days alone during the Orthodox Christmas holiday. Thanks to Adrian, I have already seen more of Poland than any other single country other than my native USA. I am eternally grateful for this kind man's generosity in showing me around.

That day in the car, I discuss with Adrian the idea of organizing an undergraduate student trip for my *Contemporary Europe* course during spring break of 2009, which we later decide to repeat and adapt for 2011. Twenty-two fortunate Bentley students are forever changed thanks to Adrian's hospitality and native expertise about his homeland. We take our students from Warsaw to Kraków and other cities where Adrian arranges company meetings, as well as visits to museums, churches, and the engineering marvel of Wieliczka Salt Mine and the horror of Auschwitz.

Operational from 1940-45, Auschwitz is notorious as the Nazi concentration camp where more than one million people were murdered, mostly Jews from Hungary, Poland, France, the Netherlands, and Greece, but also political undesirables, homosexuals, Roma, Jehovah's witnesses, and prisoners of war. The students are visibly shaken by the evil of this place, which is now a UNESCO World Heritage site. I have been to this sad location several times, but I keep coming back to help others witness the darkness that can reside somewhere deep in the heart of mankind, and the results it can bring to the landscape if left unchecked.

At the end of our intensive emotional roller coaster of a week, my students recognize the good fortune they met in Poland. I can see that they fully appreciate Adrian's gift to them. For me, it has been a pleasure to observe this exceptional person proudly sharing his knowledge and love of Poland with my students.

Adrian Grycuk is one of the most remarkable people I have ever met and his generosity is beyond my comprehension. While I plan my fall 2010 sabbatical travel to Zagreb, Croatia to study foreign direct investment there, Adrian insists that I add on a few days in Poland "to learn more about (his) country."

Once more, I fly into Warsaw "on my way" to somewhere else. Adrian picks me up at the airport and shows me "Hidden Warsaw Part II" then complements it with "Hidden Poland Part II." From Warsaw, Adrian drives me to the death camp monuments at Treblinka and Bełżec, notorious places in the system of Nazi camps that are given little or no attention in most guidebooks. Treblinka is famous for being the second deadliest extermination camp, with estimates of 700-900,000 murdered. Bełżec, near the Ukrainian border, is unique because it was completely dismantled by the Nazis before the end of the war, and although nearly half a million people were killed there, it nearly went undetected by the victorious Allies. Sensitive to death camp overload, Adrian then arranges a private professional tour for both of us in the city of Zamość, then we travel to Sandomierz, where he helps me pick out a ring that becomes my wife's favorite, striped flint set in silver, fashioned by a local artist. With the bit of free time remaining, we decide to drive to Wrocław, a city that I have long wanted to visit. Enchanted by its Oder River location, and its fusion of Polish-Germanic architecture, Adrian and I agree that Wrocław should be added to the next student trip's itinerary.

As Adrian drops me off at check-in at Chopin Airport in Warsaw, he shakes my hand with a smile. I detect a hint of local pride as he says, "Joel, the next time you come to Poland, our new train will connect the airport directly with Central Warsaw."

Sure enough, eighteen months later, I find my way back to Warsaw by registering to give a paper at an economics conference there. Adrian greets me at the airport. We ride the shiny modern train into Central Warsaw, capital of the largest and most populous country in "New Europe." The sleek new train is painted red and yellow, the colors of Warsaw. I am here for work, but the purpose of my trip is less about the conference and more personal. I chose a conference that will help me continue my friendship with Adrian and learn even more about Poland.

Each day after my conference, Adrian again makes time for me out of his busy schedule. My series of discoveries on this visit might be called "Hidden Warsaw Part III." He takes me to see the *Battle of Grunwald*, an 1878 painting by Jan Matejko on display at the National Museum in Warsaw. We then check out Warsaw's *fotoplastykon*, which has remained in *situ* since 1905. This device could be described as a musical machine that scrolls three-dimensional photos from the pre-cinema days of the 19th century. Later, we visit the Mausoleum of Struggle and Martyrdom, on Szucha Avenue. The latter is located in the former Warsaw's Gestapo headquarters, notorious as a former Nazi interrogation and torture site. To end the visit on a more positive note that evening, we explore the interactive Frédéric Chopin Museum, refurbished in 2010 to celebrate the 200th anniversary of the composer's birth.

Thanks to Adrian, I have developed a more in-depth appreciation for Poland's proud and rich history than for any other country I've visited. When I ask Adrian why he is so generous with his time, he repeats what he has often told me before, "Oh come on Joel, we know that you are a friend to Poland." It is deeply gratifying, indeed, to be considered a friend of Adrian and his beloved Republic of Poland.

8

CHINA: SEEING IS BELIEVING

See the World in Green and Blue
See China Right in Front of You

"Beautiful Day"– U2
(All That You Can't Leave Behind), 2000

It's a cold Wednesday at the end of December. The holidays are still in full swing, but I'm leaving my home, my wife, and three kids aged seven, five, and three. My excursion to China is long in the making. My grant application for experiential learning about Asia Rising has been approved. The rationale for this educator is China's importance as a global player. I teach about China in a university, but like an emperor with no clothes, my knowledge is limited to my textbooks I adopt for my classes. So, I found a compelling reason to visit an exciting country that is about as exotic as can be imagined for a grown-up kid from rural America.

My new colleague Shiping Zheng is a native of Shanghai, and he supported my request to participate in his undergraduate travel-study course. Shiping is fond of saying, "seeing is believing," and there's no better way to see than to go. China has interested me since I was an undergraduate, when I took an East Asian history course and completed a geography paper on China's "Tiger" economy. At that time Deng Xiaoping's reforms had begun transforming China's economy, but the 1989 Tiananmen Square crackdown in Beijing brought political rights to a sudden stop when government forces massacred protesters, ironically at a place called the Gate of Heavenly Peace. Finally, I see China right in front of me, and I am ready to meet China.

I force myself from the comfort of the Christmas flannel sheets on our warm bed. It's 3am, and I went to sleep just a few hours ago. Caffeinated and half-rested, I drive to Bentley to park my car, and then take a cab to Boston Logan, where at 5:40am I meet Shiping and his class at the United Airlines check-in counter.

Our departure to Chicago is at 8:15am. Sitting next to me is a vibrant and lovely ninety-year-old woman on her way home to Grand Rapids, Michigan. She is upset. She tells me she has survived two world wars and traveled the world, but she said she has never seen anything like the week's tsunami in Southeast Asia. She needs comfort, so I empathize with her consternation about the expense of our president's fourteen inaugural balls in the aftermath of the tsunami and while U.S. troops in Iraq lack adequate supplies. Trying to remain neutral, I suggest that the tsunami might offer an opportunity for the US military to play a positive role in recovery efforts, counteracting the bad press we're getting for Iraq.

In Chicago, I finish my Christmas thank-you notes and join Shiping at Chili's. He's sitting with a small group of students who are eating full menus as if it is their final meal. Good grief, how bad can food be in China? Upon boarding United 851, I am entranced with excitement about my destination. This is my first trans-Pacific trip, but as it turns out we hardly fly over the Pacific Ocean at all. Our jet makes a great circle northward over Green Bay, Hudson's Bay, and across the Arctic Circle, then southward across Siberia and Mongolia. It's a snow-covered world beneath a clear blue sky. My new neighbor is a Chinese guy who writes software for Motorola in Chicago; we exchange business cards.

I manage to get six hours of sleep, despite being in the last row of the 777's tail, unable to recline.

We cross the International Date Line and arrive in Beijing at 3:40pm, having lost nearly a full day. I try to get my head around that. Shiping has arranged for our local guide Wu Yin ("Evelyn") to meet us at the arrivals hall and guide us seamlessly to our coach, which we soon find out has a broken heater; nevertheless, it delivers us to the New World Courtyard (Marriott) Hotel on Chong Wen Men Wai Street. On the way, I drink the 32 ounce Gatorade that I packed for rehydration. We check in at the hotel, and I begin my decompression: I have a beer to wash down the trail dust while unloading my suitcase, grabbing a shower, and dressing for dinner.

In an hour, we meet in the lobby as requested by Shiping, then travel by coach to a restaurant for our first real Chinese dinner, our "welcome banquet". The blue and white tiled walls of the restaurant and aquariums with live fish are absolutely stunning. We are amazed by the dishes, selected by Shiping for the group; all manner of meats, vegetables, and rice. I guess I expected Chinese noodles in cartons and wonton soup in Styrofoam bowls with fortune cookies for dessert. I estimate that this meal is special because it is our first, only to find out later that each restaurant selected by Shiping is similarly upscale. Chopsticks are not my forté, nor have I ever been particularly fond of Chinese food, but I am ready to embrace the challenges of the next two weeks. As a carnivore in China I can count my blessings. I'm traveling with four vegetarians, for whom precious few choices exist, as most vegetables are served with a meat-based stock.

As we finish dinner, a group of our Latin American students arrives, having just landed from Miami. Their tardiness is excusable, dismissed by everyone. Sadly, I know only three students in the group, so this meal at a large round table is a great chance to get to know more of my travel companions. Our group remains politely quiet, but I cannot help but notice that our presence has drawn a great deal of attention from the local upper-class clientele.

On our first full day, it's New Year's Eve and I am in Beijing, China! Beijing, China! As our daily morning ritual, the class meets in the hotel's conference room. Shiping officially welcomes the group to China. He distributes a sheet of fifteen to twenty useful expressions he calls "Basic Chinese." After he pronounces each one, we practice them aloud in turn. This is really fun, and like the students I take notes. Words include "*hao*" (good), "*ni hao*" (hello), "*zaoshang hao*" (good morning), "*bu yao*" (no, I don't want it), "*zai jian*" (goodbye), "*xie xie*" (thanks), and "*zou ba*" (let's go). I'm quite new at running my own short-term programs in Europe, so I like the idea of daily morning study sessions while abroad.

The session is so much fun that I don't immediately notice the absence of several students; after all, this is a large group. I wonder if Shiping has noticed that a few students are missing. Soon, the same group of Miami-origin international students that was late last night ambles through the door unapologetically. "Miami Vice," I think to myself. As they find seats in the back of the room, Shiping is speaking to our group from the far end of the table. I know he notices them, but curiously he chooses not to acknowledge their late arrival. Trying not to be critical, I later tell Shiping I'm curious why he didn't admonish Miami Vice. He chuckles, as he immediately recognizes and appreciates the pseudonym I chose for them. "Joel, sometimes you say more by saying nothing." I nod in agreement, adding that maybe their homes and grades seem sufficiently distant so there is no incentive to be punctual. "Don't worry, Joel, they will pay the price," he assures me. I hope they ultimately do. On a daily basis, we wait for Miami Vice in conference rooms, hotel lobbies, and the drafty unheated tour bus, which is not a pleasant place to sit while enduring stiff Siberian winds that intensify Beijing's already-frigid January. By the end of the fourteen day trip, I estimate that an entire day has been lost waiting for this small, inconsiderate group.

Our first faculty meeting is at *Renmin* (the People's) University of China. The professors share a lecture about their beloved "China rising". They immodestly highlight several important changes in global rankings over the past year supporting the notion of China as a superpower. First, China surpassed the USA as South Korea and Japan's #1 trade partner. Second, China surpassed the USA as the world's largest recipient of foreign direct investment. Finally, China surpassed the USA as world's largest recipient of students. But the USA should not worry because China was never a communist country. Rather, they explain why it is better described as a socialist country with Chinese characteristics.

It becomes abundantly clear to me that better communication and mutual education needs to take place between the USA and China. "This is exactly why we're here," I respond to a host professor, who is concerned that Americans don't understand China. Similarly, the Chinese students seem very troubled about US impressions of China. Are Americans able to distinguish between China and the former Soviet Union? Don't both countries have more common interests after September 11th? What are the other problems with Sino-US relations that must be overcome? Why have US demands on China increased faster than Chinese demands on the USA, as claimed by the slightly nationalistic and very sanctimonious professors? Why do the American media ignore North Korea's progress that was made under the guidance of China? Why is the USA more suspicious of China than ever before? Wow- I'm really blown away by this parade of suspicion. I find it fascinating; we really do need to get to know the Chinese to allay mutual fears. However, I am content to listen to the students on both sides as they discuss their opinions. It's my second day in China, and I take comfort in know that as a professor I am unlikely to be called upon. We end the discussion with a friendly photo shoot and quick lunch. Personally, I feel that a friendly drink would have helped to relieve everyone's tension before going our separate ways.

Led by Miami Vice, the students convince Shiping to take the bus to the Red Bridge Market, an excursion that was originally planned for the following day. The ring leaders of Vice argue compellingly that in this frigid cold, it is an "emergency" to buy coats today because some of them didn't pack adequately warm clothing for their trip to Northern China. One of them—a student at Babson, near Boston—claims he doesn't even own a winter coat. On the way to the market, Shiping speaks over the bus microphone to point out a few of Beijing's landmarks. Oblivious to this learning moment, Miami Vice's heads bob to Latino beats that are so loud they escape beyond the normal range of ear buds.

We arrive at Red Bridge Market. I have little interest in shopping, so I pass my time watching the students haggle and interact at the sales stalls. The market's cacophony offers lessons in negotiation. In the din of the busy market, local shoppers settle on prices with merchants by touching each other's fingers secretly under cover of coat sleeves. Those, like us, who lack the skills to do this, pay more. Several of the students buy North Face coats of dubious authenticity, haggling with each Yuan as if it were their last. Ironically, the wealthiest students seem most concerned with how much they spend on fake designer goods.

Jen, another class chaperone and the co-director of our education abroad office, is standing next to me, also watching the students passively. Aside from name-brand knockoffs, low-quality pirated CDs and DVDs seem to be in high demand with the students, especially porn and feature films that are still in US theatres. As we gaze down the stalls of virtually useless merchandise, we see something neither of us can do without: warm-looking Chinese border patrol hats. Jen and I haggle with the vendors until the price drops down to 290 Yuan, or about $12 each. This is a bargain at only 40% of the asking price. Contented, we walk away congratulating each other for the good work, or so we think. Days later, Miami Vice finds the same hats for just $1.30 each from street vendors.

Having endured enough of the market's chaos, and satisfied that the students will be fine without us, Jen and I leave with Nick, one of the students, to venture onto the street and road-test our warm border patrol hats. For the first time, we abandon our comfort zone to leave the group and observe the urban scene for a little while. I see passersby spitting on the street as they walk swiftly in the cold. Then I do an involuntary double-take when out of the corner of my eye I think I see a man squatting along the roadside. Yup, he's leaving a dump, right here on a Beijing street! Across the street, construction workers raise the Chinese flag over the backdrop of an Outback Steakhouse.

At the appointed time, the still-heatless coach arrives. We sit and shiver during the ritual wait for Miami Vice, all of whom show up predictably late. This time, we wait thirty minutes for Octavio and Craig, who seemed to have lost their way at the market. They show up with new suitcases for carrying their other acquisitions. Again, the professor says nothing, and I'm puzzled. As we begin to move through tangled traffic, I hear Miami Vice and some others complaining about Beijing being "too fucking cold." It's 10 degrees Fahrenheit outside, and even with my thick winter coat I am chilled to the bone.

By the time we arrive at a Tai (not Thai) restaurant an hour later I feel a fierce sickness coming on like a powerful storm. Our drafty restaurant has only heavy hanging blankets as barriers to protect its enormous dining room from the cold, dark Beijing street. For entertainment, this restaurant features traditional Tai dancing, which only for a moment takes my mind off how incredibly rotten I feel. After dinner and a show, we travel again on the frigid bus to our evening cultural event: Kung Fu theatre; a fusion of Buddhism, ballet, and martial arts. The air in the theatre is slightly warmer than the air outside. Bewildered by my present level of extreme discomfort, I'm quite sure that there is no warmth to be found in the entire city of Beijing.

Shiping announces that it is simply too cold tonight for our planned celebration of New Year's Eve on Tiananmen Square. Some students announce that they are too tired anyway, so Shiping dismisses the entire class and offers to meet anyone who is interested at the adjacent shopping mall at 11pm. A party stage has been assembled for the Chinese celebration of the Western New Year. I drop my winter coat and wool cap in my room, then wait in the hotel lobby for any interested students. Together, we navigate the labyrinthine indoor passageways to the mall's epicenter, where a barrage of confetti bombs explodes over a Confucian "wish tree." After midnight I crash hard.

Rise and shine? No way! I rise at 5:30am but fail to shine; I have a dreadfully sore throat. What a way to start 2005! I spend the pre-breakfast hours reading my tour books, then writing in my travel journal. The only thing that keeps me going is the palpable exhilaration of knowing I'm in China. The nearly exact exchange of nighttime with daytime has caught up with me. It was a rough night of sleep, and after thirty-six hours on the other side of the world, the chickens have come home to roost. Morning television news doesn't help my feeling of disorientation. The Southeast Asian tsunami death toll currently stands at 135,000. I can't even fathom that number—what does it mean?

After breakfast, Shiping runs an engaging study session for our entire group. He asks the students for their first impressions of Beijing. Responses include "industrial," "construction," "restrained," "orderly," "chaotic," "friendly," "cosmopolitan," "communal," and strangely enough "Western-like." I should write these down. This drill impresses me, and I make a note to try it with my own future travel classes. The exercise is followed by a discussion of the ideology of communism, a term that Shiping proceeds to dissect. China suddenly doesn't seem very "communist" to anyone at the table.

During the afternoon Evelyn leads us on our visit to the Temple of Heaven and Lama Temple. She explains the many Buddhas as I try my best to stay quiet while filling facial tissues with germs and sucking on hard candies to soothe my throat. The huge lama temple has a seventy-foot Buddha that was carved from a single tree. In the 1700s, it took ten years to haul that tree here from Nepal using rivers, ice, and log "wheels." Throughout the excursion, Shiping reiterates to the class his ostensibly favorite expressions including "seeing is believing" and "don't miss the boat, you'll pay the price." These divulge his pride in China and smug confidence as leader, earning him the nickname, of "The Emperor." He wins further admiration for dinner; we carnivores eat slices of duck on mini fajita-style breads at Qianmen Quanjude, a famous roast duck restaurant. I should have taken a cab back to bed, but instead join the group for the Peking Opera. As the venue offers the first warmth our group encountered after a long, frigid day, several of the students fall asleep immediately. The folks—other than Shiping—who manage to stay awake, find the shrill music unbearably hilarious. There is no way to adequately describe the scene. Gesturing with her thumb and forefinger, Jen compares the twanging sounds to painful pin pricks. The look on her face doesn't help control our pent-up laughter. Listening to the fanciful singing and twanging in view of the sleeping students, we both struggle to avoid an outburst. Desperate for a break and some fresh air, we escape to the gift shop, where I clamor for tissues in my coat pocket to dry my eyes. After the stress of this trip, sickness, and physical exhaustion, it feels so good to have a laugh. I only hope that my lack of composure didn't offend any other spectators at the show.

I'm going in the wrong direction with my jetlag corrections. On the second day of the New Year, I am up at 3:30am, two hours earlier than yesterday. We visit the Forbidden City in Central Beijing, the Chinese imperial palace from the Ming Dynasty to the Qing Dynasty. With nearly one thousand rooms, it housed emperors and their families for more than five centuries! Next, we continue to Tiananmen Square, which translates to the Square of Heavenly Peace. Unfortunately, the square is now known more for the massacre that occurred here in 1989. At the corner of the square I enter what must be the largest and most malodorous public restroom the world has ever known, emitting an intense and curiously sweet-smelling steam to the frigid outdoor air. Thankful that my business there will be quick and simple, I attempt to hold my breath as long as possible, only to run out of air and ultimately ingest the vapors even deeper into my lungs. As I dash toward the open door for fresh air, I cannot help but notice a long row of men sitting side by side while squatting over completely public toilet bowls. My frigid fingers have a chance to struggle with my zipper only after escaping the squalid mist and returning to Tiananmen Square.

As we walk farther, my colleague Shiping points out a Catholic church on the skyline. "Look," he says, "you can even talk to Jesus from China." Quietly impressed to see a Christian church in China, I glibly respond "I heard you can from anywhere—you don't need a church for that."

On the ninety minute frozen bus ride to the Great Wall, Shiping picks up the microphone to discuss the Chinese perspective on the issue of Tibet. In short, while the final nation states were being established last century, Tibet "missed the boat." As I listen, I look out the window and I am befuddled by the scope of new construction taking place in this city of fifteen million. We make a quick stop at a jade factory and gift store, where I purchase a small jade globe for my office, a family "happiness ball," and blue jade bracelets for my wife and daughter.

At the Great Wall, Shiping announces that we have two hours of free time climb to the sixth watchtower, at the top of the first section, which only a handful of students accomplish. The cold, dry air defeats me in my weakened condition, and I advance only to the fourth watchtower in this section. For the first time in my life, I have a bad sense of equilibrium and I start to experience a slight fear of heights. Making matters worse, the steps are large, steep, and well-worn by weather and shoes. Nevertheless, the views of the mountains and Great Wall are breathtaking. When we return to the bus, Shiping presents each of us with a personalized souvenir certificate stating that we climbed the Great Wall of China. This guy thinks of everything, and I should start to do similarly in my own courses. We climb aboard the coach to drive to a large park on the outside of Beijing, where the class breaks into small self-selected groups to explore the trail of monuments near the Thirteen Tombs of the Ming Dynasty. Miami Vice goes directly to a café. The tombs are arranged according to Feng Shui principles to protect them from evil forces of the North, and are guarded by a long row of stone animals and officials.

Our class stops for meetings at Beijing Geely University's Euro-American College, a private college funded by Geely automobile manufacturers. Shiping, Jen, and I meet with members of the administration and faculty, while our students interact with Chinese counterparts in another room. I'm puzzled at first when we are served cups of plain hot water, but then pleasantly surprised. Somehow, this simple treat provides welcome relief from the cold air and sore throat.

That night, we're off to Xi'an by train. Beijing's disorderly main train station makes the Red Bridge Market seem tame by comparison. I've never seen so many people in one place, and I struggle to find a single sign in the Latin alphabet, let alone in English. I'm sure I would have a rough time finding my way through this enormous zoo alone. Even the names of destination cities are listed only in Chinese characters. Every queue seems to be assaulted by constant pushing and shoving from both sides. Presumably because we are *dabizi* or "big noses" (Chinese slur for Westerners), our group is waved directly through security. Even Miami Vice's largest bags get excused from the scanner. Apparently, big noses don't enter into Chinese security's profiling of bad guys. We say a sad farewell to Wu Yin ("Evelyn"), our fabulous, friendly, and competent local coordinator. Our ride from here is a "tourist" night train, with no stops until Xi'an, China's "capital of the west," home to thirteen Chinese dynasties spanning from the Sui to the Ming, and over more than a thousand years.

There are four beds in each compartment. My bunk buddies are Shiping and the two most tolerable students: David and Nick. Still fighting my cold, I am pleased with the prospect of not being kept up all night by Miami Vice. Shiping, Jen, and I spend an hour or two enjoying the enchanting Chinese night train ambiance and checking in with the students. I explain to Shiping and Jen that I also try to put my own students on at least one long distance train in Europe, preferably overnight, as it saves one night of hotel expense and gives them a memorable experience they probably won't get in the USA. As we chat, Shiping passes around Chinese candies with large shrimps printed on their outside wrappers. I don't know if I'm more relieved or surprised to discover that the sweets taste like peanuts rather than shrimp. Some students refuse to try them, dissuaded by the wrappers. The Emperor knew the train would be popular with the students, and he seems to take pleasure in our collective positive spirit. I leap at this chance to break the grip of my cold from hell. Rocked gently like a baby in a cradle by the train on its rails, I fall asleep by 10pm and enjoy a restful, if short, night.

We arrive in Xi'an, shrouded by dusty air thanks to windblown loess and valley pollution. I know these fun facts from my textbook, and accordingly I try to breathe selectively. This city exudes antiquity, and I am entranced by its ambiance, at least until we enter the glamorous and modern Hyatt Hotel. Our elaborate brunch feast includes both traditional Chinese foods and a Western buffet.

Our first excursion of the day is the Sha'anxi Historical Museum. It offers exhibits from some of the most important Chinese dynasties, and I appreciate that the Emperor provides a basic historical framework to help my historically shallow American mind contend with the depth of Chinese history. I write the following on a scrap of paper and carry it me in my jacket pocket for the remainder of the trip...

- Qing (221-207 BC), Xianyang
- Han (206 BC- AD 220), Xi'an
- Tang (AD 618-907), Xi'an
- Song (AD 960-1279), Kaifeng/Hangzhou
- Yuan (Mongols; AD 1206-1368), Beijing
- Ming (isolationists; AD 1368-1644), Nanjing, Beijing
- Qin (AD 1644-1911), Beijing.

Our day continues with a visit to the Bell Tower and the Great Mosque, which to me looks like a Buddhist temple without any Buddha statues. We then visit a dumpling restaurant that features an elaborate dance show. The restaurant offers every imaginable filling for the dumplings: lamb, pork, beef, chicken, duck, turkey, shrimp, and fish. I pity the four vegetarians in our group, as bean paste filling is the only listed vegetarian option.

I wake up in Xi'an refreshed and well rested for the first time since arriving in China; I realize I've beaten the jetlag but not my cold, which continues to terrorize me in the densely polluted frigid air. Our first activity of the day is a visit to the Museum of the Terracotta Warriors and Horses, dating back to 300 BCE. We are 30km east of Xi'an, and we have the privilege of "meeting" (seeing) the farmer who is credited with discovering the site in 1974 while working in a field. I find it interesting that this rock star is on display like this, and think it's pretty cool that people can shake his hand. After all, everyone has heard of the Terracotta Army! How strange, though, for a common guy to randomly dig up a brick soldier one day and from that accomplishment become a celebrity like this!

Another excellent lunch goes unappreciated by Miami Vice and some vegetarians, who together sneak off to McDonald's for some less exotic nourishment. Eating at fast food joints is now the norm, at least for Miami Vice. We all climb to the top of the Big Wild Goose Pagoda, then visit Xi'an Fine Arts workshop, and finally make a quick stop at the Old City Wall. Given the freezing temperatures, we decide not to hike along the top of the extensive 13km long fortification. It is possible to rent bicycles to explore the wall also, but this would be difficult in such insanely frigid weather. Next time, I will visit Xi'an during a warmer season. Our cold but incredible day is concluded with yet another excellent smorgasbord dinner accompanied by Tang Dynasty dancing.

We depart Xi'an for Hangzhou on a two-hour direct flight. I reflect upon our quick visit to Xi'an, and I'm ever so grateful that the Emperor included this historical masterpiece of urban habitation in the class itinerary. Heavy rain pelts the jet window where I rest my head during the entire bumpy flight. The pilot never climbs above the clouds, and this flight might represent one of my more religious travel experiences. I put my trust in God, the pilot, and radar. As I discuss the flight later with Shiping, he speculates that the pilot remained below the clouds to conserve fuel. Nice. As we exit the Hangzhou airport and I drink in the cleanest, softest air imaginable, my cold seems to evaporate into memory.

Hangzhou's climate in the winter might remind you of coastal South Carolina; the air is temperate and the vegetation is lush and green. We explore the park that surrounds Lingying Buddhist Temple and the mountain trail. In this mild air, we board a coach (ironically with a functioning heater) to visit a tea village where a demonstration is underway. We have the chance to sniff samples of varying grades of tea leaves. All visitors must exit through the gift shop where authentic souvenirs and specialty teas are offered for "special prices." I begin to recognize a pattern. It started at the jade factory demonstration: come as our guest and leave as our customer. "Seeing is believing" what the professors at Renmin University were arguing: capitalism is alive and well in China. Disney couldn't have designed these places more effectively for business!

Speaking of theme parks, this evening we visit the Song Dynasty Historical Culture Park. My cheat sheet says the Songs ruled from 960-1279. This dynasty-themed park is fascinating, even if a bit tacky. We sit in a moving section of seats in front of an enormous stage to watch a colorful cultural extravaganza. Upon the Emperor's urging at the end of the show, I join a small crowd of tourists that climb onto the stage to have their pictures taken with the performers. The Song City is a realistic-looking re-creation of Song reality, and is China's first and largest theme park.

In the morning, we take a boat ride on Xi Hu (West Lake), Huagang Park. Cold air on the water keeps Miami Vice and most of the other students inside the vessel, providing an excellent chance to "talk shop" outside with Shiping and Jen. The gardens around the lakes are replete with murky little ponds, which are teeming by enormous goldfish. Our final stop is a visit to a nearby silk factory, which ends predictably with the opportunity to purchase silk clothing and other local items.

Eager to experience more of Hangzhou, I explore a few nearby streets with some students. There are interesting things to see here. We pass a bar with a sign declaring in English, the words "NO JAPANESE ALLOWED." We explore a market street, just one street off the main thoroughfare. Here, we find some exotic food items I had read about in my guidebook, but that we hadn't been (un)lucky enough to encounter at the excellent restaurants chosen by Shiping. Among them are whole live and dead snakes, eels, and sundry meats and organs from all imaginable creatures of the sea, land, and air. If only our vegetarians were here to see this! We experience fascinating sights, sounds, and smells of the Hangzhou market place. I leap over a small river of blood, sewage, and feathers as it slowly makes its descent into a street drain. Right now, I could really use a scotch. On the way back to the hotel, I set off on my own to locate and purchase a pair of nail clippers, an undertaking that should not be underestimated for an American in the small shops of China! Mission accomplished, good night!

I wake up in enthusiastic anticipation of our bus trip to Shanghai, China's economic capital... if it's possible to name just one. Thanks in part to clearer and warmer air, the worst cold of my life is gone. As a result, it's not as unpleasant to wait on the coach for two of Miami Vice, who emerge from the hotel thirty minutes late, then stagger up the steps. They pass me and Shiping without making eye contact, looking pale and reeking of alcohol. Sitting across from me, the Emperor again refrains from acknowledging them, just tells the driver to start moving. When I later ask Shiping why he puts up with them as he does, he responds, "Joel, remember what I told you, sometimes you say more by saying nothing." Shiping's quiet confidence is why he is the Emperor.

Wuzhen is an old village just off the main route from Hangzhou to Shanghai. Some say it is reminiscent of Venice. Wuzhen was built as a market for silk trading during the Tang dynasty (618-907) along China's Grand Canal.

As we approach Shanghai on the highway, I chat with the Emperor about this home town and his thoughts on this trip so far. I reflect on the ever-intensifying sequence of spectacular surprises, which I know he planned with great care. I tell him, "I can't imagine how you might keep up this pace in Shanghai, let alone up the ante." Having embraced his nickname, he responds with "the Emperor is full of surprises." Those of us who aren't sleeping stare out the windows in awe at a city that is twice the size of New York. Shanghai offers a skyline that seems to have no end. The Emperor explains that Shanghai already has two thousand existing skyscrapers (defined as buildings of at least 18 stories), and two thousand more are currently under construction. Those might seem like hollow statistics until you see it for yourself. Indeed, seeing *is* believing.

Shanghai's historic Peace Hotel has a spectacular location on the Bund, named in German to reflect the riverfront district's government role during the days of European colonization. Many foreign dignitaries have stayed here, and their photographs are prominently displayed on the walls in the lobby and Dragon-Phoenix Hall restaurant, where we will have the pleasure of eating breakfast during our stay. The downside of the dated hotel is the slow and expensive dial-up internet service. Bentley and personal correspondence will have to wait. Although a world famous five-star hotel, the Peace Hotel has several limitations and the Emperor declares that he would not bring another group here. The hallways are dark and poorly marked, and many corridors seem unused or otherwise out of service. Moreover, it seems that the cleaning crew fails to do a thorough job. One of the students aptly compares it to the hotel in Stephen King's "The Shining." Still, the only thing that inconveniences me personally is the lack of a coffeemaker in the room, a luxury I grew to appreciate at our other hotels.

After our first dinner in Shanghai, I join Jen and a group of students to visit the bar of "Three on the Bund" in the Union Building. We enjoy drinks and dessert with an excellent view of *Puxi* (west of the river) and *Pudong* (east of the river). As I return to the hotel with some students, street salesmen offer us "Rolexes" for $5. Some of my companions insincerely promise that they'll consider buying one in the morning.

The next morning, we leave the Peace Hotel to find the same "Rolex" vendors waiting for us, only now the price is $4. We board the coach for Pudong, and the Emperor intimates a story from his youth. He routinely swam across the Huangpu to the rice paddies on the other side, where ultra-modern glass-and-steel Pudong now shimmers in the January sun. Pudong's centerpiece is the Oriental Pearl TV Tower. We take the elevator to its top and stare in awe at the magnitude of this Chinese megalopolis. The Emperor must be in his forties, so during his lifetime these towers must have appeared to blossom like enormous trees out of the rice paddies.

Miami Vice still wants to shop for more stuff, so during their afternoon free time they gather counterfeit goods and more knockoff high-end luggage to pack them in. After browsing $3 Rolexes with Shiping and a handful of students, Jen and I check out the pedestrian shopping zone that lies just west of the Peace Hotel on Nanjing Donglu. Jen needs shoes and I have nothing much to do, so I accompany her to a Chinese shoe store, which is packed almost beyond comprehension with customers. As Jen browses, crowds gather to watch this "big nose" try them on. "No offense, Jen, but they must think you're someone famous," I say. I clandestinely take photos of dozens of Chinese people watching Jen try on her shoes. After she completes her purchase, she and I meet Lei—the local coordinator in Shanghai—and the rest of our group go to dinner.

At dinner, our group is joined by Wing Yin Chan, a former student of mine and alum of Bentley's Global Studies department. Wing—who is Cantonese-American—shares with us stories about the challenges she faced in moving to and working in Shanghai, which she equates to Paris or New York in the sense that people tend to be elitist and closed toward outsiders. Everyone is captivated by her thought-provoking anecdotes of culture shock, as we sit dwarfed by the forest of buildings that surrounds us.

We close the evening at an acrobatic show at the Shanghai Grand Theatre. What an unbelievable spectacle! The show's finale features four motorcycles that crisscross at implausible speeds while making simultaneous 360 degree loops inside a 25-foot diameter spherical cage.

After dismissal, Jen, Wing, Igor and I check out the observation deck at the Hyatt hotel. It costs 110 Yuan (about $15) to take the elevator to the top, but we can apply the cost to drinks or desserts. We reflect upon the day's events. Then, someone notices a single Euro-American woman as she quietly takes a seat next to a Euro-American man with a ring on his finger. He has been sitting alone at the bar in silence for some time, against the backdrop of the brightly-lighted skyscrapers and night-time sky. In a scene reminiscent of *Lost in Translation*, the man repeatedly checks her out, which is clearly what she wants. With nothing else to discuss, we ponder the stressful life expatriates must endure while working so far from their homes. After considerable time, the man pays his tab and walks away alone. The woman remains, sitting on her stool and looking dejected. She tries to pretend that she was never paying attention to him. Just as we get up to leave, a large group of our students—led by Miami Vice—arrives to take our place. Timing is everything.

January 10, 2005 is a pristine day for taking photographs of "China Rising." The sky is blue and the weather spring-like. The days in China are winding down, and I can't help but be excited for home. After breakfast we visit the Shanghai Museum, famous for porcelain, clothing, sculptures, paintings, and calligraphy. At lunch, a large group of students petitions the Emperor to be excused from tonight's dinner. The finish line is on the horizon for the students as well. I confess that it bothers me to see that they aren't trying.

We make the one hour bus ride to the China Europe International Business School in Pudong to hear a lecture by a British professor, entitled "From Mao to the Market: China's Industrial Policies." Her tedious monologue about post-revolution government policy in the People's Republic fails to excite, and I can see that even Shiping seems to be having trouble staying awake. The day concludes with dinner at a riverside floating restaurant followed by a boat cruise on the Huangpu River. This is one of the highlights of our trip: an opportunity to view Shanghai, a global city of blinding lights, at night as it surrounds us on both shores.

On our final full day, we visit the Jade Buddha Temple. I still cannot grasp the merits of jade, but I purchase souvenirs anyway. Afterwards on the bus, Jen and I sit together across from Shiping. Studying my phrasebook, I struggle to pronounce some words in Chinese, asking Shiping to correct me. "*Xia*," "she-uh," is shrimp. "Good," the Emperor approves. "*Yu*," "YU," "yU," "yoooooooouuuuu," I repeat, trying to say "fish." I notice that the driver keeps looking up at me in his mirror. "Shiping…," I ask, "…did I just say something wrong; did I utter a bad word?" "No," he responds, "Driver's name is Mr. Fish."

Jen, Shiping, and I have lunch with a small, self-selected group. We visit Yu Garden and its requisite shopping bazaar. This nice tourist trap is within a short walk of our hotel, and offers lots of crafts, electronics, and tea for purchase. If I've learned nothing else from this trip, I now know that capitalism is alive and well in China. As we leave the parking lot, our bus driver Mr. Fish gets pulled over by a motorcycle cop for trying to nudge his way into gridlocked traffic on the main street. Shiping translates the violation as "causing traffic jam," which seems to me exactly what the cop is doing by stopping us in the middle of the intersection. Shiping remains coolly seated in the front of the bus, but tells the rest of us to get off the bus and encircle the policeman to watch the interaction. The cop, visibly uncomfortable to be surrounded by a dozen curious foreigners, rips up the ticket he just wrote and throws it to the ground.

We all climb back onto the bus, satisfied to have helped out Mr. Fish. As we take our seats, Shiping explains that many people from Shanghai—including policemen—hold superiority complexes like those Americans often attribute to New Yorkers. This incident echoes what Wing told us a few nights ago. Our bus license plates identify Mr. Fish as an out-of-towner. As such, he is an easy target for harassment.

At our closing dinner that evening, our entire group is present. However, only the usual crowd of faculty and the "immersive" students partake in the local cuisine. The others wait politely to be excused so they can go to another restaurant. At dismissal, Shiping announces that the rest of the day is for packing, adding that "Miami Vice will need time to pack up the half of China they bought." They have literally acquired more bags than they can carry to the airport. Making things even more complicated for these bargain-hunters, several of them are traveling to Bangkok for a week of vacation before returning to the USA.

Wednesday, January 12 is our date of departure from China.

Shiping leaves us to our own devices while he makes a final university visit by himself. I take a walk on the Bund with a group of four students, and then agree to join them for the Bund's "psychedelic" tourist tunnel to Pudong, an attractively named outdated tourist attraction. In Pudong, we explore the river walk and observe workers on a garbage scow as they try to clean up China. Shiping returns for lunch, then we visit a Confucian temple, giving us the chance for calm contemplation before the long flight home. Finally, Shiping takes us to a market area where most venders seem to specialize in unauthorized DVDs. More out of curiosity than anything else, I buy a few hand-made copies of movies that are still in theatres. I later find that many of the copies aren't worth the media they're burned onto; some fail to play at all. Others were recorded in theatres with distracting background noises and views of tops of people's heads.

An hour drive from Shanghai, the Pudong International Airport is ultra-modern and almost completely vacant. It seems as though our flight is the only one taking off today. Most of the stores have not yet been occupied, and there are precious few places to find hot food before our flight. I notice that one student pays 28 Yuan (nearly $4) for a bag of microwave popcorn. With few options, I reluctantly part with $12 for a cold club sandwich onion rings.

Departing Pudong at 7:10pm, United flight 836 somehow approaches Chicago at 7:05pm, five minutes earlier. According to my watch, we'll be landing at about the same time we took off! Outside the plane's window, what used to be a sprawling Windy City now seems like an insignificant cluster of downtown high rises. I'm on sensory overload, and as we touch down at O'Hare, the world suddenly seems different. It seems strange to hear everyone speaking English as we go through customs and await our delayed connection to Boston. At last, our short connecting flight is pushed eastward by a tailwind, then we make an easy descent to Logan Airport just after midnight.

Boston is now just a small New England village. My senses are full of China, my perspective has changed, and I don't think I will ever look at the world in the same way again.

9

THE WAITING PLACE:
NEVER CROSS A BORDER WITHOUT YOUR PASSPORT

You'll be on your way up! You'll be seeing great sights!
You'll join the high fliers who soar to high heights.

….Except when you don't because, sometimes, you won't.
I'm sorry to say so but, sadly, it's true and hang-ups can happen to you.
You can get all hung up in a prickle-ly perch.
And your gang will fly on. You'll be left in a Lurch.
You'll come down from the Lurch with an unpleasant bump.
And the chances are, then, that you'll be in a Slump.

…The Waiting Place……for people just waiting.
Waiting for a train to go or a bus to come, or a plane to go or the mail to come…Everyone is just waiting.

….NO! That's not for you!
Somehow you'll escape all that waiting and staying…

from *OH! THE PLACES YOU'LL GO!*[xviii]

It is May 2007, the school year is over, and I am feeling a bit euphoric. I am in Český Krumlov in Southern Bohemia with a group of thirteen students. This is one of the best groups of students I've ever taken overseas. They are inquisitive, respectful, well-behaved, and fun to be around. Many of them enrolled in an "overload" *Cross-Cultural Understanding* class I taught a few years earlier. That venture really paid off for me, both as extra income and as a "feeder" of great students for my short term travel programs. The week has gone flawlessly in Prague and Terezín. Now we are enjoying the ambiance of this quaint UNESCO World Heritage site of Český Krumlov —a walled medieval city in the ox-bow curve of the Vltava River. We are staying at the four-star Hotel Seneca, and everyone has a room with a view. Times like these—when everything is going well—can be dangerous.

"Petr the Czech" is my local coordinator, and he has been instrumental especially for translating to my students and communicating with Milan, our Czech minibus driver. Milan speaks neither English nor German, so without Petr, I'm cut out of the deal. Unfortunately for me, Petr is leaving us today to return home at the request of his girlfriend Lucie. I am a bit uneasy about losing him as our local (Czech) coordinator, but I am sure Petr would stay with us if he felt he could. I give Petr a "bro hug" goodbye, and he is clearly embarrassed as he walks up the narrow alleyway to catch his train back to Prague, with suitcase wheels rattling on the cobblestone[xix].

Siniša Ubiparipovic is the class clown on this trip, or maybe one of several. He entertains his peers with impersonations of Borat, a character that was recently introduced in the movie by the same name. Siniša is a native of Bosnia-Herzegovina, and he is fluent in Serbo-Croatian. When planning this trip, I asked him to help me out as a "local expert" beginning with the drive to Croatia later today. I am also satisfied with the apparent competence of our Czech driver. Petr and I have prepared him with the itinerary, and he knows where to go: first to Hotel Park in

Ljubljana, Slovenia, then tomorrow on to Hotel Pula Resort, in Istria, Croatia. After that, Milan the driver is free to return to the Czech Republic, and my class will travel to our final destination of Zagreb by train and intercity bus.

Following an early wake up call, my class finishes *snídaně* (breakfast) and boards our minibus to leave the Czech Republic and cross the Austrian Alps. Austria is rainy today, but nevertheless picturesque. I ask Milan to make a stopover in the idyllic village of Bled, Slovenia, which is right along our route. I give the students two hours of free time, suggesting they get something to eat or simply walk along the lake. I instruct them to stay in groups and meet me at the minibus at 3pm sharp. This should get us to Ljubljana by 5:30pm to check in and have a relaxed group meal. I'm picturing some charming outdoor restaurant along the Ljubljanica River. It's 3pm at the minibus, and I do a head count. Everyone made it back except for Charles. I divide the students into mini-detachment search parties. We spend more than two hours tracking down Charles. It turns out that he doesn't have a watch, and then he got lost trying to find the bus. "What happened to the buddy system, Charles?" I ask, discretely. I am frustrated because we should be in Ljubljana by now; however, given the otherwise positive atmosphere, it makes no sense for me to chastise Charles in front of his peers. My philosophy in the field is that "everybody gets a pass," which I quietly impart to Charles at my first opportunity to pull him aside. Things have been going extraordinarily well, and this shouldn't bring us down.

My class minibus approaches Ljubljana—Slovenia's capital city—with our Czech driver Milan at the wheel and our Bosnian local coordinator navigating from the guide's seat. It's dark and gloomy out as we notice the large Hotel Park's brightly-lighted letters in the distance. Ljubljana is not a large city, and the hotel is situated prominently on a hilltop not far away. Siniša has a print-out of driving directions from Prague, but getting to our hotel is not so simple: the maps don't show that many of Ljubljana's streets are one-way. In addition, with Hotel Park in sight, Siniša tells the driver "*pravo*." This means "straight" in Siniša's native Serbo-Croatian, but in Czech it means "right," so Milan turns right every time we are headed in the correct direction, almost as if he is deliberately defying us. It doesn't help matters that I point and say in English "the hotel is right there!" You can imagine how frustrated everyone becomes. One might assume that simple words like "right," "left," and "straight" are mutually intelligible in Serbo-Croatian and Czech, both of which are Slavonic tongues. Alas, we discover that this is not the case. Because of this confusion, we drive around Ljubljana for nearly an hour without reaching our hotel. Between this and the Charles snafu, we pull up to Hotel Park's entrance hours behind schedule.

By the time we enter the lobby it's close to 11:00pm, most everyone in our group is ready for a *pivo* (beer), a hot meal, and sleep as soon as possible. As I approach reception with our voucher, the Manager Rado asks for everyone's passport. I point out that we arrived late, we are exhausted from travel, and many of the students' passports are stowed in their luggage. I suggest they hold *my* passport on behalf of the entire group, and if necessary we'll be happy to produce the other documents later. Rado takes another look at my travel-weary class, and acquiesces to my request. He tells me he will photocopy my passport and return it in a few minutes; this is standard procedure for hotel guests in this part of Europe.

Wow—what a relief after a long day! I thought we would arrive too late to get our first hot meal of the day, but Rado makes some calls and finds a table at what turns out to be a very posh restaurant. Imagine that. Of course, I can't make the students go to bed without dinner. From the prices on the menu, I wonder what Rado's referral fee is. This will stress my budget, but Siniša assures me that we can eat inexpensively in Croatia, and proclaims in his best local accent that the cheap and wonderful local fast food of *civapi* is "all you need to eat" there. We eat and drink to our delight, and likewise to the delight of the restaurant owner and servers, who earn ample coin this evening. I think the fourteen of us alone enable them to consider their entire day a success.

As I pay our bill, several of my students raise their glasses and propose a toast to Professor Deichmann. I thank them for the gesture, but suggest it is they who deserve the salute; they have been a pleasure to lead. After all, I know from experience that things can go horribly wrong at any moment while traveling. Blushing with modesty, I silently relish their appreciation and think to myself how gratifying it is that they would propose a toast to me. Although we're not home yet, things have indeed gone well so far. In order to move on from the awkward moment, I tell the students that actually, *their* work in the program gets much harder in the Balkans. After dinner, we return to the hotel and I ask Rado for my passport. He tells me the photocopier is broken, but he will return it to me when I check out tomorrow. I am too tired for an argument.

The next morning—or should I say a few hours later—we make the short walk into the Old Town and ride the new funicular railway up to Ljubljana Castle, which towers over this small city. The recently re-built fortification offers informational historical plaques in Slovenian and English for self-guided visitors. I give the students an hour to explore the museum, and then gather them for a few dramatic group photos from atop the tower. Afterwards, I dismiss the students and tell them to explore Ljubljana *as a group* and then meet at our nearby hotel in ninety minutes. Then, we will take the final language quiz and depart for Pula, Croatia by noon. Back at Hotel Park, the students complete their quizzes. I collect and turn in everyone's room keys, close out our bill, and collect the receipt, thanking the manager for our comfortable stay.

As we leave Ljubljana, I compliment the students on doing a good job of staying on track in spite of the crazy hours and demanding program. Two hours into our drive, we reach

Slovenian wine country near the Adriatic Sea. The scenery is simply breathtaking. We are approaching the border of Croatia, so it's time to prepare the students: "Please have your passports ready, in a few minutes we will leave the European Union. As we've discussed, Slovenians and Croatians aren't the best of friends at the moment… there can be difficulties crossing the border." As instructed, the students begin to get out their passports. To protect my passport from being lost or stolen, I keep it in my *Geldbeutel*; this small belt-loop bag has saved me more than once. When I reach for my passport, however, I realize that my *Geldbeutel* is conspicuously thin. I check again; no passport.

The torment that comes with this revelation cannot be expressed in words. My mind begins to race, my heart starts to pound heavily, and my face is most certainly bright red. I am responsible for thirteen students who are having the time of their lives and—at least until now—they have full trust me as trail boss. How do I tell them two hours into the journey that I left my passport at the hotel reception desk in Ljubljana, and that we'll all have to go back?[xx]

Moments later, as our minivan pulls up to the border station, I'm still deliberating how best to respond to my predicament. As devastating as it would be, my impulse is to show my losing hand and turn the minibus around to get my passport. I look around at the students, prepared with their passports in hand. Our driver Milan collects his own passport and his paperwork, then exits the minibus. Siniša and I follow. The border guards are giving the driver a hard time about his Czech insurance papers. You've got to be kidding… a minibus licensed in the EU is inadequate for Croatian standards? Why do some people in power like to make trouble? I notice that the Croatian border police are giving Milan a really hard time; maybe they won't bother with the passengers! In support of our driver, Siniša and I flank him as he enters the police office, as if there were actually anything we could do to assist him.

In Serbo-Croatian, Siniša explains to the police that we are a traveling class of American university students on our way to Zagreb. The police gaze toward the passengers on the minibus with disinterest, then wave off our driver Milan. I breathe a deep sigh of relief. It is at this moment that I decide to stay quiet about my passport. Now that I'm safely in Croatia, I can have it overnighted to me.

I just crossed an international border without my passport, which I'm pretty sure isn't legal.

Two hours later, we arrive at the Hotel Pula Resort. The students get off the minibus and I pay Milan, who climbs behind the wheel to return to the Czech Republic. I take our printed hotel reservation to the Croatian receptionist, who immediately asks for everyone's passport. "Do you need one passport per room?" I ask, in a hopeful tone. "No, one passport per person," is the response. Good grief, I'm in a tight spot. "Let's get the students into their rooms first so that they can unpack, shower, and meet back in the lobby at 4pm," I say to Siniša. He and I move away from the reception desk and send the students forward in pre-assigned roommate pairs. The students all receive their room keys and disappear into the elevator.

Now it's my turn to exchange my passport for a room key. Anxiously, I approach the reception desk. "Sir," I begin, "I am responsible for this group. I left my passport in Ljubljana, Slovenia this morning. I have a copy of it with me on my laptop computer, and I'd be happy to show you." As the receptionist looks at me with suspicion, I notice "LARIS" on his name tag. "If you wish, you can also call Hotel Park in Slovenia to confirm that they have my passport…." Laris appears pensive and skeptical. After a pause, I continue… "The moment I get into my room, I will call Hotel Park and ask them to send my passport here with DHL overnight….immediately." At this point, I'm still naïve enough to think my biggest problem is that this guy might not give me a room key. "What do you mean you don't have a passport?" demands Laris. You've got to be kidding, I think to myself. These days, most hotels don't require a passport for proof of identity, except in Croatia and a few other countries. Still thinking, Laris seems rather proud of the pen he's twirling between his fingers. I take another deep breath and wipe the sweat off my brow. Taken completely by surprise with the problem at hand, I start again from the beginning, calmly explaining to the man I now address as *Mr.* Laris exactly what had happened with my passport. "So I will call POLICE," he interrupts, picking up his telephone headpiece. "Please, wait," I plead, gesturing to put the phone back down on its receiver. He interrupts again "If you do not have a passport, you are in Croatia illegally… I MUST call police," he repeats. "Please Mr. Laris, let me check into my room and I will get you my passport as soon as possible." His suspicious gaze moves to his computer screen, he re-types my name from the paper reservation I had given him, and he finally hands me a room key. "If I don't have your passport by tomorrow, I will call police." "Thank you very much, Mr. Laris."

I lift my backpack and pull my suitcase to the elevator, then continue to my room, inserting the key in the door. Wow, that was a close call, I think to myself. I never would have expected this! I am shocked by the reaction of Laris, as if I were an American criminal traveling in his country with a group of students. For good measure, I feel as though I need to show this guy that I do have a valid passport, so I begin to boot up my computer in order to open the .pdf document that I travel with as a precaution.

Bang, bang….bang, bang, bang! I'm not sure if someone is pounding with the palm of their hand or trying to kick in the door. I am startled. Trembling, I open the door just a crack, keeping my shoe firmly behind the bottom, and leaning on my right foot for leverage. It is Laris. "I WILL call police if you do not show me your passport NOW," he demands. Great, the Boston Globe headlines read, "Bentley Professor Detained in Balkan Prison," and his students have no idea what happened to him. Confident that my .pdf with mollify my impulsive assailant, I remove my foot from the door, open it, and gesture to Laris to look at the laptop computer that is open on my bed. I kneel next to the bed, log into Windows, and pull up the scanned picture of my valid passport. "Thank you for understanding Mr. Laris," I say, calmly. "I know that you are doing your job. Can you help me call Rado at Hotel Park in Ljubljana and ask him to send my passport immediately?" "No, I will only call *POLICE*, RIGHT NOW!" Unsure of what to do, I reach into my pocket and retrieve a 20 Euro bill. "Please, Mr. Laris" I repeat, "I do have a valid passport, and here is its number and expiration date." He takes the bill and responds, "I will call Hotel Park in Ljubljana to make sure they have your passport. Come with me."

I follow Laris back downstairs to the reception desk and give him the handwritten phone number of Hotel Park in Ljubljana. Laris repeats or translates—I'm not sure—Rado's confirmation to me. "Yes, Mr. Deichmann's passport is here. He forgot to ask for it." I ask Laris to please instruct Rado to send it as quickly as possible; I will pay for the shipping, overnight please. Laris assures me that Rado is leaving work right now to go directly to the post office in Ljubljana before it closes. He hangs up the phone. "Thank you so much for your patience and understanding, Mr. Laris." I exhale with relief. "Enjoy your stay, Mr. Deichmann." As I return to my room, key in hand, I take comfort in the timing of this unfortunate incident. Ljubljana is only 203 km away. Today is only Wednesday, and we don't fly back to Boston until Sunday. We will be in Pula for two nights, and we'll remain in Croatia for two days after that. If, for some reason, my passport doesn't arrive tomorrow, it will certainly be here before we leave Pula for Zagreb on Friday. I need to take a deep breath, regain my composure, forget about this for now, and meet with the students for dinner in 15 minutes.

On Thursday, the class meets again for an early breakfast. We discuss our first impressions of Pula and I give our Croatian expressions quiz. Then we walk into the city to have a look at the

Roman amphitheater, Dvojna Vrata (double gate), and other architectural relics. Visiting the amphitheater is an unplanned event, and my class budget cannot bear the weight of a guided tour. Because Siniša speaks Croatian, I have asked him to lead our walk with an audio guide and translate the salient facts for the rest of us. As class clown, Siniša channels the tour through Borat's voice: "this is where we throw Christians and Jews to lions." Afterwards, we enjoy a group dinner at the hotel. Siniša assures me the staff told him dinner is included in our hotel price. I was not aware of this, and although skeptical, I want to believe it is true. Dinner ends, and I dismiss the class for free time at the beach. I return to my hotel, and Laris informs me that my passport did not arrive today. Damn, we're cutting it kind of close. I sure hope my credentials arrive tomorrow. Fearing another threat to call the police, I ask Laris to phone Hotel Park in Ljubljana and ask when and how Rado sent my passport. I hope—and indeed expect—that as I requested it was sent DHL, FedEx, or at least express mail. Rado isn't there, but after hanging up the phone, Laris tells me he thinks that my passport might have been sent to Pula privately with a (bus) driver. "Or maybe they couldn't send it before the end of business yesterday," he adds.

No problem. I am beginning to take some comfort that I've developed enough of a rapport with Laris so that he'll refrain from having me arrested. To my relief, I find out that the hotel's mail usually arrives before our scheduled train departure for Rijeka, where we'll connect to Zagreb with a bus. Effectively, this gives me one more day and an additional chance. In the morning, Siniša and I give the students some free time at the beach while we walk to the train station to buy their tickets. No point in dragging everyone along for this. I return to the hotel. Yes, the mail arrived! No, my passport is not in today's mail! The tension mounts, and I ask Laris where the Pula Post Office is located. Following these directions, Siniša and I walk there quickly to check on my passport. As politely as possible, we attempt to get some information about what might have happened if it was mailed from Ljubljana on Wednesday. The hefty bulldog of a woman behind the glass responds to us tersely, as if we are accusing her of stealing the mail, or, at least being less than helpful. I get the feeling that if she had my passport behind the counter she would make me miss today's train then demand 100 Euros before handing it to me in time for tomorrow's train. I get it: the passport will arrive when it arrives. As we walk away from the counter, Siniša mutters some disparaging comments about people who grew up in the former Yugoslavia, the Communist system that shaped their mentalities, and the sort of workers who wind up in this type of "public service" job.

I reach a new low as my students gather in the lobby to walk to the train. Laris is visibly nervous about something. I tell him the class is leaving, but remind him I will stay here and wait for my passport. Laris wants us to settle our bill, so I present my Mastercard. The bill shows a charge of $400 for two buffet meals for fourteen people. I ask Siniša to discuss this with Laris, and they do so in Serbo-Croatian. It turns out that I was correct: those meals are *not* included in our room rate. Siniša points out that the staff told us they *are* included. I do my best to follow the heated argument that ensues. Finally, I propose that we meet half way and pay them an additional $200, an amount that Siniša assures me is good business for the hotel's mediocre kitchen. Although I just shelled out two hundred dollars I didn't expect to spend, I'm feeling somewhat satisfied to have reached a compromise. "Welcome to the Balkans, Professor," says Siniša as we head for the train station. "This is a normal way for them to get money" he adds.

I have full faith in Siniša leading the students, but I pull him aside to make sure he is comfortable with what I've asked him to do. He will take the class to Zagreb, get them settled at Hotel Central across from *Glavni Kolodvor* (the main station), and introduce them to Zagreb, a capital city that he's never been to before. I've asked him to facilitate the routine class first impressions discussion over dinner tonight. "I'm happy to help, Professor. Don't worry, my *Tetka Stoja* (Aunt Stoja) is going to meet us when we get to Zagreb. She and my cousin will show us around."

Today is the first hot, sunny day of our visit Pula, Istria. The students perspire as they pull their luggage along the twenty minute walk to the station. "Where's your suitcase, Professor?" asks Petr the Slovak, one of my students. "I'll tell everyone as soon as we get to the station," I assure him, quietly. Having held out to check today's mail, I have yet to tell the class that I won't be traveling with them. I need to remain in Pula to wait for my passport. I contemplate what might be the best face to put on this. Standing on the train platform, I explain exactly what happened the morning after they proposed their toast to me in Ljubljana. I clarify to them that I waited two days to tell them because it was reasonable to expect that my passport would be here by now. Also, I didn't want to ruin their time in Europe with unnecessary concerns about something that is now beyond our control. I bid my students a good journey to Zagreb and assure them they are in great hands with our "local expert" until I see them tomorrow night. I wave goodbye as their train pulls away from the platform.

Walking back to the Hotel Pula Resort, I again hit a new low. I'm devastated, and exhausted from the stress. I've spent two days waiting for my passport under threat of arrest, and it's just two more days until we fly. The passport *must* arrive tomorrow, or I am screwed.

I'm not hungry but I need to eat something. After that, I might as well try to keep my mind occupied by seeing the rest of Pula's sights. I sit down at an outdoor table and order a Greek salad with a beer. I ask myself a series of "what ifs"… what if in Ljubljana I had refused to leave reception until Rado returned my passport to me? Is Rado even trustworthy? What if he had returned my passport the first two times I asked for it? What if I had remembered to ask for it again in the morning?

What if, when I checked out, Rado had returned it without my asking? What if Petr had been with us at the border? He could have continued on the bus with the students while I returned to Ljubljana for my passport. What if Rado had sent my passport overnight? Would we be better off if the Croatian border guards had checked our passports and denied me entry to Croatia? Is Laris trustworthy? What if the post office bulldog in Pula took time to check her mail bags like we asked? What if I had given her some "coffee money" to do so? Through it all, and especially seeing me without my students that night, Laris becomes a sort of confidant to me. We chat briefly each time I pass the reception desk. He is the only hope I have left in Pula. He could have had me arrested (another "what if?"), and I suppose it's still possible that he might if I don't keep him on my side.

Alas, the buck stops with Joel, and a new round of self-deprecation begins. I appreciate that this all could have been avoided if I had stuck with my original plan and not dragged the class across too much geography. Why didn't we stay in the Czech Republic for all twelve days, or at least the EU? As if hotel checkout weren't already chaotic enough, why did I make the students take a silly language quiz in the hotel lobby? I should have been focused on collecting my passport, not their quizzes. This experienced traveler screwed up on so many levels.

Reflecting on my present situation twists my stomach up in knots. I'm in The Waiting Place now. I think about that Dr. Seuss story *Oh! The Places You'll Go!* My memory takes me back to another low point— as an undergraduate at Geneseo. Karen—my girlfriend at the time—gave me the hardcover book when I was experiencing great self-doubt, and right now I'm trying to remember the story's exact words. They fit both situations perfectly. As I beat myself up, I take a moment to write down my feelings.

Here I am, stranded in Pula, a city where I wouldn't normally mind being stranded. I left my passport at the

214 | Passion for Place

*hotel in Ljubljana, Slovenia. When I called from Pula,
Rado the receptionist told me he would take it to the post
office immediately and that it would be here in one day.
After waiting two days I lost my optimism but still held
out some hope. Tomorrow is day three. With or without my
passport, I need to go to Zagreb tomorrow alone to meet the
students and see them off on their return to Boston Sunday
morning. Worst scenario is that I will get a new passport
from the US Embassy on Monday, and then fly home alone
on Tuesday. It makes me sick to think about that scenario,
but now it seems to be the most likely one.*

Tomorrow comes, but the passport doesn't. After the mail
arrives at Hotel Pula Resort, I thank Mr. Laris, shake his hand,
and pay my bill. I give him an attractive but inexpensive Bentley
pen as a parting gift—it's all I have to offer. I leave by myself and
buy a bus ticket to Zagreb. My last chance of returning home
tomorrow is to track my passport down at Croatia's Central
Post Office in Zagreb when I arrive tonight. I am taking a
chance of missing my passport by leaving Pula, but I'm out of
time for waiting and I need to return to my students.

*I have time on the bus to write some thoughts. First, the
scenery is spectacular and Rijeka's setting is incredible. Very
quickly this morning, Laris and I figured out that when
Rado sent my passport in the regular mail on Wednesday,
there was never any chance that it would get to Pula in
time. The Pula Post Office was open, but the person who
sorts the mail does not work on Saturdays, and nobody had
the key. Maybe I should have paid some "coffee money" to
find another key. The burley woman at the Pula Post Office
wasn't at all helpful when I stopped in twice on Friday.
So, Laris told me he would go to the post office at 7am
on Monday. I gave him 100 kuna (about $20) to send it
with a bus driver to Zagreb. I have the bus schedule- they*

leave about every hour and take about five hours to get to the capital. Laris will call me at my hotel to tell me which bus it will be on, and I will meet the bus at the station, then I'll fly on Tuesday. This is the plan—the best scenario left after a series of catastrophes, or "katastrofa" in Croatian. Things could be worse. I keep reminding myself that nobody is physically hurt, and it comforts me that, as one of the students pointed out, if this happened to a student, two people would be screwed, and whatever the ultimate damage would be twice as costly.

These events seem so unlikely that there must be a divine reason why they happened. I think of a U2 song "Elvis Presley and America," based on Psalm 31. It includes a prayer asking God to "drop me down but don't break me." Things really could be much worse right now, and I'm thankful they're not. What if, instead, something terrible had happened, something I often caution students against when I dismiss them: "be careful, and don't get hit by a bus." Then, I think of another scenario that could yet unfold. My class traveled here on a group ticket, and we're all supposed to travel together. What if Air France does not permit any of the students to fly because one person is missing? This is a very real possibility. I'll hope for the best, but I make a mental note not to purchase this sort of ticket again.

Several hours later I arrive in Zagreb and go with Siniša to the Central Post Office of the Republic of Croatia. It seems to us that any mail coming from another country would first arrive here. With Siniša explaining, the post office gatekeepers take us directly up the chain to the facility's supervisor, who proceeds to escort us into the enormous sorting room. We go to the corner that is designated for mail from Slovenia, and search thoroughly for envelopes large enough to contain a passport. This is my last card. I want to give the postal men "coffee money" for allowing us the chance to sift through the mail—something that cannot possibly be entirely authorized—but I'm very concerned about cash. After an hour, we thank the men politely and leave.

Siniša is more supportive than I could even remotely imagine. He's seen me succeed, and now he is here by my side in a pretty dark hour. He and I meet the class again that evening for an excellent farewell dinner with Tetka Stoja and her son, Siniša's cousin. This is the students' final evening in Zagreb. The students seem slightly concerned, but with Siniša's reassurance, they take our suboptimal situation in stride.

Early on Sunday morning, I take the students to the airport and see them through the security screening. Thank God and Air France that they were all allowed to board the plane without the final group member (myself) being present. It was hard to leave the students this morning, but the worst part is calling Karen and telling her I won't be home tonight. "Why didn't you say anything about this?" "I was holding out hope until the end." It's likely that my stubborn optimism comes from being a Red Sox, Bills, or Sabres fan; I don't give up until it's over. Thankfully, I didn't say *that* to her! After the call, my emotions gauge goes from "stranded" to "shipwrecked."

I am back in Hotel Central Zagreb. I took the students to the airport at 4:30 this morning, and they should be in Paris by now. They fly back to Boston at 1pm. I am attempting to keep my chin up. After a late final night out with the students, I tried to go back to sleep but failed. In any case, my spirits lifted momentarily as I worked on my course budget. I had entered admission tickets into the spreadsheet twice (estimated at $900, but actual itemized receipts for $300). This put us back in the black. The fact that I'm not $600 over budget does raise my spirits.

So, I am still "stuck in Croatia and I can't get out of it." This situation seems so unlikely that it must have been part of somebody's plan. Now I'll get back to the story, chronologically. It seems to help me feel better to write

*everything down. I feel incredibly sad and abandoned in
the Waiting Place, although two students—Andrew Saxe
and Siniša Ubiparipovic—are still in town as a starting
point for further travels in Europe.*

I help Andrew buy his train tickets to Vienna on Sunday,
and spend some time with Siniša and his *Tetka* (Aunt) Stoja. He
has a nice family, and stayed in Europe to visit more relatives
in Bosnia. At the end of the day, we say our farewells, and I
spend my final night in Zagreb. If not a test, this situation has
got to be a sort of lesson: God's boot camp? I am slated to go to
Russia on a Fulbright in fourteen weeks and live there for four
months, and I cannot even handle being stranded for three
days, and counting. Right now, I seem to be spending a lot
of time talking to God. Now my dilemma is whether to wait
out my passport here in Zagreb, or to go to the US Embassy
tomorrow and declare my passport "lost or stolen" and pay for
a new one. Not quite sure what to do, I decide to sleep on it.

On Monday morning, the world is full of new possibilities, but I am still stuck here in Zagreb. I check my email
using my laptop and the hotel's Wi-Fi—a great luxury to have
nowadays. I'm in the habit of hunting down an internet café
for such a simple chore. Thankfully, as I requested, the students
all reported back that they made it home safely. I search on
expedia.com to find the cheapest hotel for tonight near the
Zagreb airport.

After breakfast, I walk to the Air France/KLM ticketing office
in Zagreb. I am hopeful that I can have my plane ticket reissued;
however, the most pleasant and lovely looking ticketing agent
ever is the bearer of more bad news: it can't be done. A new
one-way ticket back to Boston will cost $900. While booking
my ticket, the agent confirms that according to the rules of
our group ticket, the other passengers should not have been
allowed to board the plane without me. It doesn't matter that
they are all adults. The ticket fine print states that all fourteen

of us must travel together. My situation could have been much
worse.

After paying for the ticket, I go to the US Embassy to
document my situation and interview for a new passport. While
in the waiting room, I find another reason to feel fortunate.

*Things could be worse! In the Embassy's waiting room, I
just spoke with Richard, an American from San Diego.
He and his wife were also waiting to apply for passports.
The boat they chartered burned in the Adriatic, and
they managed to survive. In the fire, they lost all of their
belongings, including passports, money, credit cards, and
luggage. She had to jump into the sea fully clothed. This
puts things into perspective for me. At least my students got
out of my burning boat and I managed to hold on to my
money and luggage!*

Three hours later, I leave the US Embassy in Zagreb with a
brand new passport! I worked hard to fill up my old passport
with stamps, and I don't know if I'll ever see it again. I take
the city bus to Zagreb's Pleso Airport, and then find my way
on foot to my cheap and nasty fleabag hotel. I don't feel like I
deserve anything more. There's no lobby to relax in and there
are no English language channels on my television. There's not
much to do but write in my journal.

*This place is inexpensive but malodorous. It smells like eggs
in my room, but it's evening and I can sleep soon. I spent
the day getting my plane ticket at Air France, my passport
at the US Embassy, and then finding this dump of a hotel.
It's a cheap place for 299 kuna ($60). Now I'm watching
Serbian news on the television as I type. My KLM flight
leaves at 8:25 tomorrow morning, then onward to Boston
with Northwest/KLM. I am relieved, to say the least, in
spite of the anxiety and financial blow that will result.*

When all is said and done, I expect this fiasco to cost me about $1500.

The next morning in the Zagreb airport, I notice a sign for a Museum of Naïve Art. I remember walking past that museum in Kaptol also. I'm not sure what is on display there, but I chuckle at the thought that maybe I should be an exhibit for spending the past four days expecting my passport to arrive.

This chapter is about living a Dr. Seuss story. I got caught being overzealous, trying to do too much. Is this an important lesson for me just before leading Karen and the kids to Europe next month, or before heading to Russia on a Fulbright shortly thereafter? Yes, it could be. Take care, Kid. Stay humble! Try to find ways to help other people who make innocent oversights, and don't threaten to call the authorities. Don't overextend yourself, Man. Why, after a successful eight-day program in Prague with a nice group of students, did you complicate things by dragging them as far as Croatia? You had barely been there yourself. Finally, appreciate your time with the wife and kids, and remember how profoundly you missed them while you were stuck in the Waiting Place.

The day after I return home to Nashua, NH, I receive an email from Laris in Pula that my passport arrived in that day's mail, the very day I had left. Laris dutifully sent it to the US Embassy in Zagreb. Days later, the well-traveled passport arrives in my Nashua mailbox, with a cancellation hole through the entire document. I keep it in the top drawer of my dresser as a nice souvenir and conversation piece.

In June, I drive to campus to meet with two administrators at the Cronin Center for International Education. I'm here to tell my story and settle up with a blank check for the overage related to my two stranded days. Despite a strong track record in the past, my hunch is that the decisions I made won't be well received. When all is said and done, to my relief I get congratulated for another successful program. My student evaluations are strong, and the course is on budget… except for my two extra days in the Waiting Place.

The following year, Siniša completes his Liberal Studies Major capstone project by designing a short-term program entirely for Croatia and Bosnia. Applying the lessons learned from doing too much, he and I exclude Slovenia from the new Balkans course, and instead develop a plan to take students to Sarajevo and other locations in Bosnia, which we implement successfully in 2009, 2011, and 2012.

When I say it's remarkable that the (2009) trip even happened, I mean that even the students told me they had their doubts about signing up. Croatia is a place that a few Americans have heard of and might be remotely curious about, but Bosnia? Isn't there a war there? These students came from Vermont, Connecticut, California, New Jersey, (Buffalo) New York, Maine, Massachusetts, Rhode Island, Slovakia, Czech Republic, Dominican Republic, and Argentina. They were in elementary school while Yugoslavia's war of dissolution was going on, and their parents remember the conflict quite well I'm sure, as I do. Why would their kids want to go there, and why would any parent consent to it? From my perspective, it's really quite humbling that these students showed up. Yes it is a risk for all of us, but the saying "nothing ventured, nothing gained" is very true at many levels.

Of course in reality, Croatia and Bosnia are rather safe places. My experience in Sarajevo is in line with Lonely Planet's description "safer than most large cities in Western Europe." Having observed a drunken rabble in Venice on our way home from Sarajevo, my students observed this contrast first-hand.

My course to the Balkans seems a little unorthodox because

traveling there requires some improvisation and local adaptations. For example, in 2009 we flew into Venice rather than Zagreb because flights to the latter were outside the scope of our course budget; this resulted in an enchanting day in the sinking "City of Water." Similarly, in 2011's Version 2.0, prohibitive flight prices into Zagreb caused us to make a delightful stopover in Budapest. We can put transparency on a pedestal, but as we've seen, in the Balkans it is sometimes necessary to pay "coffee money" to get things done or to stay out of trouble. And trouble will find you if you're out there traveling, especially in the Balkans. Still, I think most of my companions would agree that traveling Balkan style, or being challenged to "Slav up" can be incredibly enriching and educational because it requires creativity, flexibility, and resilience.

10

AFRICA FOR BEGINNERS: GHANA

*Travel is fatal to bigotry, narrow-mindedness, and
prejudice, and (I) need it sorely on these accounts.*

Adapted from Mark Twain

The very first time I run into Diane Kellogg is in a classroom
after a spring 2006 open presentation by Carol Gray. Diane
is my colleague in Bentley's Management Department, and she
is hosting Carol on campus. Carol is a retired housewife and
philanthropist; a mother of eight and founder of HUGS International, a Salt Lake City based aid organization. As I introduce
myself to Diane, she immediately detects my interest in Ghana. I
confess to the reader that my presence at this event is attributable
to the publicity U2 and other celebrities are currently giving to
problems and opportunities on earth's second largest continent.
The questions that come to mind are: "Can I, as a professor,
make a difference for the better?" and, if so, "What can I do
without getting in the way?"

Diane calls me at home frequently that summer to encourage
me to join the "Ghana team," and eventually lead a group of
students there. My kids are young—8, 6, and 4—so any time
that I'm away from home is still a challenge for our entire
family. As a parent herself, Diane understands my constraints,
and assures me that there is a place for me in the future of

her larger project. For now, our objective is for me to obtain a grant to travel to Ghana next winter break and complete my "Ghana training," and then eventually get involved with taking students to Ghana to participate in service-learning activities.

I am elated to be part of the Ghana team. Africa is the logical next step in my journey around the world. On January 3rd 2007, I board a Delta flight at JFK bound for Accra to see what it's all about. My brother Jonathan had asked me why I'm going to Africa, and I responded that I'd tell him when I get back. I know why I *want* to go to Africa, but I'm not sure at this point what I have to offer. In other words, I'm uncertain why everything fell into place. Of course, I am curious about the world, but this opportunity came along far too perfectly to be my own doing. I sense that few big steps in life are random, and I ponder whether this could be part of a bigger plan. Maybe I'm rounding out my education a bit to become a better educator or global citizen, to assume a new role, or maybe there's someone that I'm supposed to meet. In any case, I feel like I was put here on this plane; all I have to do is embrace the opportunity.

Diane and I are traveling with a sizeable Bentley entourage. Our companions include Diane's husband Ed; Sue: another management professor; Charles: lecturer in accounting; Shawn, director of service learning, and his partner Susi; Duncan, director of diversity and his wife Beth; and Kojo, Bentley's very first PhD student. My two checked bags—like everyone else's—contain a few warm weather clothes, but mainly donations that we have collected: clothing, pencils, and candy that can't melt. On our persons, we each carry wads of crisp new $50 bills, specially-ordered from Diane's bank. Diane imparts to us that credit and ATM cards are not yet useful in Ghana. She adds that Ghanaian banks and hotels are fussy about the condition of cash. I have no reason to disagree; full of experience she has my complete confidence. So, my travel journal pages are laced with $400 in cash in eight bills.

After the jet's door closes, we wait on the JFK tarmac for

two hours. We hear a wide assortment of explanations over the intercom, but ultimately the flight attendant reveals that we are waiting for a VIP. Delta just began service from JFK to Ghana, and flights run only three times a week, so anyone left behind will spend two days in The Waiting Place. As the VIP boards and enters the first class cabin, a wave of applause erupts and we hear the door close and lock. Almost immediately, we hear "Ladies and gentleman, we are prepared for take-off." Our ten hour and forty-three minute flight will begin at last.

Curiously, long after the captain announces our initial descent to Accra, we remain high in the air in a circling pattern. I look out my window to observe nothing but dirty gray air. Expecting to see the Gulf of Guinea, I cannot distinguish land from water. "ladies and gentlemen, unfortunately we are unable to land at Kotoka International Airport due to the weather." Hmm… must be that dust cloud. "The aircraft is running low on fuel, so we are seeking alternative landing arrangements." After twenty more minutes, the captain announces that we have been cleared for landing at Cotonou airport in Benin. I'm not even sure where that is. As we land, I pull out my guidebook, and Benin is not on the map of Ghana and its neighbors. I later discover that it is the next country east after Ghana's immediate neighbor Togo.

Our Delta flight lands on the dusty airstrip without incident, makes a 180 degree turn, and parks near an austere-looking brick and steel terminal. The Gulf of Guinea is faintly visible behind the building. The captain returns to the intercom. "Ladies and gentlemen, please remain seated. Nobody is permitted to leave the aircraft. We are making arrangements to purchase fuel, and then we will continue to Accra." I look out the window and see half a dozen uniformed guards armed with rifles and looking toward the plane. "Great—now they're probably going to pass the hat for gas money," says a passenger a few rows back. His son corrects him "Dad —you mean *jet fuel*." The captain comes back on the intercom. "Folks, as Delta doesn't have a business account in Benin, we cannot purchase fuel, so we're on the phone with Atlanta right now making arrangements to have money wired in. I'm turning the fasten seat belt sign off, feel free to move about the cabin." The new film *Last King of Scotland*, which played as I slept last night, begins to re-play. The air in the plane is hot, but the passengers remain calm. After several hours, the captain instructs everyone to take their seats for a thirty minute flight to Accra.

At last, seven hours late, we land at Accra-Kotoka at 3:15pm. A smiling man named Holy meets us in the arrivals hall. A native Ghanaian, Holy chews a toothpick incessantly. Diane gives him a hug and presents him with a Red Sox cap as a hello gift, as the rest of us gather around to shake his hand. Holy is the official driver for the school Mmofra Trom that we will visit. He helps us load our luggage and carefully-weighed fifty pound care boxes from the USA into the rear bus seats, then drives us to the Afia Beach Resort, which I discover has already become Bentley's headquarters in Accra.

Helen and Kofi run the Afia, which comprises a lovely open main building with a high roof and no walls. The two are very much in love with one another. Kofi is the Ghanaian name given to boys born on Friday. In addition to the front desk and lobby waiting area, there is a shop selling locally-made furniture and handicrafts, and a restaurant that offers views of the small bedroom bungalows below and the Gulf of Guinea beyond. The bungalows contain two bedrooms, each with its own bathroom. Chickens run loose in the yard, and waves crash violently against the not-too-distance beach. At 7pm, the members of our group meet for a group "planning" meal, which costs 2,150,000 Ghana cedis for twelve of us. I'm too tired to wrap my head around that amount in dollars, but I'm sure Diane knows what she's doing. Exhausted, we retire to our respective rooms. A nice nightcap of scotch really hits the spot for me. My bed is hard and smells sweaty, but it's far more comfortable than that Delta jet I slept in last night. There's no television in the room, so I'll be able to focus upon writing. This situation is hardly roughing it, and I am relieved that my worst fears—about sleeping under a mosquito net—are not realized on the first night. I can't believe I'm in Africa.

On my first day in Ghana, my senses immediately surge toward overload. Everything is more extreme: the colors, the scents, the sounds. The air is heavy and dusty, thanks to the Harmattan winds, which blow in from the Sahara every January and coat otherwise lush and green Ghana with a layer of reddish dust. The local clothing is colorful, and the air is full of smells: stale urine, automobile exhaust, burning garbage, and untreated waste in the open sewers. On our short, dusty morning walk from Afia to the National Culture Center, we pass a dirt field where kids are kicking around a homemade football constructed from paper and tape. Next to this park is a large dump, and some of it is on fire! People of all ages sort through the rubbish, and only a few are equipped with footwear. Along our path, I observe windblown piles of empty water sachets and assorted trash, as well as a double-edged Wilkinson Sword razor blade.

It might be a long week for me. I expected Ghana to be doing well by African standards, but I don't know what African standards are. Diane had instilled romantic expectations. If Ghana is Africa for beginners, what is the rest of Africa like? I feel a bit uncomfortable and self-conscious as the rare white person, and at first I try to avoid eye contact. Damn, I wish I had my shades. Despite the poverty, I can't help but notice not only the smiles on most everyone's face, but also their smiling *eyes*. Everyone seems happy and full of life. Businesses have religious names: "GLORY TO GOD MUSIC SHOP," "ALLAH IS GREAT CHOP SHOP," and "PRAISE HIM FURNITURE." The latter sells only coffins from what I can see. I notice immediately that nearly every passing vehicle is adorned with large yellow letters across the back window sharing a religious inscription: "GOD IS GOOD," "PRAISE TO GOD," "CHRIST THE KING." I puzzle at one sticker that states "EXCEPT JESUS." Is this a misspelling of "accept," or just something that's far over my head? Only half way through my first day, some profound cultural contrasts with America have already appeared. People here seem focused upon family, relationships, and anticipation of rewards that are not of this world.

As I walk down the main street, a little boy walks toward me carrying a baby goat. Our eyes meet, and he asks me to take his picture. I oblige. He then extends his hand and asks for "something small, mister." As I don't have any coins, I give him ten thousand Ghana cedis. At a value of about one dollar, this is the smallest bill I have. I'm relieved that Diane armed us with such "small change" as we left Afia this morning, instructing us to use it for tips when we see fit.

As we reach the markets, we are approached by two Ghanaian men, who smilingly introduce themselves as Abraham and Colin Powell, the latter of whom is wearing a black t-shirt with a large American flag on the front. The two gentlemen remember Diane from her last visit. "Hello, my friend! What would you like to buy?" they ask each of us repeatedly. "Just looking, thank you," we respond in turn, except for Diane, who has specific items in mind. She leaves in one direction with Abraham, Beth, and Duncan, while Colin Powell takes the rest of us around to show us shops full of all manner of handicrafts. We walk through the stalls of ebony wood carvings, bracelets, tables, Djembe drums, and other items, all for incredibly low and negotiable prices. I soon discover that these men view themselves as our personal market escorts, and they protect us from other goods hustlers and possible tricksters. For their services, Abraham and Colin Powell will later receive from the venders a portion of the sale of anything we buy.

On the bus to Mmofra Trom, an hour's drive northeast of Accra, I observe that in Ghana, the road is the center of all activity. It is full of cars, trucks, lorries, tro tros, goats, chickens, barefoot children, and women wearing vibrant colors and carrying on their heads heavy baskets laden with bread, fruit, water sachets, and other items. All of these participants interact busily and chaotically on the asphalt. This is true of the cities, the villages, and all roads connecting them.

Mmofra Trom was established by Carol Gray, a Mormon woman from Salt Lake City. When her eight kids reached adulthood, she busied herself by filling transport containers with donations in the UK, then personally loading them onto trucks and driving them to Bosnia-Herzegovina. Now that the Balkan war has ended, Carol is working on several aid projects in Africa. The school was founded as a boarding school for children of AIDS-infected parents, many of whom are orphans. Today, a large portion of Mmofra Trom's enrollment represents tuition-paying families, and the rest of its funding comes from contributors such as HUGS and Bentley (via hosting fees and donations).

Our bus breaks down on a hillside along the road to Aburi, a mountain village that specializes in ebony woodcarvings. Thankfully, we have cell phones—if primitive—and the coverage in Ghana is remarkably strong. While we wait on the roadside for a mechanic to arrive, we make use of our first chance to venture away from our protected environments: the resort, the school, and the bus. I suggest to the others that we hike along the roadside to the hilltop to try to catch a glimpse of the hazy plains. Trucks laden with cassava pass by. We sweat profusely along the hike as our eyes scan the grassy roadside for reptiles. I sense the weight of the potential seriousness of our situation if something were to go wrong. Wow– I am in Africa! Two hours later, we are back on the bus and on our way. There is no rush, and there is no need to worry about anything. We are on relaxed "*Ghana Time*," and everything shall pass in due course.

I complete my week of Ghana training, establishing many new friendships with our Ghanaian hosts and fellow traveling Americans alike. In addition, our group visits the slave castles in Cape Coast and Elmina as well as completing the canopy walk at Kakum National Park. Although I'm not yet fully comfortable with the idea of co-leading a class here, I feel like I will be able to grow into developing a successful program.

Ghana is hard for me to describe on my first visit. In many ways, it seems like a model for Africa. The people here are friendly and cheerful. They have been through hell at the hands of their enemies, which in the past included the Europeans, but they are incredibly forgiving, and it is nice for me that most of them like Americans. Their pro-American disposition is in large part thanks to the generous aid provided by US President George W. Bush, who is currently taking a beating in the polls at home due to the bloody and expensive US-led war against Iraq's Saddam Hussein, which he initiated. Ghana is not an easy place for me to be, but it is certainly fascinating and ultimately I feel safe. As I await my flight to JFK, I know I'll be back sometime. In fact, I am quite sure I'll be called upon to lead a class here next year.

I return to Ghana fourteen months later, this time with ten students that Diane picked for me: six women and four men. The women—all Americans—are strong, bright, and enthusiast. One of the guys is Ghanaian, one Canadian, one African-American, and the other from Botswana. The four men's combined character and fortitude might equal that of the weakest of the women. Things in Ghana have changed. The Ghana cedi has been devalued: the new Ghana cedi is equal to 10,000 old Ghana cedis. After just one week of Ghana training, I could certainly be better qualified to bring a group here. But of course, that didn't stop me the first time I took students to Prague. In any case, my Nigerian co-leader Charles makes me more comfortable with the idea.

Our travel study takes place over spring break, but also cheats us out of one day of class. We leave on a Thursday night in March, to return on Sunday night before Monday classes. Half way through our first flight to Amsterdam, a female student visits my seat. One of the other students collapsed in her seat and is not responding. We'll call her Nancy. I bring Nancy water and confer with Charles. He and all of the other passengers disembark in

Amsterdam. The flight attendants deliver a wheelchair for my incoherent student. We're off to a great start! Luckily, our layover at Schiphol Airport is five hours long. Charles stays with the group, while one of the female students helps me take Nancy to the airport's infirmary, where we spend several hours. It turns out Nancy is overtired from studying for the past week's mid-term exams and work, and has overdone it with travel medicine, birth control pills, Benadryl, and whatever else. The doctor competently gives her a shot in the ass to bring her back to life, and declares that she is fit to travel. I pay the receptionist 60€, and we push Nancy to the boarding gate in a wheel chair at last call. The gate agent refuses us at first. "No, she may not travel in this condition." After I present her doctor's note, we're permitted to board, but I have to wonder if this was a mistake on my part. After all, we're bound for Africa.

Holy, Mmofra Trom's bus driver, meets us at the arrivals hall in Kotoka wearing the Red Sox hat Diane gave him last January. After the flights it's good to see a familiar and kind face. Thankfully, Nancy is alert now, and she has become the life of our jet-lagged group. Holy drops us at Afia Beach Resort, where we eat a welcome dinner as a group. After a brief discussion of expectations for tomorrow, I dismiss everyone to their rooms for a much needed rest.

Over breakfast in the morning, Charles and I facilitate a discussion of first impressions in Ghana. Some students impart their displeasure about seeing random small reptiles and insects in their bathrooms. Others complain about a lack of air conditioning, and a few comment that roosters woke them up at sunrise. Trying to reign in their expectations without coming across as glib and unsympathetic, I respond with a smile and "Akwaaba…welcome to Ghana!" I thought Charles and I had prepared them better. This is no bed of roses. The class meets at 9am in the lobby for a visit to the nearby Accra Cultural Center. The bus is parked out front, but I tell the students that this is our only day of activities close enough to reach on foot. We're not going to start up and cool off the bus just to drive half of a mile. This is no pleasure cruise. I want my students to observe their surroundings: see the sights, smell the scents, hear the sounds, and feel the dust. This is Africa, and we are here to experience it.

As director of Ghana programs, Diane lines up a "service" project for each Bentley student group that travels to Ghana, and my spring break class will help set up Mmofra Trom's football (soccer) field. A regulation-sized space has already been cleared from the thick bush, and it is our task to demarcate the perimeter and the goals. In our suitcases and extra boxes, we have uniforms, balls, and goal nets from Bentley and local community teams in eastern Massachusetts. After laying out the field, the students and I measure and hand-dig four one-meter deep holes for the goal posts. With Holy our driver, two volunteer students and I take the school's bus into Somanya to find and purchase eighty feet of pipe in four sections for the goals. The pipe alone costs nearly $500, and is too long to put inside the bus, so we strap it to the roof. On the way back to Mmofra Trom, we track down and hire two welders, who load their equipment into our bus. As the welders cut and weld the pipe to FIFA regulation size, I notice that neither of them is wearing eyewear to protect them from the bright welding arcs.

Another of the course highlights is an excursion to the monkey sanctuary Tafi Atome, in eastern Ghana. As we travel on a dark road to Ho in the Volta region, I try to keep the students' interest by sharing a recent true story. On a gloomy night not unlike the present one, bandits felled trees onto this lonely road in order to block traffic. When the logs forced vehicles to stop, the bandits emerged from the forest and robbed the travelers, many of whom were foreign tourists. The students don't appreciate this story. Thankfully, they are optimistic young people. When we arrive safely in Tafi Atome and feed bananas to the monkeys, they forget all about the bandits.

We also travel to Cape Coast, stopping at Mabel's Table for

a formidable lunch and close-up visit to the violent riptides along the Gulf of Guinea, where the students collect shells. At Cape Coast University, we meet Foster Frempong, a geography graduate student whom I have hired to provide a "living lecture" of the city. Foster is gentle, timid, and soft spoken, and has difficulty maintaining the attention of our students. They struggle to understand Foster's English, which is actually his second language, as I later clarify to the students.

Generally, my class responds well to the many challenges. Every group is different, but in this pack, the women are strong and the men are less so. The women embrace the struggles of heat, humidity, and being surrounded by friendly but sometimes overbearing Ghanaians. The men in our group seem to avoid all possible discomforts. They are just a bunch of rich kids mainly from poor countries, plus one college football player with US roots. They seem less interested in Ghana. They pass up amazing optional activities including a mountain hike in Shai Hills Game Reserve where we encounter an enormous baby python. Later in the week, as the men sleep in after a late night out, the rest of us enjoy a pleasant early morning cruise on Lake Volta. There is some dissent on the part of one male student in particular, who tries unsuccessfully to turn the others against me. My role is to line up opportunities for the students. After all, they are adults as well as someone else's kids, so I cannot force them to do anything just because I think it might be worthwhile. Even Africa for Beginners is not for the faint of heart. My advice to visitors to Ghana is to embrace opportunities; be prepared for everything, and don't resist getting hot, sweaty, and dirty.

Six years later, I'm going back to Ghana to collect data for a research project that should result in two academic papers. As fellow geographers, Foster and I have remained in touch since my trip with students, and as second author I helped him publish some of his own research in *Tourism Studies*. In our current work, we are interested in what attracts people to Ghana and what barriers they face in getting there, as well as the economic, social, and environmental impacts of their visits in the eyes of Ghanaians. Tired of being the trail boss on so many adventures, I ask Foster to plan our five days together and make all the arrangements.

Again in the arrivals hall of Accra-Kotoka International Airport, this time I'm greeted by Foster. I'm pleased to see that his fiancée Paulina is waiting in the passenger's seat of the Hyundai Santa Fe that he had shipped from New Jersey to Ghana a couple of years ago. They are getting married in May, but I didn't realize I'd have the chance to meet her on this trip. Foster hands a liter of chilled water to me in the back seat and says, "You must be thirsty, Prof." "Please, Foster, we're friends and research partners… call me Joel, and thanks for the water."

It is dark out as Foster drives purposefully away from the airport. I don't remember such an elaborate highway anywhere in Ghana, and I remember a younger Foster who behaved more timidly than this driver. The four lane is just like one you would see in the USA or Europe, except that our vehicle must compete with assorted other users such as pedestrians, bicycles, and animals, and even some cars driving in the wrong direction on the shoulders. When I comment on the new highway, Foster explains that it was named to honor George W. Bush for his contributions to Ghana.

Within a half hour of the airport, Foster's Santa Fe suddenly knocks into a near-standstill in the fast lane, and loud banging ensues from the front axle. Foster calmly moves to the side of the road, and we both step onto the busy highway's shoulder to take a look using his cell phone light. Unable to identify the problem, Foster phones his brother Augustine, who in turn calls his personal mechanic. The mechanic arrives to drive the Santa Fe the rest of the way to Nsawam, and the rest of us ride in Augustine's Chinese version of a Nissan Frontier/Navara pickup truck. I am informed that our new driver is actually *Father* Augustine, priest of St. Joseph the Worker Catholic Church in

Adoagyiri-Nsawam.

We arrive at St. Joseph's church, and Father Augustine directs me to the rectory, where he has vacated his bedroom for me. The room features a wide-screen TV and a surround sound system, and the walls are covered with pictures—equally allocated to Jesus and the Frempong family, the parents of which are visibly very proud of their son Father Augustine.

In the morning, while Foster deals with the mechanics, Augustine takes me to visit a rehabilitation center for amputees, complete with a workshop for making and adapting prosthetics. We then travel to a medical clinic, where scores of women and children are queued up to be seen. At the end, I am introduced to the director of the latter, who asks Father Augustine if he has asked me about "sponsorship". Ah—so THIS is what the visits are about! I shake the director's hand and bid him farewell respectfully, later to leave a small donation with Foster for his brother to use as he sees fit.

The mechanic is unsuccessful at fixing Foster's car problem. "Prof, please collect your suitcase and backpack," says Foster. Augustine drives the three of us to the roadside of the Accra-Kumasi highway, and Foster directs me to wait in the shade with his fiancée Paulina while he attempts to hail a ride to Kumasi. As we wait, Foster purchases and hands me a fresh bottle of chilled water. After twenty minutes, a tro tro finally pulls off the highway and stops in front of Foster. As it does, a dozen women laden with boxes and platforms on their heads converge upon the vehicle, offering water and snacks to its twenty-or-so passengers. After five minutes of negotiation with the "passenger-getter," who in turn interacts with the driver, Foster gestures to me and Paulina to board the bus. The driver opens the back doors so that we can stuff our bags—including laptops—under the already packed rear seat of the tro tro. The back row passengers willingly lift their feet to make a bit more space.

The tro tro is full of scorching, dusty air and sweaty passengers, including a gorgeous baby boy and his proud parents.

As expected, there is no air conditioning. This is more of an observation than a complaint. Thirty minutes into the drive, we approach our first police checkpoint and slow down for a vehicle inspection. The four armed officers don't notice the white guy at first, but when they do, they gesture the driver to stop, and direct me to get out of the van. Foster does the same; I'm not sure if they know we're traveling together, or if Foster decides to go along to protect me. Our bags are searched, and I receive a thorough pat-down that probably warrants a tip. For some reason, I'm not worried. I don't have any contraband to hide. I'm pretty confident in the rule of law in Ghana, even though I'm sure the policemen could probably use some "coffee money." When finished molesting me, the police nod to each other in agreement that this white guy is no threat to society. The interaction concludes to everyone's satisfaction, and we climb back on board our trusty ride. The sliding door slams shut, and nobody says a word. The passengers are all entranced by a Ghanaian film preview called *Devil Voice 2 and 3*, which the onboard VCR plays over and over again.

As night falls, Foster requests our tro tro to stop on a busy street on the east side of Kumasi. We grab our luggage and Foster hails a cab. The fare is too high for Foster, so he waves the driver away and hails another. The three of us climb in, then ride over unpaved residential streets in the dark, dodging potholes, children, and dogs. The only light is from our headlights, dim streetlights, and trash burning in the street.

Our taxi pulls up to a building with a gate. Wow—I am pleasantly surprised. Foster jumps out to unlock the gate, and the cab drives across the deep drain and into the courtyard. The apartment is sparingly decorated but tidy. There are two bedrooms, a living room, a study, and a kitchen in the back, which is divided from the neighbors' kitchen by a temporary wall. I will be comfortable here. Most importantly, I am relieved to have survived the tro tro "ride of certain death." This is no time for me to feign temperance. I offer a nightcap to Foster and Paulina, who dilute the Johnny Walker Red I provide with Coca-Cola.

I awaken to the sound of a rooster crowing, a baby crying, and a mother singing beautifully to try to sooth the baby's pain, probably from teething. Shortly, Foster knocks on my door and invites me to come to the living room for hot Nescafé and Milo, a chocolate drink. And then, my inevitable morning routine: shave, poop, and shower. As I was warned, there is no running water. I flush the toilet by pouring in a bucket of water, drawn from the large trash can in the hallway. My damn hair is too long to wash easily with a bucket; I'd never get the soap out. So I splash on some water from the bucket, apply a little more gel, and I'm good to go.

Cleaned up and ready for a day at the Kwame Nkrumah University of Science and Technology (KNUST), I watch Joy News on the flat screen in the living room as I await further instructions from Foster and Paulina. The top stories are about missing Malaysian Airlines 777, which disappeared the day I flew to Ghana, and a deadly accident on the Accra-Kumasi road. A coach bus collided head-on with a tractor trailer yesterday. Now that I hear the report, I recall seeing the smashed-in vehicles on the road side. Five were killed and dozens injured, including a Ghanaian movie star and a national team soccer player.

At KNUST, I meet Foster's colleagues and students, then sit in on three of his classes: one statistics lecture and two tourism classes. The students are well-dressed, well-groomed, well-prepared, respectful, and eager to learn. Foster is also prepared and happy to be in charge; he teaches authoritatively and confidently.

We return to Foster's place after eleven hot hours at the university. The few streetlights—normally dim by my American standards—are off. I remember it being dark here last night, but not this dark. Foster unlocks the door and enters the house to turn on the lights. No electricity. No problem. I'm up for this. Day 1: breakdown, day 2: no water, day 3: no electricity.

I cannot wait to see what happens tomorrow! I break out some granola bars and scotch, and walk with Foster and Paulina in the dark, dusty streets to buy pre-paid cards for their cell phones.

Foster makes phone calls as Paulina and I converse, discussing our respective days. I met far too many nice people today to remember, so I'm afraid their names will blend together: Amos, Ebenezer, Jacob, Eric, Esther, Samuel, Robert, Pinto, and Josephine…how will I put names to their faces if I see them again?

Day 4 begins with Nescafé and a shot of evaporated milk. We're going to Cape Coast today, but as one might guess, Foster's car is still getting fixed. As I was having my bucket shower, Foster already trolled the neighborhood for a reasonably-priced taxi. This cab is emphatically not roadworthy, but the driver is young and cool. He explains that because of heavy traffic on the Kumasi highway, he will take a detour through a largely Muslim slum. I feel rather insecure as the white guy in the back seat of the taxi, as I see people on the streets staring at me, probably making assumptions. I shake my head just enough for my shades to fall from the top of my head onto my nose, and my hair falls forward over my eyes for good measure. I'm safe now.

Kumasi is about the size of Accra, but seems larger and more chaotic. We get out of the cab at the Kumasi bus station, and I'm comforted to see a fleet of clean red VIP buses. I follow Foster as he walks purposefully right past them. Confused, I stand by feeling stupid as he negotiates in the Twi language with some apparently random people on the street. These are the "passenger-getters" for some vehicle that I just can't wait to see. I'm thinking in expletives now; words I refuse to utter out loud. "F&S%. He's trying to save 50 cents, and we're both going to die because of it. F&S%, what the hell!" I'm relieved when Foster ushers me on board a nearly-full air-conditioned van. By luck of the draw I get the seat with the fender hump, and I curl up comfortably in the fetal position, squeezed so tightly around my backpack that I cannot even access its contents.

We sit and wait, then wait some more. All the while, the motor is running and the air conditioner is blasting slightly cool air our way. "Just wondering, Foster, what time do we leave?" "As soon as the tro tro is full, Prof," he responds.

One hour and fifty minutes later, our twenty-fourth passenger finally appears, so we are free to depart on a five hour ride to Cape Coast. The roads are slightly better than between here and Accra, and the driver is slightly safer. And there is air conditioning. As we pass through towns and villages, I am in awe. I take covert photos of people outside the window, trying not to offend anyone by getting seen with my camera out.

If one considers the Trans-Atlantic Slave Trade, Cape Coast is probably the African city most closely associated with this shameful human era. One of Ghana's most prominent universities is located in Cape Coast also, where Foster did his Master's degree. We arrive on the well-manicured campus and greet his favorite professor, Professor Kofi, whom I've met before. As a Kofi, he was also born on a Friday. Straightaway the professor invites us to spend the night at his house. I am embarrassed. I am dressed to travel, in sandals, my plaid shorts, and a t-shirt. I have no better clothes in my small backpack. Covered in sweat and mosquito spray, I haven't washed my hair since leaving New Hampshire four days ago. But there is no choice but to accept his generous gesture. Foster informs the professor that we will take a taxi to his house after we complete our surveys in Cape Coast.

At a restaurant across from St. George's Castle, we identify some foreigners as potential candidates for our surveys. I approach them as Foster seeks Ghanaian service providers to interview. I feel as though we should buy something from people who are helping us, but I'm overruled by Foster, who correctly reminds me that if we buy a drink from one respondent for helping us out, we'll need to buy from everyone.

As I wait for a German lady to fill out a survey, suddenly my stomach begins to turn. Within minutes, I am in a desperate situation. I realize what the challenge of Day 4 is. I ate fresh fruit confidently yesterday. I'm confident now too—suddenly confident enough to search out a stall in a public restroom in Africa. The washrooms (as they call them in Ghana) are downstairs. Men's room is to the left. Thankfully, nobody is in there. There are two stalls, but damn, both of them are locked. I glance under the door. Nobody is there. Damn! I'm in a tight spot. Out in the hallway, I notice through the open door that nobody is in the women's room. There are two stalls there also. Without hesitation, I enter one and barely get into position in time for the inevitable. Unbelievable. I am so fortunate this didn't hit during the five hour bus ride! Now I just need to get out of the women's room stall without being seen. I attempt to flush. There's no water. The F-word slips out. Precisely at that moment, *knock-knock* is the sound on the stall door, just inches from my face. What should I do? I can't feign a woman's voice, and the restaurant isn't very busy—I'm sure someone saw me go downstairs. My impulse is to respond with the same *knock-knock* to let the intruder know there's a lady in here. After we repeat this interchange, I hear his footsteps walk away. Confident that he is gone, I emerge from the stall. Much to my embarrassment, he is waiting in the hallway with his tool kit, prepared to fix something—maybe the water supply. Not knowing what to do, I enter the men's room and knock on the locked empty stalls, shrugging, then gesturing to him that I had an emergency. The worst part is that I need to remain in the very same restaurant for another hour until our respondents complete their surveys, and neither of us even buys anything. The traveler's diarrhea behaves for another hour or so… until we arrive at the professor's house.

Professor Kofi and his wife Josephine live in a beautiful home overlooking the town of Cape Coast and the Gulf of Guinea. It took them seven years to build it. They are incredibly hospitable hosts, and offer an excellent dinner of boiled plantains, cassava, and tilapia with tomato sauce. Sadly, I feel sick and I have no appetite; it's very difficult for me to eat anything. The saving grace is that I thought to stop to buy the hosts a bottle of wine on the way here, and that takes the edge off. I am humbled to be a guest in this home, and embarrassed about my limited wardrobe and current condition. How thrilled I am when I find out I have my own guest room with a washroom and shower. Still, even after four exhausting days and nights of hard traveling, I still have trouble sleeping.

Our tro tro trip back to Kumasi is long and hot; nearly identical to the ride here, but without the novelty of terra incognita. On my final day in Kumasi, Foster and I visit the city center, the zoo, and a cultural center, where I obtain some excellent Ghanaian handicrafts. As we shop, Foster explains that his brother Father Augustine invited me to stay over at the church again, then he offered to take me to Kotoka for my flight tomorrow night. I thank him, but firmly insist that I must stay at a hotel near the airport on my final night. After many rough nights with a head full of traffic, I need a chance to stretch out, rest, and shower before my twenty-four hour trip back to New Hampshire. I am distracted by things at work, and I need time to think and write things down before thrusting myself headlong back into a busy semester and home life. Graciously, Foster says he understands, and tells me he will get me to the station and put me on a comfortable bus.

The VIP bus to Accra from Kumasi is air conditioned, but the ride is six hours long, dusty, and bumpy. As we approach Accra that evening, I ask a female passenger where to alight for a taxi to the airport, as I know my hotel is nearby. She is headed for the airport, so we agree to share a cab. As I get into the taxi, I tell the young driver I have only 25 Ghana cedis left, and ask him if that will be enough to get us both where we're going, which he affirms. After we drop the woman at the terminal, I discover that my driver does not know this part of town, cannot understand the map I show him, or cannot read at all. On top of that, he doesn't have a phone to call the hotel. An hour later, and after pulling over several times for me to ask directions to the hotel, he's still driving me around the city, as lost as I am. Aware that he cannot keep driving me around for free, I ask nicely at first, then demand resolutely to return to the airport terminal, where I will call for the hotel's free shuttle. He stubbornly refuses to let me out of the car and eventually— miraculously— delivers me to my hotel. Embarrassed that it's my last cash, I hand the driver all 25 of my remaining Ghana cedis as he lifts my suitcase out of the taxi's dented truck. I'll be back in my comfort zone momentarily, but Africa's harsh realities go on and on.

Sometimes when I'm in Ghana, I wake up deep in the night, physically and mentally disturbed. It's close to 100 degrees Fahrenheit and humid, and there's no air conditioning. I am dirty, itchy, sweaty, and I haven't washed my hair in four days because this week there is no running water in the building. I have diarrhea from something I ate yesterday, and no food I can buy tastes good to me right now. I'm sluggish, and I can't help but wonder if I might have picked up malaria or some other tropical disease. Woe is me—I'll need to live like this a few more days. Then I think about the millions of people outside, many of whom have no real roof over their heads, nor indoor plumbing, let alone electricity or air conditioning. There are many arguments about how things got this way in Africa, and many of them are plausible, at least as partial explanations.

Being in Africa makes me want to tell everybody in North America how fortunate they are—rich or poor. Your parents knew it and told you about it, although they probably never experienced Africa for themselves. If you think your lot in life sucks, or things could be better, you might be right. But in this world if you are American or European, you are among the fortunate minority. Use your passport to check out the way most people live. An American or European passport is the most important tangible item anyone can possess. Everyone who can do so should get themselves a passport and use it to go abroad, not just to Caribbean resorts and London. Take a tro tro through the countryside of a developing country, or take a meal in a local chop bar. With your passport, you can go to any place and return safely to your comfortable home. Your passport is the key to appreciating physical comfort, abundance, and unlimited opportunity by going to places where difficult to find. These are things that we in a handful of rich countries far too often take for granted, yet most human beings will never know.

11

NASHUA LAMPOON'S ZOOROPA[xxi]: EUROPE WITH KIDS[xxii]

Today, June 20th, is Karen's birthday. As she and I race to prepare to take the kids on their first family adventure in Europe, I take a moment to glance in her direction and appreciate how fortunate I am to have her as life partner. This trip has been an enormous undertaking already, and we haven't even left home yet! I hope we didn't forget anything while packing for three kids, ages ten, eight, and six. The morning of our departure, it is painful for us to drop off our yearling puppy-love Tessie for two weeks with friends, but she will be well attended to by their gentlemanly golden retriever Hercules.

This family trip to Europe is designed to be very lean, financially speaking. I got all five of our plane tickets with award points, and our rule of thumb for hotels is to spend no more than 100 Euros ($130)/night. We'll eat only one sit-down restaurant meal per day, and we'll rely mainly on public transportation. The objective is straightforward: I want to show my family four parts of Central Europe over two weeks, and so I've planned a trip that will allow them to sample these distinct areas, which I refer to as travel "phases:" I. The Rhein; II. Bavaria, III. Bohemia, and IV. Berlin. This involves more traveling than most people would want to do, but I don't know when—or indeed if—I will have such an opportunity again, so I want to maximize what I show them. But is Europe with three kids really a good idea?

Right now, life is rushed like never before. I've been traveling for work and pleasure, we all just finished school, and Karen has a job interview today. I make some last minute hotel reservations the morning of our departure, and then pre-pay for Bavaria's Neuschwanstein castle tour tickets. We cannot print our hotel vouchers or ticket confirmations because the details are still "pending." After loading our suitcases into the car's trunk, I take the kids with me to Bentley to finish some work. Karen meets us there after her job interview. We share a ride to Boston Logan and make our 3:20pm flight to JFK. At her JFK departure gate, Karen hugs me and the kids and we wish one another a safe flight. Karen will fly to Frankfurt with Singapore Airlines, and I will take the kids on Delta. We fly separately because all of our points on two different airlines were necessary to make this trip possible. As the parent most comfortable flying to Germany, I get to take the kids *with me*!

As Karen boards her flight, I give her my travel journal, inviting her to "guest author" if she feels so inclined. As for my flight, the kids will keep me busy. And with that explanation, I introduce Karen, my dear wife of fourteen years:

When I boarded I was greeted by beautiful flight attendants wearing intricately wrapped skirt uniforms. One of whom gave me a water bottle, and another guided me to my seat. Those attendants didn't stop working the entire flight. I had the window seat at an emergency exit, but the door slide stuck out about a foot so I didn't have room for my left leg. I ended up sleeping most of the flight—that was a nice surprise. I had very good food but did not opt for the "dog spread." I also had my first Singapore Sling. It was very tasty and useful for bringing on drowsiness.

I was very proud of my independence as I followed the baggage claim signs. But then I experienced a sudden

*change in blood pressure when I handed my passport to
the customs agent. He said, "Ah...Frau Deichmann...
your passport is not valid!" (I forgot to sign it). Fortunately,
rather than deporting me he allowed me to sign it on the
spot. When I exited into the arrivals hall, I was so happy to
see the kids, who were waiting there to greet me.*

The kids do well on their first flight of this duration, but the
most important bag is not here yet. It's Jack's bag containing
his beloved "bean bag" (sleeping bag), car seat, and everyone's
Oscar Mayer Lunchables snacks, which I bought for the flights
but had to gate check. After waiting a reasonable amount of
time, we put in a report with Lufthansa and request that the
bag be delivered to our hotel in nearby Mainz.

Maybe it's the German blood in me that causes me to put
things into boxes, trips included. In the interest of regional
coherence, I planned this trip in four phases, having explained
them to Karen and the kids at the beginning to elevate their
enthusiasm.

Phase I is "The Rhine," beginning with Mainz. We take the
Schnellbahn (fast train, or "S-Bahn") number 8 from Frankfurt
Flughafen (airport) to nearby Mainz. In Mainz, Karen and I
drag our bags and children around the puddles and through the
driving rain and check in at Hotel Königshof, directly across
from the *Hauptbahnhof* (main rail station). I never stayed here
before, but the location is great and it fits our budget at $100
per night. Karen and I get our tired and hungry kids ready for
a nap, and I run outside to the street to buy a few *Bretzl* (large
soft pretzels) and *Bier* to wash down the trail dust. She and I
decompress as the kids nap.

After some rest, we follow our plan to explore Mainz by foot,
including the Römergasse, Altstadt (Old Town), and the Rhine
waterfront. The kids are not used to European walking, but
ice cream at Café am Dom seems to give Charlie and Isabela
some life. Unfortunately, Jack falls asleep at the outdoor table

and the rest of us have to finish his ice cream. I have no choice but to lug Jack all the way across Mainz and back to our hotel. Even though I'm tired, it brings me pleasure to walk with my family and carry my own youngest son along the streets of the city where I lived as a young adult. I remember how badly I wanted the very situation that has become my reality: to have a beautiful wife and family, and to have the means to return to Europe with them.

Unaccustomed to crossing so many time zones, the kids get cozy quickly and go directly to sleep. Although Jack is awake again and pining for his trusty "bean bag" (sleeping bag), his resistance is no match for the power of slumber. As Karen watches the kids, I go out again to buy us some takeout herring sandwiches at Nordsee, a German fast food chain that serves raw pickled fish on fresh crusty rolls.

When I return with the food, Karen overrules my habitual attempt to check out what's on television. So, we sit together on the bed of our hotel room sipping Bitburger Pils, quietly comparing our separate flight experiences and watching our children sleep in the dim light. I'm beaming inside because I am able to be here in my beloved city of Mainz with my entire family. Thank you, Rotary, for exposing me to this enchanting place twenty years ago! My mind is full of happy thoughts. It still seems that for me, the chance to study abroad in 1987 defied all odds: a self-conscious farm kid of modest means embarks on an improbable adventure, and that short experience continues to drive my *Passion for Place*.

The next day is our first complete day in Europe, but I promised everyone there will be no alarm clocks for us. I give a miss to the Rhine river trip and winetasting in Rüdesheim because the ship was scheduled to leave Mainz at 8:30 am, which would have been 2:30 am Boston time for our jetlagged kids. We sleep to our hearts' content, then have breakfast. As we explore more of Mainz today, the weather is cool, cloudy, and at times leaky. Little Jack is dressed in short sleeves, so we search for a place to buy him a sweatshirt. Not only has Jack's suitcase been lost in transit, but he left his navy blue fleece jacket in his airplane seat, where it must have blended in with the blue Delta blankets. As the day goes on, Isabela and Jack develop coughs; I really didn't expect this predicament in June.

We return to the *Altstadt* (Old City), where Karen and I are able to email our parents from an internet café to let them know we landed safely in Germany. We then visit Mainz's famous and imposing *Dom* (Cathedral) and enjoy a small glass of wine at Vinzerfest in the market square while the kids chew on *Bretzl*. Last night, we saw the traveling carnival midway on the Rhine riverfront, so we promised to bring the kids there today. This is the kids' first real bout with jetlag, and it's a bit of a challenge to keep them enthused. Charlie begs me to try a ride called the Virus with him. The 360 degree ride looks like it will test my upper limits, but I acquiesce because I hope it will also pay dividends in making me a cool dad. I wonder if Charlie feels like I do… unsettled as we await blast off. While riding, I experience déjà vu. I realize I did this same ride here in Mainz as an eighteen year-old in 1988.

I guide Karen and the kids onto Tram #5 to Mainz's suburb of Gonsenheim. My memory barely passes the test to find the correct stop. We arrive at Beers just in time for dinner, which is fortunate because *Pünktlichkeit ist die Höflichkeit der Könige* (punctuality is the politeness of kings). It has been thirteen years since Karen and I retreated from Central Europe to wash our clothes with a hose in this same backyard, hanging them out to air dry. Steffi, Susana (Susi), and Sabine—all three host sisters—are present to belatedly celebrate Mutti Beer's 65th birthday. Steffi and her husband Stefan are here with their four kids: Max, Konstantin, Anna, and Johanna. Susi lives in Stuttgart with her husband and their daughter Julia, and another child is on the way. Sabine is visiting alone; she explains to me that she got married to Christian just this year. At the end of a fantastic reunion with my second host family, Karen, the kids and I squeeze into two cars— driven by Stefan and Sabine— and return to our hotel. Thankfully, the airline delivered Jack's "beanbag," so he'll sleep like a baby tonight.

Today is Saturday, and Karen and the "LBKs" (little blonde kids) pack up our room. Charlie and I walk farther than I had planned to pick up our rental car, which we will keep for three days on Phase II of our trip: Bavaria. It turns out that the rental place is 3km from our hotel, and it also turns out that I erroneously made the reservation for our initial arrival on Thursday, which was two days ago and before we even landed in Germany! The Germans couldn't have made that mistake! Now, the only car available is an Opel—a sort of mini version of a minivan with a standard transmission. This mini-mini vehicle has a mini spare tire on one rear wheel and a flat tire on the normal wheel, which is sitting in the trunk. It's the only car available, and it's big enough for the five of us, so there is really no choice but to rent it.

This is my first time driving in Germany, but I am happy to be on the move and comfortable after just a few minutes. By noon, we are finally on the Autobahn out of Mainz, headed in the direction of Bodensee (in English known as Lake Constance).

The Eckes are my third German host family from 1988, and their vacation home is in Dingelsdorf on Bodensee. Driving from Mainz, we reach Dingelsdorf at 4:30. We meet my host brother Maximilian, his wife Federica, and their baby son Alessandro. We've left the rain behind, and now it's a beautiful evening. Federica and Max's delightful friend Cynthia ("Chinsee-uh") is a surprise guest. It is so good to see Max again. He and I hang with my older kids, while the girls swoon over Alessandro, Max and Federica's adorable little baby.

The adults watch the "Black Pearl" on the lake, which in this case is a yellow paddle boat. We listen to the kids playing out scenes from *Pirates of the Caribbean*. Charlie becomes Jack Sparrow, Isabela is Elizabeth, and Jack is William Turner. At first, Karen and I are nervous about our kids going out so far onto the big lake, but gradually with Max's reassurances she and I relax—there is no real danger. Speedboat traffic is minimal, the waves are small, and the water is shallow here. Max has a phenomenal prepared mixed grill meal delivered to the lake house. The feast at hand, fabulous company, and spectacular view of the lake will forever remain in our memories.

We sleep through sunrise on Sunday morning, having finally adjusted to the local clock. Karen goes to Catholic Mass with the Eckes in Litzelstetten, the next village. Cynthia relaxes in the sun while I sit on the deck reading the newspaper. I watch my kids as they paddle out into the lake again. We've been to plenty of churches on this trip already, and anyway the kids wouldn't understand Mass *auf Deutsch*.

When Karen, Max, and Federica return from Mass, Eckes' yacht appears magically at our dock, and Max becomes our skipper to Meersburg via the small lake villages of Birnau and Minau. We stop to tour the historic castle, built by King Dagobert I in the 7th century. My boys marvel at the knights' armor adorning the ancient rooms. Afterwards, Karen photographs the village's architecture, red tile roofs, and colorful window box flowers. Cynthia treats us all to gelato, which for me and Max turns out to be beer. The weather on Lake Constance is idyllic as we travel back across to the dock. Cynthia bids farewell to us and heads for her home in Switzerland. Shortly thereafter, Max departs for Munich so that he'll be in position for work in the morning. Karen, the kids, and I stay one final evening with Federica and Alessandro.

Feeling guilty about still being here, Karen and I take care to help Federica put things away on Monday morning so that the cleaners can do their thing. We get the car loaded and leave quickly to avoid getting in the way. I neglect to make time to study my map sufficiently before getting behind the wheel. While driving, I make an off-the-cuff decision to circumnavigate the lake counterclockwise in order to pass through a swath of Switzerland and Austria on the way to Neuschwanstein in Bavaria. The thought of taking the kids to two additional countries on this trip is simply irresistible to me.

Why the rush? Just before leaving Nashua, I purchased online tickets for a Neuschwanstein Castle tour for any available time slot after noon; however, at the time of our departure from Boston, we still hadn't received an email confirmation and exact time for this must-do tour. We thought we could check our status on Max's computer, but alas, the computer was *kaput*. So, we are still in the dark about whether we even have a tour appointment, but we need to be in position for any afternoon time slot because pre-payment was required for a reservation.

Through magnificent scenery under clearing skies, we race toward King Ludwig's fanciful castle. We pull off the road at Linburg so that I can check the map. It's raining, so Karen takes this opportunity to quickly buy an umbrella. I am tired of driving, and I'm starting to question the logic of hiring a car rather than simply traveling by train. I reassure myself that getting Karen and the kids to Neuschwanstein will be worth the effort, and the castle is not easily reached by train. We arrive by 4pm to check in, and manage to get on the 5:45pm tour—the final one of the day! The kids deserve kudos, as they assault the hill on the arduous trail. Upon our arrival at the castle gate, we realize we still have an hour to wait. The kids are exhausted, so I use my most polite German to ask the gatekeeper lady if we can jump onto an earlier English-speaking tour. "*Ja, freilich*" (yes, of course) she responds in her cheerful Bavarian dialect.

Neuschwanstein is a Romanesque revival palace built by King Ludwig II in the late 19th century, not as a defensive fortification, but rather as an architectural icon. The short tour of this colorful and storied castle is indeed worth the effort on all of our parts. Fortunately, Jack only needs a piggyback ride a short part of the way. The tour ends in King Ludwig's spectacular ballroom. We exit through the castle's kitchen and requisite gift shop. We reward the kids with Fanta and *Bretzl*; Karen and I have Bier and *Wurst* (sausage). After taking a break from our feet, we make our way downhill to the car for the long four- to five-hour drive northwestward back to Frankfurt.

It feels like we are racing to keep up with the sunset on the drive to Frankfurt; the sun keeps reappearing between intermittent spells of clouds and heavy rain. I am tired, and concerned because my entire family is in this small car riding on wet roads on a spare tire. Energized just enough—maybe by fear of death—I carry on toward *Mainhattan*[xxiii] to complete the drive and put us into position for our 8:54pm train to Prague. It's about 11pm, and we don't have a hotel reservation. I stop at a gas station to refill the car, which we need to return to the airport in the morning before catching our train. I ask at the gas station where I might find inexpensive basic accommodations for a family, and obtain a fantastic suggestion just down the road: Motel One.

There is absolutely no problem finding our way to Motel One. The glitzy lights compensate for the lack of clarity in driving directions. The gas station lady tried to give them to me in dreadful English, and I didn't want to offend her by switching to her language. I do hope that my German is somewhat better. Motel One is a bright, neon-signed, run-of-the-mill German budget motel, where a clean, simple room costs 59 Euros ($83). Prayers of thanksgiving for safe passage rise from our room to the dark sky above Frankfurt. We survived hours of fatigued, rainy, crazy-with-trucks Autobahn travel in a mini-minivan with a mini tire. This certainly cannot be a vacation for me if I need to drive anymore. Tomorrow, we will surrender our car keys and begin traveling by train!

On Tuesday, we are up at 6am and out by 7am. I return our rental car at Frankfurt *Flughafen* (airport). As Hertz promised, we aren't required to pay a drop fee, even though I had picked the car up thirty kilometers away in Mainz. With ease, I find coffee and snacks for the family's train ride before going downstairs to the *Flughafen's* train station. I just love German intermodalism; everything here makes sense to me! Happily caffeinated and fed, we board our train and depart on time at 8:54am.

I admire the kids' excitement as they look out the window at Frankfurt's disappearing skyline. We are all enjoying the kids' first train ride in Europe. We have a scheduled train-change in Nürnberg, which normally would be no problem; however, after the conductor checked our family ticket leaving Frankfurt, we seem to have misplaced it. I took the ticket out a couple of times to study it and explain its specifics to the kids. I must have put it back in the top of Karen's bag without re-closing her zipper. The train jolted once while Karen was asleep, and Karen's bag dumped out on the floor. Either the ticket fell out then, or I folded it into the first train's *Fahrplan* (itinerary) and left it there, on the train. Whatever happened to our ticket, it's gone now. There will be a twenty-five minute layover in Nürnberg, and I'd better think fast about replacing it. I don't want to risk delaying our arrival in Prague, where Tomáš will meet us on the station's platform. The moment we arrive at the Nürnberg station, I reluctantly fork out 85 Euros ($120) for the second and final leg of this trip. This turns out to have been a good decision, as the new ticket is checked by both German and Czech controllers as we cross the border. We arrive in Prague only a few minutes late, challenging my beloved expression that "in Germany, the trains run on time."

Tomáš and I help Karen and the kids down from the train's high steps and into Phase III: Prague. Prague is my favorite city in the world, and it contains some of my favorite people, although none of them are actually originally from Prague. Having been spared from destruction in World War II, the Old Town is full of architectural masterpieces, and this rainy weather will only enhance this place's ambience. I hope the kids like it, but first they'll need to overcome initial impressions of Praha Hlavní Nádraží, the main train station, and its sketchy surroundings.

Tomáš leads this American-looking American family through what he calls "Sherwood Forest." He explains this is the local nickname for the "park of thieves and bums" in front of the train station. We use Žižkov Tram #9, then alight near Cahlíks' flat on Borijova, just two stops up the hill. Dinner is a sauerkraut-based goulash, which pleases the adults and scares the kids. Charlie (10) hits it off very well with Vojta (12), and Isabela really likes the teenage girls Jana, Zuzana, and Marketa. Tomáš hands me and Karen two 90 minute transport passes and he and Ivana insist that we go out as a couple to see some of Prague. "Joel knows Prague like a local, and the kids will be fine" Tomáš assures Karen. Our marching orders take us by surprise, but of course we oblige gleefully. Our short getaway takes us to Charles Bridge and ends with a quick overpriced drink at a bistro in Old Town Square. For the first time on this trip, Karen and I are actually outdoors to see darkness fall upon Europe! As we sip our red wine, we admire the lighted Týnski Church and Old Town Hall. It is so good to catch our breath. We reflect upon the past few days, appreciating our first return to Prague together, thirteen years after we discovered this magical city.

Our first full day in Prague begins with a quick stop at the Hlavní Nádraží station to purchase three-day transportation passes and let the kids expend energy at the playground in Sherwood Forest. This new playground features replicas of eight of Prague's most famous landmarks. I lead us to Wallenstein Gardens, which I discovered for the first time on the most recent (May) short-term program with students. I recall that it was hot and sunny. The kids enjoy hiding in the hedge rows. "Do you know what they call those bushes in Paris?" I ask Charlie. "No Dad, what do they call them in Paris?" "*Pissoires.*" Exiting the gardens, we hike up the hill to the Prague Castle, stopping for pizza at Restaurant Tusco. The hill can be strenuous, but thankfully (or not—I do prefer the sun), this time the weather remains cool and mostly cloudy. Prague Castle is a big hit with the kids.

My intention for the next day is to show my family Český

Krumlov, a UNESCO World Heritage village nestled in a South Bohemian stream meander. However, this gives way to better judgment as I hear my mother's voice in my head saying "Joel, sometimes less is more." Český Krumlov not easily reachable by train, and I really don't want to drive again. Moreover, the best deal I could find for one night of family accommodation is 670 Kc ($320). Anyway, there's still plenty to see in Prague.

Jana Cahlíkova joins us to visit the Czech National Museum in the morning. After lunch, the weather is cool and wet and it just feels like a good "movie day." Karen suggests that we reinforce the kids' enthusiasm for pirate adventures that we witnessed at Bodensee, so we take them to see *Pirates of the Caribbean III: At World's End*. Jana hasn't seen it, so we invite her to join us. The movie is a letdown for the adults, but Charlie is visibly enraptured. After that, we hike to Petřín Hill, which has as its centerpiece a 63.5 meter tower built in 1891 to resemble the Eiffel Tower. As a major downpour begins, we take refuge in the Maze of Mirrors, a nearby indoor children's labyrinth.

We've been staying at the Cahlíks' flat, and as a small gesture of appreciation for their incredible hospitality I ask Jana to call her family and invite them to meet us for dinner. Na Klarové on the Malastrana (the Vltava River's "Lesser Bank") is one of the few restaurants in Prague that I know by name because I've eaten there many times with my students. Even better, Cahlíks have never been there. After dinner, we take the subway back to Žižkov, where Tomáš negotiates a "family" tower entrance rate of 140 Kc. The elevator takes us to the 360 degree observation deck, where we witness stunning sunset panoramas of the City of a Thousand Spires, complete with a rainbow.

At the end of another full and rewarding day, we return to Borijova, where Karen and I share a second bottle of Bodensee red wine with Tomáš and Ivana. Meanwhile, the kids watch *Cheaper by the Dozen* on my laptop and fall asleep in their beds. After one week in Europe, Hollywood's familiar point of reference is a relief for the young kids, and they giggle relentlessly. That night, the nasty cough that has had Isabela in its clutches since school ended begins to spread to the rest of us.

Petr and Pavel Vacek are the two Czech brothers, slightly younger than I, who assisted me with my short term programs in Prague. Pavel, a former student of Tomáš at Charles University, also helped me collect data for a research project. Without their friendship, Prague would not have become my most-visited city outside of the United States. In the absence of professional collaboration with them, it's possible that I might never have advanced in my job. The plan was to drive to visit the Vaceks at their home in the village of Vemerovice; however, the memory of the hellish Autobahn trek is still fresh: driving in Europe is too expensive and not enough fun for me while on vacation. Once again we take the kids for exercise at Sherwood Forest playground before the trip. I put our suitcases in lockers at the main station, and Jana and Marketa help me buy tickets for the bus. Say what… a bus? This is one of the first intercity buses I've taken in Europe, and after this brutal experience I don't care to again. Thinking of the lyrics to "Synchronicity II" by The Police, the minutes tick by torturously as we spend three hours packed "like lemmings in (a) shining metal box."

Petr and his girlfriend Lucie meet us in Žamberk to pick us up. When I see Petr's small Škoda, I suddenly realize that neither he nor I had thought this plan through. All seven of us have to squeeze into the four passenger car and drive 15km to the house of Petr's mother. None of us thought of car seats, so we squeeze the kids into the car with the smallest ones on our laps.

I just can't believe Petr's house! I had been here before, but he's made improvements that I never could have imagined. He welcomes us with a *pivo*, and presents the kids with "sweeties" (Petr's preferred term for candy). In the evening, we all enjoy a refreshing stroll along Vermerovice's main road, then through a nearby meadow and up a hill into the forest. Petr, an affirmed agnostic, shows us an outdoor chapel that had been secretly built by Catholics for clandestine worship during Communist times. It features a pathway marked with the Stations of the Cross. When the Czech Communists discovered the chapel, they destroyed it immediately, but villagers restored it in 1991 after religious freedom returned. Although the Czech Republic is the most atheistic country in Europe, some (mainly the elderly) remain strong in their faith.

When the kids go to bed, Karen and I revel in a fantastic evening of eating and drinking with Petr, his mother, Lucie, and Alan the dog. Even when it is time for the fun to end, I don't want to go to bed. I just don't know how to express my appreciation for the friendly hospitality and fantastic feast of great food! As I nod off to sleep, I try to think of ways that Karen and I can raise the bar to European standards when friends and family visit our home.

After an elaborate breakfast *chez Petr et Lucie*, we return to Prague by a train that we catch in Usti nad Labem. To their delight, the kids convince us to allow them to play in Sherwood Forest for yet another hour. How odd that the nicest play gym in Prague is located in a hive of thieves and drunkards, just outside of a decrepit train station! Karen and the Cahlík girls take care of the kids while I fetch our bags from the lockers. For our train to Berlin we must transfer to Nádraží Holešovice, Prague's other international train station. In the interest of nostalgia, I remind Karen that dreary Holešovice is where she and I first alighted from a train in 1994. Put off by that station's surroundings and ignorant at the time of Prague's treasures, we nearly jumped right onto the next train leaving the City of a Thousand Spires without experiencing it. If we had done that, we certainly wouldn't be here right now.

I don't think Nádraží Holešovice has changed in the past dozen years. I position the family with our bags on the platform fifteen minutes prior to departure, then dash away to a small market just outside the station to get some supplies. I buy an assortment of drinks, snacks, and treats for the four hour train ride to Berlin.

We board our train to Berlin at 12:34pm. On the scenic trip north along the Vltava and Elbe rivers, Karen and I enjoy a few Pilsner Urquells. A rare move by this frugal traveler, I treat the kids to ice cream from the restaurant car as we approach Berlin. Our unpaid hotel reservation is guaranteed only until 6 pm, and I'm concerned about losing the room because it was difficult to find an affordable vacancy for tonight. So, I pass up my intention to show the family Berlin's incredible new *Hauptbahnhof* (main station), a spectacle of engineering built from steel and glass. Instead, we alight early and take a more direct U-Bahn route from Südkreuz to Heidelberger Platz. The escalator to daylight ushers in Phase IV of our trip: Berlin. After walking at a brisk pace, we arrive at Winters Hotel just moments before our reservation expires.

We approach the reception desk to check in. Overjoyed to be back in a country where I can speak the language, I confidently flaunt my best German: "Hello, I have a reservation for Herr Deichmann." Handing over my passport and credit card, I notice a 90 Euro (about $130) sofa bed surcharge on our bill and ask the receptionist if I can speak with the manager. Great, now I get to dispute a charge; just what we all need after traveling all day! It might be to my advantage if I can switch the conversation to English. Manager Frau Eigensinn arrives, and I raise the issue of the surcharge. On my printed reservation, the price includes a queen bed plus a sofa bed for two kids. That's all we want. I argue that 90 Euros for a third child is outrageous, especially given that it nearly doubles the price of our room. Don't these Germans have kids? What happened to the American notion that "kids stay for free" or at least that "the customer is always right?" Meanwhile, the kids are starting to melt down. Displaying her displeasure, Karen takes the room key and the kids, while I remain at the reception desk and continue my argument. I explain to Frau Eigensinn that by his own choice, Jack has been using his *Schlafsack* (sleeping bag, or as he prefers his "bean bag") on the floor this entire trip. I add that it is expensive to travel as a family and that we are not made of money. I offer to go without use of our room's kitchen, and without the breakfast that is included in the price, but I don't want to pay a 90 Euro surcharge for a bed that I didn't request and we won't use. After considerable time, she relents and switches back to German: "So, Herr Deichmann, you get your wish". I am exhausted and angry when I return to the room, but at least I "got my wish." Clearly, Karen and the kids grew bored and frustrated while waiting for me. It's also obvious that Karen does not care for the hotel's suburban location.

With Karen and the kids already pooped, at 7:30pm I drag them onto the *U-Bahn* (Underground) and to the Center of old West Berlin. We emerge from the underworld at the Kurfürstendamm stop. Karen is all hunger and no happy, and declares that she is going to get us something to eat. She leads us into the first restaurant she sees, but it turns out to be a buffet with a lot of things the kids won't eat. With all of us being tired and hungry, the trip's stress level peaks. At the risk of making the situation worse, I suggest "Hey, let's just get pizza." I win the kids over, and reassure Karen by reminding her that German pizza is excellent. Near the *Gedächtniskirche* (Memorial Church), five travelers feast on pizza and Fanta to their tummies' delight. Estimating that the downtime and food bought us some strength to carry on, I push the envelope by taking everyone on Berlin City Bus 100, which offers a quick and economical tourists' glimpse of Berlin's main attractions: the Philharmoniker, Alexanderplatz, Brandenberg Gate, the Reichstag and Victory Column, then past the Gedächtniskirche and back to Zoo Station. We return to our suburban Winters Hotel before 11:00pm. Tonight, for the first time, our kids are actually still awake to witness darkness on a trip that takes place at about 50 degrees north latitude during the summer solstice!

Karen and the kids appeal not to rush out of bed in the morning. I comply, as I'm very satisfied to have gotten the family out to see a bit of central Berlin last night. When we do get going, I suggest that the nearby German Museum of Technology would be fun, interesting, and easy on the feet. We spend at least three hours there exploring trains, planes, and boats, a few of the things Germans design very well. There is also an exhibit on the Berlin Airlift, which I enjoy explaining to the kids.

We exit the museum to find that it's still raining lightly. The weather continues to do its best to detract from this trip! After a nice hot German lunch of sausage, sauerkraut, and potatoes, we collectively decide against our planned Spree River boat tour; it's not much fun to be on the water while it's raining. Instead, we walk through Berlin's central park known as Tiergarten to the *Siegesäule* (Victory Column), and nearby Reichstag (parliament).

The German Parliament's Reichstag building is a must-see in Berlin. The dome is symbolically transparent, and citizen visitors can look down into the chamber of the Bundestag to keep watch over the politicians. Thanks to the kids, two of whom are still eight years old or less, we are permitted to use the handicapped/children entrance and elevator. Score! Although the drizzle impairs our view somewhat, the kids enjoy climbing the circular ramp to the top of the glass dome for a spectacular panorama of Berlin.

KaDeWe is shorthand for *Kaufhauf des Westens*, Europe's biggest department store, and I feel compelled to show it to Karen and the kids. Among other things, they have an excellent toy department with an enormous selection of Playmobil, as well as several electric train displays. Sadly, we arrive too late to eat dinner at the pleasant food court on the top floor. In response, we try to piece together a respectable dinner at a kiosk on Wittenberg Platz. The photo of shish-kabobs looks delicious, but alas, there aren't any left. So, it's currywurst and fries for all of us. If I never taste curry spices again in my life it will be just fine with me. To make up for our unsatisfactory meal, later on at a Turkish *döner* station near our hotel, we have some delicious kabobs, and the kids enjoy *Riesenschlangen* (big gummy snakes) for dessert.

We wake up early on Monday, our final day. We're all a bit tired of traveling. I think we're ready to go home. As the kids watch German morning cartoons, Karen shares her dissatisfaction with the location of our hotel, the weather, the food we've eaten, and Berlin in general. Why do we need to travel in the subterranean world with the U-Bahn to get anywhere? Nothing against Berlin, but she liked Bavaria and Bohemia much better. I am a little surprised and sad to hear this. When putting this trip together, I thought I was saving the most exciting city for last. Maybe I was wrong about Berlin, but at least everyone keep their chin up. At the end of the day, we stick together as a family!

After getting packed for our final day in Germany, we descend once more into the underworld to meet the U-Bahn. The Berlin Zoo—saved for last— turns out to be our best family activity in Berlin. We spend hours meeting a wide range of exotic animals. Even better than the animals, the kids love the enormous *Spielplatz* (playground) featuring a large fort, trampoline, and an ark with lots of places to climb, crawl, and slide. After a light lunch in the outdoor zoo café, our second attempt to visit KaDeWe is successful. Duly mesmerized by its magnitude, the kids aptly nickname it "the big store."

In the morning, we're up and out of our hotel early. Karen flies first with Lufthansa, and has a layover in Munich. I fly at 3:10pm with three kids directly from Berlin to JFK. We arrive at Comfort Inn near JFK, and at the kids' request I order Dominoes. Home sweet home USA! Even at $1 per can, the soft drinks in the hotel lobby soda machine seem like a bargain compared to European prices. As an experienced traveler, I had the forethought to bring two Berliner Kindl beers back with me in my suitcase for washing down the trail dust. Everyone is asleep by 7pm, long before Karen arrives at 8pm. I wake up, kiss her hello, and show her a text message I received from her sister in Atlanta: while we in Europe, Lynne gave birth to her baby Alexis Marie on the front seat of her minivan!

We're all still fighting the sore throats we took with us to rainy and cold Europe, but intermittent coughs soon give way to sleep. We are ready to be home, and the weather forecast there is phenomenal. It is nice to have a hotel room in New York for partial recovery, but we are all disappointed that we could not manage to home from Berlin on the same day.

It's morning just outside of JFK airport. We Want to Go Home! I'm thinking it, and I see it in the faces of my wife and kids. "Short visits are best;" "Everything in moderation;" these are some of my mother's fondest expressions. Indeed, even for all the natural marvels of our world, excessive exposure to the outdoors can be fatal. That's how I feel about travel right now. It just became excessive for me. For the past eight weeks, I have been mostly away from home: California, New York State, Virginia, and North Carolina in April; Washington in May; Prague, Slovenia, and Croatia in May; and now in June… **Nashua Lampoon's European Vacation!** I am spent, both physically and mentally. As we fly from JFK to Boston, we discuss our re-entry to-do lists. Personally, I just want to sleep in my own bed, open my pool for the summer, work in the yard, read *The Economist*, and sip a cold beer in the hot sun with our faithful black lab Tessie by my side!

We land at Boston Logan at 2:50pm. We collect our luggage and board the Boston Express coach back to Nashua. All three kids fall asleep on the bus. I look over to Karen, sigh, and say in an American accent "damn, talk about yer trains, planes, buses, and trams." "Yes, it will be so good to be home," she replies. The kids will remember this, the many flavors of Fanta, the German *Bretzeln*, and the exotic shapes of gummy candy upon which they subsisted. We will all remember the incessant drizzle, the periodic downpours, and the nearly perpetual clouds over our heads for most of fourteen days. I also appreciate my wife's loathing of the U-Bahn—too many trains make Karen a *kranky* Frau. Isabela and I—and now Jack also—agree that it stinks to travel with a cough. Would we do it again? In a heartbeat; maybe to Italy, and of course I'm already thinking about how to pull that off.

12

TO RUSSIA WITHOUT LOVE

I'm jolted awake by the sound of screeching tires, followed by a loud crash. Now what's going on in St. Petersburg? Passersby on the busy street turn toward an intersection that lies just out of my view. Unable to see the source of the commotion, I focus instead upon the bridge over the Griboedova canal. A white-haired babushka makes her way to the center of the arched bridge, her gaze cast upon her own waddling feet. She coyly pulls two white plastic packages from her shoulder bag and drops them into the canal. I squint in an effort to make out what might be inside; household trash, excrement, unwanted kittens? I rub my eyes. They sting a bit as I wipe away a firm crust that accumulated during sleep. I remember now… I went out yesterday for a long walk, but the air seemed more toxic than normal. Maybe because the city is socked in with fog, trapping the poisonous vapor cocktail of industrial waste, emissions from 72 octane gasoline, and tobacco smoke. I see the two plastic bags again, now bobbing in the murky wake of a canal boat. They're on their way to the Neva River, then ultimately into the Gulf of Finland and onward to the Atlantic Ocean.

I desperately need coffee, so I reach under the bed and put on my house shoes. In my Griboedova flat, I wear them to honor the wishes of my tidy Russo-Austrian landlord. Street shoes must remain at the front door to protect the faded hardwood floors from street filth: mud, dog feces, phlegm, cigarette ash, broken glass, and dust from the city's innumerable construction projects. Although fall brings rain nearly every day, it's never enough to cleanse St. Petersburg's streets. As I sip my first cup of morning coffee, I notice that more than a few people are already into tall cans of Baltika beers. As the crowd slowly disperses from watching the aftermath of the car accident, another day in St. Petersburg begins.

Excerpt from personal "Russia Diaries"
St. Petersburg, 10 October 2007

My initial ten and a half month experience in Germany left such an indelible imprint on my life that I always wanted a second shot at cultural immersion outside the USA. While touring Warsaw, Poland in May of 2005, my friend Adrian Grycuk draws my attention to a bust of William Fulbright in the university library. Fulbright was the founder of a US- funded program for cultural and educational exchange. It occurs to me that it would be ideal for me as a budding *Slavophile* academic— hopefully freshly tenured—to spend a semester or more in Central Europe. As soon as I return to the US, I begin inquiring with the Council for International Exchange of Scholars (CIES) about Fulbright programs.

I believe that it would be practical to do this with my family. If she wished, Karen could take a leave of absence from work. All ten or under, the kids could be excused from their US schools in order to share the benefits of such a priceless opportunity. The challenges of cultural adjustment would also be great for family bonding. Ideally, I would like to spend a semester in the Czech Republic or Poland. I've done research in both of these countries, and taken students to the former. I also have several faculty contacts at Charles University in Prague. After three of them agree to write letters of support and a formal invitation, I submit my application to CIES to teach at Charles University, to be hosted by the Faculty of Geography.

As the 2005-06 academic year passes, I'm ecstatic to learn that my tenure application moves successfully through all four review stages. Periodically, I follow up with the CIES officer about my Fulbright application. As summer approaches, he informs me that I occupy the first alternate position for the Czech Republic. Hearing nothing before the end of July, I come to terms with rejection. Frustrated, I call my liaison in hopes of getting at least a partial explanation and feedback that I can use to inform my re-application for the coming year. He explains to me that there are only seven awards for Americans in the Czech Republic. Because of the country's popularity, assignments are extremely competitive. I ask about neighboring countries, specifically Poland, Slovakia, or Russia. All of the positions have been filled for the upcoming school year; contracts have been signed and plane tickets have been purchased. All he can offer is to fast-track a revised, more flexible application for next year's competition.

Having sensed my interest in Russia, the CIES officer encourages me to apply for an award to spend one semester there rather than in Central Europe. He adds that there are about one hundred faculty positions in Russia during a typical year, and given that I was a runner-up for the Czech Republic, I would have an excellent chance, even without a local invitation. After some thought, it seems to me that Russia would be exciting, a natural next step in my exploration of Greater *Slavia*. As an added perk, I'm told that I will be able to select my host city, even if I don't have any professional contacts anywhere in Russia. I quickly decide that I would want to be in St. Petersburg or Moscow because of their accessibility, size, and significance. I certainly don't want to be isolated in a small village in Siberia, it might be like returning to my youth on the farm! My liaison assures me that if I receive an award, one of these two cities can be arranged.

As my spring 2007 classes end, I take a travel study class to the Balkans for the first time. I return home to find a congratulatory letter for a Fulbright award in Санкт-Петербург, Россия (St. Petersburg, Russia). The excitement mounts. I love this stuff, but I am suddenly confronted with the need to work out logistical details. Do I take my family? Do we take our dog Tessie? My fall classes are already scheduled at Bentley; what about them? How will the money work out?

I check Mercer consulting's "cost of living" rankings. They list St. Petersburg as the 12th most expensive city in the world, even pricier than #16 New York, and I know things aren't cheap there. My award for travel and living expenses is just under $18,000. Is this enough to relocate and support Karen, the kids, and Tessie, while paying our mortgage and other bills at home? This scenario is getting complicated. We would need to deal with the kids' schooling and buy plane tickets for them out of our own pockets. As for me alone, my instinct says that I'm crazy to do this, but I know deep down I would never forgive myself for backing out and skipping such a rare opportunity. After all, I am a self-proclaimed *Slavophile*, and St. Petersburg seems like it would be a remarkable place to spend a semester. Indeed, a Fulbright would undeniably be prestigious for my professional vita. I need to do this.

After a long talk with Karen, we concede that it would be logistically disruptive and financially imprudent to drag the kids along for four months in a dramatically different place. At the same time, she wants to hire a contractor and have some major home improvements done. I've been dragging my feet on those. Our settlement is that I will go to teach in Russia, and she will stay with the kids, continue working, and get her new kitchen, sunroom, and deck.

I have several concerns about my time in Russia. I fear that my absence will be too much for Karen. She and I share a pretty heavy load of domestic responsibilities. She is a full-time professional and will need to do her job plus all of the family errands, driving the kids around, cleaning, and cooking, and this while the kitchen and sunroom—the busiest rooms in our house—are being torn apart and rebuilt. However challenging Russia turns out to be, my time away from home will be even more difficult for her. As for me, I am concerned about finding a place to live in one of the world's most expensive cities. Can I trust the real estate agent? I'm also anxious about violent crime in Russia. Is it as bad as its reputation? Becoming a victim while living in Russia by myself would be psychologically devastating.

My final few days in the USA are busy beyond belief. Karen and I finalize home improvement plans with the contractor and sign on the loans. I get help from Karen and the kids to winterize and close the pool. I run to Bentley for some last-minute meetings, stock the refrigerator and freezer for the family, and finish packing my bags. I feel only partly prepared for my teaching assignment. I have two contacts where I'm going: Irina, the international relations agent with whom I've been corresponding on email, and Kirill, a sociology professor and my academic liaison at Smolny College. Neither one of them has been able to tell me much about my forthcoming duties. As a result, I'm frustrated that I can't even finalize and print my syllabi before leaving the USA. I have Russian instruction books, CD-ROM language programs, and Russian literary classics, but so far I haven't found much time to put them to use. On my musician brother Jonathan's recommendation, I also bought a mini Martin (travel) guitar and named it Natasha. Natasha will be my only mistress in Russia—an enjoyable activity to diversify the days during my self-imposed exile.

It's September 1st, 2007. As the Beatles song goes "it was twenty years ago today…"xxiv when I left the USA on my first flight for a life-altering year as a Rotary Exchange student in Germany. My seventy-six year old father rightly pointed out recently that if I hadn't gone to Germany, I would be doing something entirely different today than teaching in a university global studies department. Will this semester in Russia leave an equally profound impression?

Karen, the kids, and Tessie all drop me off at Boston's Logan airport. As we exchange emotional embraces and kisses, Karen tells me something my heavy heart needs to hear, that "angels are all around me."

I board my flight from Boston to JFK as optimistic as a Buffalo Bills fan at the opening kickoff of a new season's first game. I completely expect that the challenge of a semester in Russia will pay off. I will miss Karen and the kids, Tessie, the baseball playoffs, the NFL season, and mostly my truck, as Karen would add, jokingly. St. Petersburg will be colder and darker than home, both literally and figuratively. More than culture shock, I anticipate lifestyle shock. Without my domestic responsibilities, I will have a lot more time to myself, and this will be nice. I will use this time to learn as much as I can about Russia and its language, catch up on reading, and develop my elementary guitar skills. Hopefully I can also figure out my next steps in my career, and a more peaceful pace of life will give me a chance to develop spiritually.

Boarding the Moscow-bound Delta flight at JFK, the guitar case I carry makes me feel like a pretender. Natasha is brand new, and she competes for the shoulder space normally occupied only by my laptop computer's backpack. As I carefully place Natasha in the overhead compartment, the Lithuanian lady in the window seat asks with an accent, "Are you a musician?" "I wish," I respond with a smile. "I'm going to St. Petersburg alone for four months, and I hope to make time to learn how to play." "Wonderful, winters are cold and dark, but St. Petersburg is beautiful," she says.

As we await takeoff, the captain announces that a passenger in the first class cabin has become ill, so we'll need to leave the queue and return to the terminal. The passenger is removed from our plane, and a cleaning crew boards the plane to cleanse the soiled seat. By the time we take off, this sets us back more than two hours. Knowing that my connection to St. Petersburg will be tight keeps me uneasy throughout the flight. In Sheremetyevo I airport in Moscow, I'll need to pass through customs, collect my bags, and find my way to Sheremetyevo II airport, which handles Moscow's domestic flights.

As I get off the plane, I see a sign that says Добро пожаловать в Россию, which with the benefit of time I can make out to read *Dobro pozhalovat' v Rossiyu*. Given the context, it must translate to "Welcome to Russia." Thankfully, my Lithuanian neighbor on the flight was nice enough to prepare me for the task now at hand: getting past the aggressive taxi drivers to find a public bus to the domestic terminal, just five kilometers away. The problem is that I have no rubles for bus fare, and there are no ATMs in sight. So, my first act in Russia is the illegal exchange of currency "on the street." I trade $5 for 100 rubles. I need to repeat "*Nyet, Spasibo*" in an increasingly assertive tone to aggressive taxi drivers, some demanding as much as 40 Euros for the fare. I jump aboard a passing airport bus, quickly confirming with a young lady that it's headed to Sheremetyevo II, then paying my fare.

Sheremetyevo II is Moscow's Soviet-era airport still used strictly for domestic flights like my "connection" to St. Petersburg. My guess is the USSR and its satellite states used separate facilities for international flights to help control passenger movements. There is a long queue of people at the front door waiting to have their suitcases scanned, and I need to get through this *before* I can even check in. I have less than 40 minutes until my departure. A woman behind me spots the itinerary I'm holding, and in broken English she urges me to cut the line. She mutters something in Russian to the queue's other members. I gather that she is explaining that I need to move up. "*Bolshoy spasibo*" I mutter, embarrassed. Then I offer the Croatian "*oprostite*" (excuse me) a few times, hoping it works in Russian. As the counter agent hands me my boarding pass, I realize maybe "*pardon*" would have been more internationally understandable. Then it comes to me… "*Izvinite*, that's the word I was looking for," I say out loud as I dash from the counter to security, relieved of my freshly re-checked bags. It's unlikely that my luggage will make it to the plane in time, even if I do.

I board the plane and collapse into my antiquated uphol-stered seat. My tray table is made of stained wood. As boarding ends, I turn around to observe that the plane is less than one-third full. A handful of passengers change their seats, and one of them grasps a freshly-opened bottle of Russian Standard vodka that he apparently just procured at Duty Free. Welcome to Russia indeed.

As the plane reaches cruising altitude, the flight attendant approaches my row with her beverage cart. She utters some Russian words in an unfriendly tone as I take a few photos out my window. Having prepared my request for a beer, I confi-dently declare "*pivo, pozhaluysta*." Looking directly at me now, she repeats whatever statement she just made, and I realize I might be getting reprimanded for taking photographs out the window. Good grief, I guess the Russian authorities haven't yet heard of satellite imagery! Satisfied that my camera has been put away, the flight attendant hands me a beer with Cyrillic writing on it. Looks like it says "*Baltica 3.*" I think I can manage this foreign alphabet, but what about the language? As I enjoy the beer, I entertain myself by browsing the Aeroflot in-flight magazine. In the final section, an English translation of airport instructions states that "Upon landing in Japan, passengers will be fingerprinted and shot in the face."

As we land in St. Petersburg, the pilot applies the jet's brakes with great suddenness and force, and the rough tarmac causes half the tray tables in the cabin to shake free, rattling violently as they do. I notice that the vodka is still being passed around between my fellow passengers, who seem to take the bumpy landing in stride. As we slow to a stop, several passengers leave their seats and rush to the jet's exits, long before the "fasten seat belt sign" has been turned off. Evidently, in-flight seatbelt and liquor rules are less important in Russia than the restriction against taking aerial photos of the countryside. I just landed, and my trip has already been interesting and educational!

I collect my luggage and reach the arrivals hall in Санкт-Петербург (St. Petersburg). As instructed by Irina's email, I scan the waiting crowd for a driver holding a sign that says "Fulbright- Deichmann," then scan once again in vain. To make a simple call, I need to find an ATM, get cash, make change for coins, and locate a payphone that accepts coins or buy a pre-paid phone card. One hour later, I manage to get ahold of Irina. "The driver was waiting for you, but he left because you did not arrive," she explains. It seems he had my arrival time right, but wrongly assumed that I would arrive at the *international* terminal of Pulkovo because he knew my trip began in the USA. Well, that's excusable I guess, but why the hell didn't he check my Aeroflot flight number? I recognize that I'm getting tired and cranky after three dramatic flights. "Remain where you are," Irina instructs me. "I send driver back to fetch you."

Twenty minutes later, I'm sitting in a smoky unmarked taxi behind a Russian driver who speaks no English, and I know barely any of his language. It's dark out, and the rain is falling in sheets. As we pass a large factory I recognize the words Русский Стандарт, or Russian Standard. This must be its vodka distillery. Wanting to test some of the few Russian words I know, I say to the driver "*Russkiy Standart, eto khorosho?*" "*Da, eto khoroshiya vodka,*" is his response, and that is the end of our conversation until my final "*Spasiba*" as he drops me off at the curbside and points to a building that I infer holds my reservation. I gesture to the driver that I need to use an ATM to get rubles before I can pay him, but he waves me off. Apparently, he was pre-paid by Irina. Now I just need to find a place called "Hotel Arena."

I stand on the sidewalk with my large suitcase, my backpack, and Natasha. It's cold and dark out, rain is still falling, and the streets are foggy, messy, and noisy. I search the streetscape for

274 | Passion for Place

clues, trying not to look lost. There are more revelers out than
I would have expected for a Sunday night, and quite honestly
I'm uncomfortable carrying my worldly valuables here. Where
do I go from here? Fortunately, several businesses are still open.
In the well-lighted Vodaphone store, I ask a young woman if
she knows of a nearby hotel called Arena. She says she's heard of
it—it might be close. The store's internet connection is down,
so she cannot look it up. Now I'm angry that I don't have better
information. Irina simply told me the driver would pick me up
and take me to my hotel. She gave me no address and no phone
number. I walk the street looking for Hotel Arena for the better
part of an hour. While doing so, I manage to find an ATM
and withdraw some more rubles. Aware that the Vodaphone
store won't stay open all night, I return to it and ask the same
woman if she will dial Kirill for me on her business phone. I
describe my surroundings to Kirill and put him on the line
with the Vodaphone woman. She gives him our street address
then explains to me that he will call back with the address of a
nearby hotel.

Kirill instructs me to walk down the main street to the right
to building number 1056, enter the courtyard, and ring the
bell for the 5th floor. At last, safety and rest are within sight!
Five minutes later in front of 1056 I find a gate leading to the
courtyard, and it's locked. I cannot get inside the courtyard to
ring the bell and have the receptionist unlock the main door.
Crap- what should I do now? Just then, a young couple approaches me from behind, opens the gate with their key, and I
follow them inside the courtyard. Angels? I approach the main
door and ring the bell for the 5th floor. Moments later, I hear
angry feet stomping down the concrete stairs. The woman
produces a ring of keys that would make a jailor jealous and
proceeds to unlock two doors and a gate, letting me in. Apparently, the doorbell I rang interrupted whatever she was doing.
She re-locks the gate and the doors behind us, and I haul my
bags up five flights of stairs to what I assume must be Arena[xxv].

This doesn't seem to be a proper hotel at all; more like a pension. The angry woman at the reception desk requests that I pay right away for my room: 2400 rubles, or about $80. St. Petersburg is indeed expensive. I pay her 3000 rubles, and she hands me my change. When I get to the room, I count my change and realize she handed me 2400 back instead of 600. Trying to be a good ambassador, I return to the desk and give her 1800. I'm shocked that I don't even receive a "*Spasibo*" in return. This miserable woman either has a problem with her own lot in life, or with her American guest. Given the price of my austere room and the attitude of the receptionist, I'm determined to find another place to stay tomorrow. I'm relieved to be safe and dry for now, but I struggle to sleep. My mind is spinning from today's sensory overload. I'm puzzled by this entire situation, and I'm so looking forward to daylight.

I awaken to the alarm of my travel clock, far from recuperated from the long trip, and eight time zones to the east of home. Today's got to be better! At the desk is the same woman as the night before. I ask her if breakfast is included with my rate, and she gestures that I should sit at a small table in the hallway and wait. She disappears through a doorway, leaving me alone in the reception area. Minutes later, she reappears to serve me white bread, boiled bologna sausages, and a cup of Nescafé. No problem, I'm just happy to start the day with something before going out.

I had planned to walk to Smolny College, located on Vasilievsky Ostrov. Using my map, I figure the walk should take about forty-five minutes, but breakfast ate into my plan. I'll need to figure out how to take a bus there. Confident in my route, I ask a young woman at a bus stop if I can buy a ticket on board, which she confirms. I step onto the bus with change in hand, but as the front door closes I realize that the driver's window is completely sealed. Great! I'm on a Russian bus without a ticket! A uniformed woman taps me on the shoulder and utters something in Russian. Crap! I'm about to get busted for riding without a ticket! I present the 100 rubles that I had prepared for the driver, and she says something to me angrily. I tell her that I want to buy a ticket. She takes the money and gives me change of 86 rubles. Whew! And 50 cents is not bad for a bus ticket. I guess this is the system here: each bus has its own cashier, but passengers aren't supposed to wait until the cashier approaches to buy a ticket. It's evident that my inability to pay in correct change didn't go over well either. As I exit the bus, I notice an enclosure labeled кассир, which I quickly decipher to mean "cashier." Aha, next time!

There's no problem finding Smolny College on Lieutenant Schmidt Embankment. It occupies two floors of a large building, each organized around long corridors. I manage to find Irina, who is in charge of my resident registration and faculty identification card. There is a framed photograph of Vladimir Putin on the wall of her office. I fill out some paperwork with her, and then ask her where I might find Kirill. "He doesn't have an office here. Some faculty share offices at the palace building," she explains. Fair enough, Smolny occupies another building somewhere as well. Irina explains that most of the professors are gathered with students for registration in the conference room down the corridor, and Kirill should be there. I enter the room and behold the chaos. I can't help but notice a photograph of Putin on this wall as well. Students are dressed to the nines. Girls are wearing skirts, scarves, and high heels; many of the boys are wearing dress shoes and ties. Professors, dressed in suits, are seated at desks covered with name lists, and students are lined up to register for their favorite classes and professors. Shouldn't I be part of this action? Did I miss something? I try not to feel slighted that I wasn't invited.

By asking around, I eventually identify Kirill. He's a young professor, also dressed in a suit and busily signing students into his courses. When I manage to make eye contact I introduce myself and reach out my hand. "Hi, you had a difficult arrival I think" he says. "We can talk later." "Don't I need to be part of this?" I ask. "I will have some students for your class," he assures me. "Okay, I see how busy you are; can we talk later then?" I ask. "Yes, let's meet at 2 pm."

I leave the undergraduate cacophony behind and find a payphone on the street. I pull out the number for the property agent who was recommended by Irina at Smolny, and make a call. Her name is Irina also. She suggests meeting me in front of Smolny at 3pm so she can show me some apartments. Perfect! This will leave an hour for me to meet with Kirill first.

Temporarily free of the bedlam that is Smolny College on registration day, I find a nearby pizzeria and catch my breath over a slice of pizza and a Sprite. Over the past twelve hours I've lost my happy feeling. At 2pm I return to meet Kirill as he suggested. He's still surrounded by students. I try to attract his attention, but he doesn't seem to notice me. He *must* know I'm here. At thirty-seven years old and wearing jeans, I stand out among the young, well-dressed students, some of whom hail from Bard College in New York State. I am still standing by the door waiting to talk to Kirill as 3pm approaches. My free time is gone, so I am forced to interrupt his conversation. Excusing myself, I explain that it's 3pm, and apologize that I have an appointment with my real estate agent. "No problem, we'll have tea soon," Kirill responds.

Irina doesn't look anything like the beautiful blonde woman on her agency's web site, but she is very knowledgeable and helpful. She and I walk swiftly through the drizzle and wind. She insists upon using an umbrella, holding its drip edge over my head. I don't do umbrellas, especially in the wind. Eventually, however, some force of chivalry prevails and I hold the umbrella over Irina with my left hand, which quickly gets exhausted as we dance the gauntlet of puddles and abundant dog feces on St. Petersburg's uneven pavement.

This must be a standard real estate agent strategy: show one acceptable property and two that are clearly unworkable. I settle for a dated single bedroom unit with a pullout on

Kanal Griboyedova, or the Gribeodov Canal, within view of *Lviny Most* (Lion Bridge). It costs $800/month, and the agent receives $560 as standard 70% commission. The owners need the entire sum of $3,760 in advance, before I move in. The bad news is that I have only $1,000 in cash, and it will take me forever to withdraw that kind of cash in rubles when constrained by a $400 daily limit. And then of course there are significant transaction fees!

The apartment's owner is an Austrian named Vincent who is married to a Russian woman. They have one son, Konstantin. Vincent stops by to meet me while I'm touring his flat, and he clearly likes the fact that I speak German. He tells me he is willing to rent to me, and explains that he would like my money in cash US dollars so that he does not need to claim it as income. Karen quickly comes through for me by transferring a $3,200 MoneyGram, and I am able to sign my lease, agreeing to let the current tenants remain until September 10th. Irina offers to help me find a reasonably-priced hostel where I can stay until then, which turns out to be Hostel Zimmer on Liteniyya Prospekt. This will get me out of the $80-a-night "Arena" and into something more affordable at $20 a night.

Hostel Zimmer is not a bad place to spend time. It has several rooms of assorted sizes surrounding a shared lobby. The lobby features a large picnic table, and in the back of the hostel are lockers, communal toilets, and showers. My room has four bunk beds, and for now only one other resident, a young Canadian named Jordan. A lone tourist, he is clearly amused to walk in and see me studying Russian while sitting inside the deep window frame. "You're wasting a rare sunny day in St. Petersburg," he observes. "Yep, the sooner I crack the language code, the sooner I immerse myself here," I explain. "Yeah, good luck with that. Lovely city, though," is his response. "Yes, I know, it's going to be difficult as an American in Russia." In the aftermath of Afghanistan and in the midst of Iraq's bloodiest days, US travelers abroad face greater than normal suspicion and abuse. "Everybody loves Canadians, though," I tell Jordan. "That's why you all sew your flag onto your backpacks. I'll bet you have one too….show me your backpack, Jordan." Sure enough, there's the beloved red maple leaf, front and center.

At Hostel Zimmer, I also meet backpackers from Mexico, Germany, England, and Australia. The Mexican returns one evening to report that he was just jumped by three Russians in a dark stairwell while visiting St. Isaac's Cathedral. The perpetrators opened his backpack and removed his new $500 digital camera, then pushed him and ran away. A little later the same evening, Jordan returns from Peterhof and tells us that as a non-Russian, he was charged double for his palace entrance ticket. He complains that little information was available in English or French, and he was treated with contempt for even asking in English. He was then scolded for taking photographs, and charged a "photography fee."

Jordan returns to Canada the day before I leave Hostel Zimmer. He is replaced by an inquisitive young Russian named Aleksey, who introduces himself as a doctor. Really? How many doctors stay at hostels? Then again, how many professors stay at hostels? In any case, all foreigners in Russia must register with the police within the first days of their visit, so the authorities know that I'm here. It wouldn't surprise me if Aleksey was sent by the Russian government to check up on me and make sure that I'm not a subversive element. I've since been told that some US Fulbright scholars have been deported in the past, but I am no threat to Vladimir Putin and Dmitry Medvedev.

The eight days of my life spent at Hostel Zimmer pass swiftly and comfortably, except for the showers. After the first one, I realize that I will probably stay cleaner by not exposing myself to the pungent city water. My days are dominated by self-directed Russian studies; work now, play later. My Russian resources are Pimsleur CDs, a *Talk Now!* CD-ROM, a small dictionary, and a Lonely Planet phrasebook. These materials contain more Russian instruction than anyone can reasonably manage in four months. Around the picnic table in the common area, I meet some very interesting people. In the evenings, I learn a lot from the stories of the tourists, most of whom are backpackers. By September 11th, my date to move into the apartment on the Griboedova Canal, I've pretty much worked through the Russian exercises and grown bored with the interactive language lessons. What I need now is direct human interaction.

On the morning of September 11th, I arrive at the street-level entrance to my apartment with my large suitcase, my backpack, and Natasha. Two minutes after I ring the doorbell, my landlord Vincent appears and lets me in. In German, he instructs me how to use the four keys for the doors and the security gate. He offers house shoes to replace my street shoes and protect his worn and faded hardwood floors. I am aware that Vincent's wife and son returned to Vienna last week, so as I pass the open bathroom door I am surprised to see a different woman drying her hair in front of the mirror. Of course, I ask no questions. Just as Vincent begins a new load of laundry, the power goes out. "Oh yes," says Vincent. "I want to show you the power breaker that you will need to turn sometimes." He grabs a flashlight and a step ladder and ushers me back through three locked doors to the dark stairwell, climbs the ladder, and flips an antiquated switch to bring the apartment's power back to life. "You are welcome to use the linens in the washing machine when they're finished," he explains. Vincent and his mistress show themselves out the door, informing me that a technician from "Doktor Komputer," will come before noon tomorrow to set up the internet. At last, this lovely—if dated—apartment is all mine for the next four months!

Doktor Komputer does not show up in the morning, but after I call Vincent in Vienna, he does appear in the afternoon. The young, competent technician speaks English quite well. He connects my computer to the internet though the single phone line, and installs the required software. He then shows me how to make inexpensive calling card calls to the USA. I must switch the jacks back to the phone, then type in an eigh-teen-digit phone number followed by a twenty-four-character code. I thank him profusely for helping me connect to work and home. After almost two weeks, I will finally be able to interact with my family in Nashua and my employer in Mas-sachusetts through Skype, and maybe even follow occasional audio broadcasts of the Buffalo Bills and the Boston Red Sox.

My first call to Karen in more than ten days lasts nineteen minutes. I ask her if she can see her way through my four–month, self-imposed exile. She thinks so, and I assure her that I can. "A lot of people are praying for us," she adds. My response is, "I can feel it." Truly, everything has fallen into place. I can finally say this now that I'm safe and sound in this apartment.

The queen-sized bed is comfortable, but on my second night I cannot seem to fall asleep. A bit sweaty and curiously itchy, at 2am I move to the mango IKEA couch to write down events and impressions so far. My personal rule for Russia is that if I cannot sleep on any given night, I must work—either read or write. It turns out I'm not alone in my bed; I share it with some kind of tiny biting mites. Maybe the English tenants who just moved out of the flat had pets. The next day, to my chagrin I discover dozens of bites on my neck, arms, and legs; fortunately, I also find a bottle of *Made in England* flea spray in the drawer of the small bedside table. I call Vincent, who says he wasn't aware of a problem; nevertheless, the onslaught of bug bites persists for several nights.

My commute to work takes about thirty minutes on foot, past the Mariinskiy Ballet Theatre, across two of St. Petersburg's canals, and then over the Neva River to Lieutenant Schmidt Em-bankment. I've been assigned to teach my course *Cross-Cultural Understanding*. Ironic, isn't it? I am here to learn cross-cultural understanding. At the beginning, my class has five students: Sergey, Anna I, Anna II, Diana, and Julia. Periodically, other people simply appear in the class and ask permission to sit in. During the second week, Anna II approaches me to apologize because she needs to drop my course. An English class she wants to take is offered at the same time. One of the more pleasant visitors is Olga, Smolny's librarian. Probably twenty years my elder, she addresses me with the utmost politeness and respect, and hangs on every word I say. She is auditing my class to learn conversational American English, as she is an English language consultant to Russians. "I would also like to audit Russian classes," I mention, and she offers to put me in touch with the appropriate professors. When I inquire, it turns out that the other professors don't want me in their classes, but the director of language studies tells me I can get a Russian tutor for $20 an hour, the same rate charged to the US students from Bard. I'm sorry that this sort of thing is not in my Fulbright budget, and I can't justify paying that out of pocket. Maybe someone would teach me Russian in exchange for learning English. Frustrated, at the moment I feel like being an "older" married professor limits my options. If I could be more socially included or single, I could more easily find my way to getting some help with the language.

On that topic, my student Julia mentions that I talk a lot about my wife Karen in class. "Yes, there needs to be a lot of cross-cultural understanding in marriage," is my response, not sure what she means. The attention of the class turns to my wedding ring. "Then why do you wear your ring on your left hand like you are single?" she asks. Again, I become the student in my own class as my new teachers explain that in Russia, men wear wedding rings on their right hand. Good stuff! The class material itself examines cultural differences: language, religion, alphabet, ways of life, ethics, political ideology, and the role of women in society. Toward the end of class, Sergey asks me how my life in Russia so far compares to back home. "I like it here very much, and I'm learning a lot," I respond. "The people are quite nice," I say politely, "especially the students." I continue, "And the city of St. Petersburg is beautiful, except for the air pollution and litter." I shouldn't have been so candid.

Sergey seems offended now, and he immediately gets defensive, retorting that Russian news shows that the environment in the US is in a much worse condition, then criticizing our leaders for neglecting the international Kyoto Agreement.

After two weeks in St. Petersburg, I finally manage to secure a one-on-one appointment with Kirill, my faculty liaison at Smolny. Over tea, he gives me an overview of the institution. With just 400 students, Smolny is the Arts & Sciences wing of St. Petersburg State University, Vladimir Putin's alma mater. The college is only temporarily being housed at this location while the Bobrinsky palace site is renovated. Smolny is struggling financially, and enrollment is low; there are typically only eight or nine students in each class. Most of the professors are in their fifties or sixties. Educated in the Soviet Union, they are struggling to demonstrate their usefulness in the "New Russia," so they need to compete fiercely for students. Because Smolny is state funded, its future is uncertain. The issue is that last week Putin dissolved the Russian *Duma*, and this is the parliamentary body that makes state appropriations for education. Bard College in New York State provides financial support for Smolny by maintaining a group of about 20 students here as well as offering faculty exchanges.

Over time, I find my way around Smolny's two floors of barren white corridors. A few specific seats in the student lounge pick up Wi-Fi, and several Russian students are watching streaming video of boxing with great passion. I ask two Bard students about Wi-Fi, and they direct me to Svetlana, who sets up access for me. I discover that I can also go to Svetlana for logistical support with teaching: she keeps the key to the huge classroom on the top floor, as well as the key for the LCD projector closet. She informs me that Anatoly—assistant to the dean—can make photocopies for me when I need to distribute handouts to the class. This is valuable information I would have liked to have on my first day here.

As I leave the Smolny building for the day, I hold the door

for a nice looking Russian lady and her young daughter. The daughter asks me something and without thinking I panic and respond in my pathetic Russian "I'm sorry, I don't speak Russian," feeling satisfied that someone talked to me and that I had a chance to say anything back in their language. After a few more moments of walking in the crisp evening air and replaying the scene in my head, I realize that the girl was simply asking "*Gdye Tyaleta?*" Man, I could have managed to point out the restrooms to her. Frustrated, I chastise myself aloud, "Kid, you've got to relax."

The next week, the US Consul General in St. Petersburg hosts an elegant reception for US Fulbright scholars positioned throughout Russia, as well as some past Russian scholars who spent time in the US. We are briefed about international relations in the context of the US-led war in Iraq, which is currently at its height. We also discuss personal security issues, and the scholars are informed that every imaginable crime has happened to Americans in Russia since the present calendar year began. Several amiable people are present, sipping wine. A thin American runner tells me that he stopped jogging while living in Archangelsk because the air is so thick with pollution he was afraid running would do more harm than good for his health. An incredibly articulate and friendly Russian political scientist named Viatcheslav seems to empathize with my comments about feeling isolated. It's normal for foreigners in Russia, he says, and offers to include me in future faculty gatherings. I thank him, and respond, "That's very kind of you, I would love to join you sometime. I'll be happy to contribute some beer or other libations for the party." I detect a bit of snobbery in his response, "Actually, friends at my parties don't normally drink beer; only wine or liquor." A bit put off by this comment, I am elated when weeks later I receive an invitation from Viatcheslav for a party at his flat across town; unfortunately, I get lost in the dark and rain trying to find the address from the nearest subway station, and I have no cell phone. Even if I had one,

I would not want to show up late and soaking wet at a classy party too good for beer. When I later apologize for missing the event, Viatcheslav informs me that there are taxi cabs in St. Petersburg, and "the drivers are good at finding the addresses." I didn't bother to remind him that the Consul General just finished warning us about cab drivers and going out alone after dark.

Given the newfound luxury of my own place, my daily routine evolves quickly. I wake up every morning at 6:30 to the sound of a garbage truck as it lifts and tips two dumpsters to empty them. Invariably, this prompts me to start water for coffee in my treasured LL Bean stainless steel French press my mother gave me for my time here. I return to bed with the coffee, watching the busy street while practicing Russian with the Pimsleur lessons. Then, I sit on my mango-colored IKEA couch to eat breakfast and watch Russian news, trying to recognize a few words. Next, I read a bit of *Natasha's Dance* by Figes, Peterson's *The Message*, Massie's *Peter the Great*, something from C. S. Lewis, or any other literature that I think might help broaden my intellectual and/or spiritual scope. To feel like I can afford a little time for reading every day is a novelty. Following that session, I do my daily exercises: one hundred jumping jacks, twenty-five sit ups, twenty-five pushups, arm circles, and toe touches. Then I grab a quick shower before calling home. By half past noon, it is 4:30am at home, so I can connect with Karen as she starts her day. Sadly, given the time difference there aren't many opportunities to talk to the kids on Skype, and when I do my connection is too slow for sustained video coverage. After a light lunch, I get out into the streets of St. Petersburg. I plan my walk around whatever needs to be done that day: teaching class, errands such as buying groceries or a train ticket, or simply exploring a new district of the city. Finally, I return to the flat before dark to make dinner, play Natasha, do email, and check in again at home before I go to bed. It makes me a little sad that the kids don't seem to miss me more than they do, but at least they don't appear to be having difficulty with my absence. They are used to me traveling.

My apartment is located near Сенная плóщадь, or Sennaya Ploschad. This square is unexceptional on its own, but it's a very busy transportation hub, and features pretty much every store I'll ever need while living here. Facades facing the square are adorned with enormous television screens that silently stream Russian news shorts and commercials. One day, as I return home with two bags of groceries from a store called *Норма* (Norma), two men begin screaming at me angrily in Russian. I continue to walk swiftly, and try not to flinch. I have no idea what they said, but I feel pretty unsettled. Luckily, they don't follow me far. In five minutes I'm back in my flat. What the heck was that all about? Granted I don't look very Russian, but I don't look non-Russian, do I? I'm wearing jeans, a leather jacket, a beret, and I just left my dress shoes at the door. I look in the mirror to figure out what gave me away. I have a normal mid-length American haircut. It could be the hair, but more likely it was the beret. I won't wear that thing around here again! Now that I think about it, most Russian men either have military-length hair like the strangers who just berated me on the street, long Euro-trash hair, or shaved heads. As I start to cook dinner, I wonder how fast I can grow my hair.

I structure my day to meet the goals of returning from Russia in better physical, intellectual, and spiritual condition than I was in this past summer. On days when I don't need to go out, I create errands just to get exercise: I'm committed to doing at least one hour of intense walking every day. Often, this means going to a park such as nearby *Yusupovkiy Sad* in the wind and rain, then walking laps around its pathways.

One day, possibly thinking I am looking for the park's exit, but maybe out of concern for the many young mothers pushing their prams in the park, the security guard yells "*Vychod!*" (exit) to me, pointing toward the gate. Another day, on my way home from *Yusupovkiy Sad*, I see a man lying on the muddy street in military uniform. He has one arm, no legs, and there is a begging cup positioned next to him. Instinctively, I look straight ahead and pass him by. What am I thinking? I turn around and place a five ruble coin in his cup. He reaches his hand toward me, and for some reason I fearlessly grasp it. "*Sbasibo! Otkuda ty…?*" I know that he thanked me, but I don't understand what he asked. He switches to German, "*…Deutschland?*" Aha- I get it! "*Nyet, es-sha-ah*" (No, USA), I reply. I squeeze his hand again. As I walk away, I feel like an idiot. He probably got maimed in Afghanistan or Chechnya by an American-built weapon, and here I am giving him 18 cents to make myself feel better about his situation. I return to my flat and open my dictionary to look up the Russian word for peace. It is мир (*mir*). It's all I could have said to that man; it's a good "word for the day" that I'll probably remember from now on.

I consider myself a positive person, so I am disinclined to over-report the negative. My days in Russia are structured and satisfying, but I came here for cultural exchange. Sadly, I eventually realize that my attempts to reach out aren't going far. I feel that my first month was spent trying faithfully. I am grateful to my friendly students and Olga for being receptive to me, but I was hoping to be better integrated by now. At the end of September, in deference to my short timeline in Russia, I begin to revisit my pre-travel hopes and dreams of excursions to places nearby. From the start, train trips to Finland and Estonia, then Latvia and Lithuania were part of my plan. Given my cold reception in St. Petersburg, now might be the right time to get away for a weekend. At least I'll have the chance to practice Russian by buying my ticket at the train station's international sales counter!

My first jailbreak is to Tallinn, Estonia, and Helsinki, Finland at the end of September. When I get off the train in Tallinn, I can't believe the cleanliness that welcomes me. It's a cool and dry autumn day when I kiss the ground Es-ton-I-eh. My first impression of Estonia is not so much about Estonia. Rather, it's: "What the hell is the matter with Russia?" In Tallinn, the air is clear, the parks are litter-free, and people seem to be tolerant of my English and feeble Russian alike. I'm pretty sure they don't mind that I'm not Russian!

In my effort to remain money-wise, I stay in a hostel. There is another adult guy there, and he's staying in my room of four bunk beds. He sits at his notebook computer and listens to "Everybody Hurts" by REM over and over again. How strange. Let's call this guy Stephen, maybe forty-five years old. He introduces himself and proposes to explore the sights of Tallinn with me. Fair enough, it would be nice to have someone to explore with. As we walk through the capital of this reluctant former Soviet Republic, Stephen and I discuss our respective jobs and lives. He tells me he is psychologist who deals with troubled youth. He visits schools and tries to help kids who come from broken homes. He is particularly concerned about girls from families without fathers. I first realize something is awry when Stephen stops to pick up a scrap of wire from the street and begs my patience as he mends his sandal with it. It's a chilly day in October, why is he still wearing shorts and sandals?

After a few hours, Stephen confides that he is here in Estonia as a sort of American refugee. Seems he's a sex offender who is wanted in the United States and Argentina, at least. Stephen divulges that there are warrants out for his arrest in the states of Washington and Georgia. He had sex with the underage daughter of a CEO in Seattle, and he let a young girl "sit on his lap on a swing" in a nudist camp in Georgia. From there, he fled to Argentina, where he visited schools in order to meet more teenage girls, and ultimately he escaped to Europe.

As a parent, I'm disgusted by these sudden revelations. "Aren't you interested in women… women *our* age?" I ask Stephen, a bit generous knowing that he is close to ten years my senior. "In my work I've learned that many young girls have been hurt by their fathers—either by neglect or abuse—and they need a *real* father figure…they are hurting inside." The most awkward of silences ensues. I don't want to spend another minute with this creep, and I suddenly regret that Stephen knows my name.

Two more hours pass as we wander between landmarks, but there's no longer much to discuss. How can I shake this guy? When Stephen reveals that he is completely out of cash, I make plans to go to a restaurant. I tell him that I haven't eaten since I left St. Petersburg. Predictably, he says he cannot afford to eat at a restaurant. With that, Stephen goes his own way, indicating that he has "a youth event" tonight, a dance party. He met with the school principal about it this morning. Apparently, the filthy animal is still on the hunt for new victims.

In spite of my troubled mind, I enjoy the best imaginable seafood soup in the restaurant Emilio Hidalgo, just inside the fortress wall of Old Tallinn. Grilled chunks of shrimp, mussels, scallops, and what I think might be squid on rice noodles for just $8!

I can't get this predator out of my head. These creeps really do exist, and they don't always look like criminals. I have three kids. Where is this asshole heading next? At 10pm I return to the hostel for a quick sleep before my morning ferry to Helsinki. Stephen doesn't return to the room that night. Hopefully he was picked up by the police, but I fear that he was otherwise engaged.

The ferry to Helsinki is loaded with revelers who bring their own inexpensive Estonian alcohol on board with them. No worries if they run out—there is a duty-free store on the second level. The revelry is a sad sight, like what you might see at the end of the night at a middle-aged fraternity party; grown men drinking until they pass out in the hallways and on the deck, some in their own vomit.

When the ferry docks in Helsinki, the very first thing I do is visit the public library. I need to get internet access so I can leave a tip about this guy Stephen. Conveniently, internet access in Finland is considered a basic human right, and is already without cost in 2007. I file an anonymous report with the FBI about Stephen, and let them know he told me that he's headed next for Kaunas, Lithuania.

Later that day in Helsinki's Sibelius Park, I meet a gray-haired English gentleman named Peter (the) Martin, who carries a cane that he uses more for costume than for walking. As he sits on the bench, dozens of noisy Chinese tourists take photos of his well trained and beautifully groomed dachshund, who wears a mini top hat. After China climbs back onto its tour bus and drives away, the park returns to its peaceful state. I ask Peter if I may take a photo of his dog. "His name is Mr. Tim," Peter clarifies. Peter becomes friendly to me either because I *asked* permission to take a picture, or because I'm another rare English speaker in Helsinki. He invites me to tea, and I gratefully accept.

At tea, Peter explains that he is an English expatriate who married a Finnish woman, whom he still loves dearly after decades of marriage, despite having to live in her native Finland. He immediately earns my respect. She is a retired school teacher, and he still teaches English for business as a corporate consultant. He is noticeably homesick for England, but he's making the most of his time in Finland. I mention Monty Python's skit "Finland" that sarcastically trumpets the non-virtues of his adopted home. Immediately, Mr. Martin's eyes light up. "Exactly, young man!"

In his spare time, Peter the Martin is a poet. He published a poem called "Exile." I'm not a poet, but his poem inspires me to write my own piece about my voluntary self-exile in Russia.

Exile in Russia[xxvi]

Imposed by curiosity
Dreaded but enjoyed
Wandered away from
The things I love most

Exiled from the home I made
With the one I love. The bed we share

The children whose lives
We're entrusted with.

Time to catch breath
Explore, imagine
Reflect, think, rest
Try new things, digest

Become a student again
Reading, writing, music
Language, gym class
And social acceptance

A city of superlatives
Among Europe's largest
Newest, dirtiest, meanest,
Priciest, loveliest

Number the days
Document the details
This time is mine but
The race will begin again

I return to St. Petersburg with renewed determination to make my time here a success. Like an answered prayer, Olga the librarian offers to meet me after my Wednesday class. She leads me around the city for three hours to show me architecture from the street, opulent hotel lobbies, and stunning foyers of public buildings, places I'd be hesitant to enter on my own. Olga and I help each other with the respective languages we are trying to learn. She explains that her husband and son are both pilots, and her daughter is an accountant for Price Waterhouse Coopers. From the beginning, I notice that Olga refuses to walk and talk at the same time. If I ask her a question, she stops in her tracks, turns to me, thanks me for the question, and provides a thorough and thoughtful response. Of course, this means that I need to stop walking too. So, Olga and her American friend stand in the middle of the sidewalk talking as busy Russians rush around us. My Type A personality has a real hard time with this situation, and we fail to cover much of the city. Just before nightfall, Olga introduces me to *bilini* (pancakes), sold in specialized chain restaurants at all hours of the day. In Russia, you can order anything on these thin, crepe-like pastries: salmon, cheese, mushrooms, jams, or fruits.

That night, I talk to Karen on Skype. I already bought plane tickets for her and Charlie to visit me in two weeks, but she is having a difficult time getting a Russian visa. It seems that the US Department of State made a typo on her passport: it identifies her as a man. I've been married to her for fourteen years, and I never suspected her to be a man. She's already used that same "male" passport to enter Germany, the Czech Republic, and the United States. Nobody in these countries seemed to notice, or at least they didn't fuss about it. As there's only two weeks before her trip, Karen needs help expediting a new, gender-correct passport, so she calls New Hampshire Senator John Sununu. After two trips to Boston to apply for and pick up her next-day passport, she has to reapply for a Russian visa and pay the application fee of $160 all over again.

One of the most exciting days of my life is when Karen and Charlie arrive. I track their flight in my mind: Maine, Nova Scotia, Newfoundland, the British Isles, then connecting in Munich for St. Petersburg. The first embrace at Pulkovo Airport is beyond description. As I confidently lead my venerated guests into the sketchy *marshrutka* shuttle to Sennaya Ploshchad, it occurs to me that maybe I have actually made some progress since I arrived in St. Petersburg after all.

I spend the next few days entertaining Karen and Charlie and showing them rainy St. Petersburg's main sights: The Hermitage, the many churches, cathedrals, parks, and the *Swan Lake* ballet at Mariinskiy Theatre. They come with me to my class, which I organize as a round-table discussion, putting any cultural questions on the table as fair game. Each rainy evening, we watch DVDs with Charlie on the IKEA mango-colored pull-out couch then enjoy some much-needed marital recharging. We then travel to Moscow to see Arbat Street, Red Square, and some other attractions. A Citibank ATM eats my cash card, and the bank manager refuses to return it to me, even when I present my passport as proof of identity. He explains that he also needs telephone verification from the bank headquarters in the USA, but right now it's 3am on Saturday morning there. It will take until Monday morning in the USA — more than forty-eight hours—to get my ATM card back, and we are all leaving Moscow tomorrow. Low on cash, we are forced to eat at one of the few places in Moscow that takes credit cards, so we choose the overpriced Hard Rock Café. Even though rain has been falling in sheets the entire week, this visit has been ever so important for our marriage and mutual sanity. Already, it's time for me to accompany my wife and son to Sheremet-yevo I airport and say our very sad goodbyes. As they disappear behind security, I take the shuttle to Sheremetyevo II for the one hour flight "home" to St. Petersburg.

After Karen and Charlie leave Russia, the St. Petersburg air remains cloudy and polluted, but it suddenly seems much colder. The canals freeze by the end of October. Unable to float out to the Neva, the daily deposits of trash and litter begin to accumulate on the ice. With the streets becoming icy, all but the freshest dog feces are frozen too, so walking ironically becomes less treacherous. I teach my class, finish up a paper for an academic journal, and return to my daily routine of studying, reading, exercising, and playing guitar. I return from my class on Monday to a handwritten sign on my building's front door. I sit down with my dictionary and translate it as "the water will be shut off from Tuesday until Friday." I ask my neighbor Anton to confirm that I understand correctly, which he does. I shower that night and fill some pans with water for cooking, noticing for the first time the dark color of my tap water.

November 4th is Russia's National Unity Day, and it will be observed as a national holiday on November 5th. I write an email to one of my Russian colleagues to ask him about the significance of the holiday. Will there be parades, other festivities, maybe some fireworks? Here is his response:

Dear Joel:

The first thing I would mention in conjunction with the Day of National Unity is the necessity to exercise caution. On Russian holidays, people are getting drunk quickly and becoming aggressive. I would suggest that you keep distance from any large groups, especially nationalists. Militsiia (police) can be quite aggressive too..."

I read this as "In other words, Kid, if the drunks and skinheads don't get you, the police will." I decide I will stay safely at home today and relax.

During my Fulbright assignment, I write several reflections for family, friends, and colleagues. After two months, it seems to be in order to write a short report for general audiences, and I submit it to my local paper *The Nashua Telegraph*, to use if and as they see fit.

"ANGELS AND DEMONS" - St. Petersburg, Russia

Russian suspicion toward foreigners is well known. As an American, I was warned by my Fulbright officer that if were placed in a major city like Moscow or St. Petersburg I will likely receive "very little welcome." After exactly nine weeks of living in Russia I've concluded that he was wrong; I've received no welcome at all. At best, my treatment has been benign neglect, at worst rejection. But the human coldness is okay with me because I'm having a blast here at 60 degrees north latitude as winter arrives! Even colder than my reception in Russia is the damp breeze sweeping off the Gulf of Finland, sending ripples along the surface of the Griboedova Canal outside my window in St. Petersburg, a city itself known as Peter's Window to the West. Many Russians would have preferred to keep that European window sealed off. Yesterday I observed hundreds of faces on the escalator down to the Metro—the world's deepest subway system—before observing a single smile. The smiling woman was on a cell phone, probably talking to a non-Russian. I had to grin. Sometimes I think of gleeful smiles on the faces of Russian drivers as they accelerate and force pedestrians to run for their lives across "zebras," local slang for crosswalk.

So, after nine weeks of self-imposed Russian exile, is it possible to speculate on where the country is headed? Since I've been here, Vladimir Putin's popularity has soared as he dissolved the Duma (parliament) and hinted that he will be continuing in political leadership after his second Presidential term, either by changing the Constitution to allow a third term, or by becoming the Prime Minister and shifting more power to that position. Before putting all of the blame on Putin, however, we should remember that Russia has never experienced anything close to sustained, functional democracy. Its history is riddled with the abuses of its leaders, from Czars to Communists. Even Peter the Great, namesake of this city and Russia's reformist Europhile, was a tyrant who with his own hands tortured his son Alexis and had him put to death for the crime of being deemed an unsuitable heir. Tens of thousands of others suffered even worse fates under Peter, while untold millions starved under Stalin's imposed famines. Relative to Russia's past, the present is a safe, happy time, and at least some semblance of stability is assured under Putin. So, why wouldn't Russians want to allow him to bend the rules and stay in power?

Today, Russia's soul is up for grabs. It is being torn between angels and demons. Their presence is especially palpable on the street. There is so much to sense everywhere. One sees devout Orthodox babushkas genuflecting in front of a cathedral. One hears the moaning, then smells stench of a drunken disabled man. He fell on the uneven, grimy sidewalk and he can't reach his crutches. A timeworn pensioner throws a bag of trash into the canal, apparently to wash it out to sea. A team of young trash collectors noisily gathers empty beer bottles that were left carelessly on parked vehicles, the canal's railings, and the window sills of buildings. A young mother and her child feed scraps of bread to the ducks in the pond of a nearby palace. The good and the bad overwhelm the senses every day in St. Petersburg, and the city's soul, like that of Russia, hangs in the balance.

The life expectancy for a Russian man is 58, a result of poor diet, alcohol abuse, and smoking. However, I noticed a conspicuous absence of vodka in the streets. I suspect it's consumed at home during the evenings, and then people drink beer in the streets all day in order to "rehydrate." At any hour of the morning, passersby can be seen with half-liter cans of beer and mixed drinks in hand. This level of consumption cannot be healthy. In short, Russia's high death rate and low birth rate result in population decline of one million every year. Natural selection might "solve" some of the social ills, but economic times are relatively good in Russia—what if times get hard? In spite of population loss, Russia's economy is sailing with 2006 growth of 6.7 percent, thanks in large part to lucrative petroleum exports. What would the USA, Japan, and Germany do for that kind of growth nowadays? Moscow and St. Petersburg are undergoing some of the most extensive urban renewal and new construction projects ever experienced anywhere.

Entire sides of streets such as Liteynyy Prospekt are covered in scaffolding and safety netting. Thanks to what's known as "wild capitalism," Russia now has sixty billionaires. This can't be all bad, can it?

So, what does all of this suggest for the future, for the soul of Russia?

In short, it depends. Russia's hope lies in its bright-eyed youth. I have listened to them in the classroom. They are intelligent, energetic, friendly, and optimistic. They value tradition but embrace technology and globalization. They are curious, unafraid to ask challenging questions, and not automatically suspicious of foreigners. They are developing the technical, leadership, and communication skills that can build Russia's future. And threats? They can all be found in the street: the pollution, the drivers, the drunks, and the skinheads. Russian nationalists are perpetrators of daily hate crimes against minorities and foreigners, in retaliation for vile offenses like looking non-Russian or speaking English with one another. Enemies of Russia's future can be found at any hour, but after dark it is their turn to rule the streets, and in the long Russian winter, nighttime dominates the day.

Quite often, on my way back from class to my flat, I buy a few groceries at a small shop on the city block next to my own. It's called *Produkty Magazin*, which makes me laugh, because it translates roughly to "products store." What do they sell? Products! Barely the size of my garage at home, it employs one cashier, one stocker, and like most other urban shops in this city, it has a full-time security guard. When I ask the security guard in broken Russian for help finding something, he asks in very bad English if I'm German. "*Nyet, ya Amerikanets,*" I reply, satisfied to have understood him and responded in Russian. We exchange introductions in my broken Russian and his broken

English. His name is Fyodor, and he invites me to McDonald's on Sunday so that we can practice each other's languages. He says we can then go together to get babies. I show him my ring and tell him I'm married. He looks confused.

On Sunday morning, I walk to *Produkty Magazin*, just 100 meters from my flat, to meet Fyodor and his brother Timon. Timon shows us to his car—a rusty yellow Lada with a cracked windshield. Explicit American hip-hop music plays, far too loud for the low-grade stereo. I sit in the back, as Timon drives to a gas station, where he pumps a few liters of 76 octane gasoline. "*Gdye McDonald's*" I ask, starting to get a little nervous about where we're going, while reassuring myself that Fyodor is a security guard. From the passenger seat, Fyodor responds by showing me a shopping bag that contains a bottle of cognac, a tube of sausage, and a jar of pickles. I gather that they want to party.

After driving around a few blocks, Timon returns to park near *Produkty Magazin*. It becomes clear to me that the brothers intend to bring their feast to share at my nearby flat. Reluctantly, I let them into my apartment, but manage to keep them in the kitchen area and out of the main part of my flat.

Fyodor and Timon are from Tajikistan, where the rest of their family remains. Timon has two golden teeth, which, through charades, he explains he received following a street fight. We have a good conversation over the libations and snacks. Fyodor produces a huge knife from a belt sheath for chopping the sausage and pickles. Timon leaves periodically to smoke a cigarette. I show the brothers photos of Karen and the kids, and they again mention going for "babies." Puzzled, I'm not sure if they are trying to say "babes" or "boobies," but from their gestures it soon becomes abundantly clear that they mean both. I pound my right hand to my heart. "*Amerikanets*" they laugh, indicating that they think I am silly; they assure me that I should feel free to chase women with them here in Russia. Timon explains he has two girlfriends and one child. Fyodor doesn't want to "settle down" like his brother; he's working all the time at the store. "I go with you to *Amerika*?" Fyodor asks, repeatedly throughout the afternoon. As the Russian cognac pours, I catch myself making a mistake by using my left hand to put ice cubes into our glasses. Within minutes, Timon leaves to buy more cigarettes and doesn't return. I notice that Fyodor stops drinking, and when he leaves at 2:30pm, his glass remains half-full on my kitchen table. So I surmise I just offended two Muslim womanizers who drink like fish, but won't accept ice that I touched with my left hand. Little do they know, my left hand is not my "cleaning" hand.

Relieved that the Tajik brothers are gone, I am kicking myself that they were here in the first place. Nevertheless, I appreciate the cross-cultural interaction, even if it is driven by their hope to get to the USA or help them "get babies." It's mid-afternoon on Sunday, and I'm sporting a considerable buzz from cognac— the first hard liquor I have consumed in Russia. I regret that the brothers know where I live. For the first time, I take comfort in having four keys to three doors and a gate that protect my flat from the street.

Dave Schoenl, a close friend of mine, frequent travel companion, and county collector extraordinaire from previous chapters, comes to Russia to visit me during the first week of December. Because Dave is staying with me rather than in a hotel, we find it difficult to register him with the Russian authorities within seventy-two hours of his arrival, as required by law. We walk across St. Petersburg to Hostel Zimmer to pay for one night's accommodation in return for registering Dave, but the hostel is gone: it has been replaced by a construction site for high-end apartments. Managers of several other hostels, including the one that registered Karen and Charlie, look at us suspiciously and refuse to assist, even in return for one night's rate. I guess they don't want to be associated with an American who isn't actually going to stay with them. While we're sightseeing and trying to get Dave registered, his seventy-two-hour grace period expires. Without being officially registered through a place of accommodation, Dave now risks arrest if the police ask him for his papers on the street, which is a regular occurrence for foreign-looking people in Russia. Even if that doesn't happen, Dave might get detained when he tries to leave Russia this weekend if the police discover that he wasn't registered. After a prolonged search, Dave and I finally locate a hostel that is willing to register him, but we won't know if he was too late until he attempts to leave the country this weekend!

Dave and I repeat all of St. Petersburg's notable sights that I recently showed to Karen and Charlie. In addition, unencumbered by children, Dave and I manage to go farther afield to Tsarskoe Selo (Catherine the Great's Imperial Estate) and Veliky Novgorod, a fortified historical city replete with Orthodox Churches. Through strength in numbers, we also decide that together we can stay out safely in St. Petersburg after dark (which now begins mid-afternoon) and we are rewarded for our bravery with a spectacular view of the main avenue of Nevskiy Prospekt adorned with Christmas lights. Dave and I run out for some beers and snacks at the nearby *Produkty Magazin*, and bump into my Tajik acquaintance Fyodor. Fyodor is just getting off work, and he wants to go out with us tonight. He will stop by to get us in two hours.

With Dave present, I feel slightly better about allowing Fyodor in my flat. After all, Fyodor already knows where I live, and he didn't stab me with his gargantuan machete the last time he was over. This time, I have food to offer, but Fyodor again brings cognac, which clearly isn't his first of the day. He is using his cell phone to text his friends, but he cannot seem to dial correctly, and he repeatedly drops his phone on the hard floor. The first few times, the plastic case pops off, but eventually, smaller metal parts fall out of the phone. Fyodor kneels down to pick up the parts, and Dave and I need to steady him as he struggles to get back to his feet. Dave says, "Let's get him the fuck out of here before he pukes in your kitchen." "Damn straight." He needs food. "Fyodor, we are all going for *yeda*."

On the way to Sennaya Ploschad, Dave and I stabilize Fyodor enough to keep him on the sidewalk and safe from passing vehicles. As we approach the square, three of his friends appear: two male and one female. We exchange introductions with Fyodor's leather-clad friends, who smoke like chimneys and offer us cigarettes. We enter a nearby self-serve diner that is enclosed with smudgy glass walls. Fyodor and his friends sit down immediately and continue to smoke. I ask Fyodor what he wants to eat. "*Pivo!*" Great, he'll take a beer. I offer to spring for the three of us, and walk to the counter. Nothing here looks appealing to me either. The beer seems to help sober up Fyodor. He and his friends take us to a multi-tiered, high-end shopping mall, where we meet some more tattooed, male ruffian friends of Fyodor's. Dave and I probably stand out like circus clowns here, but it is sort of nice to be included in anybody's social plans. Fyodor's group is starting to look and act like a street gang, and our Tajik associate seems far too quick to introduce us as his "American friends" to his growing crew of knife-toting buddies. Dave and I are getting more uncomfortable by the second, and we start to gesture to each other that it's time to ditch this group. I extend my hand to tell Fyodor, "*do svidaniya*, we have early morning train tomorrow." With his composure deteriorating again, Fyodor pleads with us to stay out on the town. He parts with his buddies to go with us; he wants to go for one more drink, which I am sure will put him over the edge.

At the metro stop Sadovaya near Sennaya Ploshchad, the three of us are just a five minute walk from my flat. Without being able to communicate discretely with Dave, it's unclear to me how we might be able to lose Fyodor. Luckily, Fyodor says he needs to piss. The three of us climb the steps to the surface and Fyodor stumbles to the port-o-lets, begging the man collecting piss money to allow him to go for free. While he's arguing, Dave and I whisper that it's time to make our break by splitting up. "Do you know how to get to my flat from here, Dave?" "Sure

302 | Passion for Place

do." Dave runs back down into the Metro Station, then up the stairs on the other side as I dash across the street. I look across the square and see that Fyodor has noticed our flight. I wait for Dave at the outside gate to my flat, and fortunately he arrives within seconds, explaining that Fyodor spotted him in the subway and started to follow. Fortunately, we both make it back before any chance of seeing our drunken pursuer. Nervously, I fumble for my key and open the gate. That night, for my own safety I decide I can never shop at *Produkty Magazin* again, I will also need to change my walking path to Smolny, and I'll have to keep my eyes peeled for Fyodor whenever I'm out in this city. Luckily, I'm leaving St. Petersburg for my December jailbreak in a few days, and I have only two classes left to teach after that.

Periodically, I express frustration about my situation to Fulbright's leadership, explaining that I didn't come here to be isolated. They respond with profuse apologies. I am happy with the Joel time, but I cannot experience cultural immersion alone. I love the location and the students, but I have no colleagues, and I'm still waiting for someone to show me around my host city and help me find assistance with the language. Eventually, my American Fulbright liaison in Russia invites me to travel to Moscow to interview Russian applicants for US programs. They also put me in touch with a woman name Denai, who runs a cross-cultural forum in St. Petersburg called American Corner, and I offer to lead an interactive presentation, which turns out to be well-received by the mostly-Russian audience. In addition, I finally receive a callback from Anna Etkind, who is in charge of orienting and supporting the international faculty at Smolny. We arrange to meet at Bobrinsky Palace in January, on my final full day here in St. Petersburg.

I'll be home for Christmas in Nashua. On my flight to Boston, I ponder my state of affairs. I was assigned a position in Russia to break down cultural barriers, and the only people who seem to want to hang out with me have ulterior motives.

In Russia, I have been ignored in the workplace and threatened on the street; I've even been yelled at angrily by a cashier because I didn't understand "do you want a sack?" in Russian. Over Christmas break, it occurs to me that the best way to make the most of my final three weeks in Russia is to visit Poland, Lithuania, and Latvia. Because Russia's Orthodox Christmas celebration is some days later than the Catholic and Protestant holiday, there won't be much I can do in Russia. I only have one remaining class to teach and then the exam. When I broach the idea to my close friend Adrian in Poland, he invites me to see some "Hidden Poland in Winter." Ecstatic about the idea, I convince Delta Airlines to change my flight destination to Warsaw instead of Moscow. I will work my way back to St. Petersburg using surface transportation.

Flying back to Europe a third and final time, I reflect upon my four months in Russia. This is a short time to learn about a country, especially when you consider a few weeks spent with visitors and leaving on jailbreaks; nevertheless, I find the four months straightforward to sum up in stages. September: confidence; October: patience; November: perplexity; and December: resignation. Russia is a unique place, and it's also exceptional in my catalog of travels. Still, unlike most of the places I've visited in the world, I fail to find much here to love, or any compelling reason to return in the foreseeable future.

As my final days in St. Petersburg approach, I think that more time here would have been helpful for breaking into this xenophobic society. I confess that my Fulbright agent was probably correct when he said I would be better received in the provinces than in the huge cities of St. Petersburg or Moscow.

Trying to make the most of the home stretch, after giving my final exam I invite my Russian students to a friendly goodbye drink *or* dessert at their favorite restaurant, Chimidan. I order a beer, and they order the menu's priciest mixed drinks *and* sundaes, requiring my last few thousand rubles. Are you kidding me? I feel as though they took advantage of a well-intentioned parting gesture. Nevertheless, we have a really great time talking about the semester and each other's future ambitions. Now, I've got to withdraw more rubles to get myself to the airport.

Just before leaving St. Petersburg's Vasilevskiy Island for the last time, I barely remember to ask Svetlana how to submit grades. I have three registered students, and they earned an A-, a B+, and an F. The latter student—a generally pleasant human being—had perfect attendance and participated meaningfully, but turned in absolutely no written work all term. When I told her she was falling behind, she defiantly told me that she didn't need to turn in work because her parents would arrange her grade directly with the administration. For what it's worth, I report her "F" anyway.

I cross the Neva for the final time and locate the Bobrinsky Palace, which, I learn, belonged to the illegitimate son of Catherine the Great. The building is completely under construction, and it will be a worthy home for Smolny College in a few years. I knock on Anna Etkind's door, and she greets me with a professional handshake and a friendly smile. She is young, kind, and extremely attractive, and she speaks perfect English. I feel like I just left Russia as I walked into her office. I scan the walls for a photo of Vladimir Putin, but I don't see one. Anna offers me a quick tour of the palace, showing me the dusty future classrooms and offices, littered with construction tools, ladders, paint buckets, and tarpaulins.

After the tour, Anna and I discuss my time in Russia over tea. I tell her I find it very difficult to behave as a malcontent with someone I just met. I assure her that I'm pleased with the time I spent in Russia. She apologizes profusely about the isolation and tells me that I was subjected to several unlikely circumstances. First, Irina, the International Relations Coordinator quit her job on August 31, two days before I arrived. Second, Smolny's temporary current location on the island is inadequate compared to its future home here at Bobrinsky Palace.

Third, she is aware that Kirill was too busy this semester to help me, as his wife lives in Berlin and he is preoccupied with his upcoming promotion case. Fourth, she admits to seeing email event announcements that were intended for me returned to her because of an incorrect address. Finally, she adds that last year she hosted five Fulbright scholars, but three of them felt pestered and preferred to be left alone. She thought I might be one of these "less-social" scholars. This makes me feel only slightly better, but I am so happy to have some closure. After this debriefing, I recognize that St. Petersburg is a less hostile place than I thought at times. After all, although my four months were not what they could have been, I am very grateful for the opportunity and I'm pleased that so many people, especially my wife Karen, turned their lives upside-down to make my Fulbright experience possible.

13

WINTER INTO ARAB SPRING: BAHRAIN & NEIGHBORS

One day I find myself in a small island kingdom across the Gulf from Iran, a country that is increasingly the prime nemesis of the USA. My Bahraini students correct me when I refer to the adjacent body of water as the Persian Gulf. Persian means Iranian, Iran is the enemy, and the enemy has no naming rights over that body of water. Iran is a very close and real threat, and Bahrain's royal family is very friendly to the United States, friendly enough to host the American Fifth Fleet.

My employer Bentley University has a cohort program in this small island kingdom, and for four years members of our faculty have been sent here to teach three weeks at a time. Now, a more senior colleague in my small International Studies department who happens to be a friend of mine really likes to teach in Bahrain. He has done so several times, and I thought my chance would never come. However, after returning from my Fulbright semester in Russia, I am asked by our dean to serve as interim department chair. Chairs are the ones that decide who teaches which classes when and where, so I decide that 2010 is finally *my* turn to go to Bahrain, just as the final cohort of students is finishing up. A few weeks after this decision, the same dean leaves Bentley, and her associate dean is left to take her place. After I set the department teaching schedule, the rising dean makes an appointment with me and asks me to take over as her 2nd in command, interim associate dean of arts & sciences. I am flattered that someone would think highly enough of me to make such a request; however, I thank her and respectfully decline. As is my nature, I already have my upcoming year mapped out, including my first ever Buffalo Bills season tickets, a family vacation in Florida to fit my teaching schedule, three weeks of teaching in Bahrain, and plans for May travel study to Central Europe. When Dean Durkin returns a few days later and says she could work around my pre-existing commitments, I relent and accept her offer, embracing the opportunity to get a taste of administration. This will be another busy year.

The year of "deaning" is just another academic year of constant motion, to which I've grown accustomed. Sometimes I wonder what typical professors do with all of their free time. Everything I try to accomplish seems to get done in a hurry, if it gets done at all. I worry about the quality of what I do. I am concerned about being a reluctant dean, but even more about being a half-ass professor. Administrative service is tipping the balance away from teaching and scholarship, let alone family life and a very demanding travel program. By the time I board the flight to Amsterdam on the March Thursday before my Sunday teaching begins, I am exhausted. I'm also as sick as I've ever been in my life with a deep, productive cough, and I can hardly breathe. Two long flights and changing air pressure wreak havoc with my sinuses. In Amsterdam I maximize my layover by taking a two hour walk in the brisk, fresh early morning air. The same evening, I arrive at Al Manámah International Airport in Bahrain, and exit the air-conditioned airport into a wall of choking, dusty heat to meet my driver, who rushes me to the five-star Gulf Hotel that I will call home for the next twenty days.

A small army of porters waits at the curb to compete for my suitcase. One even carries my laptop backpack. The lobby of the hotel is modern opulence of a quality far removed from anything I ever saw in Allegany County, New York. High ceilings with elegant crystal chandeliers hang over marble floors with carpet runways. Signs in the lobby point guests to about a dozen ethnically themed restaurants on the ground floor. In jeans, a dress shirt, dress shoes, and a "scholarly" jacket, I feel underdressed and provincial. I check in with ease, and retreat from this dazzling hall to my room. The large bedroom has a king-sized bed, a generous working area with a desk, large flat panel television, and ample dresser storage for extended stays. First thing's first…thanks to my rehydration efforts, I need to return the water I just drank. I turn on the bathroom light to reveal marble floors and walls, a designated stand-up shower stall with glass walls and embedded ceiling faucet, a large tub with jets, and yes, a flat-screen television installed overhead. This room will be a good place to recover from my cold and fatigue. All I need to do is teach my three-week intensive class, keep up on associate dean emails, and prepare next week's invited presentation for Ankara University in Turkey. I'm this close to Turkey, why not go there too?

I wake up late on Saturday only when my eyes pop themselves open; eight time zones from home, the clock simply doesn't matter today. Thankfully, there is no pressure because Saturday is the Muslim day of rest. Outside the window are the Al-Qudaibiya Palace and Al Fateh Grand Mosque. Manama's skyline is impressive, but engulfed in a dusty haze. Below in the hotel parking lot, I see several dark-skinned Indian men in t-shirts dusting off BMWs and Lexuses. Through the insulated glass, I can vaguely make out the sound of the Muslim call to prayer that emanates from loudspeakers atop the minarets of Al Fateh, the national mosque. It's a beautiful sound that will become eerily routine to me over the next twenty days. Directly below me, Bahraini men in white *thobes* and *keffiyehs* (robes and headdresses) drift like elegant ghosts into and out of the Gulf Hotel's main entrance. I spend the day recovering from the long trip and trying to steam, sweat and bake out my cold. First, I enjoy a long, hot bath while catching up with *The Economist.* Next, I explore the hotel grounds and find the fitness center and the pool. Then I venture outside the hotel into the neighborhood of Adliya, which I later learn is among the city's oldest and most diverse quarters.

My daily routine will be to prepare for class over coffee, enjoy a fantastic breakfast buffet, teach, return to jog in the hotel's fitness center, then grade homework and prepare for the next class by the pool. In the evening I will make use of the top-floor lounge where free Wi-Fi, hors-d'oeuvres, and wine are offered from nine until midnight. The Filipina women who keep my wine glass full and whisk away my empty snack plates are the same ones who serve me breakfast each morning in this elegant room. Saturday ends with the usual pre-semester trepidation about meeting a class of new students, but this time with the added element of major cultural differences.

Bentley classes are offered on the premises of the Bahrain Institute of Banking and Finance (BIBF), a modern facility built on land recently reclaimed from the sea. My classroom is even more recently reclaimed from a parking garage. The room's acoustics are dreadful on their own, but the loud and inefficient overhead air conditioner makes them worse. Zahra, a very friendly Lebanese woman, is the local program coordinator. The class I will teach is called *Global Tourism and Transportation*, an upper-level elective that I normally teach during fall semester. Class runs from 9am until 12:30ish on Sunday, Monday, Wednesday, and Thursday. I have ten students in my class; all of them Bahraini, with the exception of one Syrian girl, Zanubiya[xxvii].

As a learning cohort, the students have known one another for four years, taking mostly identical classes in Bahrain. The idea is that the students get a Bentley education without living in the USA. This means they miss out on all of the hedonistic fun that goes along with the university experience, like living on campus, extra-curricular events, and going to parties, which might corrupt their Muslim sensibilities. The arrangement of Bentley in Bahrain is especially attractive to the parents of young women. Knowing one another so well, the students have a very interesting social dynamic. All of the students suffer from what is widely known in education circles as senioritis. Only half of the women in the class observe the Muslim dress code of *hijab*. Alia, who does not, is more or less the class ring leader. At least I have been warned by my colleagues. She is an attractive, omni-smiling girl who is always asking for less work, lighter standards, more time for assignments, and so on. The class's atmosphere is respectful but extremely laid back. Every student addresses me as "professor" or "sir," but the students pay little attention to punctuality and deadlines. I attribute this not only to the Arab culture, but also to the expectations that have set by my colleagues. I am in no position to change four years of precedent, although it troubles me that our 9:00am class begins for most students as late as 9:35, and our twenty-minute break often extends beyond a half-hour. Alia also dilutes the class time by bringing snacks to share. Our class time is part lecture, part discussion, part picnic.

The Gulf Hotel is less than one mile from BIBF, and I don't mind the half-hour walk in afternoon oven heat, despite the blowing dust and the sweat that ponds between my dress shirt and laptop bag. I am walking home from my second day of class when I feel like I'm being followed. A white Land Rover with darkened windows slows down behind me, and pulls up to the curb beside me. Oh no, here we go! The tinted window rolls down.

"Excuse me, professor…" I suddenly recognize that the driver is one of my new students and breathe a sigh of relief "…please let me give you a ride."

"Thank you, I enjoy the walk—it's my exercise program."

"But it is so hot and dusty out… professor, it's not healthy," he adds. I concede; he has a good point.

"Thank you very much Mohammed," I say, telling him

I'm living at the Gulf Hotel. I notice that he is not wearing a seatbelt. As I pull mine across my lap, Mohammed laughs and says "In Bahrain, you don't need to wear a seatbelt."

"But isn't there a seatbelt law?"

"Yes, of course, but nobody listens to the police," he says, driving far faster than what I consider to be a safe speed. "You see, the police are not respected in the kingdom, they are common people… usually immigrants."

I change the subject. "You have a very nice car, Mohammed."

"Yes, thank you professor, this one is my favorite."

"Really, what else do you drive?"

"I have a Mercedes, but I don't like it so much… it's a convertible and it gets too dirty inside"

"Yes," I agree, "I suppose it's not ideal for the desert."

Only minutes later, I thank Mohammed as he pulls into the Gulf Hotel's parking lot. He drops me off at the curb. "My pleasure, professor. I hope nobody recognizes me here," he says. "See you on Wednesday, sir."

I revel in the fact that I don't need to teach tomorrow, but dread that I haven't started preparing my presentation for Ankara University in Turkey. No worries, now it's time for the treadmill and the pool before going back to work.

It's Thursday night, and I have only one hour to sleep before returning to the airport. I haven't been in Bahrain even one week, and I'm already off to Turkey. I will not pass up such an opportunity to maximize my temporary base in the Middle East. My Turkish Airlines flight to Ankara leaves at 2am and connects in Istanbul. I will present in Ankara, meet a fellow geographer named Nuri Yavan who organized my colloquium, present my paper, and return to Istanbul late tomorrow night to enjoy two days of sight-seeing in a city that I've always wanted to visit.

Still under the weather, and not fully adjusted to the proper time to be awake and asleep, I oversleep and barely get to BAH airport in time for my flight to Istanbul. The airport terminal is filled with South and West Asian migrant workers—mainly male, short, and dark-skinned. My colleagues who taught here before told me to watch for plane loads of tall, blonde, Ukrainian sex workers being brought in to Bahrain, but I don't notice any.

After my three and a half hour night flight to Istanbul, it's already time to start the day. I've never seen such a chaotic airport; it seems worse than Charles de Gaulle or JFK. I know that I need to buy a visa, but which one of these tangled lines is for visas, and where can I exchange US dollars for the requisite Turkish Lira? How will I get my visa, make it through customs, and onto my connecting flight to Ankara in one hour? I have an 11am appointment in the capital to meet Selin Sayek for coffee. Selin is an old friend, economist, and former Bentley colleague who left the USA to start a family with her husband in her native Turkey.

I locate an ATM, withdraw local cash, wait in line for a visa sticker, and choose my best guess of a line for customs. I hear "American" being spoken by the person in front of me in line. I ask the man what he thinks my chances are of making my connection. "Not very good in this line" he responds, suggesting that I should jump to the shorter, faster-moving "Turkish Citizens Only" line. Fearing an official admonishment, which would really kick me while I'm down (overtired, sick, disoriented), I stay put at first. A few moments later, the American turns around again to tell me that he was a customs officer at Seattle-Tacoma International Airport. He assures me that travelers often do this when their connections are close, and officials don't mind. I decide it would be good to agree with him. I enter the Turkey with my adopted countrymen, and find my way to the gate for a very short flight to the capital city of Ankara.

Exiting Ankara's airport, I have instructions from Selin. I manage to find the crowded city bus that travels to Ankara's main bus terminal and city center. The problem is that I don't know where to disembark, and while the bus is moving I'm not able to find anyone with whom I can communicate. To my frustration, I cannot identify the correct stop with any reasonable amount of certainty, so I stay on board until the main bus stop in the city center. In the meantime, Selin is waiting for me at Ankara's main bus terminal, which must be the largest bus station on our planet. Immediately when I get off the bus, I search for an internet café or any store where I can make change for coins and call Selin. When I do reach her from a pay phone, she explains that she has meetings starting at noon, so even if we were to meet up at this point, we wouldn't have time to visit.

Such a disappointment; Selin and I go way back to our first years as Bentley professors. We published several journal articles together on research teams, and I felt honored to have been invited to her wedding in Turkey a few years back. Sadly, I could not attend at the time because of small kids and small finances. This is a failed opportunity to maintain a friendship and professional association that has been very important to me.

Ankara is a chaotic place. My first impressions are not positive. There is a lot of noise, heavy pollution, and the streets are crowded with thousands of police in riot gear. Seems they are there to ensure that ongoing labor strikes and protests remain peaceful. I see two police officers carrying cardboard cases of teargas canisters from their patrol van to their post. One of the boxes rips open at the bottom. Dozens of canisters fall to the pavement and roll down the sidewalk, clinking off the curb and into the street. There is a lot of action in Ankara today; so many things to see everywhere!

Although I missed Selin, I do manage to meet up with Nuri Yavan. Until now I had never met Nuri in person, but we had corresponded for years via email about our shared research interest in foreign direct investment. When I got the chance to go to Bahrain, I thought it would be a good time to do a side-trip to his fairly nearby country. I wrote Nuri to ask if there were any conferences in Turkey during my time in the Middle East. Nuri responded that he would prepare one. He organized a "conference" with me as the speaker, and promoted it to his faculty and students. So, this event—something Americans would call a colloquium—is a different kind of conference.

Nuri and his friend Erdem meet me in the city and take me to lunch in a historical district of Ankara. They then show me to a large lecture hall at the university. With about seventy attendees it is the largest group that I have spoken in front of in my life, and it is my first time addressing an audience through a microphone. My paper is about the distribution of foreign direct investment in Sub-Saharan Africa, a paper that I wrote with friend and colleague Charles Malgwi. After the presentation, I receive some healthy criticism from an engineer in the audience, a senior faculty member who admittedly knows little about FDI or Africa, but apparently is quite advanced at quantitative methods.

After the presentation, a beer, and an unintentional but much needed nicotine rush from secondary cigarette smoke, I return to the airport with my small backpack and board my flight for Istanbul. Into and out of Ankara in one day! I don't know how much more there was to see, but I feel like I didn't really have enough time to find out, and the nice visit with Nuri and Erdem was too short, let alone the non-visit with Selin.

I arrive in Istanbul late at night, and the airport seems like a different place from this morning. The signs are well marked and there are hardly any people. A clean, modern train takes me from the airport to the city center. I exit the train, which somewhere along its route into the city becomes a subway, then emerges from underneath the street. The city is a bustle, even approaching midnight on Friday. More or less competently, I find my way to Hotel Zagreb.

I present my hotels.com, pre-paid reservation receipt and passport at the reception desk, and the receptionist regrets to tell me that the hotel is completely full. "How can that be?" I ask politely, trying not to be an ugly American. "We are sorry," I will find you another hotel and our driver will take you there. Five minutes later, I am at another hotel—far inferior to Zagreb. I wade through the smoke to check in at reception and catch a glimpse of the posted rack rates. I notice that they are much lower than what I paid for Zagreb. After finding my room, I return to the bar for a nightcap of Efes, the Turkish national beer. I count several Russians in the lobby, and hear their language as they come and go. I've been in constant motion for over a week, and this is no way to live. I'm tired, sick, and angry. I decide to return to Hotel Zagreb first thing in the morning to meet the manager and demand a room for my pre-paid reservation.

Hotel Zagreb's manager Matta is young and very friendly. There is no need to demand anything. Matta apologizes profusely and offers to set me up immediately in a superior room with a view, including complementary wine and fruit. I graciously accept and thank him for fixing the situation. "You are most welcome, Mr. Deichmann, we want foreigners to think favorably about our country," he adds. Outside my top-floor room is an indoor roof-pool, sauna, and Turkish bath, all of which I will check out this evening. Today, however, is for exploring this enormous and invigorating city. I do this on my own by walking the main street Ordu Caddesi to the Grand Bazaar, Sultanahmet, and finally Topkapi Sarayi.

As I look around, Istanbul impresses me as one of a handful of very special cities that I've seen in my life. It is on a short list of cities with incredible geography—peninsulas, hills, water, bridges, and as I tell my students its position at a pivotal location straddling Europe and Asia, linking Thrace with Anatolia. The position is really a good base for running an empire. Its buildings and crooked streets are replete with history and grit. Equally welcoming is the hospitality of the Turkish people. Yesterday I learned this by interacting with Nuri and Erdem, and today I continue to meet friendly people who quickly melt away any anxieties that I have about walking around alone, even after dark. The day ends with a nice private session in the Turkish bath… warm water and hot rocks. Finally, I've reached a turning point against this late winter New England cold that has been tormenting me.

I needed to reschedule today's (Sunday) class in order to make my presentation and side-excursion to Turkey possible. My students don't seem to mind. After an entire day of exploring Istanbul, I return to Bahrain, almost as run down as I was upon my initial arrival nine days earlier. A very short sleep barely rejuvenates me for my Monday class. I let my students convince me that it would be good to plan a "tourism" field trip—a first-hand analysis of Manama's *souk* (market), which I myself am eager to see.

My Syrian student Zanubiya is very quiet and doesn't seem to fit in with the rest of the class. I'm starting to notice that she misses about half of our class meetings. I email her directly with my concerns. After no response, I email other Bentley professors who have already taught her. My colleagues tell me yes, they know all about Zanubiya's problems. With the benefit of their insights, I chat with Zahra, the program coordinator. It seems that Zanubiya has been sick and is therefore behind with everything. Zahra cautions against giving Zanubiya any breaks. I wonder if she has been "babied" throughout the Bentley program and/or in her home culture. I want to remain consistent but also culturally sensitive.

A few days later, Zanubiya's father—also a professor—phones me and invites me out to lunch at Trader Vic's, a posh Polynesian-themed restaurant chain. I find myself in an awkward position, but of course I accept the professor's invitation. At lunch I take my host's suggestions on food and drink. I then learn about some family history, health issues, and Syrian politics that of course must have detrimentally impacted Zanubiya's academic performance. A US-trained Syrian academic and government minister, Zanubiya's father takes me off guard by informing me of his firm support for the US-led military intervention in Iraq. I wasn't going to bring that topic up. Apparently, he assumes that I'm on board too. He appeals to me to give Zanubiya a break by excusing her from missed assignments. Delicately, I try to reach a reasonable solution given the circumstances. I tell him that I can offer his daughter some extra time to complete the work, but she still needs to turn in everything. I add that despite her missed classes, my standards for her work will be just as rigorous as those for the students who have attended class regularly. He seems satisfied. I'm in unfamiliar territory here, and I hope I didn't concede too much.

Upon my return to the Gulf Hotel, I take the elevator to the lounge at the top and look through dozens of emails. I receive a message from Bentley's Admissions office asking me to save their staff a long and expensive trip to Bahrain by hosting a dinner for accepted students at Trader Vic's, the same high-end restaurant I visited today. Immediately, I reply, "Of course." Afterwards, I feel unsure of my own ability to interact skillfully with a group of bazillionaire, royal-family Bahrainis and their veiled daughters. The good news is that my co-host will be a former student of mine, Abdulla. He and his wife are both survivors of one of my very first courses at Bentley: *Comparative Government*.

Abdulla is an excellent salesman; he's extremely enthusiastic about Bentley. At the restaurant, I do my best to follow his social cues. However, I might be too egalitarian and student-centered for this task in the Arab world. I fail the first test as the young female student enters the restaurant. I approach her and offer her a handshake. D'oh! I know better than that! I inadvertently focus the conversation toward the man's daughter, the person who might attend Bentley. Again, I know better than that! C'mon, Kid, *she* won't be the one to decide whether she'll study at Bentley! Then I notice that her mother isn't even part of the conversation. *This* conversation is only for the men. Increasingly tentative for fear of offending the girl's parents, I back off and let Abdulla handle the sales pitch. After all, I'm not trained for this. After all this, I could use a glass of wine, but of course that would be *über*-taboo. Fortunately, I think we're all impressed by Abdullah's ability to articulate his love for our academic institution. To my relief I survive the dinner, but I never do find out whether any of this group of accepted students decides to attend Bentley.

On my final day off from teaching in Bahrain, I hire a driver to take me to the main *souk* (market), where for my safety he encourages me to remain in the car, then to the Seef shopping mall. My students recommended the mall, but I find it sterile and oppressive just like the ones at home. On a stroke of good fortune, I get an Imam-led tour of the Al Fateh Mosque—Bahrain's main religious site that broadcasts its services on national television. Given my appreciation for Abrahamic ecumenicalism, I feel culturally more similar to the Imam than to the other tourists. They are rather loud women with intense Texas accents. I presume they are here at the mosque to entertain themselves while their husbands are working at the Fifth Fleet naval base.

The students and I muddle through the rest of the course material, which I do my best to adapt by making it less "Euro/American-centric" and more "Middle-Eastern" with regard to examples and case studies. We even visit the Salman Cultural Center in Manama together. On the day of final presentations, Zahra and many of the students present me with gifts of local sweets: various forms of gelatinous candied nuts. After the final presentations, I invite the entire class out to a restaurant of their choice, which turns out to be a "fish restaurant." Unlike in Russia, in this case I am authorized to expense the cost to Bentley. I take the students' advice on what to order. Following our meal, I bid them farewell. There is precious little time to relax and reflect on the class I just taught. It is Thursday, April 15th, and I leave tonight for Jordan, not to return to Bahrain.

I'm checked out of the Gulf Hotel and checked in at the BAH airport after repacking my suitcases in front of the ticketing desk. I had carefully packed my luggage last night, but then I received additional gifts today. The standard allowance is 23 kg (about 50lbs), and my heaviest bag—hastily re-packed—was eight pounds overweight. I put everything I could into my carry-on, but still had to forfeit some of the sweets; they are as heavy as bricks. Even after giving up some of my Bahraini treasures, Gulf Air charges me $95 for the eight pound overage. Ironically, only today a team of my students presented a glowing paper praising Gulf Air, where one of their parents works. In Bahrain, which I view to be a country of excess, Gulf Air is unnecessarily stingy, and decidedly unfriendly to its passengers, who might as well be cargo.

That evening as I fly from Bahrain to Amman, Jordan I watch the large, modern skyline of Manama disappear. I admire the distinctive features of the Arabian Peninsula. As I drift in and out of sleep, I ponder my overdue introduction to the Holy Land, at least a small piece of it. Concurrently, the Eyjafjallajökull volcano erupts thousands of miles away in Iceland, closing airspace over much of Europe, and shutting down some of the busiest airports in the world. It will be interesting to see if I can make it home to Boston in two days. Any delay after my extensive absence would be detrimental to my domestic situation, if not my professional one.

Amer's taxi is the second cab I attempt to hail when the airport express bus drops me somewhere near the center of Amman. It is nearly midnight. I am carrying a backpack and an "overflow" bag of books, and pulling two heavy suitcases on the uneven, pothole- ridden streets. I'm traveling on my own budget now, and the first cab wanted too much money. I am genuinely famished, tired, and pissed off about my current situation, born of over-zealousness. The cab stops before me and out comes Amer to fetch my bags. I ask him how much for a ride to the Caravan Hotel. "Where?" He asks. "Caravan Hotel…It's next to King

Abdullah Mosque," I reply. Of course now he knows, and he offers 5 Jordanian dinars (JD). I bid him down to 3 JD. On the ride, Amer gives me his life story in decent English, telling me that he was born in Palestine. He then moved to Kuwait, but was forced to flee when Saddam invaded his village. His brother is a doctor in Portland, Oregon. Like me, he has three kids- two boys and one girl, or the other way around. When we arrive at the hotel I pay him 4 JD, and he waits near his car until I check in. He exchanges greetings with the manager and helps me carry my bags up the steps.

My room in the Caravan Hotel is probably the worst I've ever stayed in. For 21 JD (about $30), I have a small chamber on a noisy street facing the mosque. In the bathroom, the toilet drips incessantly and emits the stench of the city sewer. Yet it is probably my ceaseless hunger pangs that contribute most to the sleeplessness of that night. Just as I begin to fall asleep, the mosque across the street calls me to 4:30am prayer. To think that I was afraid of oversleeping! My bus to the UNESCO World Heritage Site of Petra leaves at 6:00am, and before I go, I need to obtain local currency to pay for my hotel and bus ticket, as neither one is payable with credit cards.

I arrive at Petra mid-morning. Petra is by far the most visited tourist attraction and certainly the most interesting place to see on a short visit to Jordan. I can't decide if it's more exciting to walk in the footsteps of Moses, or to walk onto the set of *Indiana Jones and the Last Crusade*. Petra's origins are 2300 years ago as the capital of the Nabateaens, who managed to create an artificial oasis by learning how to control run-off and store water. The surrounding mountainous desert scenery is spectacular. Satisfied with the use of my day, on the bus ride back to Jordan I observe cars pulling off the highway so that travelers have the opportunity to kneel and face Mecca for sunset prayer time.

Upon returning to Amman, I elect to abandon Caravan Hotel and its leaking toilet for the Toledo Hotel just down the street, which costs 60 JD/$100. This hotel has an indoor pool, but not for me. At least I have a chance to utilize the included internet access and get some rest.

I spend my second and final day exploring Jordan's capital of Amman, which interestingly had previously been known as "Philadelphia." I am most impressed by its citadel and amphitheater. As I promised Amer, I phone him when I'm ready to go to the airport. I am happy enough to see this pleasant driver again that I pay him 18 JD for the agreed-upon 15 JD fare.

It's 9:52pm on April 17th, and my Delta flight is scheduled to leave in two hours. *In sha'Allah* (if God wills it), I will be back in the USA in fourteen hours, and then it's just a short flight back to Boston. I'm in an internet café, enjoying a glass of St. George cabernet, *Grand vins de Jordanie.* I'm devastated that this internet café's Wi-Fi is down. To ease my re-entry shock, I had hoped to pass the time waiting by following the play-by-play of my beloved division champion Buffalo Sabres, who at this moment have an afternoon playoff game against the upstart Boston Bruins.

As I prepare to fly back to the USA, I think about the past three weeks. I'm not sure how to tell the whole story of this adventure. In short, this experience has added the Middle (and Near) East to a geographer's mental map. Now I have experiences to report from this fascinating region. I might have time to reflect in more detail tomorrow if I'm still here in Amman. My flight is overbooked, and Eyjafjallajökull has shut down most of Europe's airspace. Most major airports have been closed for two days already, with no end in sight. The BBC reports that "the volcano is intensifying its spew." If I hadn't decided to come to Jordan, it's almost certain that I would have booked my flight through Europe. As it stands, I avoid European airspace by flying back to Boston via a direct flight to JFK. Good things beyond my control happened on this trip—I'm not an extremely religious person, but I really feel the hand of God. I've met some really great people on this trip—my students in Bahrain, Nuri and in Turkey, Amer in Amman. I am really quite blown away by each of the three distinct and positive experiences I've had with new countries: Bahrain, Turkey, and Jordan. I notice a pattern of rapid adjustment to each country: on my arrival day I was nervous and suspicious venturing out into the street, but by the second day I was already out walking the streets with confidence, even after dark. I am thrilled to have met some Arabs and Turks. The ones I met clearly value friendship, honesty, and the chance to be hospitable. In particular, in this broadly defined region of Southwest Asia, I've noticed the role of eye contact, handshakes, and family, and I am in agreement about their importance.

Finally homeward bound, Delta Airlines couldn't have possibly paid me enough to bump me from seat 34C. As I board my flight to JFK, the fascinating events continue. Boarding winds down, the seat next to me remains empty, and I notice a confused-looking woman in a *hijab* searching for her assigned seat. Her boarding pass indicates that she has 34B, the middle seat right next to me. I get up to make way for her. "Boarding completed" is announced. Although it's time to take off, the veiled woman refuses to sit down, attracting the attention of the Delta flight attendants, who try in vain to re-seat her. I come to realize that the conservative Muslim woman simply refuses to sit next to me, being a male infidel. As she struggles with the flight attendants, a Jewish girl leaves her seat in front of me to translate between English and Arabic. The flight attendants take the Muslim woman to the front of the plane. As we take flight, I wonder if they re-seated her in first class, or if she abandoned the plane rather than sitting next to me. It turns out that she must have been put in a jump seat, because she re-appears during the flight to again pace the aisles in search of an acceptable seat. Meanwhile, the seat next to me remains empty for the entire twelve-hour sold-out flight.

14

AUSTRALIA AND NEW ZEALAND: THE YELLOW BRICK ROAD TO OZ

Stand up in a clear blue morning
Until you see what can be
Alone in a cold day dawning
Are you still free can you be?

"While You See a Chance"
Steve Winwood, *Arc of a Diver* (1980)

This lyric could work for nearly any chapter in this book. I put it here because it played on my running mix this morning while my heart was pounding with excitement at the prospect of doing this trip. It's almost inconceivable that such a trip would fall into place, so "while you see a chance, take it," the cheerful song repeats. During that late summer jog with Tessie, I had a conversation with myself, and we agreed that I might be dead or unemployed tomorrow. "Are you still free, can you be?"

It's September 2nd, 2010. This semester is my first sabbatical after eleven years at Bentley. Sabbaticals normally come after seven years, but my opportunity was postponed by a Fulbright, a year as chair, a year as interim associate dean, and a year as director of a sustainability-related program. Our kids just went back to school this week. In a flurry of activity, I spend two morning hours making breakfasts and lunches, and helping Karen and the kids get out of the house for the day. I then begin my own work day with good intentions of making progress on my new research on international flows of tourism to Croatia. When the day begins, I certainly have no intention of booking flights to New Zealand and Australia. This is how an adventure can begin.

We are at the end of our (northern hemisphere) summer, and I am intent on preparing well for my appearance at next week's faculty research showcase event. It has been raining for four days, and the lack of sunshine should help me focus on my work. This is the first such drenching all summer, and I intend to make the indoor time work for me.

The curse of distraction begins with an incoming email message with the subject heading "U2 360° Down Under". Ticketmaster is announcing a pre-sale for U2.com members. I've known about the shows for weeks, but I never considered seeing U2 in Australia. Distracted from what I should be doing, I succumb to the temptation of entertaining this idea. I'll just take one minute to check prices for flights on Kayak… $1600- $2000 from Boston. Wow! I guess they're so high because it's the beginning of summer there. Wait a minute… No way! I'm interested to see that Air New Zealand has much cheaper flights from California cities, at $1000 plus taxes and fees.

I dismiss the idea for a few minutes, and read a journal abstract aloud as if doing so might help me concentrate on what I'm reading. It's probably impossible to get tickets to the show, and I'm not going around the world to see a band I can (and will) see much closer to home.

I muse as I struggle to decide what maps, tables, and other illustrations to include on my poster board presentation. Yes, Australia and New Zealand…I've wanted to visit both countries for as long as I can remember. Since I decided to write this book, I thought it would be incomplete without their inclusion. After all, at least on the surface, this book is supposed to explore places around the world, which means that the stories should be as representative as possible. Such a trip would also be beneficial for my job, I think to myself, seeking further justification. I know little about these places other than what I can teach from my textbook. Australia is arid, with twenty million people reputed to be culturally even less formal than my own countrymen. I know the capital, the major cities, and the fact that like Canada, the country is resource rich and relatively less-industrialized. I am aware that New Zealand has far more sheep than Australia has people, with only one person per twenty sheep. Australia's native people are Aboriginals, and New Zealand's are the Maori. Australia is flat and brown like Texas; New Zealand is green and mountainous like the Olympic Peninsula of Washington State. Brilliant, right? Pleased to meet you, my name is Joel Deichmann, PhD in geography!

To clear my mind, I take a break and grab the dog leash. Tessie knows what's going on, and she meets me at the front door ready for a run. As we start up the hill, "While You See A Chance" by Steve Winwood plays in my ear buds[xxviii]. Our run along the hilly residential streets of South Nashua is only two-miles long. Pathetically short I know, but it gives me exercise and peace of mind almost every day. Any longer would kill Tessie from heat exhaustion, and probably her owner too. With my mind racing and heart pumping like seldom before, I wonder if the run would end with me in a heap on the side of the road. And why not, after all? Heart attacks happen to plenty of forty-one year olds who are in better shape than I.

Having survived the run, I shower and return to my home office. I remind myself that I'm on sabbatical. I've been told that sabbatical means more than just writing; from the same roots as "Sabbath," it means rest and rejuvenation, which as far as I'm concerned doesn't preclude travel. I need to finesse a way to get approval! I can rationalize this, just give me time. I toy around with the Air New Zealand web site. Wow—I could go from

San Francisco to Auckland to Melbourne, then take surface transport to Sydney, spend two days there, and continue back to New Zealand, where I would spend four more. I even check all of my frequent flyer accounts and itineraries to get to San Francisco and back to Boston. Just after Thanksgiving, we'll be driving from North Carolina back to New Hampshire, so I'd better consider a departure airport along the route that won't pull us out of my in-laws' place any earlier than normal. Because I'm not teaching this semester, I had promised Karen an entire Thanksgiving week with her family in Kannapolis.

Australia and New Zealand have even been on my mind for a family trip. Back in May, I priced the trip for five of us at $11,000+ (airfare and hotels), and aside from the prohibitive price I wasn't really sure it's even a good family vacation idea at such a great distance. There are plenty of closer places to go for now, for my wife and kids at least! Even Karen and I alone won't be able to pull off a "couple trip" so soon after my conference with her in Brazil earlier this year. The kids are in school until the weekend before Christmas. My brain scans for friends who might be willing and able to join me. David J. Schoenl. Yes, Dave might do it! I email and text my idea to him at once, acknowledging that I know this is a long shot. There's no immediate reply. Very well, I've got to get to work!

I'm being entirely unproductive today. So while I'm waiting for Dave to reply and putting together my petition to Karen, I renew my U2.com membership for good measure, making me eligible for today's Australia ticket presale. I decide quickly if I can manage to get two general admission floor tickets, it would be a clear indication that I should pursue the trip further. To my surprise, my experimental search ends with two tickets in my Ticketmaster shopping cart! Crap, I have less than one minute to act or the tickets will be released to other customers. My fingers are shaking as I enter the encrypted pass codes. Two minutes to finalize the sale! Two tickets for $99 Australian each—comparably priced to shows in the USA. I *must* do it! I fumble for my wallet and pull out my American Express card.

Later that day, in my beloved four-year-old red Nissan Frontier on a Home Depot run, I follow up with a call to Dave. "Did you get my message?" I ask. "Yeah, I'm all about it, let's go," Dave responds. Dave is always prepared to commit spontaneously to a trip. I've been to half the counties in the USA with him, as well as Germany, the Czech Republic, Russia, Chile, Argentina, and soon we will add the South Pacific. Now comes the hard part: getting the wife's blessing. I have the coolest wife in the world, and she's always *über*-accommodating of my *Passion for Place*. A pair of short phone conversations with Karen alerts me to the fact that she's having a hard day, so timing might be bad. The seventy-two-hour airfare sale ends at 9pm Pacific Time, or midnight for me on the East Coast. Tonight is the night—I would hate to wait until tomorrow and see higher fares, then face the dilemma of backing out right after getting Dave on board.

While cooking dinner, I pick up my cell to text Dave and let him know that I don't think I can ask Karen tonight. While I'm typing, she immediately sniffs out that I'm up to something, and asks to see what I'm typing on my cell phone. Although Karen and I pride ourselves on not keeping things from one another, with great trepidation I refuse to show her. Instead, I tell her that I want to talk to her about something after dinner. I'm not yet prepared to make my strongest case. Should I talk about this book, and how essential Australia is to its completion? I don't want her to think it's all about U2. Her suspicious eyes morph into smiling eyes. Her heart has been softened, as she asks "what are you up to now?" I snicker to myself, then cannot resist singing out "every night, I have the same dream, I'm hatching some plot, scheming some scheme…"[xxix] Yes, there's a U2 line for every situation in my life. "Karen, let's discuss it after dinner."

After dinner, I tell Karen about the scheme. She loves my buddy Dave—a college friend of us both— so his involvement helps my case. The fact that Dave is going probably compensates for the revelation that U2 will be there. Before I book the trans-Pacific flights that night, I go for a walk and take in some quiet time for soul searching. I see a golden opportunity but I also feel some guilt. Is this trip overly indulgent? Why should I be able to travel to the other side of the world when so many people never even leave their home state? Here's why: I've been in that situation too and I might be in it again. I found a way to make this trip happen. If I can make it happen, I *should* make it happen. Who wouldn't take this opportunity? Another line from Winwood's "While You See a Chance" comes to mind....

Don't you know by now
No one gives you anything
Don't you wonder how you keep on moving
One more day your way, go your way

So with Karen's blessing I'm going to Australia and New Zealand in December, period. While on the phone with Dave, I book my flights from San Francisco and Dave books his. Can the timing be better than at the end of my sabbatical? No. Can the season be better than summer, with long days for maximizing exploration? No. Can I beat the ticket price on offer by Air New Zealand? No way. The only bummer is that I'll miss more precious time with my lovely wife and great kids. Although I like to travel, I simply enjoy being home, especially as the holidays approach.

I log onto my frequent flyer accounts to try to find a free award flight to San Francisco the weekend after Thanksgiving. This is challenging on a holiday weekend. I cannot risk rocking the boat by impacting our time with Karen's family at all. In other words, leaving the family in Kannapolis so that I can fly from Charlotte to go on this trip is *not* an option. Having Karen drive 900 miles home with the kids and the dog is also a no-go. After hours of researching award tickets, I eliminate the possibility of flying out of Boston, Manchester, or even

New York. I'll spare the details on why other options do not work, but they have to do with flight schedules and getting to Melbourne by December 1ˢᵗ, then back to New Hampshire in time for Charlie's Christmas play and other holiday events. I float the idea of Baltimore to Karen, but that is still an eight hour solo drive for her on I-95, which wouldn't fly…figuratively or literally. Finally, I find only one workable option, and it is to drive Karen and the kids 550 miles north to Allentown, PA and fly out early the next morning. They will only need to drive about five additional hours on Sunday, and they should be able to do that before traffic gets too busy on I-84 and I-90. God forbid they get stuck in snow, heavy rain, or traffic. This would be very bad in my absence, and so much worse if anything happened to the family while they are driving. The cost for the only workable option is ten dollars and 42,500 miles, nearly twice the miles I want to use for an award, but a small price to pay to protect my marriage and minimize the risks to my family.

The Saturday night after Thanksgiving, we arrive at Red Roof Inn on Airport Road in Allentown, Pennsylvania. As tradition dictates, the family winds down with beer and Domino's pizza and we fall asleep quickly. I'm up at 4am, and I'm at the airport by 5:30am for my 6:30am flight to Atlanta.

It's a five hour flight from Atlanta to SFO with Delta's free holiday trial Wi-Fi on board. Surprised by the quality of the signal, this is a nice chance to catch up on work emails and listen to the live (but spotty) Buffalo Bills game broadcast. Of course, football without beer is like Thanksgiving without turkey, so I buy a couple of Heinekens.

San Francisco. I made it this far. And only now after traveling all day, the real journey begins! I just returned from a research trip to Europe, followed by fifteen hours of driving to Kannapolis via our friends' place in Maryland, then nine hours to Allentown, a two-hour flight to Atlanta, another five-hour flight here, and now I'm ready for a fourteen-hour flight to Auckland on the other side of the world, a two-hour layover, and yet another

332 | Passion for Place

two-hour flight to Melbourne.

Karen leaves me a message that Charlie (13) is concerned that I travel too much, so I text him that he makes a good point; however, the more I travel the smarter I get and the better I do my job. I miss doing things and having talks with him. I'm always busy and he's always on the PS3. He likes to talk about guns and I like to talk about music and travel. Our bond hasn't broken, yet, but I feel estranged after being away so much recently and I'm sure he does too. Karen says that Charlie is anxious about his grades after being away from school for more than one week, and he's stressed about being Ebenezer Scrooge in his school's play *A Christmas Carol*, worried he has forgotten his lines over Thanksgiving break. I do my best to respond appropriately with a conciliatory email message.

Dave joins me at SFO's Star Alliance lounge and I greet him with a handshake and bro-hug. He and I enjoy a few libations while discussing plans for our trip.

As we board our Air New Zealand flight the crew greets us. "I think we're already half way to New Zealand," I tell Dave, alluding to the well-dressed flight crew and their kiwi accents. Short haircuts, trimmed beards, pale skin, and freckles, very friendly and talkative. Dave and I have aisle seats across from each other, and we revel in the fact that there are empty seats next to each of us for our fourteen-hour flight. Air New Zealand's dinner of chicken and sides is excellent by airline standards. I pass out completely as the half-read *Economist* falls from my hands to the floor.

November 29th 2010 barely exists. At 2am, we cross the International Date Line, thrusting us directly into November 30th. I last an entire day of traveling without even thinking about drinking anything! I attempt to soak up some New Zealand popular culture by selecting *Goodbye Pork Pie* and *Parking Lot Contest* movies from the seventy-four offerings on the flight. Flight attendants circulate the cabin for most of the flight, alternating between "Coffee at all?" and "Water at all?" I do my best to throw in a few "cheers" and "sorries;" the latter when I don't quite understand what they're saying. As we approach New Zealand, I am amazed that it's possible to travel at such speeds for so many hours and remain on the same planet!

December 1st begins at 5:00pm on a plane approaching Melbourne, Australia. I can't sleep anymore—too much on my mind, and I'm too many time zones ahead of home. Today is yesterday in America. It is 7pm in Auckland (where I was yesterday at this time), and 10am in San Francisco, 1pm in Nashua, where I belong. Dave had a chance over the weekend to adjust to the Pacific time zone, and it's clear that he and I remain a couple of time zones apart. We check into Enterprise Hotel, then leave again to explore Melbourne. I begin getting tired during a mid-afternoon stroll through Melbourne's well groomed Botanic garden. "Watch out, Dave, you're next," I warn him, referring to the onset of fatigue. We return to the Enterprise hotel at about six to get catnaps before dinner and neither of us wakes up until the next morning. I hear only the sound of traffic in my head, a few cars on the street, and a very loud man in a nearby courtyard room hacking up a lung.

I awaken knowing that today is U2 Day. It's their first show in Australia since 2006, and Dave and I have general admission tickets for the floor right in front of the stage.

After spending a day in Melbourne, my first impressions aren't really earth-shattering. Melbourne is a large, modern, clean, rather nondescript city. It has a population of 3.2 million and seems to have every bit of the bustle of Boston without as much history. It reminds me of Toronto. I'm amazed that it grew so large so fast, beginning with the Australian gold rush of the 1850s. A museum and pedestrian bridge over the Yarra commemorate the city's immigrant history, one that celebrates new Australians from what seems to be every country in the world.

The traffic in my head this morning is about the class meeting I need to get covered on Friday night, and the research manuscript that's waiting to be submitted to a journal. I would really like to have some time on the internet to handle these issues this morning- one of them is urgent and the other I consider to be merely pressing. Wi-Fi, however, is not available in our hotel, and it seems to be difficult to find on short order. Using my iPod touch, I send out a few essential emails from a café across the street from our hotel.

Dave and I have an excellent day at the Melbourne Zoo, which is purportedly the oldest in the world. The range of species is a great surprise! I thought the zoo would be okay, but it's simply amazing! We check out a wide array of bizarre animals, and I find myself taking lots of photos I'll probably never use for anything. From this American's perspective, some of the coolest are the tortoises, monkeys, koalas, and red kangaroos. Buying a few souvenirs for family and friends, I'm shocked at how pricey things are in Australia.

Dave and I split up for a few hours. I walk in the rain to explore Federation Plaza and take care of my other souvenir shopping, then endure another drenching on my way back to the hotel. It looks like we're taking the train to Sydney tomorrow. The trip costs $69 and takes eleven hours, but it will provide a chance to rest, write, and see some scenery, which based upon the map we expect to be less than dramatic. As the gates of nearby Etihad stadium open at 5:30, I watch the news and recuperate alone in our hotel room while Dave explores another of Melbourne's districts. I can't believe how great it feels to be off my feet. The news shows that it's raining just about all over Australia, but it looks mainly dry with occasional showers for the outdoor concert here in Melbourne.

Dave returns to the room and asks when I want to leave for the U2 show. I respond that 7pm should get us into the ellipse. I hope that's not too late to get a good spot. I'm sure there are throngs waiting in the rain at this very moment. We don't want to wait three more hours on our feet for the show. I'm confident that I have the drill down: get into the stadium toward the end of Jay-Z, the opening act, and as fans abandon the stage area for beer or a pee break, we'll make our way around to the ellipse in-between the stage and the catwalk. This approach works in the USA, and I hope it translates well to Australia. I put on a playlist of U2's Atlanta 2009 show and pour some happy hour Yellow Tail Merlot for myself and Dave.

As Dave and I head to Etihad Stadium, I am pretty pumped up and tuned up. The plan to get a spot to stand inside the ellipse works perfectly, although to our surprise, the opening act Jay-Z does not attract many fans; nevertheless, if we had arrived any later we would have been hosed.

As normal, the lights go down as the band takes the stage to "A Space Oddity" by David Bowie. The set list is standard for the tour, except it includes two new (unrecorded) songs: "Return of the Stingray Guitar" and "Mercy." They also play "Scarlet" ("Rejoice") for Aung San Suu Kyi, who was just released last month from house arrest in Myanmar. Other highlights are "Amazing Grace," "Streets," "Bad," "Unforgettable Fire," and "Moment of Surrender." Rain threatens to close Etihad's retractable roof, but the band announces they promised an open-air concert. Then I have a pretty cool special moment with Adam Clayton, U2's bass player. Bono and the Edge move to the front of the ellipse behind me to perform a song. All eyes follow them except for mine. Thinking Adam might feel neglected as he stands alone center stage in front of Larry's drum kit, I turn to face all the eyes looking past me and at Bono and the Edge, reach up, and give Adam a big goofy smile and two thumbs up. He acknowledges me with a smile and nod. Yes! That was nice of a rock star! Energized by my special moment with Adam, I forget for a moment that I can't hold a tune to save my life. A couple songs later, a lovely Australian girl in a halter top turns around as I belt out the chorus of "Streets." She looks at me with a grin, mocking my tone deafness. I shrug, smile back, and apologize. The scene reminds me of my most recent U2 concert with Karen, when she pleaded "Joel, let Bono do the singing." But Bono keeps encouraging the crowd to sing. He's just not close enough to hear how bad it can be. Rain holds off during the entire show, and it's a rare pleasure to have accommodations within easy walking distance. I've never seen so much pedestrian congestion leaving a show, and I'm glad we didn't have to deal with public transportation or driving in this mess.

The next morning, Dave and I are on the CountryLink train that left Melbourne for Sydney at 8:30am. Last night's concert was fantastic, although I confess it would have been better with one less glass of wine. Armed with nearly every one of U2's recordings on my iPod, I'm determined to spend an entire day free from U2. Dave and I are subsisting on snacks that we brought with us. This is hour eight of eleven, and we're due to arrive at 7:54pm. As expected, the ride is scenic but not dramatic. Rolling hills, trees, sheep, and red earth. The hills look like California's Sierra Nevada foothills, the farms remind me of Bandera County, Texas, and the color of the earth and rocks are somehow reminiscent of Utah. It has been uncharacteristically rainy in southeastern Australia these days, and the rain is cramping our ambitions to explore.

There's no better place to contemplate one's juncture in life than on a train. I really miss home, and I fully appreciate everything that fell into place to make my presence here possible. I miss the fires in the sunroom, holiday music, and the fun surrounding the Christmas season. I can't help but ponder that it's late afternoon on a wet Australian day, but only 1am this morning in my bedroom. Maybe it's because Air Supply is crooning in my ear buds, but I start to think about her face, her eyes, her voice, and our kids. I quickly calculate that exactly one week from now we'll all be together, getting ready for Christmas. At least at this moment we're back to the same calendar date for a few hours!

Sydney all day tomorrow, then off to New Zealand for four days. Dave and I are really moving fast and seeing a lot, but this unlikely rain carries on, and it looks like it will continue to cramp our style. We talk about our first few days in Melbourne. They have been excellent; we got to know a nice city quite well, but it is not a city either of us will likely ever visit again. We just cannot think of a reason why we would. This geography lesson was great, but now it's over.

We arrive in Sydney and exit the train station, surprised to see that it's already getting dark out. The rain continues too. Having had little luck on the internet, we set out on foot to find a hotel for $100, but there seems to be nothing available for less than $250. We stop at hostels, but the first two are full. Another hostel grants us refuge. Having gone without a meal all day, Dave and I find an Irish pub and grab some appetizers with a few pints. We both agree that Sydney doesn't seem very hospitable to us on this rainy night. Still jetlagged, we return to our hostel.

The next day brings a break in the deluge. The "subway" is simply a train that goes underground in the city center, and we take it to Olympic Park. Next, we walk back across the Harbour Bridge, pausing to watch a handful of tourists scale the enormous arches high overhead. "Yeah, right….there ain't enough beer in Milwaukee," I say to Dave. He agrees, and adds that climbers need to take a breathalyzer test before starting out anyway. We complete the requisite stroll around the Sydney Opera House, but decide not to do the tour. Everything seems so expensive in Australia, and I think absent a concert, the House's virtues can be appreciated by viewing its iconic exterior. Unlike yesterday, we spend the entire day on our feet. We miss the critically-acclaimed Sydney Aquarium's open hours, and return to the hostel—again on foot. I am tired, but Dave musters the energy to venture out for a drink.

Today—Saturday—is our designated beach day. So Dave and I ask some locals for suggestions, and they tell us there is a bus route to Bondi Beach, probably the most famous beach in Australia. After taking the bus, we grab a quick breakfast at the bus stop and hike along the beach. I touch the water but decide not to go in, as I don't have a towel. Dave goes for a swim, and seems to enjoy it. We hike for an hour along a cliffside trail, looking for a place to sit down and take a meal, but we see only surfers in wet suits and topless sunbathers. The place could be less interesting, I suppose. Toward the end of the day, we make our way back to the hostel to get our bags, and then head to the Sydney airport.

Dave and I reluctantly planned to sleep in the Sydney airport tonight. We have a very early 6am flight to Christchurch, New Zealand tomorrow with low-cost carrier JetStar. The lovely young lady standing alone behind the airline's Sydney check-in counter simply appears to be a nice person. So just for kicks, I greet her and ask, "Is there any chance we might be able to get onto a flight tonight without paying a change fee?" She asks for our tickets, and without saying a word she re-books us for a flight that leaves in one hour. "Have a nice flight," she says, as she hands us our new boarding passes.

We arrive in Christchurch, New Zealand on Saturday night and make our way to the city center to look for a hotel or hostel. After Sydney, we're fine with a hostel, especially if this saves us some money. We ask around on the bus from the airport, and learn that that "Base" is a good option. Base Hostel is full, so we ask at the desk for suggestions, and we're given the names of two others. We end up getting the final available room in the New Excelsior Backpackers hostel for thirty dollars apiece. Half of the hostel is off limits, as it was severely damaged by the Canterbury earthquake of September 4th, which coincidentally occurred the day after we booked our flights for this trip.

Dave and I check in, drop off our bags, and head directly back out. The Excelsior Sports Bar is located outside our hostel on the corner of Manchester and Lichfield Streets. It is our planning headquarters for seeing what we can of New Zealand in four days.

From the looks of things, every last teenager from the surrounding villages came into Christchurch to revel on this

Saturday night. Girls are dressed in skimpy spaghetti-strapped dresses, revealing all-too much of their all-too-fair and often-too-fatty skin. They drink, smoke, giggle, and jaywalk across the streets as the tattooed boys fall off the sidewalks. Once again, the kitchens are already closed, but Dave and I manage to find a place that has cheap beer, expensive French fries, and free Wi-Fi. We chase our deep-fried dinner with another beer for dessert, and then I return to Excelsior to sleep while my energetic, single companion Dave goes out for a drink.

Morning in New Zealand! Dave and I grab coffee "to take away," then walk all around this fantastic small city of Christchurch. The city is riddled with damage from that 7.1 magnitude earthquake in September. There is so much to see here that is different from home. A long haired dude rides his bicycle past us on Manchester Street with a 2-by-4 in his hand and a cockatoo perched on his other shoulder. Naturally, the scene makes me think of U2.

At an internet café, we stop for salmon tube and orange juice, just to get the free Wi-Fi so we can check in at home. With the iPod touch and Skype, I have the chance for a nice talk with Karen. "You've never seemed so far away before," she says. Trying not to sound insolent, I can't resist saying, "That's because I've never been this far away before." David talks to her too, and makes a quick call or two of his own. This new technology that allows me to talk for a pittance to the other side of the world is amazing; I can only imagine where technology is going next.

We take City Bus 28 then hike the trail that climbs over Bridal Pass. It's a ninety minute walk with "extreme inclines and spectacular views," as advertised in a trail pamphlet. The trail begins at the base of the gondola, and goes to Lyttleton, the port of Christchurch. Dave and I hike it like champs, working up a thirst. Then two Yanks walk into a bar where a private party is being hosted. When I realize the bar is not open to the public today, I apologize and start to leave. The friendly locals insist we refresh ourselves with two "jugs" (half pitchers) of beer. Always attentive to tunes, I take note that the jukebox plays "Massachusetts" by Australia's Bee Gees and "Summer Breeze" by Seals and Crofts, as well as several Eagles songs.

We return to our earthquake-damaged hostel and order another jug to share out front while watching people and Christchurch traffic. It's not dark yet, and we're trying to figure out how best to travel across the Southern Alps tomorrow. We both favor hiring a car. We want to go west to Greymouth, which is coincidentally in the news these days because of the Pike River Mine disaster that occurred last month. After that, we'll hopefully travel southward to Franz Joseph Glacier. The train is prohibitively expensive and schedule-restrictive. Everyone we've talked to here says we should simply hire a car. Dave hikes upstairs to double check our flight information. Today is Saturday, and we leave for Auckland at 10:35am on Tuesday, then we fly to San Francisco at 7:30pm. Tomorrow morning, we're looking at forty-eight hours until the long trip home, so probably a car will enable us to most flexibly make full use of that time.

We set forth our final itinerary leg over beer, which, on an empty stomach feels pleasant this hot day. Then we go for pizza, salad, and more beers. On the radio, Tom Petty sings "Free Fallin'." Including the Thanksgiving holiday in North Carolina, it's been more than fifteen days since I left New Hampshire, so "Free Fallin'" resonates with my soul. I've got lots of stuff on auto-pilot right now. Is something good going to come of this? I'm hoping. Still haven't figured that out. And as far as an adventure goes I know that I cannot really "up the ante" after this. At the moment, I'm thinking a long time at home would be nice, and I'm sure the family would like that too. It's strange to be here in New Zealand. Sometimes I take pause and ask myself where I am—maybe it seems like a fusion of Canada, Ireland, and California. Then I really don't know where I am. Imagine if the people didn't speak English! Wow, it's late, and it's time now to wind down and get some rest. We return to our

New Excelsior headquarters and retire after a long day.

Dave and I wake up in the morning and look for a car to hire, which turns out to be a complicated task. When we finally reach the rental agency's address, we're happy that our rental car turns out to be an old one. We want to minimize flash and risk toward the end of our trip. Not knowing what to expect for roads crossing the Southern Alps, I'm a little uneasy. The road remains two-lanes throughout the trip, but it turns out to be just fine. At one overlook, we are impressed with enormous boulders that seem to have been dropped from the sky onto a lush, green landscape. At the next, we encounter the friendly kea bird with its glorious colorful plumage. We take photos of these beautiful birds before discovering that locals consider them to be a common nuisance. Silly us! As if to prevent us from leaving, keas perch on and surround our rental car until some locals chase them away. Meanwhile, an older Kiwi gentleman can't seem to start his car, so we are happy to jump the battery for him. After that, we continue down the winding road toward the sea. What shocks us more than the stunning geography is how quickly we make it through the spectacular mountain range and down to the western coastal plain.

We visit Monteith brewery in Greymouth. Dave and I are invited to pour our own beer samples. We find an amazing hostel near the Franz Joseph Glacier that is outfitted like a resort, but very inexpensive. We run to the store to buy supplies so that we keep our costs down. We will cook our own meals in the hostel's kitchen. Tonight, I will cook and Dave will clean up.

The next morning, we hike as close to the glacier as we're allowed. Unfortunately, access is limited not so much by the trail but rather by the recession of the glacier itself away from the trail. This is still an excellent hike on a misty morning. On the way back to Christchurch, we stop at Punakaiki, or the "pancake rocks and blowholes," which is one of New Zealand's natural wonders. On the coastal drive, we're astounded by the seemingly endless miles of unspoiled gray sand beaches, and by the lack of people on them. On our return over the Southern Alps, we are again struck by the beauty and the brevity of the coast-to-coast journey. We return the rental car then retire for our final night in New Zealand at the New Excelsior.

Did you ever wake up thinking, "Damn, it's going to be just far too many miles and hours until I see a bed again?" That's what I'm thinking this morning. Today, the journey from New Zealand to New Hampshire begins.

Our JetStar flight from Christchurch arrives in Auckland at 11:55 am. There is one place I need to go in Auckland, and it's called One Tree Hill. One Tree Hill is the namesake of a U2 song mainly about justice and love. The New Zealand reference honors a U2 crew member who died in a motorcycle accident while running an errand for the band. The song has been close to my heart for nearly twenty-five years. I convince Dave that it's worth visiting, and the hike will "do us good" before hours of flying.

At the airport tourist information booth, we lock up our luggage and pick up a map. I ask "How can we get to One Tree Hill?" The agent responds, "You mean Cornwall Park? You can take a taxi." "Can we take a bus?" "No, it's too far to walk from the bus stop." Dave and I look at each other in disbelief. Thirty minutes later, we step off the bus at the stop and casually hike twenty minutes to Cornwall Park.

Cornwall Park, location of One Tree Hill, is an incredible urban landscape replete with shady trees, green grass, and sheep busily enjoying both. Dave and I are content just to hike up to the monument where the tree once stood, then take a bus into downtown Auckland. Like Melbourne, Auckland reminds me of Toronto, except I don't think I've ever experienced such a bitterly cold ocean breeze in Toronto. Our final meal in the Southern Hemisphere is seafood soup and Guinness at an outdoor table of an Irish pub.

The city bus returns us to the Auckland airport in time to comfortably collect our bags from the locker and check them with Air New Zealand. We pass through security and find our gate. As we wait to board, I think about this journey. For this American, the adventure to Australia and New Zealand has been enjoyable and educational but not so much of a thrill. I know that I wasn't in either country long enough to make a very authoritative statement, but from first impressions, Australia bears some resemblance to Canada or the USA, and New Zealand is more like Great Britain or Ireland. These reflections are mainly based upon geography and culture. Australia and New Zealand are interesting pieces of the puzzle that is our world. Above all, this quick visit helps me think about geographic versus cultural distance. What seems most remarkable is the magnitude of diversity that lies in-between the former British colony where I live and these other two. In the big "global" picture, I find it remarkable how similar Americans, Aussies, and Kiwis really are to one another.

Air New Zealand departs at 7:30pm to arrive in San Francisco the morning of the same day. The trip from San Francisco back to Manchester, New Hampshire seems to happen in a blink of an eye. Our world is small, as I suspected.

15

GELATO EVERY DAY:
ITALY, CROATIA,
AND BOSNIA-HERZEGOVINA

"Gelato every day"…that's what I told my incredulous kids before we set out on this adventure, our second family trip to continental Europe. It has been twenty-five years since my own *Passion for Place* went into action, and during most of that time I have been blessed with the opportunity to grow a family with Karen while simultaneously growing my career. There are few better ways that I can think of to punctuate the end of the beginning than to dream up a trip for all five of us. The planning started two years ago and was inspired in large part by the film *Under a Tuscan Sun*. Karen has always wanted to visit Tuscany. She is also intrigued by what she's heard from me about Croatia, especially Dubrovnik. Sarajevo has become a special, non-mainstream destination for me, and I want to share it. The whole idea quickly grew legs as soon as we learned the tentative dates for the kids' final day of school, then the excitement began!

Apart from my general obsession with travel, I've been able to accumulate some specific knowledge and amazing friends in the Balkans to share with my family. I also collected enough miles for five more free flights to Europe by carefully playing the airline credit card game for a few more years. I confess that it annoys me when people resentfully suggest I fly for free because I travel a lot. It's almost the reverse: I can afford to travel a lot because I do it on the cheap. Most people probably wouldn't be willing to travel the way I do. Back to the miles: I keep mileage accounts with most US-based airlines: Delta, United, American, JetBlue, Southwest, and even USAir. I make cheap purchases every year or so, like $9.99 DVDs through airline shopping portals to keep miles from expiring. My free trips are almost exclusively from paying those $95 annual fees to credit cards, receiving 25,000 to 30,000 enrollment miles (enough for a free domestic ticket), then using my American Express card for all possible purchases. Karen and I both do this: pay for everything using our our airline cards, and as a result we've achieved Gold Medallion status with Delta, which does come in handy as you'll see later. So, five of us will fly to Europe for a total of $750 in taxes and fees rather than $7500. Our American Express Delta cards make an otherwise cost -prohibitive trip very manageable.

It is the final day of July 2011, and also our 18th wedding anniversary. Having carefully planned and waited, I book our flights the very first day award flights for next June become available, eleven months before our trip. Because we don't have enough miles to fly together as a family, Karen and I will again split up our kids and fly to the same destination on almost the same dates, courtesy of two airlines: AirFrance (using Delta miles) and Lufthansa (using miles from now-defunct Continental). Over the years, I've become comfortable with trans-Atlantic flights, so I have little reason to doubt that Karen and Isabela can find our hotel in Florence, Italy three hours before I arrive with the boys.

Months pass. January 2012. It is a rainy and unseasonably mild Sunday in New Hampshire. We had some friends over last night, and I spend my moderate hangover sketching out our destinations and surface logistics, then reserving our hotel rooms. Over the next months I work out the transportation details and encourage Karen and the kids to line up their wish lists of sights in the cities we will visit.

I'm still too preoccupied with the spring semester and an impending travel course to Europe with students to get very excited about the family trip. The semester ends in May and I travel with nine students to Croatia and Bosnia, to some of the same spots I will take my family. I like the idea that I will visit Sarajevo, Zagreb, and Dubrovnik twice in the space of one month. The group of students is among the best I've ever led. They are from India, Guatemala, Mexico, Venezuela, Russia, Ukraine, and the USA, the group dynamic is incredible, and we all learn a lot together. I finish my course grading and complete my STP expense report, barely finding a moment to catch my breath as June sneaks in unnoticed by giving us a third month of April weather.

I spend my day of departure doing yard work and snaking out the sewer lines of our house. It has become quite a habit lately, and I'm getting better at it. When the sewer backs up, I light a candle, insert a snake, and ream out the lines until my hands are bloody. Forty-five feet of the snake go into the line with minimal resistance, and then I hit some kind of blockage. The first time it happened last year there had been forty people in the house for Karen's 40th birthday party. I need a vacation. At 4:30pm I drop off Karen and Izzy at the airport bus in Tyngsboro, then return home to treat the pool, drain the hot tub, and accept an offer from my friend and neighbor Dale to take my physically exhausted and slightly buzzed carcass to Tyngsboro for the next airport bus at 6:30pm.

We are going to connect in Paris Charles de Gaulle airport (CDG), the airport where I spent nine hours with five students last month after missing our connection by ninety seconds; my third such experience there in the past five years. I am anxious about flying through this French hub, one of the busiest and most chaotic airports I've ever witnessed, but I take comfort in our one hour-forty minute scheduled layover. My sons are fourteen and ten; the older one wears a cast after breaking his arm last month. Despite booking our seats together with Air France, we are now separated, randomly dispersed around the plane. Several calls to Delta Airlines could not get us back together on Air France. At the airport, however, we bypass the long check-in line and the agent at the Gold Medallion line groups us together on the upper deck of the 747-400 airplane. All three travelers are very optimistic as we await our departure.

Charlie, James, and I fall asleep on the aircraft while waiting for departure, which is over one hour late because the Air France crew cannot seem to close the door on the plane. By the time we begin our descent over France, I become aware that our layover at CDG in Paris has been reduced to fifteen minutes. Well aware of CDG's enormity, and anticipating the challenge that lies in store when we land, to save time for the rat race I do something I never do—I take care of my morning constitutional in the aircraft's bathroom. It seems to be a fitting tribute to this airline right now. It's okay to write about it; everybody poops, even you.

When I return to my seat, I ask the flight attendant for advice on making our connection. Cherise walks me through the CDG map, informing me of my arrival and departure gate numbers, which I later discover to be wrong. Dutifully, she explains that she cannot let us off first, because everyone else on the flight is also late for their connections. Cherise assures me that we will make ours, which is the response I've come to expect from the French; just get out of my face, try in vain, and then become someone else's problem. Déjà vu, I think, is an apropos French expression. I know the odds but I thank Cherise in French with a smile.

I begin to sweat profusely even *before* we begin our sprint through the airport. I prepare the boys for what lies ahead; everything from positioning when we land so that we can jockey for the exit, to getting ready for running carefully; our only hope is to give it all we've got. Thankfully, we already have our boarding passes. As we wait at the starting gate, I am reminded that Karen is not comfortable finding her way to the small Hotel Giada in Florence, and even if she does find it, the three of us are likely to arrive only very late tonight, much later than our 3:30pm scheduled arrival. So much for our 6pm dinner plans with my former colleague Marissa, and I have no way to contact either of them from Paris.

My normally slightly-elevated blood pressure must be spiking right now. Man, either I need to change my ways, go on medication, or prepare to die early. Doing my best to follow the confounding terminal and gate signs while running, carrying my bag, and watching my boys, I lead a sprint that lasts thirty minutes, minus time in a customs line, a train, and a bus. We excuse ourselves repeatedly in English, German, or French, depending upon the case; I don't want to be a jerk, but people seem to be wandering aimlessly and standing randomly on the escalators. *"Rechts stehen, links gehen"* (Stand on the right, go on the left!), I shout in German, intermittently cursing Air France and this *freakin'* airport out loud, hoping the boys won't hear. I think I even drop an s-bomb. I don't like myself right now but I am so fed up with multiple CDG failures and I'm drained. We literally jump over suitcases, strollers, and sleeping bodies trying to keep hope alive in this seemingly endless race. Drenched in sweat and finally at our designated terminal, I spot an overhead screen that announces a closed gate—ours. I don't have the time or the spirit to yell to the boys, who are now dashing ahead of me. It is still 200 meters to that gate.

As we arrive in the nearly deserted end of the terminal, soaked with sweat and out of breath, we confirm that out gate is indeed closed. Here we go. Standing at the neighboring gate are two female mechanics. I approach them, and do my best to make my case. To get their attention while pointing to Charlie and Jack, I mutter something to the effect of *"excusez moi, s'il vous plaît... J'ai un handicapé et un bébé,"* then gesture toward the plane parked on the tarmac. One of the women says she speaks English, so I ask her if we can board that plane just outside the window. A hefty woman we had passed during the later stages of our dash catches up, and she's also late for our flight. She is from Atlanta, which I could have guessed from her accent. Now we have strength in numbers; she is first class, and so we are in good company! We await our new boarding passes. I cannot express in words how relieved I am. The Georgian lady looks at her new coach class boarding pass, puzzled, then exclaims in an uncommonly angry southern drawl, "But I paid Delta $6000 for a first class ticket; what happened to my seat?" I butt in… "Ma'am, let's just get on the plane while we can, and I'm sure you can work the rest out with Delta later." The mechanics scan their badges to open the door to the tarmac for us. I feel like I am on the last plane out of a war zone, pissed off that the situation happened in the first place, yet also immeasurably grateful to our deliverers.

Our plane sits on the tarmac for more than an hour. While waiting to take off, I wonder if Karen and Isabela made it to Florence. It turns out that this departure is delayed because an oxygen mask will not remain secured in its overhead compartment. By the time three French crew members finally resolve this issue, a baby in the middle of the plane is screaming so loudly that his father picks him up to comfort him, and refuses to put him back in the seat. A standoff with a flight attendant ensues. "Sir, international law requires all passengers to be strapped in for take-off." An ugly American in the back of the plane, who claims to be late for a (Wednesday) wedding, shouts angrily "Put the fucking kid in the seat or I'll come up there and do it myself!" The flight attendant retreats to the cockpit in tears, a moment passes, and then the captain comes on the loudspeaker to announce that "We will be returning to the gate immediately to deplane two passengers unless they are both properly seated." Our plane is in the air five minutes later. Apparently, some nearby peacemaking passengers helped to diffuse the issue.

Charlie, James, and I arrive in Florence, but predictably our luggage doesn't. I am not at all surprised and quite frankly I really "don't even give a rat's ass," to steal one of my buddy Dave's favorite expressions. After all of that, I'm just happy to be in Italy. I know the drill with Air France, so I fill out the usual lost luggage report and collect three overnight care packages from the attractive Italian Sky Team lady. Within an hour, the boys and I are reunited with Karen and Isabela, only about two hours late. Just enough time to get a shower and meet Marissa, who takes our exhausted gang on a "ten minute" scenic walk past the Duomo, through the city, and across the river. The walk goes on and on, and I cherish the opportunity for our kids to experience the sincere generosity, informed perspective, and enthusiasm of our guide, even though they would rather be sleeping. Although born American, Marissa is the picture of European hospitality who so loves her surroundings that she neglects to notice that ten minutes has become more than an hour. It's time for my kids to "Slav up," a term coined by my students in Bosnia.

Marissa leads us all to a bar that she says offers "overpriced drinks and free tapas;" a good deal in my view. We encourage the kids to eat the assortment of meats, cheeses, and salads, but to them this is exotic food. To be fair to the restaurant, I buy a couple of rounds. Marissa is articulate and charming, and it seems that she and Karen could have been friends if they had grown up together. They are ready to explore more of Florence, but the kids are tired, and I do my best to keep the factions together. We promise the kids gelato and an early bedtime, and then make our way back to Hotel Giada. Karen seems sure that Marissa wants to show us more of the city after we put the kids to bed, but I am (maybe) cautious about overstaying our welcome, or maybe just physically and mentally drained myself. And after all, Marissa is more acquaintance than friend, and I don't want to burden her. We've come to call this present condition as "hitting a wall"; after running, cutting grass, and playing in poopies (the plugged sewer) at home then sleeping on a plane and dealing with another Air France debacle, I am so exhausted that every cell in my body has targeted a good night's rest as soon as possible.

As we return to Hotel Giada, the manager asks us what time we want breakfast in the morning. "Nine thirty, please," Karen replies. The manager then tells us the only available slot is at 7am. Seems the table is small so they need to stagger the breakfasts. Surprised that breakfast is even included in the hotel price, we're are willing to take any time slot, even though it's impossibly early on our first day in Europe, six time zones ahead of Nashua.

Despite the racket of foreign revelers and street vendors tearing down and setting up their stalls outside our hotel window, we first emerge from our deep sleep at 9:30am (3:30am back home). There are open tables in the breakfast room, so we sheepishly ask for some coffee and a bite to eat. A breakfast table is set for us, and everything is right with the world.

We do a short foot tour to the Duomo and wait in the long but fast-moving entrance line, and then explore the cathedral's interior wonders. There is still some time to kill, so we visit Basilica di Santa Croce, what Frommer refers to as Tuscany's Westminster Abbey, resting place of many famous Italians including Michelangelo, Machiavelli, Dante, and Galileo. The kids know these names. We fully appreciate the presence of greatness, even if their souls have left the scene.

Karen, Charlie, Isabela, James, and I wait at the Ufizzi for our reserved 1pm entrance. The on-line reservation was costly, but it's nice to be able to avoid the lines. Isabela and James are not impressed by the sculptures of naked men, and the kids start to refer to male appendages as "Davids." Oh, well, I think to myself, this is an educational trip in ways that I did not anticipate. We see a good portion of the museum, even though the kids are again visibly spent. I tell them, "This is what we do in Europe: we walk, explore the city, and eat gelato." "Gelato" was the magic word. Marissa texts me that she can meet at Piazza San Lorenzo at 3pm, but that she is going on a trip with her boyfriend at 5pm. She offers to show us more of Florence, but the kids are exhausted and hungry. So, we find a place where the kids can sit and eat pizza while the adults sip the local wines she recommends. Charlie, Isabela, and James impress their parents with their ability to maintain an adult conversation.

After dinner, we say our goodbyes to Marissa. She is simply a remarkable person, and meeting her in Florence really set a positive tone for this trip. On our own now, Karen and I gently inform the kids that the final task for the day is to cross over to Oltrarno (left bank of the Arno) to Piazzale Michelangelo, explaining that, by the way, today is a "double gelato day." I buy "walking drinks" for everyone at a grocery store on the way up the hill. We find an excellent seat on the steps to view the skyline of Florence. Karen and I share a bottle of Chianti as we watch the sun set over the historic city, with the Duomo as its centerpiece. Noticing a teaching moment and an easy answer with the sun descending to our southwest, I ask the kids to point toward Nashua, New Hampshire. After some discussion, they confidently point in the correct direction. Nicely glowing from wine and/or sugar buzzes, we skip back to Piazza San Lorenzo, holding hands as the sidewalk width allows, and pausing to take blurry photos. Finally, one last stop for that promised double gelato.

We wake up for our second full day with a mess to clean up. All sleeping in the same room, we need to repack our bags and Charlie's backpack (remember that he is wearing a cast on his arm, so I must fill it and lift it onto his shoulders). We eat breakfast of Nescafé, toast, and fruit, put our bags in the luggage room, and walk to the intercity bus station. We board a bus for Siena and disembark a short distance from the square. Walking the steep lanes surrounded by Tuscan brick in the blazing sun feels like hell on earth, but it looks like heaven. We visit the fantastic Duomo, eat a simple lunch of *panini*, and the sun's brutal heat helps us quickly realize that climbing the tower of Loggia di Mercanzia is not on the table. Instead, we spend our afternoon in Siena guzzling fountain water, sodas, and beer while trying to hide in the shade as much as possible.

Our train from Florence to Milan leaves at 6:55pm. We arrive at 8:40pm, and take the Metro to Piazza del Duomo. We take the escalator out of the Metro to see the sunset behind the most magnificent Duomo. Was it last night we were in Florence, and today Siena? We've seen so much already. I tell Charlie to stay put with his mom and the LBKs (little blonde kids) while I try to figure out which tram will get us to our hotel. It seems as though all trams depart from the Duomo, so there are lots of things that can go wrong. Walking around the block by myself, I discover that in our direction the tram lines split along three successive streets. I find another stop with our tram number then call my companions, who have just earned patience points, maybe just because they are in awe of the architectural spectacle before them, the Duomo.

The family alights correctly at Piazza Resistenza Partigiana, but I need to scout three streets alone before locating the first street sign. I leave the family in the square; by now they understand that I sometimes need to scout, and it's better to sit tight than to follow me and then have to backtrack because I led them the wrong way. None of the people I ask seem to recognize our hotel's name. I find out later that it's because our hotel is new. I nearly knock over a large glass vase while carrying my crippled son's large backpack into in a small tobacco store to ask for directions. It turns out that we need to walk back in the direction from which we came, and the hotel is on a side street just off the main square. Good grief; it's 11:30pm, we haven't eaten, and I am at wit's end again. Why do I do this to everyone? Alas, the bright décor of the simple but modern Idea Hotel Milano Corso Genova and the cheerful receptionist give us just enough willpower to keep going until our day is complete. Rather than search for a restaurant, we elect to eat snacks and go to sleep.

Our day begins with a long breakfast and a short walk to

Santa Maria delle Grazie.

Karen really wants to see Di Vinci's Last Supper, but signs across the counter at the entrance clearly state in five languages "SOLD OUT." Then again, our connection in Paris said "BOARDING ENDED" too. I have plenty Euros in my pocket, and I don't mind spending them for things that are important, and the Last Supper seems to be ever so important to us. I encourage Karen to follow the earlier advice of our hotel receptionist and ask if there were any cancellations for today, but she declines, saying, "That's a man's job." I assure her that her intoxicating blue eyes and charm give her a better shot at it. Finally, I relent and ask the mean-looking lady. To my surprise, she responds tersely that "we can take five at 12:15pm." Did she learn her English at McDonalds? I ask how much it will cost. "Where do you come from?" she counters, and I immediately know why. "America," I reply, wondering if my longish hair could help me pass as Dutch. "32.50€, cash only." If we had been Dutch, entrance would have cost half that. Note to self: when I get home, encourage our government to charge Europeans double prices on our taxpayer-supported national treasures.

Now we have time to kill…"Take it to the Duomo!" as Bono said to the Edge in Milan on their 2005 Vertigo tour. In two hours, we walk to the Duomo to view its magnificent interior, drink Coca-Cola on its front steps, and return on a tram for our appointment with Jesus and the disciples. Our group of twenty-five viewers passes through airport-like security and some sort of air-sealed purification antechamber before our fifteen minute viewing of Leonardo da Vinci's Last Supper, which survived shelling in World War II, then was left to open-air destruction during post-war rebuilding. As I gaze upon this masterpiece, another U2 lyric rises in my brain: "We ate the bread, drank the wine, everybody having a good time, except you (Jesus), you were talkin' about the end of the world." Charlie shares his insights from Dan Brown's *The Da Vinci Code* with the family as we all pick away a bit at the less altruistic aspects of the Catholic Church. We've done this before, but the exercise seems to get more intense during our time in Italy.

It's Father's Day today, so I'm wearing my "World's Best Dad Hands Down" t-shirt that I forced my kids to make by putting their hands down in red, blue, and yellow paint many years back, then placing their handprints on a white t-shirt. The family enjoys the World's "Best Panini Hands Down" at Stazione San Giovanni while waiting for our train to Como. We spend the rest of the day using water taxis on Lago di Como, taking in the dramatic green and blue landscape and enjoying the cool breeze generated by movement over the water. Today it's all *birra* (beer) and gelato, family, and fun. This has to be one of the best days of a pretty good life. Karen is beautiful and in her glory, head tilted back and eyes closed in the sunshine. I can also see that the kids have adjusted to our European time zone and that they are taking an interest in their surroundings.

As the sun fades over the foothills of the Alps, we take a train back to Milano and eat pizza while watching Germany beat Denmark in a *EuroCopa* football game. The pizza is fantastic but this is our first lesson that in Italy the *vino della casa* (house wine) is sometimes not.

We leave tomorrow for Venice. I would like to see more of Milan. I would like to see more of Florence and Siena too. In Milan, I would start with the Castello Storzesco, the big palace we saw from the outside at 9:00 last night, when it became clear to me that I could expect the kids to walk no farther. So far, the places we've seen on this adventure aren't much like the part of southern Italy (Salerno, Naples, and Sorrento) that I experienced unenthusiastically as a youth in 1987.

On the morning express train 9711 from Milan to Venice, I pause for one of those rare moments to catch my breath and ponder who and where I am, ironically while traveling at 250 kilometers per hour. I reflect upon the unlikely fact that I am traveling in Europe *again* with the love of my life and our kids, all of whom I hope will someday read this book. Hi guys! Right now, they have no idea what I'm working on. Karen is reading our guidebook, Charlie reads a Star Wars series book on his Kindle, Isabela plays with a Smurf app on her iPod, and James drinks Coca-Cola while studying the landscape. I recall my first intercity train trip in Germany in fall of 1987 from Mainz to a Rotary outing in Heidelberg. I immediately fell in love with the strong sway and the sounds of the trains. Today, I look across to my son James and see that this fascination is in his blood also. Yet, there are 32 years of age between us. Even if he uses paper tickets, he will probably never know the joyful challenges of figuring out international travel without the help of the internet, cell phones, and electronic schedules at train stations. As the train halts in Verona and people embark and search in vain for open seats, our family sits comfortably in the seats I reserved from my laptop computer at the kitchen table in Nashua last month. Verona is home not only to Romeo and Juliet, but also to a very nice banker, Roberto Teso. I met Roberto in Croatia while leading a student program in Zagreb last year, so I tell my family about Roberto and send him fond wishes from his own train station. The train begins to move faster and faster at speeds unseen in the USA and unheard of in Europe a quarter century ago, when I first was here.

The five of us disembark with our backpacks and small suitcases at Venezia Santa Lucia. I'm so happy that I need to consciously subdue the urge to bounce as I step. Our train ride was amazing and everyone is having a great time. We leave the station via the brick wall corridor on the left and endure the smell of baked on, stale urine. After a quick left outside onto Rio Terra Lista di Spagna, we arrive at Hotel Adua, which I found on hotels.com at 100€ for a quadruple room. Karen waits outside with the rest of our luggage as the kids and I ascend the twenty steps of the narrow staircase. The lady at the desk greets me and talks me into upgrading our room to one with a bathroom for 10€ more. Instinctively, I reckon this is a good time to clear the air that she's already seen a total of five people in my party, and gesture that the "bambino" (ten year old James) will be using his own sleeping pad. I hand her 10€ and she hands me the key. She gives me the hairy eyeball but that's the extent of it.

There are no more new cities for me on this trip. Maybe this is why I am very nonchalant about what foot route to take to Piazza San Marco. Let them figure it out. I have been here before; why not let them lead rather than dragging them around behind me? I follow them without a map, eventually remembering that the signs on the buildings, can be followed to the famous covered rock bridge Ponte Realto, Piazza San Paulo, or the train station. We can tell that we are close when the noise, pedestrian traffic, and shop prices intensify. As we enter the sunny square from the shady narrow alleyways, we meet a wall of heat. I duck back into an alleyway where I had seen "bargain" drinks for 2.50-3.00€, and we enjoy one in front of the Palazzo Ducale. Nobody in our family seems to want to wait in line to enter the palace, so Karen leads us to the waterfront, where we immediately get our first gelato for the day. Already, it is abundantly clear to everyone that this will be our second "double gelato" day.

Karen and I try in vain to text our neighbor Sue and my brother Chuck to let them know we are still alive, as well as wishing Karen's father a belated happy Father's Day (my own father doesn't text). In our first five days we have really struggled to find internet access, although I confess that because my whole family is here it hasn't been a priority for me. It makes sense to wait out the worst of the oven heat by sitting down in shaded chairs outside a restaurant with Wi-Fi, and relax with some food and wine. The waitress doesn't bring us a menu, but does inform us that there are tapas inside. Sounds like the place in Florence, where we pay for overpriced drinks and snack for free. Perfect, except the food is behind a glass case. After much cajoling, I convince the hungry ones in our party to go in and point to what they want. Shortly, two small plates arrive with octopus tube sections, celery sticks, and some deep-fried items. We fire off a couple of emails to send proof of life, and then remain seated until two bottles of water and one liter of wine are empty.

We wander back toward the northern part of Venice, and my intention is to point out Ponte Rialto, which I do. As nobody really ate at the previous place, Karen proposes that we sit and eat in view of the bridge and the throngs of tourists taking their photos. I decide to myself that it's okay if it costs a little more; we'll pay for this view. They agree upon a restaurant that, to me, looks anything but authentic. The laminated menus are complete with photos of the offerings, mainly pizza and pasta dishes. I don't like this artificial place, and this time it's not about price. Although there are no drink prices on the menu, I remind myself that on this trip, I'm really not worried about minor cost differentials. Karen reluctantly follows me and the kids back out of that restaurant, and we go around the block for (also previously frozen) entrees at half the price. This is the second time today that I've "unchosen" a place that my wife chose; I must be getting on her nerves. I apologize later on. It turns out that I have a combination of motives: to let other people choose, but also to guard against choices they make when informed by experience. Call it a veto. She has the same veto power, but the kids don't. After all, the parents are paying for this trip.

To avoid being cheap, I honor Karen's request to take a boat trip on the Venetian canals. I purchase our one-hour tickets for 35€ (no discount for kids over six), and we spend the next 90 minutes on the state water taxi, enjoying the views as the sun meets the horizon. The kids are visibly exhausted, so we conclude our day with the second gelato (*melone, mango,* and *strattacelli* seem to be evolving as favorites). We put the kids to bed and then resist our own fatigue to walk out to the canal and share a bottle of mediocre wine on the canal. We have a fantastic time talking, but fail to finish the bottle. We return to our room to find that the kids waited up for us while watching Italy beat Ireland in the *EuroCopa*, as well as other Italian television shows. Luckily, our questions probing about late-night porn—common in Europe—leave us satisfied that our kids remain unexposed to it and relatively uncorrupted.

We wake up to an alarm at 7am to pack for our 9:27am train to Rome. Breakfast is not included here, so I take the family out to purchase the sort of 2€ fruit cups that were ubiquitous the day before. No luck, only whole fruits today, so I buy apples and soft drinks for the train. We can finally use up some of the granola bars I have been carrying since Nashua.

We arrive in Rome on schedule, and I lead the family out of Termini to Hotel Urbis, which is just to the right of the main train station on Via Marghera. Our hotel is on the second floor, and there are other small hotels on the first and third floors. The tiny elevator is simply a cage, and all of the moving parts are exposed. I send Charlie in with most of the bigger bags, and climb two flights of stairs with Karen and the LBKs. As we arrive on the second floor, the gentleman at the desk checks us in, and we enter our adjacent rooms 24 and 25. Tomorrow is Karen's 41st birthday, so it will be nice to have some space. Hotel Urbis is modest, not unlike its $65 pre-paid price, and all of the guests share a bathroom at the end of the hallway. The bathroom has a stand-up shower and "removable" toilet seat: one that the user needs to place on the rim and balance if sitting down is required.

We are all famished after the trip from Venice, and I know I should have bought sandwiches for the train. My response to any complaints is the same that I provide after grocery shopping at home: that I will honor requests for folks who take the time to come shopping with me.

As set forth by Karen and Charlie, the goals for this afternoon are to visit the Colosseum and then the Parthenon, both on the other side of enormous Termini station… too close to bother with the metro but nevertheless a considerable walk. Tomorrow we will see the Sistine Chapel at the Vatican Museum and some other highlights of Rome. Our itinerary doesn't seem very ambitious, but in this oven heat it is difficult just to be outdoors. There is ever so much to see just by walking down these streets, where so many important events have taken place throughout Western history!

Shortly, Karen, the kids, and I find a café that advertises Wi-Fi, air conditioning, and no *couvert* (cover charge). *Couvert* approximates the notion of tips in Italy, except it goes to the establishment rather than the server. We all enjoy the best *panini* imaginable. When we return home, I need to remember to introduce to our regular menu the simple wonder of *panini*, which Karen and I first encountered at a beach near Athens, Greece in 1993, then forgot about. I ask our server for the check with, "*Il conto por favore.*" His immediate response is, "Where are you from?" and I realize I must have failed in my attempt to speak his language. I tell him we're from Boston, and he reacts with a smile and an almost unrecognizable "Celtics! Red Sox!" When, as instructed by the waiter's gestures, I leave the table to pay at the counter, I am shocked by the prices that appear on the bill. My draft beer went from the posted 3.50€ to 6.00€, and I see similar surprises for the sodas and sandwiches! I manage to get our bill reduced by about 3€, but I'm not sure how this was recalculated. We had made our selections according to the prices posted over the food, but now I notice there is another tier of pricing that applies to people who sit down. So much for no *couvert*! Lesson learned; I brush it off.

The family walks down the avenue toward the Colosseum, and at Izzy's request we stop at a pet store, for whatever reason I'm not quite sure. I find myself in rare form. For a change, I want to give everyone a chance to pursue their own interests and I find it enjoyable to observe the kids as they do. Today, we are in no rush whatsoever.

As we approach the Colosseum, an East Asian-looking guide approaches us and offers us a guided tour and bypass of the general admission line for 25€ each, no discount for children. Karen had read about this sort of arrangement in our guidebook, and is showing enough interest to keep the female guide nearby. Right now, I am thinking it's about 800 degrees out, the kids are exhausted, and we don't want to subject ourselves to the rigors of a structured historical tour, let alone at the price of $160. The kids, to their credit, are wise to the debate between me and Karen and immediately veto any guided tour. So, the kids get a veto after all! To thank them for their good judgment, I promise them an extra gelato later.

We queue up in the regular tour line, where we'll pay 12€ per person to get in. Discounts apply for EU residents, but not for kids unless they are Europeans. As we wait, I'm thinking about the price structure, which to me seems exorbitant and uncool if not unfair. Americans are famous for being culturally ignorant, and yet we get charged nearly double to visit European sites of antiquity. Is the goal of European pricing schemes to keep Americans ignorant, or is it simply opportunism? By comparison, the taxpayer-supported US National Park System offers *annual* passes for $50 (per carload) to visitors, irrespective of their origins. I am irritated by the prices charged in European countries for simple things. Don't get me started on the standard .50€ "fee to pee" that is imposed throughout much of Europe. Peeing and potable water should be among the most basic of human rights, and yet Europeans lecture the USA about social justice!.

We are now at the front of the line, so I pay 60€ for the five of us, plus rent an audio guide for Karen (5€), inviting her to tell us if she learns anything from it that we really need to know. I've rented those audio guides, and they are the next-worst thing to real-life guides who speak poor English and move at a snail's pace in the frigid rain of St. Petersburg or the oven heat of Rome.

We tour Rome's Colosseum for less than an hour, all at once realizing how incredibly parched we are. Karen finishes up with

the audio guide, admittedly having heard very little information worth sharing with us. My pocket map shows a fresh water
fountain very close by, in front of the Titus Arch. Wow–free
water in Europe! We head directly to the Arch, but within
10 meters of the fountain, we run into a tall fence. A sign on
the turnstile gate from the ruins, our target on the map, says
"EXIT ONLY." I can't help but think of National Lampoon's
Vacation: "sorry folks, gate's closed, moose out front should
have told you." For what seems like an eternity, we use the
map to search in vain for the designated entrance, Reaching
two dead ends, I relent and negotiate five 1€ bottles of cold
water for 4€. I just saved $1.30, and Karen's embarrassment
shows. We can afford the price, but it's the principle, and I
wanted the challenge. I told the young man he does a good
business, and he is willing to make the sale. Out of water now,
he leaves his post, presumably to buy another case for 6€ to sell
to overheated tourists like us at a 400% profit.

When at last we arrive at the entrance to the Palatine Hill
ruins, Charlie discovers that he has misplaced his 12€ multi-
site entrance ticket. He is wearing a full cast on his broken arm
and is struggling with his one good hand to find the ticket in
his pockets. He can't find his ticket, so the fine young tick-
et-checkers refuse to let him through the gate. I am already past
the gate, so I hand Charlie my own ticket over the fence. He
can't scan himself in, as my ticket has already been cancelled.
Are you kidding me? Charlie is wearing a cast. These guys can't
see what's going on and help us out here? "Another 12€?" I ask
the young man, who is showing little emotion. "Unless you're
a European citizen," he responds, "then it's only 7.50€." "May
I please speak with whomever is in charge?" I ask. The young
man gestures to a small booth. Visibly pissed, like the typical
annoying tourist I ask the supervisor the embarrassing question
whether he speaks English. "Yes, of course." "Thank you," I say
as I take out my camera and display several photos of all five of
us inside the Colosseum a few minutes earlier. It's my attempt

to prove to him that we paid to get in there. "We spent 60€ an hour ago for tickets for the whole family, I have a receipt, and my son has a broken arm and dropped his ticket, I would like to show my family the ruins." "Good," he replies, nodding to the young man at the gate. "Okay, *grazie mille*," I respond, testing out a new expression I heard on a live U2 track from Milan, half surprised that this situation and my blood pressure didn't both escalate further in the scorching heat.

Wow, Palatine Hill! When Karen and I were in Rome in 1994, we didn't have money for the entrance fee. Even though our kids are pooped, I think it's fair to say that the sights reward everyone for their perseverance. We manage to find the poorly-marked exit from the ruins after the loudspeakers announce in Italian, French, German, and English that the gates will be closing soon. On the way to dinner, I push the family to see the nearby Il Vittoriano monument. In Florence, Marissa advised us to never eat at a place that shows photos of the entrees; they are frozen dinners, she says. In this section of Rome, however, it seems that's all we can find. We eat pizza and drink less-than-mediocre house red on the way to the Trevi Fountain. When we get there, we enjoy gelato and a mini-bottle of Banfi, which was suggested earlier by Marissa, but which we didn't have the chance to try in its home region of Tuscany. This excellent red wine becomes our favorite during the rest of our time in Rome.

We navigate our way back uphill to the hotel as the sun sets. Wow, what a great day! The small store at street level outside our hotel has two doors. As Karen takes the kids up to bed, I stop in, searching for juice for the kids and more wine for me and Karen. I collect the items I would like to purchase. I greet the gentleman behind the counter with "*Buona Sera*" then give him a confused look as he bags the items, hands me a receipt, refuses my money, and points to a cashier in the center of the store. I wait in line there to pay, then return to the guy with our drinks and present him with the receipt, which is now stamped with the English word "PAID." This is educational for me. I guess I understand that they must conduct business this way because the store has two doors, but wow—how inefficient to pay those extra employees for busy work and make customers wait in line three times!

Tonight we have internet access, which allows me to address a few backlogged work emails and post some travel photos on Facebook while Karen naps. With the luxury of our own room tonight, she and I enjoy a bottle of wine and some quiet time together.

It is difficult to get moving in the morning. We all really need some rest, but I had planned to get up at seven, eat breakfast at 7:30am, and get on the Metro by 8am for our 9am admission to the Vatican Museum. As luck would have it, I am up at 6am and in spite of my supplications, everyone else emerges more like 7:45am, so I am a bit agitated. We race to the Metro at Stazione Termini during the morning rush hour, and I buy McDonald's coffee-to-go for Karen. All of us struggle to board the packed train through different doors. When we get inside, we receive a massage and a sauna. The subway reaches our stop at 8:35am, and I tell the family that "we gotta wiggle," an expression my own father would use to hurry up his kids. In their excitement, Karen and the older kids move fast and lead the way, following the signs to the Vatican. But James is dragging, and he's holding me up with a tight grip of my hand. I spot the next sign to the Vatican Museum, and we are able to break away from the main-line foot traffic stampede that is headed for St. Peter's Wednesday papal appearance.

The five of us walk swiftly through the line that says "pre-purchased tickets only," past throngs of folks waiting to pay for general admission. The museum's collection is worthwhile, but as my fourteen year-old son points out, it holds many valuable items that were "acquired," "procured," "taken," or otherwise *stolen* from places all around the world. Most of the "Davids" (as Izzy calls sculptures of nude men) had been castrated, which Charlie explains was because Pope Pius XII, in his Holy wisdom, wanted to discourage lustful thoughts inside Vatican City. We estimate that he just was repressing his gayness. All told, this is a great visit, but it doesn't leave any of us feeling very warm and fuzzy about the Roman Catholic Church.

After the museum, we queue for the security lines to enter St. Peter's Cathedral. As we enter the sanctuary, I stand in awe at the enormity of the place, speculating that someone could comfortably fly a small aircraft inside this church. It is beautiful, but I know I'm not the only one in the family who is a little bit angry that the denomination fancying itself the true Christian Church would erect such opulent buildings with money from its devoted followers while keeping them in the dark and treating many of them–particularly women–so unfairly. I know that the Catholic Church stands for many good things, but I am not sure if God favors this grand monstrosity over small, modest places of worship found elsewhere throughout the world.

We leave this spectacle and hike past the Castel Sant'Angelo, then cross Ponte Umberto on our way to Piazza Navona. I realize that traveling with Karen and our own kids in Europe seems too easy. I don't need to worry about attitudes from other people's kids or any other undercurrent. We are all exploring, observing, and learning, and there are no grades or expense reports to do. We find a nice restaurant that allows Karen and me to share a carafe of water and the kids to bring in gelato from a nearby stand, which costs half the price of the gelato dishes at the present restaurant.

The last item on our Rome bucket list is the Spanish Steps. Karen is on board for the final push, and we manage to get the kids to walk there. We give the kids the option to take the Metro to Termini, which is near our hotel, or walk another mile and instead use the ticket money on gelato when we arrive. They choose the latter.

Our second morning in Rome involves packing up, eating breakfast at a Termini café, and boarding our train to Bari on the Adriatic Coast.

We arrive in Bari at 1:30pm, nearly an hour late thanks to several mysterious delays just outside town. The second largest city in the South after Naples, Bari has all of the stripes of a failed city: poverty and dysfunction seem to abound. Without looking at a map, I know we have crossed the Ancona line, and the modernity and efficiency we witnessed in northern Italy is out the window. We are more than eight hours early for our ferry to Dubrovnik, but can do nothing with our time except sit with our bags and consume overpriced beverages and microwaved food at the ferry terminal. Our efforts to visit a beach or the Old Town as a family were snuffed out by myriad issues such as 5€ per bag fees to lock our nine pieces of luggage. We might have been willing, but the luggage shop is closed for *riposo* (Italian siesta) until 5pm, leaving us precious little time to go anywhere before our ferry departs. Moreover, at this point in the day, two hours at a local beach would be uncomfortably hot and sandy for Charlie and the cast on his broken arm. So, we spend most of the time in the ferry terminal staring at our ship. Eventually, I discover that I must travel 3km in a free shuttle to another terminal to obtain our boarding passes. I wait in line behind an equally confused and angry Serbian passenger, who clearly has no compunction about telling the supervisor what he thinks of this goose chase. This might be the low point of the trip: a day wasted in southern Italy because of confounding logistics.

It is sunrise on Friday, June 22nd as we awaken merely half-rested in airplane seats on the Croatian-run Jarolinja ferry to Dubrovnik. Karen and I shared a bottle of wine the night before during our delayed departure from Bari. The present scene is magical; there is no line on the horizon, and no land in sight as the sun rises. The kids wake up and climb up to the ship's deck, where the wind turns Izzy's long, curly, blonde hair into a violent cone. Everything seems cool until we disembark at customs, where the aggressive pushing and shoving in the scorching terminal make us long for the beach. As it becomes clear that our ferry delay and a long wait at customs will make us too late for daytrip departures to Montenegro or the Elaphite Islands, any local beach will satisfy our ambitions for the day. After all, trips across Lago di Como and the Adriatic will suffice as our requisite boat excursions for this trip. We hire an angry taxi driver to take the five of us and our luggage up the hill to our rented apartment. He is paranoid about having five passengers in his vehicle and to punish us, he overcharges us for the trip. We settle into Anmar Bed & Breakfast at Andrije Hebranga 1. Anna, the manager, has the apartment prepared for us, allowing us to decompress for the next couple of hours. "Yes, I know that driver," says Anna, as she collects all five of our passports to register us with the authorities, "He's disgusting." Against peer pressure on our downhill march to the beach, I call for a stop at a small store and buy lunch items and drinks, taking some pleasure and pride in knowing how to carry on this simple business in Croatian. The local free beach is a twenty minute walk down steep cliffs, so I don't want to have to come back up for food.

After dipping his feet into the warm, salty water, Charlie spends the next four hours reading in the shade while the rest of us swim, drink ice tea and Ožujsko *pivo*, and people-watch. The most interesting group to observe is a bunch of petite Russian ballerinas in bikinis and their bodybuilder boyfriends, one of whom is African American. The Speedo-clad Russian men proudly take turns flexing and jumping from the rocky cliffs, challenging one another at successively greater heights. One of the girls takes photos of them while another tries to discourage their showing off by ignoring the jumpers, her back turned towards them.

We all return to the apartment to take turns showering, then change our clothes and walk down to Dubrovnik's walled Old City for dinner. We find a pizzeria that I remember on Kuniceva, a shady, narrow side street of Stradun. Following our daily gelato, I send Karen off to "get lost in Dubrovnik," promising to meet her forty-five minutes later after I've walked the exhausted kids back up the steps to our apartment and settled them in for bed.

Racing back down the steps to the Old City, I am momentarily startled by an owl perched on a limb overhead, and it makes me laugh to remember my Croatian friends calling this kind of nocturnal bird a "hoot." There must be a lot of hoots in Croatia!

When I meet Karen at the fountain at the end of Stradun, we endeavor to find my favorite place to get a drink in Dubrovnik, an outdoor bar situated on the rocks outside the city walls, looking out across the Adriatic. From inside of the city wall, we're literally looking for a hole in the wall. I see a sign for a place called Buža, but I think more likely it is a smaller hole marked simply by the words "DRINKS, BEST VIEWS" painted on the bricks. Yes, this is the one!

Again at the limits of our endurance, Karen and I commit to staying for just one glass of red Plavac wine from Montenegro, which turns into more than one. It's okay, we assure one another, when are we going to share an evening like this again? The evening yields a very enjoyable conversation. After Venice, this is only our second chance to reflect upon the trip. We both appreciate that very little could be going better, including the attitudes of the kids. As a precaution, I share my memories of feeling this way in the past—also in Croatia—reminding us both that nothing can be taken for granted; take great care and ward off any sense of complacency. Long after watching the sun set over the Adriatic, Karen and I hike thirty minutes back up the steps to our apartment, check on the kids, and go to sleep.

We awaken blissfully well rested. Within a few minutes Anna, who lives downstairs from the apartment, appears at the door with juice, milk, fresh bread, butter, honey, and assorted jellies. She must have heard us moving about so she knew it was time to come upstairs. I had already made coffee for myself and Karen. It is another idyllic day outside. We assure Anna we will be present to check out by noon, when our driver Branko is due to pick us up.

All five of us return to the Old City, where I buy tickets to climb the exterior fortification walls. The hike begins with steps. Within five minutes in the scorching heat, the kids are begging for refreshments, which are available at a premium at small shops along the top of the city walls. Peering over the edge and down the 80 foot shear drop into the sea, I feel a little dizzy. The heights seem to be bothering me more than normal today, even though I've done this hike with students on three earlier occasions. The kids aren't in their best form: at least one of them sabotages each otherwise incredible photo in the city that provides the backdrop for "Game of Thrones." For me and Karen, this is easily one of the most beautiful places we've ever seen, and we savor the two hour walk before returning to Anmar Bed & Breakfast.

Branko is a sturdy fifty year-old father of three from Ploče, Croatia, who drives a silver Citroen van that would comfortably seat seven passengers plus luggage. I hired him twice in the past to transport my student groups between Dubrovnik and Sarajevo, but because Siniša was present to speak to him in Croatian, I never realized how remarkably well Branko speaks English. A retired traffic policeman, we feel safe with him as a driver. Once, when being pulled over while driving my class in Bosnia, Branko relayed to me through Siniša "Don't worry, because I am also a police man in Croatia, and a snake never bites another snake." As his official interrogator approached, Branko simply flashed his badge and we continued on our way without incident. Today, Branko is driving the Deichmanns for 175€ with whistle-stop service, including a two hour sightseeing break in Mostar, Bosnia-Herzegovina. It seems reasonable to round up his pay to 200€ when he gets us to Sarajevo. Money is tight for the working man in Croatia. I've been told by an economist friend that one of the chief challenges most people face here is that they are paid in Croatian kuna, but now most of their debts are due in Euros. It is easy for us to help

Branko earn a good day's income, and for us this sure beats traveling by bus.

Mostar is Bosnia's fifth largest city, and it endured relentless bombardment during the civil war of the 1990s. In the process, its famous 427 year old bridge was pointlessly destroyed, later to be re-built through an international aid effort. The family enjoys a lunch of *ćevapi*—fresh minced meat fingers shaped like Brown-and-Serves. I help the kids buy the souvenirs they want, as Mostar is really a great place for inexpensive mementos. On the cobbled street, Karen and I are offered free samples of *rakija*, which is a broad category for local schnapps and brandy. A native Bosnian, Siniša always says that *rakija* is best when it's home-made and purchased in re-used plastic Coca-Cola bottles. I confidently purchase cherry and walnut flavors from the self-proclaimed engineer- turned distiller.

Branko meets us at the designated time and street in Mostar. It's great to see this friendly guy again on this trip. I explain to Karen that when I was here with students last month I ended up riding in the second car with Branko's younger brother, Dario. I hope to hire both of these nice guys again, in part because on the ride from Mostar to Sarajevo, Charlie falls asleep and unknowingly drops his brand new 32 GB iPod touch under the seat. Because the iPod contains a lithium battery, by postal restrictions it cannot be mailed legally to the USA. Further, removal of the battery would void the iPod's warranty, then it would cost us $100 for a new battery. I'll just have to come back to the Balkans!

As we arrive in the gritty-by-European-standards city of Sarajevo, I can tell that Karen and the kids are unimpressed. Karen comments that "it feels like we're in the Bronx. "Dude, this city was under siege for nearly four years," I remind her gently. I pay Branko and wish him a safe journey home. We unwind in a large apartment room at the Hotel Astra in Baščaršija, the historic Turkish Old Town. Next, I take Karen and the kids shopping. Enthusiasm grows as they admire the jewelry, colorful textiles, and handicrafts. The sun sets behind Sarajevo's mystical minaret-adorned skyline. At the risk of killing this idyllic moment, I warn the kids about pickpockets, especially in Pigeon Square. Satisfied with our purchases, I direct my famished and once-again exhausted family to a restaurant with outdoor seating. It's a joint where I've bought a fast and tasty meal before. Tonight, the food is neither fast nor tasty: deep-fried breaded meat patties with mayonnaise on stale rolls.

It's Saturday night, so Karen and I put the kids to bed and head back out to Baščaršija, leaving Charlie in charge and assuring everyone that we will not be eaten by the thousands of stray dogs that roam Sarajevo's streets at night. We stroll to a place called BarHana, where I am intent to have some *rakija* and introduce Karen to my friend Djana and her sister Nadja, both of whom live on nearby Logavina Street. Logavina is the namesake of an excellent book I read about life in Sarajevo during the war[xxx]. Sadly, I can't find the sisters in the crowded BarHana, and after failing to get a place to sit in the smoky bar, Karen and I settle in at a nearby street restaurant under a huge awning. Just as we do, the sky opens up and drenches Sarajevo, creating mini rushing rivers between the cobblestones under our feet. After a fun outing, but unsuccessful in meeting my friends, she and I walk back to the hotel in the continuing deluge. Tomorrow is another day.

Hotel Astra's breakfast buffet in the basement offers great variety of poor quality, and after eating I feel nauseous in the absence of windows and fresh air. "Let's go for a walk," I suggest. Today is Sunday, so the museums, including Svrzo House, are closed. It's also disappointing to me that Tramline 1, which connects Baščaršija with the new city, is closed for reconstruction this entire year. Sarajevo just doesn't seem the same without its trams. All within a few hundred meters, we visit Ali Pasha's Mosque, the Catholic and Orthodox churches, and the Jewish Synagogue. Pointing to the city's ecumenical history, I explain to my companions how Sarajevo was long considered a place of tolerance and peaceful coexistence, symbolized by the 1984 Winter Olympics that were hosted here. Throughout Yugoslavia, in fact, many marriages were some combination of Bosnian, Croat, Serb, or other ethnicities. After that, we walk to the Markale Market, where more than 60 civilians were killed and 200 wounded in a February 1994 bombing. Nearby is a monument to Sarajevo's 1500 children who were killed between 1992 and 1995 while the city was under siege by *chetniks* (The Chetnik Detachments of the Yugoslav Army). Some of these places are indeed depressing, but nonetheless the morning program is educational for us and our kids.

The sisters Djana and Nadja meet our entire family for lunch at the Pivnica HS Restaurant, where Sarajevksa *pivo* is still brewed. In my humble opinion, it's one of the best beers I've even have the pleasure of tasting. As I introduce Karen to Djana and Nadja, Djana jokes "our parents only could spell with four letters, so they rearranged these letters to name us." Remarkably quickly, the friendly sisters develop a positive rapport with my family, just as they have in the past with my students.

We feast upon meaty plates of kabobs and goulash with fresh side salads; an excellent meal at last! Next, we cross the Miljacka River via the Latin Bridge, where Archduke Franz Ferdinand, heir to the Austrian thrown, and his wife Sophia were assassinated in 1914, sparking off World War I. At the tourist information center, we meet our guide/driver at Zelenih Beretki 22a for a "Siege of Sarajevo" tour. I simply *had* to include this tour in my family visit, as my students and I considered it a highlight of the course I led. Djana negotiated a private "abbreviated tour" rate through her friend, who is part-owner of the company. I invite the sisters to come along with us, but they remind me that they were here for the siege itself and have no desire to relive it. Understood!

To my satisfaction, the kids show great interest in Sarajevo, especially as we creep though the remaining portion of tunnel near the airport, a lifeline that helped keep the city supplied during the war. Near the Olympic stadium, the former sports fields and parks are adorned with thousands of grave markers, mainly of Muslim Bosniak victims, but also Christians and Jews, as indicated by the grave styles and engraved religious symbols. In the besieged city, there was limited space for burying the dead. I can tell my kids are thinking about what it might be like to live in our city of Nashua while it's being shelled for more than three and a half years. By the time we end our tour on the hillside near Bijela Tabija (White Bastion) overlooking the amazing city of Sarajevo, everyone seems to grasp the gravity of local history.

Djana and Nadja meet us at Bijela Tabija restaurant, perched on the hillside overlooking Sarajevo. Remarkably, this is my chance to introduce them to a restaurant in their own city! Here, we take refuge from the heat and have a few drinks to rehydrate ourselves. I am quietly aware that some of our most important challenges remain ahead of us: the night train to Zagreb, getting to Pleso airport, and my overnight layover with the boys in Paris. Aside from the drinks, Djana and Nadja seem less than impressed with my restaurant idea.

Back in Baščaršija, the sisters treat us to *burek*, fried dough available with meat, cheese, potato, or spinach filling. They also buy us the best *ćevapi* in Sarajevo, loaded with creamy *ajvar* sauce. As much as I appreciate their incredible hospitality, I feel stuffed and uncomfortable beyond description in the heat. I don't think I'll ever be able to eat again. Djana jokes about how grandmothers force their families to eat too much, so I begin to call her "grandma." We say our thank yous and goodbyes to Djana and Nadja, who are off to a pub to watch tonight's Euro-Cup football match between England and Germany. It's time for us to quickly finish up our souvenir and travel snack shopping, and we still need to get to the station and purchase our train tickets.

At the hotel, I arrange for two cabs and our luggage for the ten minute ride to the train station, asking the driver to please use the meter. He seems to acknowledge my request. I put our nine bags in the trunks by myself, yet when we arrive at the station and I attempt to pay the 7.40KM ($10) fare with 8KM, the driver tells me it's 10KM ($15) per car. "Meter," I say, angrily, pointing to the 7.40 on the meter. "Luggage," he counters. "I carried the luggage myself," I exclaim in English, gesturing angrily then looking him in the eye while handing him the full 20KM he wants. This is completely normal behavior in the Balkans, but I don't have the patience or the ability to argue. I dismiss the driver as a *lopov* (thief) who isn't worth the fight. After all, he needs the money more than I do, and I am getting on a train out of this place. It's just an unfortunate way to end a nice visit in a city I love.

The train station looks like something out of a Stanley Kubrick film: cold, barren, and empty. The large sign says "SARAJEVO-CAPAJEBO." No, the second word is not the name of a suburb or district; it's "Sarajevo" in the Cyrillic script. Studying the schedule, I am surprised at how few trains serve this city of 700,000. I buy our tickets speaking only Bosnian, responding correctly with the ages of our children, who pay discounted fares. Thankfully, numbers are one of the easiest steps in another language and the friendly ticket woman seems enchanted by my efforts. After that, with only pocket change left in KM, I check prices for 1.5 liter bottles of water at the forlorn-looking snack stand inside the station: 3.20KM, or about $2. I have an hour to kill, so I'm going snack shopping outside the station with my leftover money and any volunteers. Charlie, Isabela, and I return triumphantly twenty minutes later with two respectably-filled plastics bags full of drinks, fruit, and other snacks for the ride.

My former student Siniša, traveling with our students last month as my co-leader, joked that riding on a Bosnian train is like going back in time. I would agree, and I'm guessing about 40 years. I notice the sweaty film on our compartment's window sills, and the bathroom, whose toilet empties directly onto the tracks. It has clearly never been cleaned. A large woman in the next compartment chain-smokes directly under the "NO SMOKING" sign. I want to take a photo of her, but fail to muster the courage. I pity the lone American girl sitting across from smokestack lady while she protects her belongings and attempts to sleep. A Balkan overnight train ride: what an essential life experience! I am thrilled to be on this train with my family, and I briefly, silently appeal to God for travel mercies— no train wrecks, no thefts, no problems tonight. Once again, I'm reminded that I don't talk to God enough unless I need something.

As the sun rises, we arrive in Zagreb nearly an hour late. We pull our bags through the front door of *Glavni kolodvor* and look back at the elegant train station, recently renovated and painted in bright Maria Teresa gold. Without hesitation, Karen, who didn't sleep a wink on the Balkan night train, exclaims "now *this* is my kind of city!" I love Sarajevo's grit and charm, so I never really thought about this, but I wonder how my students feel when we travel in the reverse direction. I wonder if they mutter to themselves "WTF, Professor?" Karen meant nothing by her comment, but nevertheless I remind her that unlike Sarajevo, Zagreb wasn't shelled for nearly four years.

When, after an easy ten minute walk, we reach our Valentina Vodnika apartment I reserved on hotels.com, we again enter the gates of heaven. Wow! This was 100€ well spent! The entire place is ours: two bedrooms, a pull out couch in front of a flat screen TV, a kitchen, and a bathroom. I breathe a sigh of relief, as we *need* a comfortable final night. We are almost home! Still more to experience, but nearly all possibilities for calamity are past. After a short post-Bosnian train sanity break for all of us in the apartment, I confidently show my family some highlights of Zagreb, mainly clustered in the Kaptol district. Our day ends with Croatian fare at Medvedgrad, a *pivnice* (pub) on Ilica, the city's main retail street. Near Jan Beličić Square, this street is frequented by Zagreb's distinctive locally-manufactured blue trams. As Karen, the kids, and I return to the hotel, the sky once again opens up to drench us on our final day together in Europe. "I get the first hot shower!" declares Charlie.

On our day of departure from Zagreb, I am the first to awaken, as usual. As my body caffeinates, I am eager to get people and their things moving in the direction of the door. As trail boss, the pressure on me is palpable, given what is at stake if we screw up. I know this from the pitfalls I've experienced in the past. I do my best to muster the troops, trying not to irritate them by being too pushy. But I'm getting increasingly impatient as they roll slowly out of bed, so I leave the apartment on my final food reconnaissance mission of this amazing European adventure. I return with a pretty fantastic breakfast: apples, yogurt, fresh chocolate croissants, and orange juice.

An hour later, we depart our Valentina Vodnika apartment and lock the key inside as requested. Our suitcase wheels repeat "clickity-clack" on sidewalk joints and we cross the street to catch our blue tram for the short ride to the bus terminal. Just in case we get separated, I instruct Karen and the kids to get out on the fourth stop. After that, Zagreb Airport Bus takes us to our terminal at Zagreb-Pleso International Airport, where we check in and drop off our luggage with no problems. All of us will depart from the same gate area at the fairly small terminal. Charlie, James, and I hug Karen and Isabela, then board our flight to Paris. The girls will leave in twenty-five minutes for Munich.

When I made the reservation for me and the boys to spend the better part of a day in Paris, Charlie and I were excited. Now we're in flight to Paris! How nice it will be not only to show the boys a few highlights of the French capital, but also to have a comfortable layover at CDG! Grateful for what seems to be accurate information from Air France's in-flight magazine, I map out a plan for taking a clean coach into the city center, which will cost the three of us about 60€ round trip.

We land at CDG, then experience bewilderment at the two-hour plus ordeal involved in leaving the airport for the city center. The lads and I enter the customs queue and wait there for a half hour. We are now third in line. Security guards approach the customs desk right in front of us. "Everyone must evacuate the hall!" we hear in French, confirmed in English. Someone left their laptop on the floor in front of the customs agent and entered the country without it. The Texan girl behind me in line, who just came back from missionary work in Bosnia, explains that the same exact thing happened at CDG on her way to Europe. They had to evacuate the arrivals hall and call in a bomb crew to destroy the suitcase. This laptop would need to be sealed to the floor under a heavy duty tarpaulin and exploded. With hundreds of other passengers, the Texan missionary, the boys, and I migrate to the other arrivals hall and start all over waiting in a new long line. CDG must be a cursed place for me. I can never seem to get through this airport without incident!

Officially in France at last, we locate the buses to the city center. At the bus stop, I ask where to buy tickets. They must be purchased from the machine, located back inside the terminal, and with credit cards only. No problem, I have one of those. Problem: only European chip credit cards are accepted at the ticket dispensers, and by the way the price is now 75€. "Alright, kids, where's the damn train station?" I mutter under my breath, unable to spot any signs for "*La Gare*"

At last where we need to be, I instruct the boys to sit and rest with their bags while I wait in a forty-five minute queue to purchase our train tickets. In the queue, an attractive young Brazilian woman asks me to hold her place while she tells her mother (also waiting outside) that she will be a while. She returns promptly, and during our friendly banter while waiting in line she tells me how she, her fiancé, and their two friends were robbed at gunpoint outside Notre Dame Cathedral on Christmas Eve during her previous visit to Paris. They had gone into Paris directly from the airport, and had all of their valuables with them. The Brazilian Embassy was closed for the holiday, and provided minimal assistance after that. A relative who is a banker in Rio was able to wire them money to get by until they could obtain new passports and credit cards. Seeing my boys sitting uncomfortably outside, she insists that I take the next available kiosk. Tickets to the city are about 30€ for the three of us, and include one Metro connection. That should be fine for our purposes.

As Charlie, James, and I enter the filthy, graffiti-covered train compartment, I notice the look of fear on my sons' faces. There are only scattered seats available, so I take one for the team. I sit down directly next to a tattooed, punk attired, gangsta with sunglasses. He's playing raucous, French hip-hop music on his iPod's mini-speaker for everyone's enjoyment as he sings out loud and bobs back and forth. Thirty minutes to go, and our stop won't come a moment too soon. Silently trying to focus on what is going on *outside* their window, the boys examine the outskirts of Paris, alternating between underground and surface views. As for me, I find seclusion from the racket by studying the Metro map.

We exit at *Gare du Nord* (North Station) and hike through the dank, busy, rush-hour Metro tunnels to find Line 2, which takes us to Charles de Gaulle Étoile. Thirty minutes at L'Arc de Triomphe. Photos; check! We hike nearly an hour down Avenue d'Iéna toward the Eiffel Tower. Of course, this centerpiece of Paris is on everyone's bucket list. Seeing the length of the admission lines, it's clear that that we will need to view the tower from the gardens below. "Hey guys, let's make a picnic." I say. We have three cans of Sprite that I just bought for 3.50€ apiece, a bottle of Croatian red wine that I bought for the same price at Zagreb's duty free shop, some random chocolates, and bags of peanuts remaining from the USA. For more than an hour, the three of us remain resting on the damp lawn while admiring this phallic French wonder of modern architecture that towers over us.

Rain and fatigue are both imminent, so we are best to travel underground and off our feet. We take the Metro to St. Michel, just across from Île de la Cité; next stop, Notre Dame. Karen and I renewed our marriage vows informally in this famous church years ago on our way home from our brief tenth anniversary trip to Greece. Remembering what the Brazilian woman told me about the square out front Notre Dame Cathedral, having myself been to Brazil, and knowing that it can also be a dangerous place, for Brazilians to come to Paris and get robbed here seems especially violating.

Notre Dame Cathedral closed early today for an evening concert, but we would have the option of coming back tomorrow at 8am, however unlikely that is with the kids. The next hour represents a fun and beautiful walk in the direction of our hotel and I take some pretty cool photos. We cross Ponte d'Arcole and turn left to view the Conciergerie, Pont des Arts, and the Louvre, all places the three of us have or will read about in school. Doug Mack, in his entertaining travel book *Europe on Five Wrong Turns a Day*[xxxi] , writes that the Louvre is more magnificent on the outside than the inside. Out of convenience, I'll have to say I agree with him because this is my third visit without having had the chance to go inside. In any case, for me the contents would have to be pretty amazing—better than the Hermitage or the British Museum—to beat the building itself. "We need to come back here someday," I tell the kids, which we intend to do on our next European trip. I don't pretend for a moment that we are doing Paris any justice by spending just two half-days here this trip. We are just hitting the highlights and getting a taste in preparation for a more in-depth visit in the near future. This time, Bosnia and Croatia come before France!

It is past normal dinner time, and I have my eyes open for a restaurant. We are dressed as travelers, and have our daypacks with us, which is somewhat limiting in this part of Paris. The walk along Avenue de l'Opera goes more quickly than expected. We approach the magnificent entertainment hall, flanking it to the right to find our Hotel Prince Albert Opéra on Rue de Provence hotel just on the other side. We share a sigh of relief as we put our bags in the room and head back out to the street in search of food.

There are two McDonalds within a five minute walk of our hotel. We decide it wouldn't be too much of a sin to eat there, as we have only 40€ Euros left in cash, and we haven't eaten much at all since breakfast in Zagreb. It is 9pm and not yet dark, except for inside the first McDonalds. Very well, we walk around the block to the other one. The menu has been Franco-cized, and by the time everyone selects their luscious American meal and moves to the counter to order, we are told that there are no more French fries. "No problem, we'll take Filet O' Fish and salads." No fish. No more salads. "Do you have *les hamburgers?*" Only chicken. "*Merci Beaucoup. Au revoir.*"

A short distance down this pedestrian street, I spot a "meal deal" advertised on a pink neon sign: 11€ for meal, dessert, and drink. We sit down. With 40€, I should have just enough cash including tip! Our waiter Antoine is stylish, gregarious, and respectful to us, even in our American traveling clothes, as he *should* be… after all he works under a pink neon sign, and we are trying to speak his language. We order drinks. The house wine is dreadful, which might have been excusable in the Balkans, but not here in France. Turns out not all of our meals are part of the 11€ deal, so we won't quite have enough cash, and the restaurant doesn't take American Express, the only card in my pocket. *Zut alors!* After Charlie orders for us all in French, I leave the boys waiting for the food while I dash back to the hotel room to get my Visa card. Charlie's recommendation of steak with potatoes is delicious, one of the better meals I've had on this trip. Despite initial trepidation about trying something new, James really enjoys his roast chicken.

I struggle with my final monetary exchange in France, but I think I did the right thing. To my defense, we were lured to Antoine's neon restaurant on the pretense of a 33€ meal that turned out to cost 48€. Also, I have been told by plenty of Europeans that waiting tables generally yields a fair income there, and that in some countries a 15% tip is even built into the menu prices, which on my scribbled bill I could neither confirm nor refute. Tipping is an optional reward for good service, and often a simple "rounding up" to the next whole number or "keep the change" is appropriate. So, when paying for our meal, I round up to 50€, thereby tipping the nicest waiter in the history of France only 2€. As I do, he gives me a sad puppy-dog look as if he's failed to please us. Having just arrived in France today I could have been more certain about the local customs, which I am now thanks to google. It seems the problem is that locals expect Americans to tip extra, and even though Antoine already gets tipped as part of his paycheck, he tries to play on emotions to get extra tips from Americans.

The next morning, I announce to the rejuvenated boys what I knew all along: that after breakfast I would be taking them on a hike to Basilique du Sacre Coeur, the final of five superficial introductions in Paris. My initial plan was to return to the hotel after sightseeing to get our bags, but Charlie (14) rightly asks why we should backtrack to the hotel when we can go directly to the *Gare du Nord* afterwards. So, I buy the boys fresh chocolate croissants and drinks to eat at a local *boulangerie* (bakery) while I run back to Hotel Price Albert Opéra for a quick checkout. Approaching the Paris bakery from the street and carrying our three day packs, I cannot resist sneaking a photograph of the boys conversing with one another behind the floor-to-ceiling glass wall. They look pretty grown up, and I'm so glad that we were able to come here!

The hike is hot but the incredible view vindicates me from the wrath of my exhausted kids. The boys and I are now completely "Europed-out," but I'm sure it's just a passing phase. All that remains for us to accomplish here is a short hike to *Gare du Nord*, a train ride to CDG, and a direct flight to Boston. But first, the requisite wait of dubious duration to buy our train tickets to the airport.

Thanks to another Parisian ticket queue, the boys and I just miss our train to the airport. So, we board the next one on the same track, discovering one a moment too late that this one separates from the main track and goes to Mitry-Claye rather than CDG. As soon as I figure this out, we exit the train before the tracks divide, then we wait twenty *more* minutes to board the next train for CDG. Fortunately, we arrive at the airport three hours before our flight, and the boys enjoy an extended re-entry into the world of video games by experimenting with sit-in Nintendo demos at the gates. I sit nearby and enjoy a tall Heineken while logging into my email to check on Karen and Isabela's status. The boys and I high-five when we learn that they arrived safely at home just a few hours ago.

All is right with the world, especially when we exit Boston Logan's Terminal E to meet our bus. A text message on my cell phone tells me that Karen and Tessie—our black lab—are already here at the airport to pick us up!

16

A SORT OF HOMECOMING: MAINZ, GERMANY

And you know it's time to go
Through the sleet and driving snow
Across the fields of mourning
Lights in the distance
And you hunger for the time
Time to heal, desire time
And your earth moves beneath
Your own dream landscape
Oh, oh, oh
On borderland we run
I'll be there, I'll be there
Tonight, A high road
A high road out from here…

…Oh don't sorrow, no don't weep
For tonight, at last
I am coming home

"A Sort of Homecoming"
U2, *The Unforgettable Fire* (1984)

As I step onto the *Schnellbahn* (fast train) S8 underneath Frankfurt *Flughafen* (airport) in Germany one more time, I pull the international baggage tag marked "FRA" off my suitcase and take a seat with the other newly-arrived passengers and German commuters. I reflect upon my global journey. *Passion for Place* has become inextricably linked to my career and my personal life over the past quarter of a century.

Today is the fourth day of a fresh new year, and I am returning to Mainz to breathe the magical air of inspiration where my journey began, and close the loop that has become this travel story. My initial idea was to work in Berlin, but I'm not a rock band, and Mainz is closer to the heart of my story. Almost twenty-five years ago, I graduated from Alfred-Almond Central School to become an unlikely Rotary exchange student in this city of 180,000. Coming from a farm in rural Allegany Country, Mainz was incredibly exciting to me at the time, and the months I spent in this historic Rhine River city made a lasting impression that turned me on to a lifetime of travel. That first international travel experience played a significant role in fueling my *Wanderlust* and helping me dream up the adventures that became this book.

Indeed, twenty-five years is a long time. If you rewind to a quarter century *before* my 1987 Cold War arrival in Mainz –50 years ago–you will find yourself at the height of the post-World War II reconstruction effort in Germany. *That's* incredible.

As the S-Bahn approaches Mainz, I observe that my beloved city really hasn't changed much since I lived here. Sure, the city seemed bigger when I first came here from the farm as a bashful but bright-eyed seventeen year-old, but fundamentally it still looks the same to me. As the local saying goes, "*Mainz bleibt Mainz, wie es singt und lacht*" (Mainz remains Mainz, how it sings and laughs). In contrast, I think of Berlin, another of my favorite German cities, and how it bears little resemblance today to its divided Cold War self.

I check in at the Hotel Königshof in Mainz, then sit alone in my room and think about how to approach the book. As I reflect upon the title of this chapter, I recall a clear case of déjà vu shortly after I came to live with the Kellers *Am Eselsweg* (on the donkey path) in the Bretzenheim district of Mainz. In those early September days, I rode my bicycle to school on a narrow, paved path. That gently winding trail crosses a very green meadow with a row of apartment towers in the background, a settlement prepared for Berlin refugees after World War II. The very first time I took this path in 1987, I immediately recognized the meadow from a dream that I had long before living in Germany even crossed my mind. The music in my head during the dream was "A Sort of Homecoming" by U2, from their newly-released 1984 album *Unforgettable Fire* album, a cassette tape that I was admittedly lukewarm about back then. From that day on, I thought about my incredible sense of familiarity and connection with this meadow every time I passed through it, and I continue to ponder the strangeness of this place. If I have time during the next few days in Mainz, I should go there.

I spend two days exploring at least as much of Mainz as I saw during the entire time I lived here. Mainz used to seem so big. Distance is relative, and these days I love to walk for hours in European cities. I like to explore on my own. In 1987-88, it didn't seem to occur to Mainzers to show me Mainz. They generously took me to Heidelberg or skiing in Switzerland, or sent me to Italy and Great Britain. They told me about the magnificence of Paris and Budapest, and my German classmates just wanted to get out of Mainz.

Ninety minutes before checkout from Hotel Königshof, I decide to take a stroll in the city under the January sun. I walk my old route from the *Hauptbahnhof* (main train station) to my school before pausing at an interesting-looking building. I decide to check out the parallel street behind it, where I notice for the first time in my life the Mainz Hilton City. This is only one block away from a path I've taken hundreds of times. Have I become more curious as I've gotten older? I continue wandering up a hill and toward Bretzenheim, along the way admiring so many things I've walked past before that I took for granted in my youth. Münchener Freiheit plays on my iPod; the album they released in 1987 when I lived here. I was so excited to listen to their music as a "German lesson," and I went to see them perform at Mainz's Rheingoldhalle.

Continuing on my hike, I make a left on a road closed to cars, and observe joggers, walkers, and bikers running through a huge park. This green space appears to be on the site of Mainz's former city walls, so I follow it to an enormous citadel, which I never really noticed before. I guesstimate my way back downhill to the Old Town, and stop at a shop on Augustiner-straße to pick up a nice looking bottle of Bordeaux for Mama Beer, my former host mother. I was invited to go "home" to her house for dinner tonight. Back at the hotel, I tell the receptionist how strange it seems that I lived here for almost a year but never saw the Citadel of Mainz. She responds that "it's just been fixed up, so you can go there now." Cool, maybe I can spend some more time there tomorrow.

I get off tram 50 at Kapellenstraße in Gonsenheim, a suburb of Mainz, and begin walking toward my old home. One hundred meters along, I stop and realize I forgot to buy flowers, a faux pas in Germany in general and with Mama Beer in particular. One time when I returned to Mainz from a day trip, she greeted me at the station with flowers. I return to the tram stop and try unsuccessfully to find a bouquet. Oh well, at least I remembered to get a bottle of wine in Mainz.

I walk through the former US Army base and to Max-Planck-straße 33, reaching down to twist the handle on the low gate, then ringing the doorbell as I have done hundreds of times before. Everything looks the same as in 1987, even Mama (Ingrid) Beer. I cannot believe how young she looks! After a hug in the doorway, she invites me in and fetches me deceased Papa Beer's almost-new house shoes. She and I have a fun conversation about old times, her family, and my family while she prepares a lunch of pork cutlets, potatoes fried in mayonnaise, and boiled carrots. We are having such a great conversation that I don't want to go upstairs to write. After lunch, Mama Beer shows me photographs that bring back fond memories of my short time with this fantastic family. After a while, Mama Beer announces that she'll give me some time to work, and sets me up in the loft at the top of the house.

Let me paint you a picture. The sun is breaking through the clouds and onto my face, and droplets of the morning's chilly rain remain on the glass. Through the large window in Mainz-Gonsenheim, I see the fields and orchards where I used to walk my host-dog Gypsy. On the other side of the vast fields are the Autobahn and power lines, and in the distance, Mainz Bretzenheim with ZDF (Germany's second television station), and the home of Mainz 05, the over-performing local soccer team.

For the next ninety minutes I work on the book you are reading now, mainly editing early chapters. Having read my 1987 *Tagebuch* (daily journal) over the past two days and for the first time in my life, I feel very close to the experiences and emotions that I had a quarter century ago. This is exactly why I am here in this room looking out this window, not at home in Nashua, and not in busy Berlin or Prague.

I wonder how Papa (Volker) Beer tolerated spending three months sleeping in this loft while I was an exchange student. To make room for me, my six year-old host sister Sabrina gave up her bedroom and slept with Mama Beer in the parents' room. This arrangement can't have been healthy for their marriage, but neither one seemed to mind. After all, Papa Beer spent two weeks on his own adventure in the desert of Algeria during my stay, and he seemed to enjoy spending countless hours in this very loft at the top of the house, framing and sorting his thousands of travel slides while his girls watched television on the couch just around the corner.

Papa Beer was an extraordinary human being. As I mentioned in Chapter 1, he was fun in a way that is counter to the stereo-types we often associate with Germans: always smiling, always joking, always hugging his kids and being goofy. I attribute his fun disposition in large part to the fact that he was originally from Augsburg, a city in jolly Bavaria. Likewise, Mama Beer can be thought of as being very *Mayence* (Mainz spent much of its history as a French city) as she possesses a certain *joie de vivre* that lies in stark contrast to the *Hochdeutsch* dialect and formal attitude of folks from northern and central Germany. On the rare occasion when a Beer parent raised their voice, my host siblings and I would halt in our tracks because angry shouting was so uncommon, we knew they must *really* be trying to make a point. Papa Beer died in 1997, and although it was emotionally difficult, on my most recent visit to Gonsenheim, I accompanied his widow to visit his grave. Papa Beer has been a great inspiration in my life, especially with regard to my passion for travel adventure and in my effort to create a fun family atmosphere in the home. Sadly, neither of these were part of my upbringing, so I had to learn them on my own.

Thanks to our annual exchange of Christmas cards, I knew that Mama Beer has a new partner in life, Rolf, and I am about the meet him, much to my surprise. After my ninety minutes of writing time expires and while Mama Beer and I are walking through the garden paths between Gonsenheim, Finthen, and Bretzenheim, Rolf arrives at the Beer domicile.

Rolf is a tall, gray-haired man from Kasiserlautern, not far from Mainz. He speaks in an accent that I find a bit difficult to understand. I tell him that it's a great pleasure to meet him, trying to act unsurprised and comfortable. I'm sure that he is aware of my admiration for Papa Beer. The three of us move to the beautiful living room, sit down, and open a bottle of white wine. To break the awkward silence, I mention to Mama Beer that the grand piano I used for learning the Beatles "Yesterday" is gone. Did one of my three host sisters take it with them when they moved out?

The three of us spend the rest of the evening together. I am so happy for Mama Beer, but it still seems strange to see someone else opening doors for her, fetching her jacket, and hugging her. Rolf lost his wife to a brain tumor seven years ago. At the family's favorite Greek restaurant that night, when Mama Beer goes to the rest room, I look Rolf in the eye and tell him how bad I feel about what happened to his wife. He thanks me for the condolences, and seems a little upset to think about her. Three glasses of ouzo come with the check. I am not permitted to pay for dinner, but my hosts tell me that it is my responsibility to pay for beers, and they know just the place... a nice young man Rudi down the street owns the coolest local bar. At Rudi's bar, I enjoy two of the best beers in my life, fresh from the tap.

That night, I sleep upstairs in the loft where Papa Beer used to have his "man cave." I wake up to text Petr the Czech and confirm our plans. Petr is scheduled to meet me in Mainz at 10am. He texts me back that he had car troubles in Germany near the border and must return to the Czech Republic, as he isn't comfortable having repairs done outside his home country. I brush my teeth and go down to breakfast, where Rolf and Mutti Beer are already sipping coffee. "*Guten Morgen, hast Du gut geschlafen?*" (Good morning, did you sleep well?) she asks, precisely as she did every morning twenty five years ago "*Ja, danke,*" (Yes, thank you) I respond. "Sit down, Choel, in the morning, we only eat sweet," she says, "but we have deer bacon for you." "Thank you, that is very nice of you." I am exhausted from speaking so much German over the past twenty-four hours. Now Mama Beer is going through her phone book, dialing the numbers of anyone who has ever heard of me, then handing the phone to me so that I can say hello. I speak with several old acquaintances. First, my gorgeous host sister Susana is now a doctor in Stuttgart, married to another doctor. They have three kids, plus a fourth is due in April. They are on a cell phone driving back early from a ski holiday in Switzerland for fear of getting snowed in. I also speak with my youngest host sister Sabine, and Richard, a family friend of Beers who in 1966 escaped to Germany from Communist Czechoslovakia.

392 | Passion for Place

Richard explains to me that his wife is very ill, and will die soon. This is a difficult conversation for me to hold in German with someone that I haven't talked to since I was eighteen years old. That night, I visit my eldest host sister Stefi (dentist) and her husband (also a dentist) and their four beautiful kids in their large home, at least large by German standards.

While I've enjoyed the walk down memory lane, I haven't accomplished much writing in the past 24 hours, so I withhold from Frau Beer the information I just received that Petr cannot make it to Mainz to pick me up. I thank my hosts and say goodbye, *"Auf Wiedersehen,"* then walk through the mild drizzle to the #51 tram headed back to the city.

Realizing that this tram will go through the city and close to my first host family's house in Bretzenheim, I remain on board for four more stops until *Pariser Tor*, or Paris Gate. I exit the tram and see a sign displaying the distance to Paris: 576km from here. At first, I'm not sure if I can find my way to my old bike path, but as I walk instinctively things come together.

Just before the bridge that connects Paris Street to the Autobahn, a path veers off to the right. That is my path. I pull out my iPod and locate "A Sort of Homecoming," then insert my ear buds. The song lasts about as long as it takes me to walk the path the length of the meadow, observe the row of four symmetrically arranged towers ("I see seven towers…") of the Berliner *Siedlung* (Berlin settlement). I come to a pause at the end of the music and the path. My first host family, which lost my host sister Nina from an aneurism about twenty years ago, lives just a few minutes' walk up the bike path.

My walk continues automatically; no conscious decision was made to carry on. Do I want to see Kellers this Saturday morning if anyone is even home? After ten more minutes, I arrive at the back of their cul-de-sac that abuts the bike path. I pause in contemplation. I want to say hello and thank them again for hosting me, maybe even apologize once again for the stress I caused them when I rode my bike to the hockey rink with skates and a stick and didn't return until after midnight. Then I think, would I want someone to stop by my house on a Saturday morning without calling ahead? Absolutely not, and I am only 12.5% German! I continue to the gate of their house, which still reads "Hermann Keller," but below this name is written "Leo Grundbesitz." I don't recognize the German word after Leo. Literally, it looks like "ground occupy," so it might be real estate, but I don't have a dictionary. Is Leo a renter? A partner? Has my host mother moved out? Beyond the awkwardness of an unannounced visit to people who know me, a ring of the doorbell might be pretty bad if someone else lives here now.

I take a stealth photo of the house and turn back toward the city. I have the Mainz Citadel in my crosshairs. I follow a muddy path to a soccer field that I identified yesterday as the way to the fortification. Inside is a large, muddy soccer field. On the other side, it looks like a dead-end, but soon I spot a woman and her dog disappearing through the fortress's gates. I follow them at a distance, and discover a sizable apartment complex of 1912 -built buildings, many of them offering a beautiful view of the city and the Rhine. I climb up to an overlook and then hike the length of the walls before descending back into *Altstadt Mainz.*

I follow the sound of noontime bells from St. Stephen's Church and then enter the sanctuary to admire its brilliant blue-themed Marc Chagall windows. In a sudden spiritual mood, I light a candle for my family, and for safe travel. The Christmas trees and nativity scene remain on display, enhancing the already dazzling colors of the church. I make a small donation for the new sanctuary organ and leave through the towering, leath-er-padded doors. As I walk, the rain intensifies and I'm exhausted from yesterday's intense conversation in German, so I stop for a beer at a pub on Schillerplatz. I find great satisfaction in reading through a couple of German popular magazines, periodically texting Petr the Czech about the cool stuff I've seen and how I wish he was here. I reflect upon the morning and regret that I blew off several hours of writing. Afterwards, I return to Hotel Königshof, check in to a new room, and hunker down to write at my desk. There are no instructions on how to finish up a book. I feel so much emotion just being in Mainz, but I'm frustrated that I've accomplished so little writing.

After I've written all that I possibly can and my brain is defeated, I need a diversion. I get online and book tickets for my brother Jonathan to travel from Austin to New Hampshire for the upcoming summer's Alaska trip, then back to Austin again. There are few options with the miles I can offer for his trip, so I am glad to take this time to get it booked, even while in Germany. After all, this is the guy who got *me* started flying years ago by sharing his miles with me. After that, I skip through the German television channels looking for something interesting. I give up at midnight and drift off to sleep. I am happy that I made some progress on the book.

The next day, I make one final foray on foot through a drizzly, empty, Sunday morning version of Mainz, one that I have never really seen before. Church bells ring as the raindrops splatter violently on the rectangular street stones. I insert my iPod's earbuds. It feels like I am alone in this special city with the music of Münchener Freiheit, and there is no place I would rather be.

The incredible experience in Mainz twenty-five years ago only served to ignite my *Wanderlust*. I was then imprisoned again for several years as I worked my way through college. There was little time or money for travel, let alone international travel. But my temporary incarceration only intensified my desire to see the world. One of my great breaks in life was having the opportunity to live in this historic city of Mainz, and another is now having the resources and the support of my wife to be back here today. The richness of my life has much to do with the opportunity provided by Rotary International, and the kindness, generosity, and hospitality of so many Rotary

families in Hornell, New York and from Mainz Club 50°
North. I know and freely admit that I was far from the perfect
exchange student, but I am reassured by the multiplier effect
that this Rotary opportunity had upon my life. I have been
back to Germany many times with college students, friends,
and my wife and kids. It has been my privilege to share what
Rotary began. I have traveled throughout Central and Eastern
Europe and have had the pleasure of making close friends in
many countries. My insatiable appetite for knowledge about
exotic places first led me to Mainz, but has since taken me
not just throughout Europe, but also to Central and South
America, Asia, Africa, the Middle East, Australia, and New
Zealand. Embracing these unlikely opportunities has yielded
the predictable benefits of personal and professional enrich-
ment and happiness in a life (so far) fully lived.

Conclusions

Yes, that section heading is written by a displaced academic,
attempting to do travel writing. There are no conclusions, and
the story will continue as long as I can keep it going. Nobody
could possibly live long enough to see all the places as I would
like to see. The world offers innumerable attractions. The
challenge is to reconcile itinerary depth and breadth within
the limitations of a human lifetime. Infinitely enriching, travel
is the best education money can buy. I am truly grateful for
every single opportunity that I've had to experience so much
of this amazing planet, and to meet so many of its inhabitants.
Finally, this book is to share, not to boast; I humbly appreciate
the unlikeliness of my good fortune, and the safety that I have
enjoyed while traveling to so many unforgettable places. If you
see a chance to travel in the world, take it, enjoy it, and come
safely home!

ENDNOTES

[i] "Time For Me To Fly" from the album *You Can Tune a Piano but you Can't Tuna Fish* (1978).

[ii] Nouns are capitalized in German.

[iii] "Now he's bought a gramophone on the never never"– "UK Jive" from the album *UK Jive* (1989).

[iv] I think *pivo* becomes my first-learned and most frequently used Slavonic word – it works in in Slovak, Czech, Polish, Croatian, Russian, and other Slavonic tongues.

[v] K-Mart was one of the first US investments in Slovakia; it was later purchased by the British retailer Tesco.

[vi] I met Pavel Korvín one final time in Bratislava when I brought a group of students there in 2005, and then this angel went to heaven in 2007, leaving behind a wife and two boys that I had the pleasure of meeting. Karen and I remember Pavel fondly and speak of him often.

[vii] In light of my affection for the region and its people twenty years later, it pains me to share with you such drivel written as a young guy under duress, but my perceptions at that time are part of the story.

[viii] Prior to the age of electronic ticketing, plane tickets were strictly made of paper. In the absence of electronic flight manifests, paper tickets were required at check-in, in order to obtain a boarding pass. Having had our paper tickets stolen, ours needed to be re-issued for a fee that, at the time, we could only guesstimate.

ix We haven't heard from Craig & Jane since. In Poland, they say "after three days, fish and guests start to smell."

x As of October 2014, I still haven't been to Madrid or anywhere else in Spain (except for Barcelona, which most locals will argue is Cataloña rather than Spain).

xi For more information, visit http://www.extramilerclub.org/ (current as of October 22nd, 2014).

xii Mark Twain's *Tom Sawyer Abroad* New York: Dell Publishing, (1894).

xiii William Least Heat Moon's *Blue Highways: A Journey into America* New York: Random House, (1982).

xiv This academic department is now called Global Studies.

xv The lyrics of *New Year's Day* refer to Poland's solidarity movement, led by Lech Wałęsa. Coincidentally, Poland's Communist government announced it would abolish martial law on New Year's Day in 1983. http://www.songfacts.com/ (Accessed June 2nd, 2014).

xvi PAIZ is now PAIiIZ: Polish Information and Foreign Investment Agency, but retains the original web address http://www.paiz.gov.pl/en (current as of October 22nd, 2014).

xvii When I later asked Adrian why he decided to make time to meet with me, he explained that his colleague Aleksandra told him I showed interest in Poland by asking about the atmosphere following the death of Pope John Paul II. Although Adrian is not Catholic, he is a proud Pole and a sensitive guy. He emailed me that he could meet for an hour, then generously spent that entire first day of our friendship showing me Warsaw.

xviii Dr. Seuss. *Oh, The Places You'll Go!* New York: Random House (1990).

xix Most Czech males—indeed most Slavs—resist any public behavior that could be remotely construed as gay.

xx At this point, I assume it was an innocent oversight, but as I reflect upon it later it seems fishy. Maybe not malice, but more like non-cooperation with the rich Americans on their way to

Slovenia's unworthy rival Croatia. The reason for suspicion is that the passport was not shipped DHL overnight as I requested, but mysteriously "required" five days to travel 200km.

xxi "Nashua Lampoon" is both a reference to our home town of Nashua, New Hampshire, and to the National Lampoon films, some of which have become family favorites. The name "Zooropa" is from U2's 1993 album by that name.

xxii Most of this chapter originated from notes written on the return flight from Berlin to JFK.

xxiii Frankfurt's nickname among Germans is Mainhattan, derived from its location on the Main River as well as its impressive modern skyline, which is thought to resemble that of Manhattan.

xxiv "Sgt. Pepper's Lonely Hearts Club Band," from the self-titled album (1967).

xxv I find out three months later—in December—that this pension was not Hotel Arena. The driver took me to the wrong address, and Kirill cut his losses by finding me basic accommodations near the place where I was dropped off.

xxvi I'm not a poet, so I share this with apologies and gratitude to "Peter the Martin" and his faithful champion dachshund Tim, who inspired me to capture my thoughts in a poem.

xxvii Zanubiya is not her actual name; it is a name for a Syrian Queen. Her father is a public figure in Syria, so I assigned a pseudonym for the purposes of this book.

xxviii It turns out that Steve Winwood's song happens to be #1 on my iTunes all-time "played" list, ahead of anything from U2, which populates most of the top 25.

xix "No Line on the Horizon" is the title track from U2's *No Line on the Horizon* (2009).

xxx Barbara Demick's *Logavina Street: Life and Death in a Sarajevo Neighborhood.* New York: Spiegel & Grau, (2012).

xxxi Doug Mack's *Europe on Five Wrong Turns a Day.* New York: Perigee (2012).

CPSIA information can be obtained
at www.ICGtesting.com
Printed in the USA
LVOW11s1736071217
558993LV00007B/894/P